# TEACHER'S EI

## Consultants

**Kathy W. Dames, Ed.D.**
National Education Consultant
The Intellectual Child, LLC
Flossmoor, Illinois

**Robert M. Johnson, M.S.**
Elementary School Teacher
Cambridge Elementary School
Orange, California

**Lillie Lewis, Ed.D.**
Assistant Principal
Davis-Emerson Middle School
Cottondale, Alabama

Sadlier School

## Reviewers

**Rachael Carletto**
Director of Curriculum, Instruction, Assessment and Technology
Little Ferry Schools
Little Ferry, New Jersey

**Candace Dixon**
Elementary Literacy Teacher
Arthur Dixon Elementary
Chicago, Illinois

**Jamie Leigh Ettinger**
Professional Learning Facilitator, 6–12 English
Selinsgrove Area Middle School
Selinsgrove, Pennsylvania

**Allison Greer**
Literacy Coach
Pershing School
Orlando, Florida

**Erin Kent**
Remediation Specialist Grades K–6
Montgomery County Intermediate Unit
Norristown, Pennsylvania

**Gabriela MacDonald**
Instructional Coach
Sally Ride Elementary
Orlando, Florida

**Rhonda Mathis**
ELA Curriculum Coordinator
Richmond County School System
Augusta, Georgia

**Megan Phelan**
Elementary Teacher
Germantown Central School
Germantown, New York

**Chaunte Robinson**
Middle School Literacy Teacher
Arthur Dixon Elementary
Chicago, Illinois

**Steve Rodriguez**
Middle School Teacher
The Accelerated School
Los Angeles, California

**Cover:** *Series Design:* Silver Lining Studios, Studio Montage; *Title design:* Quarasan, Inc. **Photo Credits:** *Cover:* Alamy/B.A.E. Inc.: *bottom left*. Getty Images/GK Hart/Vikki Hart: *right*; StockTrek: *top left*. Shutterstock.com/Bill Florence: *center*; nikolarisim: *background*. age fotostock/IndiaPicture/Gurpal Singh Datta: 36 *top*; JGI/Jamie Grill: 114 *top*; KidStock: 10 *top*; Michael S. Nolan: 8 *top right*; Gian Carlo Patarino: 44 *background*; View Stock RF: 106. Alamy Stock Photo/Glowimages RM: 146; jvphoto: 8 *bottom right*; John Elk III: 52 *right*; Julie Hiebaum: 44; Adrian Sheratt: 92; Dave Watts: 218; A.T. Willet: 87, 89; Blend Images/Andersen Ross: 202 *top*; Chronicle: 46; Heritage Image Partnership Ltd: 45; Science History Images: 143. AP Images/Associated Press/Tannen Maury: 90 *bottom*. Blend Images/Andersen Ross: 88 *top*. Corbis/Blend Images/KidStock: 216 *top*; Wave: 96. Dreamstime.com/Mature: 190 *bottom*; Vicki France: 140 *inset*. Fotolia/Paul Moore: 215, 217. Getty Images/AFP/Randy Johnson: 94 *inset*; Bloomberg: 102; IMAGEMORE Co, Ltd: 187, 189; NASA/SPL: 98; Stocktrek: 8 *center*; Paula Bronstein: 201, 203; Tim Hall: 61, 63; AFP/Khaled Desouki: 48; AFP/Guillermo Legaria: 38, 39, 40, 42; Business Wire: 178; Corbis/VCG Wilson: 8 *bottom left*; Jupiterimages: 134 *top*. iStockphoto.com/monkeybusiness: T18; powerofforever: 51. Media Bakery/Blend Images/Michael Poehlmann: 160 *top*. NASA: 142, 149. Punchstock/Digital Vision: 188 *top*. Robert Harding Picture Library Ltd/Andrew McConnell: 104. Science Source/European Southern Observatory: 148; NOAA: 97; Friedrich Sauer: 8 *top left*. Shutterstock.com/adriaticphoto: T11; blackzheep: T17 *bottom*; Brad Sauter: 206; cecoffman: 220; Erik Lam: 204; Jana Guothova: 36 *bottom*, 10 *bottom*, 88 *bottom*, 114 *bottom*, 134 *bottom*, 160 *bottom*, 174 *bottom*, 188 *bottom*, 202 *bottom*, 216 *bottom*; M. Dykstra: 190 *top*; Mahod84: T9, T15, T17; Nikitina Olga: 103; nikolarisim: 1; S-F: 35, 37; Santia: 140 *bottom*; SueC: 176; takepicsforfun: 54; wong sze yuen: 62 *top*; Ye Liew: 173, 175; Thomas Lusth: 52 *left*; Pikul Noorod: 133, 135; Sergey Novikov: 192 *bottom*; Chepko Danil Vitalevich: 9, 11. SuperStock/4x5 Collection: 100; Blend Images: 174 *top*. REUTERS/Allen Fredrickson: 91 *inset*.

**Illustrator Credits:** Tim Beaumont: 159, 161, 162, 164. Smiljana Coh: 122, 123, 124, 126. David Harrington: 76, 77, 78, 80. Olga and Alexsey Ivanov. International Mapping: 50. John Joven: 12–13, 14, 16. Naoko Matsunga: 18, 19, 20, 22. Kelley McMorris: 64, 65, 66, 67. Michele Noiset: 116, 117, 118, 120. Rob Schuster: 136, 137, 138, 139, 144, 150, 152, 157. Martin Wickstrom: 24, 25, 26, 28. Jason Wolff: 113, 115.



**For additional online resources, go to SadlierConnect.com and enter the Teacher Access Code: P31A22CBTS**



William H. Sadlier, Inc.
25 Broadway
New York, NY 10004-1010

Printed in the United States of America.
ISBN: 978-1-4217-1913-9
1 2 3 4 5 6 7 8 9 10 WEBC 25 24 23 22 21

# CONTENTS

## CHAPTER 3 Craft and Structure
## Literary Texts *Reading Chapter 3 connects to Writing Chapter 9*



## CHAPTER 4 Craft and Structure
## Informational Texts *Reading Chapter 4 connects to Writing Chapter 10*



## CHAPTER 5 Integration of Knowledge and Ideas
## Literary Texts *Reading Chapter 5 connects to Writing Chapter 11*

## CHAPTER 6 Integration of Knowledge and Ideas Informational Texts



## CHAPTER 7 Text Types and Purposes Write Fictional Narratives

CHAPTER 8

## Text Types and Purposes
## Write Informative/Explanatory Texts



CHAPTER 9

## Text Types and Purposes
## Write Nonfictional Narratives

## CHAPTER 10 Text Types and Purposes Write Opinion Pieces



## CHAPTER 11 Research to Build and Present Knowledge Write Research Reports



Digital Resources for *Progress English Language Arts* are available at SadlierConnect.com.

Research indicates that high-level student performance is the result of an alignment of curriculum, instruction, and assessment. ***Progress English Language Arts*** is a reading/ language arts program that puts standards-based instruction into practice by aligning curriculum, instruction, and assessment in every chapter, and at each level.

The foundation of *Progress English Language Arts* is the analysis and integration of state and national standards, curriculum guides and/or frameworks, current research on instruction, and best practices. Instruction in reading, writing, vocabulary, conventions of standard English, and speaking and listening is prioritized to create an instructional focus for each chapter. Each element of the chapter—including direct and guided instruction and independent work—focuses on these critical skills, and provides students the range of encounters, varied practice opportunities, and levels of application necessary to gain proficiencies required by the standards.

***Progress English Language Arts:***

- engages students in close reading of high-quality, challenging informational and literary texts through a **gradual release of responsibility**, leading to independent and proficient reading.
- increases students' knowledge of history/social studies, science, and technical subjects by reading rich, content-area texts.
- requires students to cite evidence from complex texts to respond to text-dependent questions and support critical thinking.
- provides instruction and practice of reading skills that reflect the structure of standardized tests.
- highlights academic and domain-specific vocabulary in each reading selection.
- contains student writing models for students to analyze and engage in constructing both informational and narrative essays with a focus on appropriate language usage.
- scaffolds student learning with easy-to-use, comprehensive lesson plans.
- supports English language learners, struggling learners, and those needing extended learning opportunities.
- provides opportunities for observational and formal assessment to inform and direct instruction.

***Progress English Language Arts*** serves as a flexible resource for supporting schools in meeting English Language Arts standards. *Progress English Language Arts* can be used as:

- an alternative core English Language Arts program that provides standards-based instruction, which can be supplemented with independent reading materials for additional practice.
- supplemental lessons to fill curriculum gaps in a current core English Language Arts program.
- targeted preparation materials for state-standardized assessments.

***Progress English Language Arts*** can be used for:

- an entire class.
- small group instruction.
- individual students needing intervention.
- Summer School or After-School Programs.

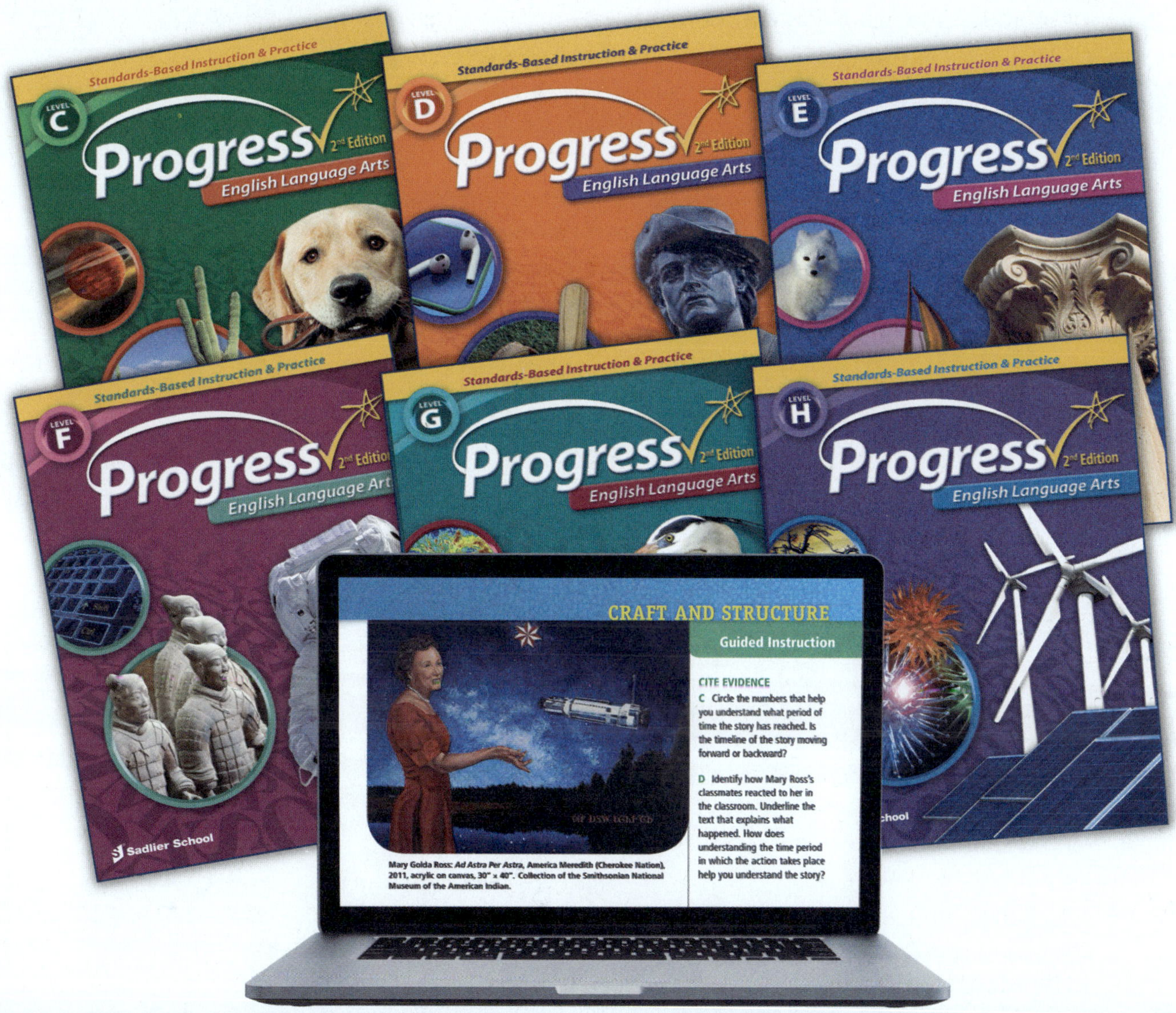

## Gradual Release of Responsibility

The *Progress English Language Arts* program employs diverse grouping and instructional models to help teachers provide effective instruction in key English Language Arts skills/concepts.

Each reading standard is taught using one continuous text following a **gradual release of responsibility** instructional model. By gradually decreasing the level of support within each text, students are prepared for independent encounters with complex texts and master complex standards.

**Guided Instruction** The program uses **whole-class** instruction to provide direct skill-based instruction and think-aloud modeling while students **read along** with the teacher. Discussion-based Comprehension Checks provide students an opportunity to engage in collaborative and meaningful discourse. ▶

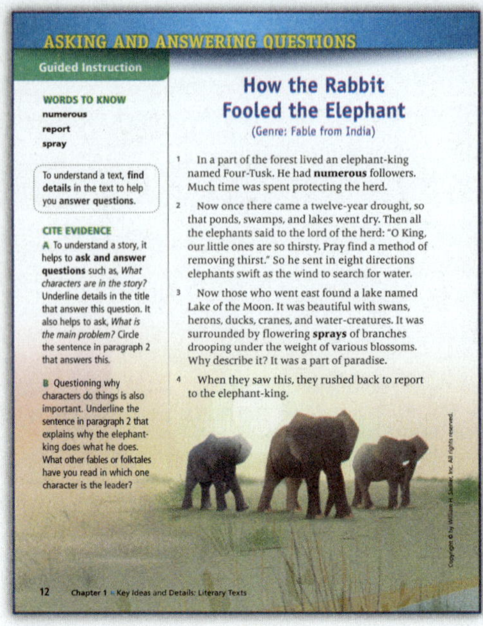
ASKING AND ANSWERING QUESTIONS

Guided Instruction

WORDS TO KNOW
**numerous**
**report**
**spray**

To understand a text, **find details** in the text to help you **answer questions.**

CITE EVIDENCE

A To understand a story, it helps to **ask and answer questions** such as, *What characters are in the story?* Underline details in the title that answer this question. It also helps to ask, *What is the main problem?* Circle the sentence in paragraph 2 that answers this.

B Questioning why characters do things is also important. Underline the sentence in paragraph 2 that explains why the elephant-king does what he does. What other fables or folktales have you read in which one character is the leader?

### How the Rabbit Fooled the Elephant

(Genre: Fable from India)

1 In a part of the forest lived an elephant-king named Four-Tusk. He had **numerous** followers. Much time was spent protecting the herd.

2 Now once there came a twelve-year drought, so that ponds, swamps, and lakes went dry. Then all the elephants said to the lord of the herd: "O King, our little ones are so thirsty. Pray find a method of removing thirst." So he sent in eight directions elephants swift as the wind to search for water.

3 Now those who went east found a lake named Lake of the Moon. It was beautiful with swans, herons, ducks, cranes, and water-creatures. It was surrounded by flowering **sprays** of branches drooping under the weight of various blossoms. Why describe it? It was a part of paradise.

4 When they saw this, they rushed back to report to the elephant-king.

12 Chapter 1 ▪ Key Ideas and Details: Literary Texts

Copyright © by William H. Sadlier, Inc. All rights reserved.

Grade 3 Page 12

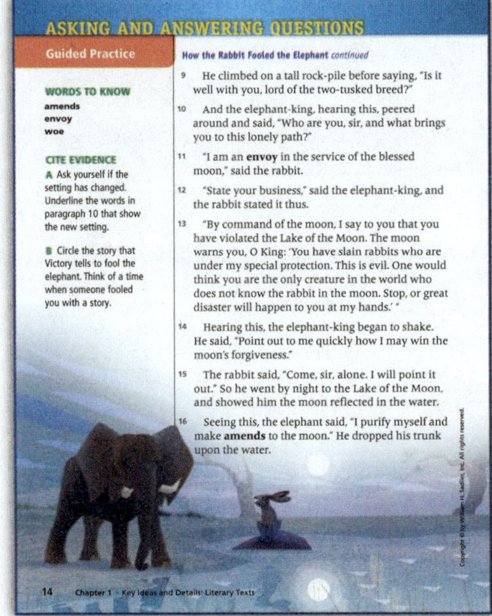
ASKING AND ANSWERING QUESTIONS

Guided Practice

WORDS TO KNOW
**amends**
**envoy**
**woe**

CITE EVIDENCE

A Ask yourself if the setting has changed. Underline the words in paragraph 10 that show the new setting.

B Circle the story that Victory tells to fool the elephant. Think of a time when someone fooled you with a story.

**How the Rabbit Fooled the Elephant** *continued*

9 He climbed on a tall rock-pile before saying, "Is it well with you, lord of the two-tusked breed?"

10 And the elephant-king, hearing this, peered around and said, "Who are you, sir, and what brings you to this lonely path?"

11 "I am an **envoy** in the service of the blessed moon," said the rabbit.

12 "State your business," said the elephant-king, and the rabbit stated it thus.

13 "By command of the moon, I say to you that you have violated the Lake of the Moon. The moon warns you, O King: 'You have slain rabbits who are under my special protection. This is evil. One would think you are the only creature in the world who does not know the rabbit in the moon. Stop, or great disaster will happen to you at my hands.' "

14 Hearing this, the elephant-king began to shake. He said, "Point out to me quickly how I may win the moon's forgiveness."

15 The rabbit said, "Come, sir, alone. I will point it out." So he went by night to the Lake of the Moon, and showed him the moon reflected in the water.

16 Seeing this, the elephant said, "I purify myself and make **amends** to the moon." He dropped his trunk upon the water.

14 Chapter 1 ▪ Key Ideas and Details: Literary Texts

Copyright © by William H. Sadlier, Inc. All rights reserved.

Grade 3 Page 14

◀ **Guided Practice** Lessons incorporate **partner reading in heterogeneous pairs** for scaffolded practice as the teacher circulates to provide targeted support as needed. Written Comprehension Checks offer multiple-choice and short-answer questions for pairs to work through together and then to share their thinking with the class.

**Independent Practice** Lessons offer **independent reading application with callout support** as the teacher circulates to ensure that all readers are on task and effectively engaging with text. Written Comprehension Checks offer multiple-choice and short-answer questions as opportunities to demonstrate standard mastery. ▶

➡ Alternative grouping models are suggested for struggling learners and English language learners, such as **heterogeneous pairing** with more proficient readers or **small group work with the teacher**.

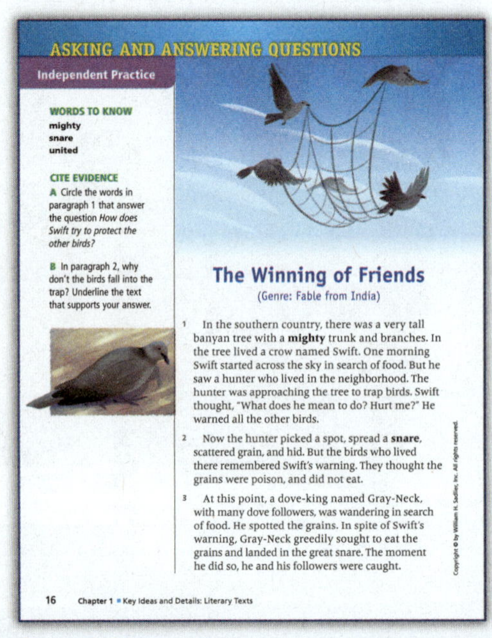
ASKING AND ANSWERING QUESTIONS

Independent Practice

WORDS TO KNOW
**mighty**
**snare**
**united**

CITE EVIDENCE

A Circle the words in paragraph 1 that answer the question *How does Swift try to protect the other birds?*

B In paragraph 2, why don't the birds fall into the trap? Underline the text that supports your answer.

### The Winning of Friends

(Genre: Fable from India)

1 In the southern country, there was a very tall banyan tree with a **mighty** trunk and branches. In the tree lived a crow named Swift. One morning Swift started across the sky in search of food. But he saw a hunter who lived in the neighborhood. The hunter was approaching the tree to trap birds. Swift thought, "What does he mean to do? Hurt me?" He warned all the other birds.

2 Now the hunter picked a spot, spread a **snare**, scattered grain, and hid. But the birds who lived there remembered Swift's warning. They thought the grains were poison, and did not eat.

3 At this point, a dove-king named Gray-Neck, with many dove followers, was wandering in search of food. He spotted the grains. In spite of Swift's warning, Gray-Neck greedily sought to eat the grains and landed in the great snare. The moment he did so, he and his followers were caught.

16 Chapter 1 ▪ Key Ideas and Details: Literary Texts

Copyright © by William H. Sadlier, Inc. All rights reserved.

Grade 3 Page 16

## Connecting Reading to Writing

Reading and Writing chapters are connected by theme and, where appropriate, by reading genre/writing type. Students are first introduced to key concepts in reading selections based around a theme, usually a social studies or science topic based on grade-level standards. In the related Writing chapter, they encounter a Student Model, exemplifying excellent grade-level output in the same theme.

| Reading Chapter | Writing Chapter | Theme |
|---|---|---|
| 1 | 7 | It Takes a Hero |
| 2 | 8 | Echoes of the Past |
| 3 | 9 | Best Friends |
| 4 | 10 | Extreme Weather |
| 5 | 11 | Searching for Answers |
| 6 | | The Solar System |

**Writing types in *Progress English Language Arts* include:**

- **Fictional narrative text** reflecting the sequential narrative structure of text within the related Reading chapter.
- **Informative/explanatory text** with the idea-detail structure of related reading selections.
- **Nonfictional narrative text** that reflects the structure of a historical text in the related Reading chapter.
- **Opinion piece** modeled after a reading selection with a structure identifying an opinion and related supporting reasons.
- **Research report** whose research topic reflects the setting/theme of the selections within the Reading chapter.

***Progress English Language Arts*** supports and recognizes the central role of the learner in the Standards for the English Language Arts* and the four dimensions of language learning: **content**, **purpose, development**, and **context**. These dimensions are integrated throughout *Progress English Language Arts*, providing a sound foundation for student success.

| Research | *Progress English Language Arts* |
|---|---|
| **CONTENT** | |
| *Content* addresses what students should know and be able to do in regard to English Language Arts.<br>The development of literacy and the attainment of English Language Arts standards depend on experience with and systematic study of a wide array of texts. | *Progress* chapters expose students to a collection of rigorous texts, fifty percent of the texts are informational and fifty percent are literary and encompass a wide range of genres and topics.<br>Through *Progress*, students learn a range of processes and strategies for comprehending and producing texts. Program instruction is centered on texts and skills rather than on related activities that draw attention from texts. Repeated readings and analysis of complex, content-area texts expose all students to new information and ideas. Writing instruction builds on student models and supports students in responding to an array of texts and becoming skilled with writing narrative, informational, and opinion essays, as well as research papers.<br>In addition, *Progress* includes study of the systems and structures of language and of language conventions, including grammar, punctuation, and spelling. Students learn how to apply their knowledge of the systems and structures of language depending on the context. |
| **PURPOSE** | |
| *Purpose* addresses why students use language.<br>English Language Arts instruction should focus on four purposes of language use: for obtaining and communicating information, for literacy response and expression, for learning and reflection, and for problem solving and application. | *Progress* integrates reading, writing, language and speaking and listening instruction with the goal of developing students who are independent learners, critical thinkers with deep knowledge, effective communicators, skilled problem solvers, and therefore, prepared for success in college and careers. With *Progress*, students' knowledge of history/social studies, science, and technical subjects and their academic and domain-specific vocabulary increase through reading rich, content-area texts. |

* NCTE/IRA Standards for the English Language Arts

| Research | *Progress English Language Arts* |
| --- | --- |
| **PURPOSE** *(continued)* | |
| | Relevant and meaningful opportunities for speaking and listening engage students in developing lifelong oral communication skills. Writing chapters ensure students develop effective written communication skills for a broad range of purposes. Integrated language instruction develops students' knowledge and use of conventions of standard English. Through a variety of carefully planned tasks that increase in their cognitive demand, students apply and extend the acquired knowledge and skills. |
| **DEVELOPMENT** | |
| *Development* addresses how students develop competencies in English Language Arts.<br>Students acquire knowledge and develop language competencies with practice over time. The quality of students' performance improves over time as students learn to use language clearly, strategically, critically, and creatively. | *Progress* is grounded in research-based learning progressions. Skill-based lessons reflect a gradual release of responsibility instructional model in which students assume increasing independence in reading and analyzing text, writing—including in response to text, developing and using vocabulary, employing the conventions of standard English, speaking, and listening. The program's scope and sequence balances instruction and practice so that students grow in their language competencies and effectively integrate all aspects of language development to learn, think and communicate effectively. For example, the readability of texts increases across chapters. Guided practice and independent practice are scaffolded and allow students to successfully engage with tasks that increase in cognitive demand. |
| **CONTEXT** | |
| *Context* influences all areas of learning and encompasses the three preceding dimensions.<br>Language is by definition social. Reading, writing, speaking, and listening take place in a context which influences the learning process and the resulting knowledge, skills, and communication. Students' interests and motivations are integral to English Language Arts instruction, practice, and application. | *Progress* is designed to engage and motivate the students who use the program. The magazine-like format was developed with today's learners in mind. The diversity of content, characters, and topics represented is inclusive and the selection was intentional. Each passage, each writing text, each speaking and listening activity was developed with the audience in mind and was purposefully selected with relevance to the participants in mind. Similarly, instruction was developed to guide students to think of the purpose and audience when communicating. |

# Program Components

The program components for *Progress English Language Arts* are designed to support a range of instructional models to effectively implement a standards-based English Language Arts program.

- Student Worktext
- Teacher's Edition
- Digital Resources

**Optional Purchase**

- Progress Monitor
- Full Access
- eBook for Student Worktext
- eBook for Teacher's Edition

## Student Worktext (in print and eBook formats)

Colorful standards-based instruction including complex, rigorous reading selections and structured writing models fuel student engagement. See pages T19–T24 for more information on the Student Worktext. ▼

ASKING AND ANSWERING QUESTIONS

Guided Instruction

**WORDS TO KNOW**
numerous
report
spray

To understand a text, **find details** in the text to help you **answer questions.**

**CITE EVIDENCE**

**A** To understand a story, it helps to **ask and answer questions** such as, *What characters are in the story?* Underline details in the title that answer this question. It also helps to ask, *What is the main problem?* Circle the sentence in paragraph 2 that answers this.

**B** Questioning why characters do things is also important. Underline the sentence in paragraph 2 that explains why the elephant-king does what he does. What other fables or folktales have you read in which one character is the leader?

### How the Rabbit Fooled the Elephant

(Genre: Fable from India)

1 In a part of the forest lived an elephant-king named Four-Tusk. He had **numerous** followers. Much time was spent protecting the herd.

2 Now once there came a twelve-year drought, so that ponds, swamps, and lakes went dry. Then all the elephants said to the lord of the herd: "O King, our little ones are so thirsty. Pray find a method of removing thirst." So he sent in eight directions elephants swift as the wind to search for water.

3 Now those who went east found a lake named Lake of the Moon. It was beautiful with swans, herons, ducks, cranes, and water-creatures. It was surrounded by flowering **sprays** of branches drooping under the weight of various blossoms. Why describe it? It was a part of paradise.

4 When they saw this, they rushed back to report to the elephant-king.

5 So Four-Tusk, on hearing their **report**, traveled with them to the Lake of the Moon. The lake sparkled in the spring sun. The elephants plunged in. But in doing so they stepped on the rabbits who long before had made their home on the banks of the lake. Now after drinking and bathing, the elephant-king with his followers departed to his own part of the jungle.

6 Then the rabbits held an emergency meeting. "What are we to do now?" they said. "These fellows will come here every day. Let some plan be made at once to prevent their return."

7 A rabbit named Victory, seeing their terror and sorrow, said with sympathy, "Have no fear. They shall not return. I promise it."

8 Victory departed and saw the elephant-king in the act of returning to the lake. Victory thought, "It is impossible for folk like me to come too near. I must seek safe ground before introducing myself."

**Comprehension Check**

What role does Victory play in the story so far?

KEY IDEAS AND DETAILS

Guided Instruction

**CITE EVIDENCE**

**C** Ask yourself, *What words does the author use to help me see the action?* Circle the words in paragraph 5 that help you see what is happening.

**D** The story's setting includes *when* it happens. Underline details that tell you when this story happens.

12 Chapter 1 ■ Key Ideas and Details: Literary Texts

Chapter 1 ■ Key Ideas and Details: Literary Texts 13

**Grade 3 Pages 12–17**

## Teacher's Edition (in print and eBook formats)

Teacher-friendly lesson plans with targeted standards instruction and supportive features suitable for both novice and experienced teachers. See page T25 for more information on the Teacher's Edition. ▼

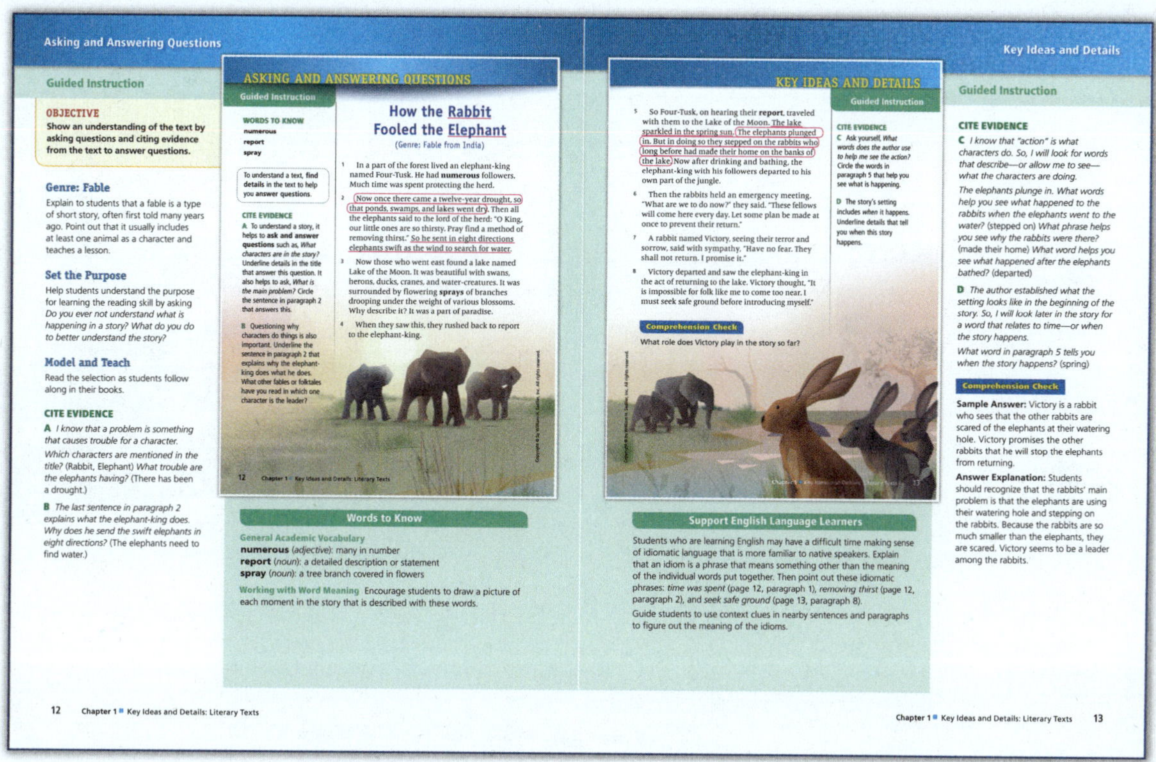

Asking and Answering Questions

Guided Instruction

**OBJECTIVE**
Show an understanding of the text by asking questions and citing evidence from the text to answer questions.

**Genre: Fable**
Explain to students that a fable is a type of short story, often first told many years ago. Point out that it usually includes at least one animal as a character and teaches a lesson.

**Set the Purpose**
Help students understand the purpose for learning the reading skill by asking *Do you ever not understand what is happening in a story? What do you do to better understand the story?*

**Model and Teach**
Read the selection as students follow along in their books.

**CITE EVIDENCE**
**A** *I know that a problem is something that causes trouble for a character. Which characters are mentioned in the title?* (Rabbit, Elephant) *What trouble are the elephants having?* (There has been a drought.)

**B** *The last sentence in paragraph 2 explains what the elephant-king does. Why does he send the swift elephants in eight directions?* (The elephants need to find water.)

ASKING AND ANSWERING QUESTIONS
Guided Instruction

WORDS TO KNOW
numerous
report
spray

To understand a text, find details in the text to help you answer questions.

CITE EVIDENCE
A To understand a story, it helps to ask and answer questions such as, *What characters are in the story?* Underline details in the title that answer this question. It also helps to ask, *What is the main problem?* Circle the sentence in paragraph 2 that answers this.

B Questioning why characters do things is also important. Underline the sentence in paragraph 2 that explains why the elephant-king does what he does. What other fables or folktales have you read in which one character is the leader?

### How the Rabbit Fooled the Elephant
(Genre: Fable from India)

1 In a part of the forest lived an elephant-king named Four-Tusk. He had **numerous** followers. Much time was spent protecting the herd.

2 Now once there came a twelve-year drought, so that ponds, swamps, and lakes went dry. Then all the elephants said to the lord of the herd: "O King, our little ones are so thirsty. Pray find a method of removing thirst." So he sent in eight directions elephants swift as the wind to search for water.

3 Now those who went east found a lake named Lake of the Moon. It was beautiful with swans, herons, ducks, cranes, and water-creatures. It was surrounded by flowering **sprays** of branches drooping under the weight of various blossoms. Why describe it? It was a part of paradise.

4 When they saw this, they rushed back to report to the elephant-king.

12 Chapter 1 ■ Key Ideas and Details: Literary Texts

Words to Know

General Academic Vocabulary
**numerous** (*adjective*): many in number
**report** (*noun*): a detailed description or statement
**spray** (*noun*): a tree branch covered in flowers

Working with Word Meaning Encourage students to draw a picture of each moment in the story that is described with these words.

KEY IDEAS AND DETAILS
Guided Instruction

5 So Four-Tusk, on hearing their **report**, traveled with them to the Lake of the Moon. The lake sparkled in the spring sun. The elephants plunged in. But in doing so they stepped on the rabbits who long before had made their home on the banks of the lake. Now after drinking and bathing, the elephant-king with his followers departed to his own part of the jungle.

6 Then the rabbits held an emergency meeting. "What are we to do now?" they said. "These fellows will come here every day. Let some plan be made at once to prevent their return."

7 A rabbit named Victory, seeing their terror and sorrow, said with sympathy, "Have no fear. They shall not return. I promise it."

8 Victory departed and saw the elephant-king in the act of returning to the lake. Victory thought, "It is impossible for folk like me to come too near. I must seek safe ground before introducing myself."

Comprehension Check
What role does Victory play in the story so far?

CITE EVIDENCE
C Ask yourself, *What words does the author use to help me see the action?* Circle the words in paragraph 5 that help you see what is happening.

D The story's setting includes when it happens. Underline details that tell you when this story happens.

Support English Language Learners

Students who are learning English may have a difficult time making sense of idiomatic language that is more familiar to native speakers. Explain that an idiom is a phrase that means something other than the meaning of the individual words put together. Then point out these idiomatic phrases: *time was spent* (page 12, paragraph 1), *removing thirst* (page 12, paragraph 2), and *seek safe ground* (page 13, paragraph 8).
Guide students to use context clues in nearby sentences and paragraphs to figure out the meaning of the idioms.

Key Ideas and Details

Guided Instruction

**CITE EVIDENCE**
**C** *I know that "action" is what characters do. So, I will look for words that describe—or allow me to see—what the characters are doing.*
*The elephants plunge in. What words help you see what happened to the rabbits when the elephants went to the water?* (stepped on) *What phrase helps you see why the rabbits were there?* (made their home) *What word helps you see what happened after the elephants bathed?* (departed)

**D** *The author established what the setting looks like in the beginning of the story. So, I will look later in the story for a word that relates to time—or when the story happens.*
*What word in paragraph 5 tells you when the story happens?* (spring)

Comprehension Check
**Sample Answer:** Victory is a rabbit who sees that the other rabbits are scared of the elephants at their watering hole. Victory promises the other rabbits that he will stop the elephants from returning.
**Answer Explanation:** Students should recognize that the rabbits' main problem is that the elephants are using their watering hole and stepping on the rabbits. Because the rabbits are so much smaller than the elephants, they are scared. Victory seems to be a leader among the rabbits.

Chapter 1 ■ Key Ideas and Details: Literary Texts 13

**Grade 3 Pages 12–13**

## Digital Resources

A rich array of digital resources for teachers, students, and parents is available at **SadlierConnect.com** to support the learning process. See page T27 for more information on Digital Resources. ▶

- Additional Practice
- Close Reading Selections
- Comprehension Checks
- Cumulative Comprehension Checks
- Fluency Practice
- Foundational Skills Handbook
- Foundational Skills Practice
- Home Connect Activities
- Instructional/Reteach Videos
- Interactive Lesson Planners
- Writing Handbook

## Progress Monitor (optional purchase)

Three Benchmark Assessments comprised of literary and informational texts and assessment items to monitor student progress toward proficiency of grade-level reading standards.

See Assessment Options, pages T30–31, for more information. ▼

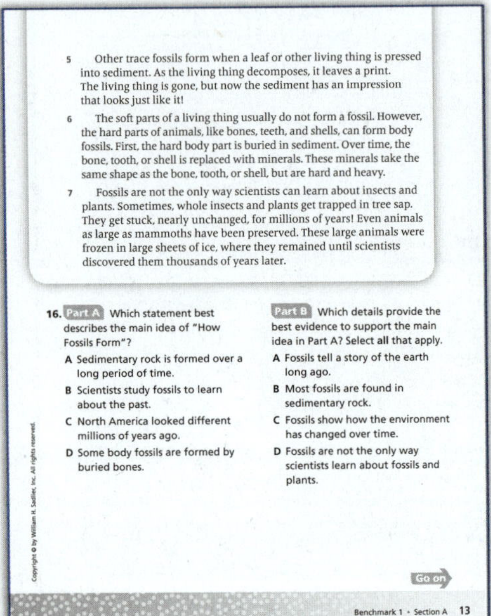

5 Other trace fossils form when a leaf or other living thing is pressed into sediment. As the living thing decomposes, it leaves a print. The living thing is gone, but now the sediment has an impression that looks just like it!

6 The soft parts of a living thing usually do not form a fossil. However, the hard parts of animals, like bones, teeth, and shells, can form body fossils. First, the hard body part is buried in sediment. Over time, the bone, tooth, or shell is replaced with minerals. These minerals take the same shape as the bone, tooth, or shell, but are hard and heavy.

7 Fossils are not the only way scientists can learn about insects and plants. Sometimes, whole insects and plants get trapped in tree sap. They get stuck, nearly unchanged, for millions of years! Even animals as large as mammoths have been preserved. These large animals were frozen in large sheets of ice, where they remained until scientists discovered them thousands of years later.

16. Part A Which statement best describes the main idea of "How Fossils Form"?

A Sedimentary rock is formed over a long period of time.
B Scientists study fossils to learn about the past.
C North America looked different millions of years ago.
D Some body fossils are formed by buried bones.

Part B Which details provide the best evidence to support the main idea in Part A? Select **all** that apply.

A Fossils tell a story of the earth long ago.
B Most fossils are found in sedimentary rock.
C Fossils show how the environment has changed over time.
D Fossils are not the only way scientists learn about fossils and plants.

Copyright © by William H. Sadlier, Inc. All rights reserved.

Go on

Benchmark 1 • Section A 13

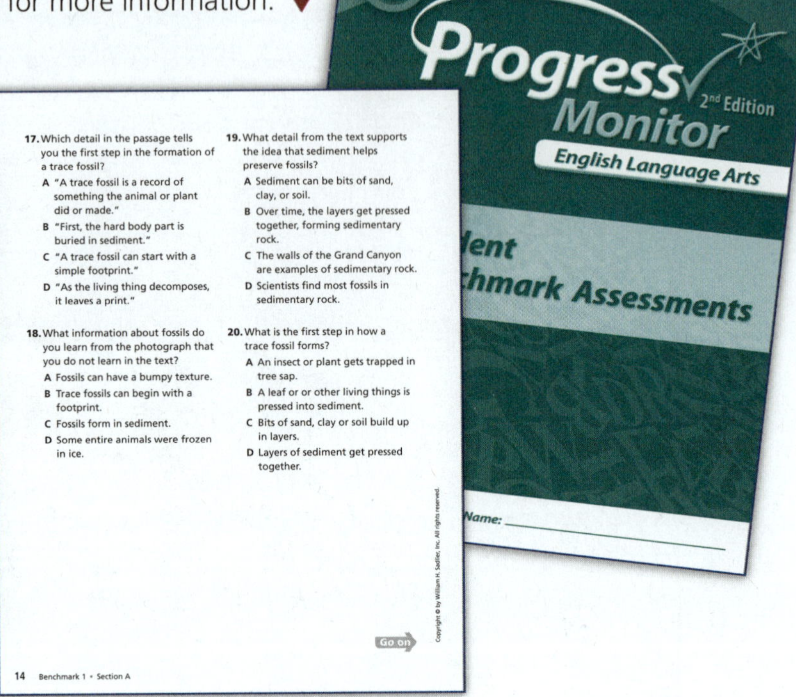

17. Which detail in the passage tells you the first step in the formation of a trace fossil?

A "A trace fossil is a record of something the animal or plant did or made."
B "First, the hard body part is buried in sediment."
C "A trace fossil can start with a simple footprint."
D "As the living thing decomposes, it leaves a print."

18. What information about fossils do you learn from the photograph that you do not learn in the text?

A Fossils can have a bumpy texture.
B Trace fossils can begin with a footprint.
C Fossils form in sediment.
D Some entire animals were frozen in ice.

19. What detail from the text supports the idea that sediment helps preserve fossils?

A Sediment can be bits of sand, clay, or soil.
B Over time, the layers get pressed together, forming sedimentary rock.
C The walls of the Grand Canyon are examples of sedimentary rock.
D Scientists find most fossils in sedimentary rock.

20. What is the first step in how a trace fossil forms?

A An insect or plant gets trapped in tree sap.
B A leaf or or other living things is pressed into sediment.
C Bits of sand, clay or soil build up in layers.
D Layers of sediment get pressed together.

Copyright © by William H. Sadlier, Inc. All rights reserved.

Go on

14 Benchmark 1 • Section A



Progress Monitor Grade 3, Pages 13–14

## for *Progress English Language Arts* (optional purchase)

Full Access offers an integrated and program-specific solution for assessing and addressing individual student learning gaps at strategic points during a school year. This unique solution includes a robust array of reports to indicate individual skill levels and recommend resources to meet individual needs.

See Full Access *for Progress English Language Arts*, pages T28–29, for more information. ▶

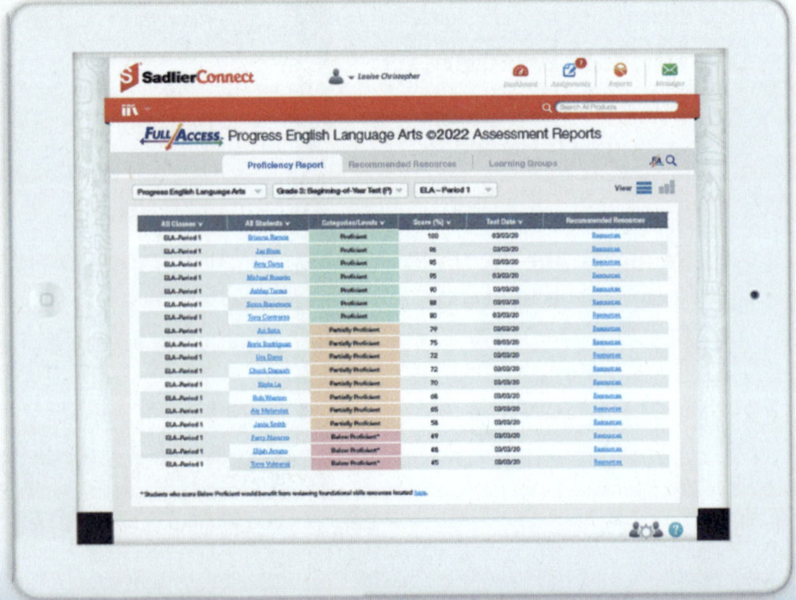

## eBooks (optional purchase)

**Student Worktext** eBooks provide the same quality content as the print Student Worktexts with added tools to make notes, highlight, search for key words, and zoom in on specific content.

**Teacher's Edition** eBooks provide the same quality content as the print Teacher's Editions with added tools to make notes, highlight, search for key words, and zoom in on specific content, toggle between the Student Worktext eBook and Teacher's Edition eBook, use full screen mode to project the Student Worktext, and assign lessons from the Student Worktext eBook to entire class or a specific group of students.

## Grade-Level Placement

The chart suggests grade-level placement for each level of *Progress English Language Arts*. These placements reflect teacher experience and recommendations but should not be taken too literally. Teachers should determine appropriate placement based on knowledge of their students' abilities, background knowledge, and reading levels.

**Grade-Level Placement**

| Level | Grade |
|---|---|
| K | K |
| A | 1 |
| B | 2 |
| C | 3 |
| D | 4 |
| E | 5 |
| F | 6 |
| G | 7 |
| H | 8 |

## Full Access™ for *Progress English Language Arts* (optional purchase)

Full Access for *Progress English Language Arts* can also be used to determine appropriate grade level content to assign to students based on Benchmark assessment data. Recommended Resources Reports identify resources within the program from across grade levels to meet individual needs.

## Student Worktext

***Progress English Language Arts*** is organized by English Language Arts standards.

**Reading Chapters** 1–6 present instruction and practice of grade-level reading skills and provide students with opportunities to:

- read literary and informational texts with a variety of genres.
- build knowledge through comprehension of texts.
- encounter increasingly rigorous and complex texts.
- answer text-based questions requiring use of supporting text evidence.
- engage in academic discourse about text.
- build academic and domain-specific vocabulary.

**Writing Chapters** 7–11 present instruction and practice of grade-level writing skills and provide students with opportunities to:

- encounter student models of key writing types: opinion, informative/ explanatory, narrative (fictional and nonfictional), and research report.
- develop effective written communication skills for a broad range of purposes.
- apply language conventions, including grammar, punctuation, and spelling to writing.
- engage in rigorous, academic discourse.
- employ speaking and listening skills.

## Chapter Overview

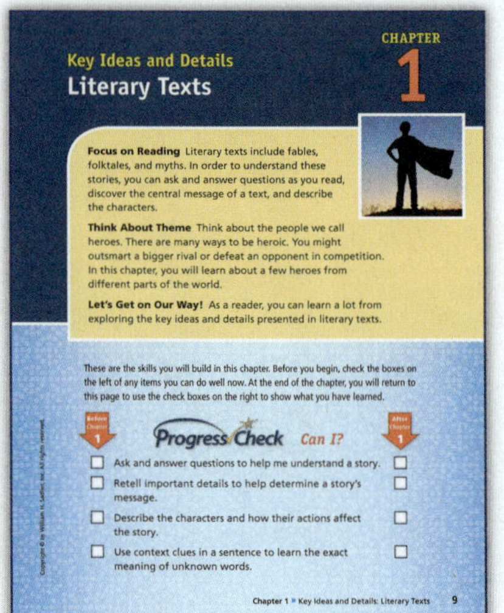

**Reading Chapter page 9**

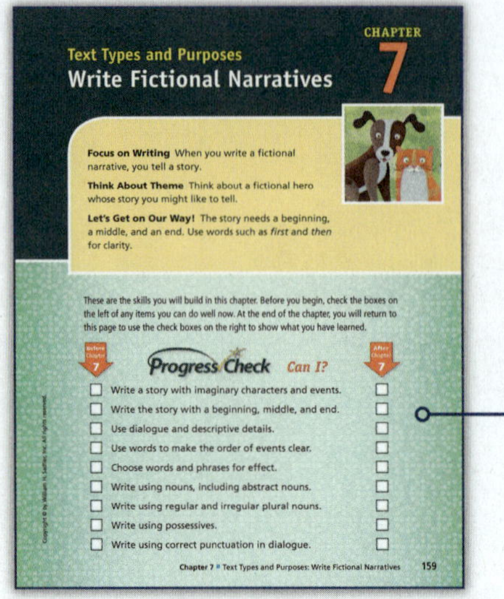

**Writing Chapter page 159**

Each chapter begins with a **Progress Check**. Students are provided with an overview of the skills and concepts presented in the chapter and opportunities to self-assess learning.

**Home Connect** activities in each chapter support learning at home.

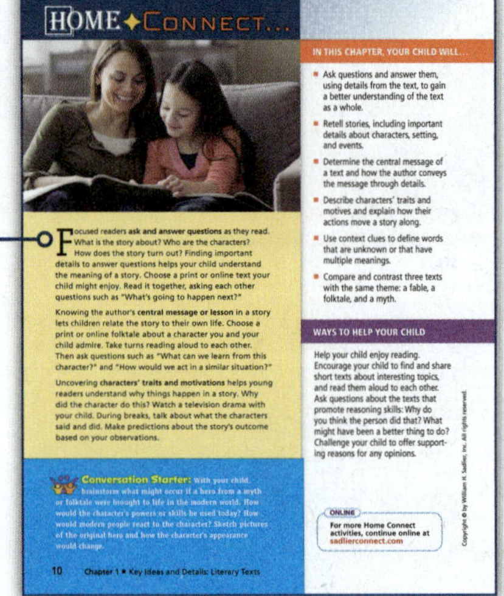

**Reading Chapter page 10**

**Writing Chapter page 160**

**Reading Chapter page 11**

**Writing Chapter page 161**

Each chapter is framed with an **Essential Question**, which serves as a focal point of academic discussion. The **Theme** and elements of each chapter are listed. Reading and Writing chapters are connected thematically.

## Reading Chapters

Each standard is taught using one continuous text following a Gradual Release Of Responsibility instructional model.

**Guided Instruction:** Direct standard instruction and teacher modeling

**Guided Practice:** Scaffolded standard practice in a partner-reading environment

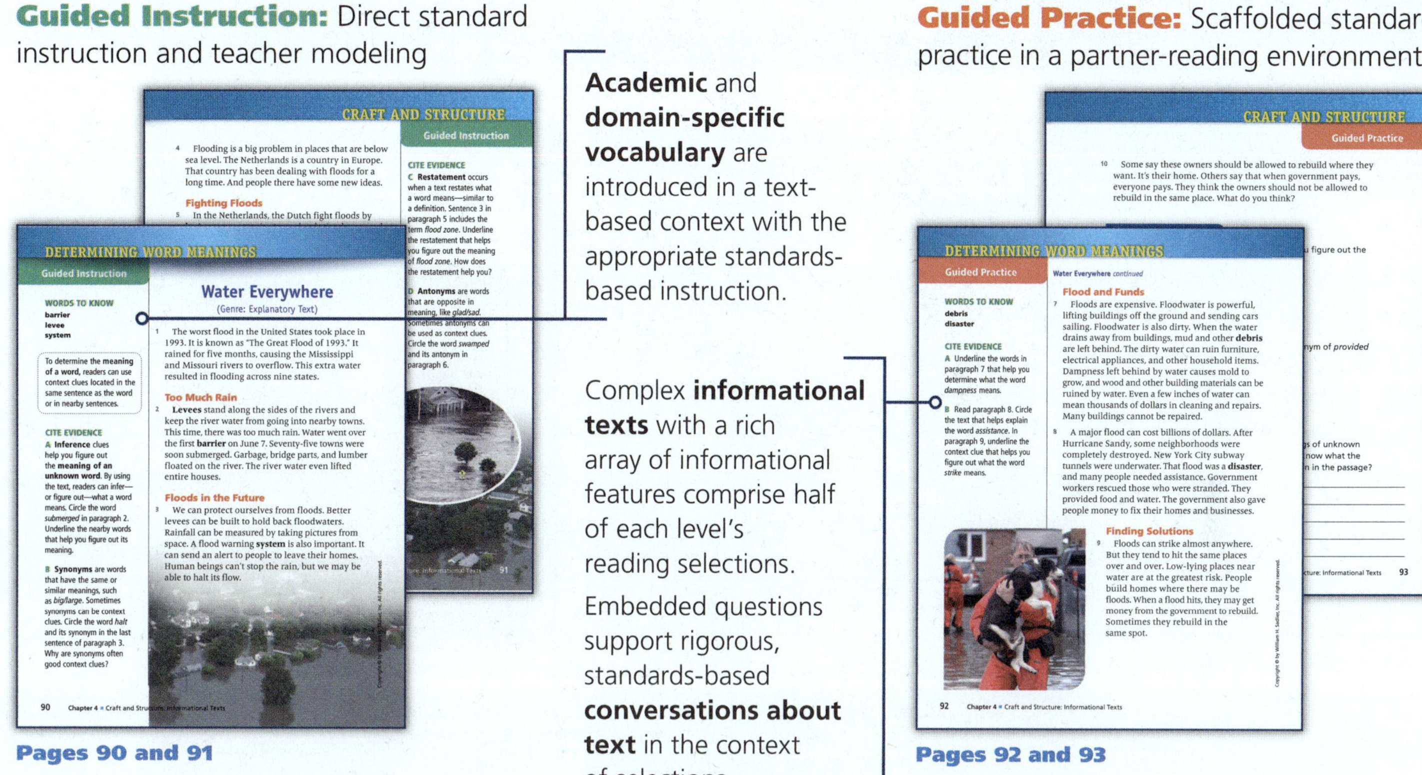

Pages 90 and 91

Pages 92 and 93

**Academic** and **domain-specific vocabulary** are introduced in a text-based context with the appropriate standards-based instruction.

Complex **informational texts** with a rich array of informational features comprise half of each level's reading selections.

Embedded questions support rigorous, standards-based **conversations about text** in the context of selections.

**Independent Practice:** Extensive independent standards-based practice enables students to build mastery.

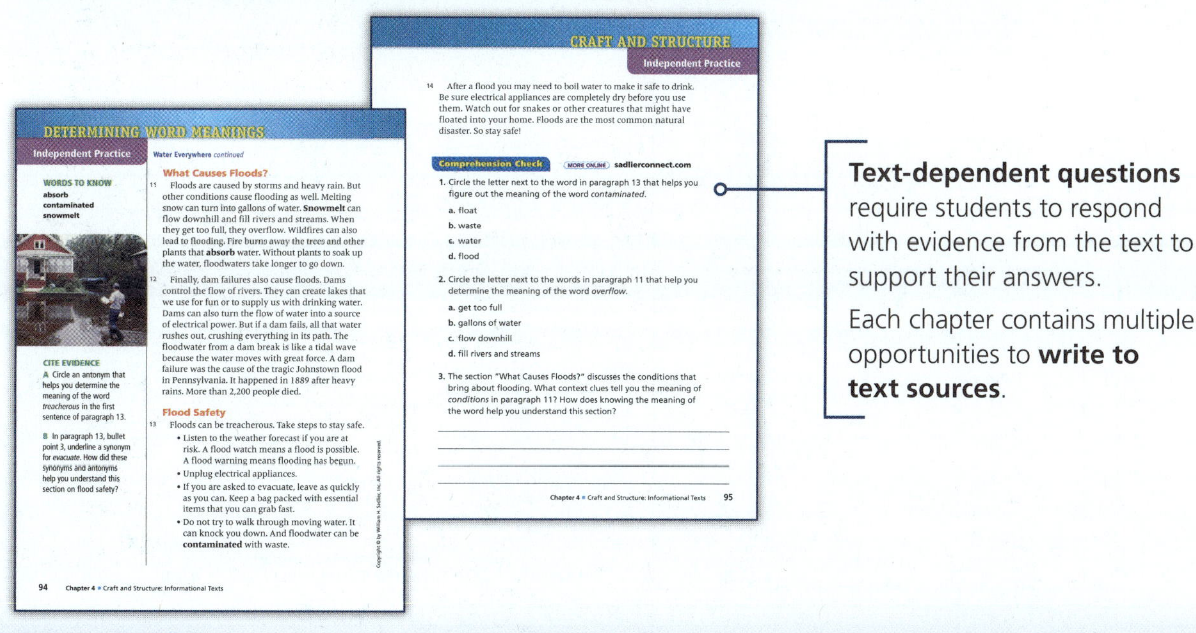

Pages 94 and 95

**Text-dependent questions** require students to respond with evidence from the text to support their answers.

Each chapter contains multiple opportunities to **write to text sources**.

## Connect Across Texts, Language, and Chapter Review

After reading the chapter's reading selections, students make connections to the texts, the chapter's Essential Question, and Theme.

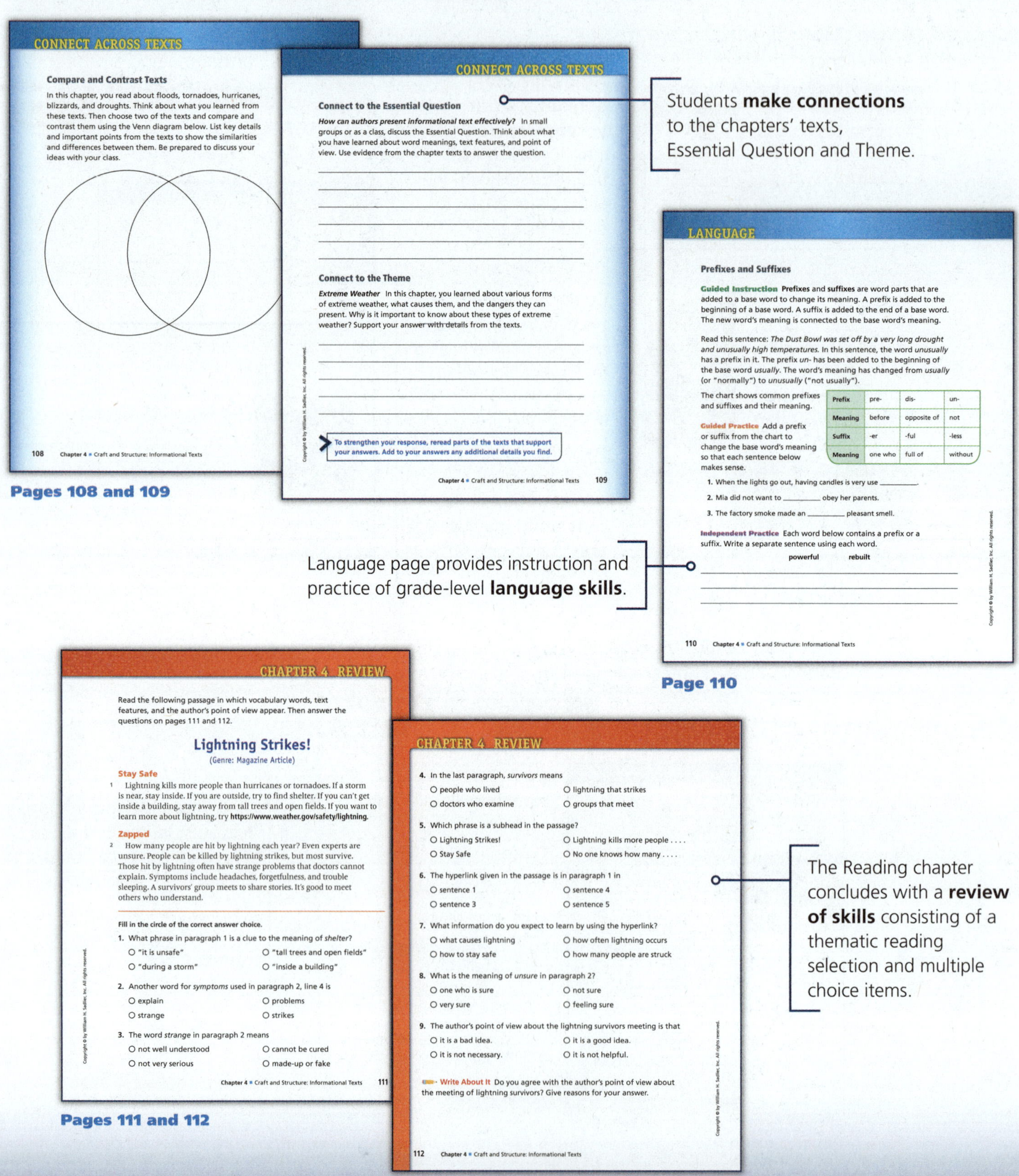

CONNECT ACROSS TEXTS

**Compare and Contrast Texts**

In this chapter, you read about floods, tornadoes, hurricanes, blizzards, and droughts. Think about what you learned from these texts. Then choose two of the texts and compare and contrast them using the Venn diagram below. List key details and important points from the texts to show the similarities and differences between them. Be prepared to discuss your ideas with your class.

108 Chapter 4 • Craft and Structure: Informational Texts

CONNECT ACROSS TEXTS

**Connect to the Essential Question**

***How can authors present informational text effectively?*** In small groups or as a class, discuss the Essential Question. Think about what you have learned about word meanings, text features, and point of view. Use evidence from the chapter texts to answer the question.

**Connect to the Theme**

***Extreme Weather*** In this chapter, you learned about various forms of extreme weather, what causes them, and the dangers they can present. Why is it important to know about these types of extreme weather? Support your answer with details from the texts.

To strengthen your response, reread parts of the texts that support your answers. Add to your answers any additional details you find.

Copyright © by William H. Sadlier, Inc. All rights reserved.

Chapter 4 • Craft and Structure: Informational Texts 109

Students **make connections** to the chapters' texts, Essential Question and Theme.

**Pages 108 and 109**

LANGUAGE

**Prefixes and Suffixes**

**Guided Instruction** **Prefixes** and **suffixes** are word parts that are added to a base word to change its meaning. A prefix is added to the beginning of a base word. A suffix is added to the end of a base word. The new word's meaning is connected to the base word's meaning.

Read this sentence: *The Dust Bowl was set off by a very long drought and unusually high temperatures.* In this sentence, the word *unusually* has a prefix in it. The prefix *un-* has been added to the beginning of the base word *usually*. The word's meaning has changed from *usually* (or "normally") to *unusually* ("not usually").

The chart shows common prefixes and suffixes and their meaning.

| Prefix | pre- | dis- | un- |
|---|---|---|---|
| Meaning | before | opposite of | not |
| Suffix | -er | -ful | -less |
| Meaning | one who | full of | without |

**Guided Practice** Add a prefix or suffix from the chart to change the base word's meaning so that each sentence below makes sense.

1. When the lights go out, having candles is very use ________.
2. Mia did not want to ________ obey her parents.
3. The factory smoke made an ________ pleasant smell.

**Independent Practice** Each word below contains a prefix or a suffix. Write a separate sentence using each word.

powerful rebuilt

110 Chapter 4 • Craft and Structure: Informational Texts

Copyright © by William H. Sadlier, Inc. All rights reserved.

Language page provides instruction and practice of grade-level **language skills**.

**Page 110**

CHAPTER 4 REVIEW

Read the following passage in which vocabulary words, text features, and the author's point of view appear. Then answer the questions on pages 111 and 112.

**Lightning Strikes!**

(Genre: Magazine Article)

**Stay Safe**

1 Lightning kills more people than hurricanes or tornadoes. If a storm is near, stay inside. If you are outside, try to find shelter. If you can't get inside a building, stay away from tall trees and open fields. If you want to learn more about lightning, try **https://www.weather.gov/safety/lightning**.

**Zapped**

2 How many people are hit by lightning each year? Even experts are unsure. People can be killed by lightning strikes, but most survive. Those hit by lightning often have strange problems that doctors cannot explain. Symptoms include headaches, forgetfulness, and trouble sleeping. A survivors' group meets to share stories. It's good to meet others who understand.

**Fill in the circle of the correct answer choice.**

1. What phrase in paragraph 1 is a clue to the meaning of *shelter*?
   - O "it is unsafe" O "tall trees and open fields"
   - O "during a storm" O "inside a building"
2. Another word for *symptoms* used in paragraph 2, line 4 is
   - O explain O problems
   - O strange O strikes
3. The word *strange* in paragraph 2 means
   - O not well understood O cannot be cured
   - O not very serious O made-up or fake

Copyright © by William H. Sadlier, Inc. All rights reserved.

Chapter 4 • Craft and Structure: Informational Texts 111

CHAPTER 4 REVIEW

4. In the last paragraph, *survivors* means
   - O people who lived O lightning that strikes
   - O doctors who examine O groups that meet
5. Which phrase is a subhead in the passage?
   - O Lightning Strikes! O Lightning kills more people . . . .
   - O Stay Safe O No one knows how many . . . .
6. The hyperlink given in the passage is in paragraph 1 in
   - O sentence 1 O sentence 4
   - O sentence 3 O sentence 5
7. What information do you expect to learn by using the hyperlink?
   - O what causes lightning O how often lightning occurs
   - O how to stay safe O how many people are struck
8. What is the meaning of *unsure* in paragraph 2?
   - O one who is sure O not sure
   - O very sure O feeling sure
9. The author's point of view about the lightning survivors meeting is that
   - O it is a bad idea. O it is a good idea.
   - O it is not necessary. O it is not helpful.

**Write About It** Do you agree with the author's point of view about the meeting of lightning survivors? Give reasons for your answer.

Copyright © by William H. Sadlier, Inc. All rights reserved.

112 Chapter 4 • Craft and Structure: Informational Texts

**Pages 111 and 112**

The Reading chapter concludes with a **review of skills** consisting of a thematic reading selection and multiple choice items.

## Reading Selections in Level C

Reading selections in *Progress English Language Arts* incorporate a variety of genres and reflect expectations regarding text complexity. The **LEXILE®** measure and brief summary for each reading selection is provided in the chart below.

As students prepare to read each selection, provide background information about the theme or topic they will encounter. Encourage students to make connections to any prior knowledge and to further explore these topics.

**Chapter 1 Theme:** It Takes a Hero

- **How the Rabbit Fooled the Elephant** and **The Winning of Friends** pp. 12–17, **680L** and **690L**: The rabbits have long lived by a peaceful lake, but the arrival of elephants threatens their home. One clever rabbit sets out to solve the problem using brains, not brawn.
- **Momotaro** pp. 18–23, **610L**: A folktale from Japan takes readers on a journey to an island of bandits. A boy, a dog, a monkey, and a bird vanquish the bandits and return to their homes as heroes.
- **Athena and Poseidon** pp. 24–29, **710L**: Athens is looking for a patron in this retelling of a Greek myth. It's god vs. goddess in the contest for Athens.

**Chapter 4 Theme:** Extreme Weather

- **Water Everywhere** pp. 90–95, **720L**: Heavy rains, failing infrastructure, and even wildfires can contribute to flooding. This explantory text includes tips on what to do to stay safe in a flood.
- **Watch Out for Weather!** pp. 96–101, **760L**: Extreme weather events happen every day. This journal article covers hurricanes, tornadoes, and blizzards.
- **Stop the Droughts!** pp. 102–107, **730L**: Droughts ruin crops and cause food shortages and wildfires. What causes droughts, and what can we do to prevent them? The answers to these questions can be found in this newspaper editorial.

**Chapter 2 Theme:** Echoes of the Past

- **Rainforest Art** pp. 38–43, **790L**: A recent discovery in Colombia has revealed a collection of prehistoric rock. Beautiful photographs give readers a look into the past.
- **King Tut: From Forgotten Pahraoh to Ancient Superstar** pp. 44–49, **770L**: The world has been fascinated by King Tutankhamun ever since the discovery of his tomb in 1922. Read more in this historical text.
- **The Mysteries of Easter Island** pp. 50–55, **770L**: Questions continue to be asked and answered about the megaliths on this island. What do the sculptures tell us about the people who made them?

**Chapter 5 Theme:** Searching for Answers

- **The Case of the Missing Fruit** pp. 116–121, **600L**: What has happened to Mrs. Moreno's prickly pear cactus fruit? Tino and Sophia aim to find out in this whodunit. Students can follow the further exploits of Tino and Sophia in the following passage.
- **A Camping Adventure** pp. 122–127, **690L**: The brother and sister detective team of Tino and Sophia is back. This adventure takes them with their family to the Sonoran Desert, where they make a spectacular discovery. Illustrations take readers out to the desert to join in the fun.

**Chapter 3 Theme:** Best Friends

- **The Secret Garden** pp. 64–69, **690L**: This excerpt from Frances Hodgson Burnett's 1911 novel shows the healing power of the friendship of Mary, Dickon, and Colin.
- **Anne of Green Gables** pp. 70–75, **NP***: This stage play adaptation of L.M. Montgomery's novel takes readers to the moment when Anne and Diana, destined to be best friends forever, first meet. (*NP texts do not receive a Lexile measure.)
- **Damon and Pythias** pp. 76–81, **NP***: This tale from Ancient Greece is retold as a rollicking narrative poem about what true friends will to for each other. (*NP texts do not receive a Lexile measure.)

**Chapter 6 Theme:** Amazing Discoveries

- **How to Make a Telescope** pp. 136–141, **770L**: Making a telescope does not have to break the bank. This technical text takes readers through the steps of making their own telescopes out of simple materials.
- **Pluto: Planet or Not?** pp. 142–147, **780L**: From 1930 to 2006, Pluto was a planet. Then it was not. Find out what changed in this magazine article about how Pluto went from planet to dwarf planet.
- **Pluto Is Our Planet!** pp. 148–153, **800L**: When Pluto lost its status as a planet, some people seemed to take it personally. The writer of this editorial makes a case for reinstating Pluto's title as the ninth planet in the solar system.

## Writing Chapters

Instruction and practice in the Writing chapters reflect the key writing types in English Language Arts curriculum: opinion, informative/explanatory, narrative (both fictional and nonfictional), and research report. Writing chapters are connected thematically to Reading chapters.

**Pages 162–165**

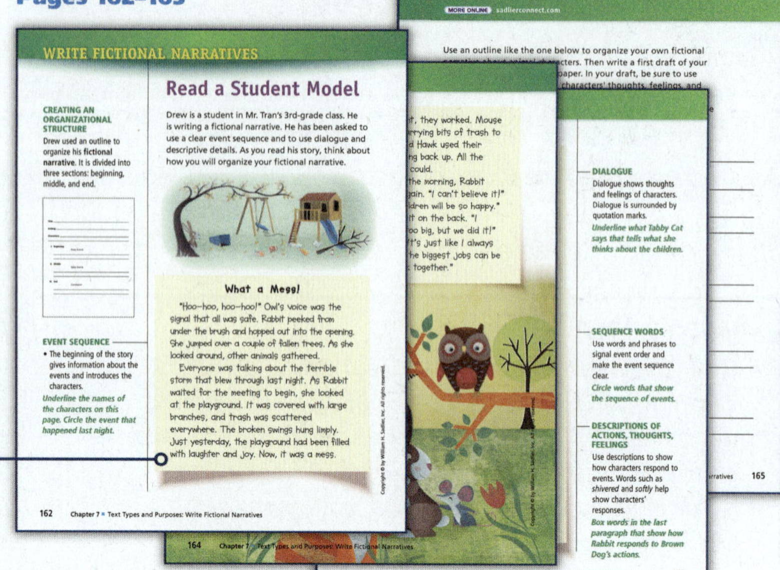
WRITE FICTIONAL NARRATIVES

Read a Student Model

Drew is a student in Mr. Tran's 3rd-grade class. He is writing a fictional narrative. He has been asked to use a clear event sequence and to use dialogue and descriptive details. As you read his story, think about how you will organize your fictional narrative.

CREATING AN ORGANIZATIONAL STRUCTURE
Drew used an outline to organize his fictional narrative. It is divided into three sections: beginning, middle, and end.

EVENT SEQUENCE
• The beginning of the story gives information about the events and introduces the characters.
*Underline the names of the characters on this page. Circle the event that happened last night.*

What a Mess!

"Hoo-hoo, hoo-hoo!" Owl's voice was the signal that all was safe. Rabbit peeked from under the brush and hopped out into the opening. She jumped over a couple of fallen trees. As she looked around, other animals gathered.

Everyone was talking about the terrible storm that blew through last night. As Rabbit waited for the meeting to begin, she looked at the playground. It was covered with large branches, and trash was scattered everywhere. The broken swings hung limply. Just yesterday, the playground had been filled with laughter and joy. Now, it was a mess.

162 Chapter 7 • Text Types and Purposes: Write Fictional Narratives

DIALOGUE
Dialogue shows thoughts and feelings of characters. Dialogue is surrounded by quotation marks.
*Underline what Tabby Cat says that tells what she thinks about the children.*

SEQUENCE WORDS
Use words and phrases to signal event order and make the event sequence clear.
*Circle words that show the sequence of events.*

DESCRIPTIONS OF ACTIONS, THOUGHTS, FEELINGS
Use descriptions to show how characters respond to events. Words such as *shivered* and *softly* help show characters' responses.
*Box words in the last paragraph that show how Rabbit responds to Brown Dog's actions.*

Chapter 7 • Text Types and Purposes: Write Fictional Narratives 163

Each **writing model** is surrounded with support, including, explanations of each component of the type of writing and opportunities for students to analyze, organize, and produce the same text type.

**Pages 166–169**

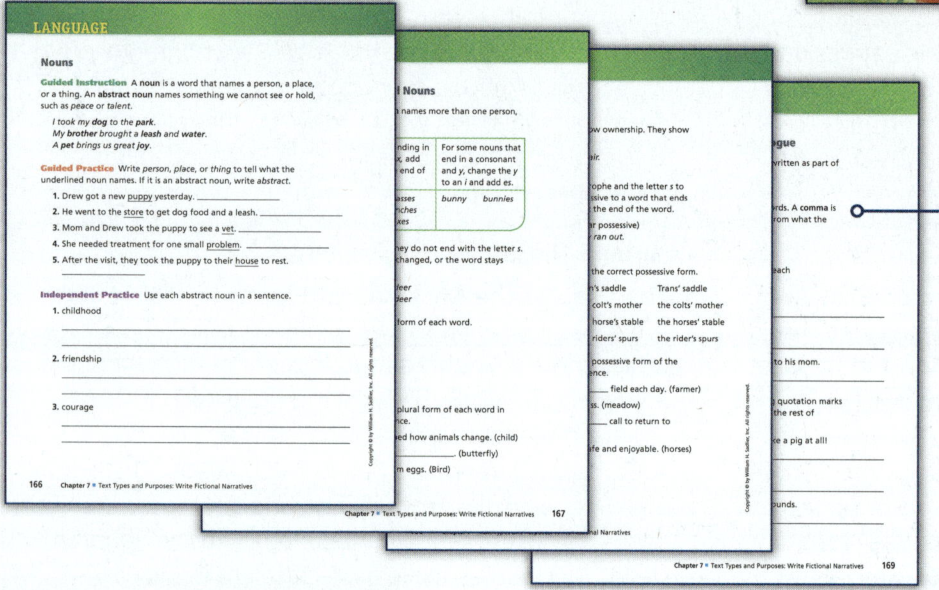
LANGUAGE

Nouns

**Guided Instruction** A **noun** is a word that names a person, a place, or a thing. An **abstract noun** names something we cannot see or hold, such as *peace* or *talent*.

*I took my **dog** to the **park**.*
*My **brother** brought a **leash** and **water**.*
*A **pet** brings us great **joy**.*

**Guided Practice** Write *person, place,* or *thing* to tell what the underlined noun names. If it is an abstract noun, write *abstract*.

1. Drew got a new puppy yesterday. ______
2. He went to the store to get dog food and a leash. ______
3. Mom and Drew took the puppy to see a vet. ______
4. She needed treatment for one small problem. ______
5. After the visit, they took the puppy to their house to rest. ______

**Independent Practice** Use each abstract noun in a sentence.

1. childhood
2. friendship
3. courage

166 Chapter 7 • Text Types and Purposes: Write Fictional Narratives

Integrated **Language** pages focus on conventions of English and knowledge of language—grammar, usage, and mechanics—through a gradual release instructional model.

CHAPTER 7 REVIEW

Assignment: Write a fictional narrative about animal characters.

On the lines below, write your final copy of the fictional narrative draft you created on page 165. Be sure to include dialogue and description to show thoughts, feelings, and actions. Make sure to choose your words carefully and use words to signal the order of events. Include a conclusion that wraps up events in your story. See the Writing Handbook (at sadlierconnect.com) for ways to improve your writing as you revise.

CHAPTER 7 REVIEW

This paragraph has mistakes in sentences and agreement. There are incorrect plural nouns and possessive forms, as well as incorrect punctuation of dialogue. Write the paragraph correctly on the lines below.

Lauren has two bunnys, Patches and Hopper. They were in a terrible flood. When the flood came, Lauren put them in boxs and carried them to safety. Lauren whispered You will be okay. Hearing her voice made them feel calm. Patches and Hopper didn't have their favorite grassies, but they did have plenty of water and food. After the flood, Laurens mom suggested that she teach other peoples how to help animals in emergencys.

Chapter 7 • Text Types and Purposes: Write Fictional Narratives 171

The Writing chapter concludes with a **review of language skills** and **on-demand writing**.

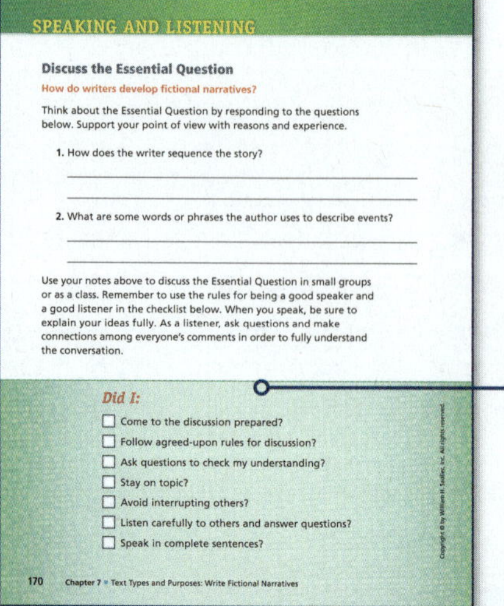
SPEAKING AND LISTENING

Discuss the Essential Question

How do writers develop fictional narratives?

Think about the Essential Question by responding to the questions below. Support your point of view with reasons and experience.

1. How does the writer sequence the story?
2. What are some words or phrases the author uses to describe events?

Use your notes above to discuss the Essential Question in small groups or as a class. Remember to use the rules for being a good speaker and a good listener in the checklist below. When you speak, be sure to explain your ideas fully. As a listener, ask questions and make connections among everyone's comments in order to fully understand the conversation.

Did I:
- ☐ Come to the discussion prepared?
- ☐ Follow agreed-upon rules for discussion?
- ☐ Ask questions to check my understanding?
- ☐ Stay on topic?
- ☐ Avoid interrupting others?
- ☐ Listen carefully to others and answer questions?
- ☐ Speak in complete sentences?

170 Chapter 7 • Text Types and Purposes: Write Fictional Narratives

**Page 170**

**Speaking and Listening** lessons support students as they engage in **rigorous, academic discourse** about the chapter's Essential Question.

**Pages 171–172**

## Teacher's Edition

Each chapter of the Teacher's Edition clearly states the learning objective and provides teachers with an easy-to-use lesson plan filled with the following instructional support.

Suggestions for modifications and instructional support are provided in each lesson:

### Words to Know

Academic vocabulary is defined and researched based vocabulary-building activities (e.g. Marzano's six vocabulary acquisition strategies) support acquisition. The *Words to Know* in each reading selection are defined in the Student Worktext's *Glossary* and at point-of-use in the Teacher's Edition.

### Foundational Skills

Foundational skill practice and foundational skill review are integrated at point-of-use in within reading selection instruction. A comprehensive *Foundational Skills Handbook* providing instruction and practice on all grade-level foundational reading skills, including phonics, word recognition, and fluency, is available at **SadlierConnect.com**.

### Support English Language Learners

Students whose primary language is not English may need modifications or additional instructional support in breaking down the skill, context, or text of a chapter.

### Discussion Skills

Based on key skills and concepts and Resnick's research-based *Accountable Talk* strategies, the *Discussion Skills'* suggestions integrate speaking and listening instructions into every chapter and support academic discussion of text.

### Differentiate Instruction/Grouping Options

Modifications and grouping options are included for struggling learners to make content accessible for all students.

### Assess and Respond

*If-Then* diagnostics allow teachers to remediate immediately when students need additional support.

**Learning Progressions** provide context and background of the critical skills and skills progressions by showing what students learned in the previous grade level and connections to what they will learn to the next grade level; building coherence within and across the grade levels.

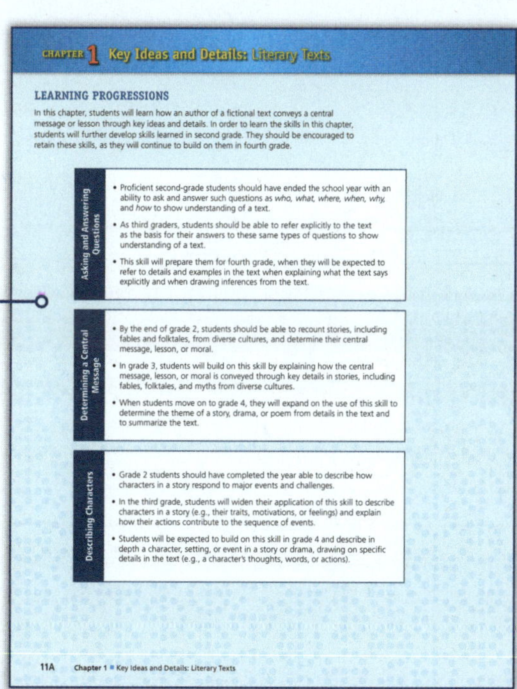

CHAPTER 1 Key Ideas and Details: Literary Texts

LEARNING PROGRESSIONS

In this chapter, students will learn how an author of a fictional text conveys a central message or lesson through key ideas and details. In order to learn the skills in this chapter, students will further develop skills learned in second grade. They should be encouraged to retain these skills, as they will continue to build on them in fourth grade.

**Asking and Answering Questions**

- Proficient second-grade students should have ended the school year with an ability to ask and answer such questions as *who, what, where, when, why,* and *how* to show understanding of a text.
- As third graders, students should be able to refer explicitly to the text as the basis for their answers to these same types of questions to show understanding of a text.
- This skill will prepare them for fourth grade, when they will be expected to refer to details and examples in the text when explaining what the text says explicitly and when drawing inferences from the text.

**Determining a Central Message**

- By the end of grade 2, students should be able to recount stories, including fables and folktales, from diverse cultures, and determine their central message, lesson, or moral.
- In grade 3, students will build on this skill by explaining how the central message, lesson, or moral is conveyed through key details in stories, including fables, folktales, and myths from diverse cultures.
- When students move on to grade 4, they will expand on the use of this skill to determine the theme of a story, drama, or poem from details in the text and to summarize the text.

**Describing Characters**

- Grade 2 students should have completed the year able to describe how characters in a story respond to major events and challenges.
- In the third grade, students will widen their application of this skill to describe characters in a story (e.g., their traits, motivations, or feelings) and explain how their actions contribute to the sequence of events.
- Students will be expected to build on this skill in grade 4 and describe in depth a character, setting, or event in a story or drama, drawing on specific details in the text (e.g., a character's thoughts, words, or actions).

11A Chapter 1 ■ Key Ideas and Details: Literary Texts

## Suggested Pacing

| Weeks | Student Worktext | Online Resources to Support and Assess |
|---|---|---|
| 1–3<br>4–6<br>7–9 | Reading Chapter 1, pp. 9–34<br>Reading Chapter 2, pp. 35–60<br>Reading Chapter 3, pp. 61–86 | • Instructional/Reteach Videos<br>• Additional Practice<br>• Comprehension Check<br>• Close Reading<br>• Foundational Skills Handbook<br>• Foundational Skills Practice<br>• Fluency Practice<br>• Chapter Test<br>Optional purchase: Full Access |
| 10 | | Cumulative Comprehension Check, Chapters 1–3 |
| 11–13<br>14–16<br>17–19 | Reading Chapter 4, pp. 87–112<br>Reading Chapter 5, pp. 113–132<br>Reading Chapter 6, pp. 133–158 | • Instructional/Reteach Videos<br>• Additional Practice<br>• Comprehension Check<br>• Close Reading<br>• Foundational Skills Handbook<br>• Foundational Skills Practice<br>• Fluency Practice<br>• Chapter Test<br>Optional purchase: Full Access |
| 20 | | Cumulative Comprehension Check, Chapters 1–6 |
| 21–22<br>23–24<br>25–26<br>27–28<br>29–30 | Writing Chapter 7, pp. 159–172<br>Writing Chapter 8, pp. 173–186<br>Writing Chapter 9, pp. 187–200<br>Writing Chapter 10, pp. 201–214<br>Writing Chapter 11, pp. 215–228 | • Instructional/Reteach Videos<br>• Additional Practice<br>• Writing Handbook<br>• Chapter Test<br>Optional purchase: Full Access |

See page T28 for more information about Full Access for *Progress English Language Arts.*

## Digital Resources

A rich array of digital resources for teachers, students, and families available at **SadlierConnect.com**, supports program implementation and extend learning opportunities.

- **Additional Practice** offers targeted skill practice for each Reading and Writing chapter.
- **Close Reading Selections** provide students with opportunities to build reading stamina, analyze and annotate texts, and support responses with text evidence.
- **Comprehension Checks** assess a specific lesson skill for each Reading chapter and two Cumulative Comprehension Checks assess a group of reading skills, chapters 1–3 and chapters 1–6.
- **Fluency Practice** provides students with opportunities to improve comprehension with repeated readings of a continuous text.

**Instructional/Reteach Video**

- **Instructional/Reteach Videos** break down reading and language skills as well as engage students to ensure success.
- **Foundational Skills Handbook** and **Foundational Skills Practice** provide instruction and practice of grade-level foundational skills including review of key phonics and word recognition skills from earlier grades.
- **Home Connect Activities** provide an overview of skills in each chapter as well as specific activities to support family member involvement.
- **Writing Handbook** contains instruction and support for teaching the writing process.

**Full Access** for *Progress English Language Arts* (optional purchase) provides site-wide access to all program-specific components—Student Edition eBooks, Teacher's Edition eBooks, Online Assessments, and digital resources including instructional videos, plus a robust array of reports to indicate individual skill levels and recommend resources from across grade levels to meet individual needs.

Full Access for *Progress English Language Arts* is designed to:

- identify and resolve students' learning gaps by assessing their skill levels through Benchmark Assessments.
- provide teachers with variety of reports—Proficiency, Skills, Domain, Learning Groups— as well as Recommended Resources to address skill deficits and track progress.
- allow teachers to create, assign, and teach personalized action plans with recommended instruction and practice.
- provide teachers with *full access* to all on and off grade-level *Progress English Language Arts* instruction and practice.

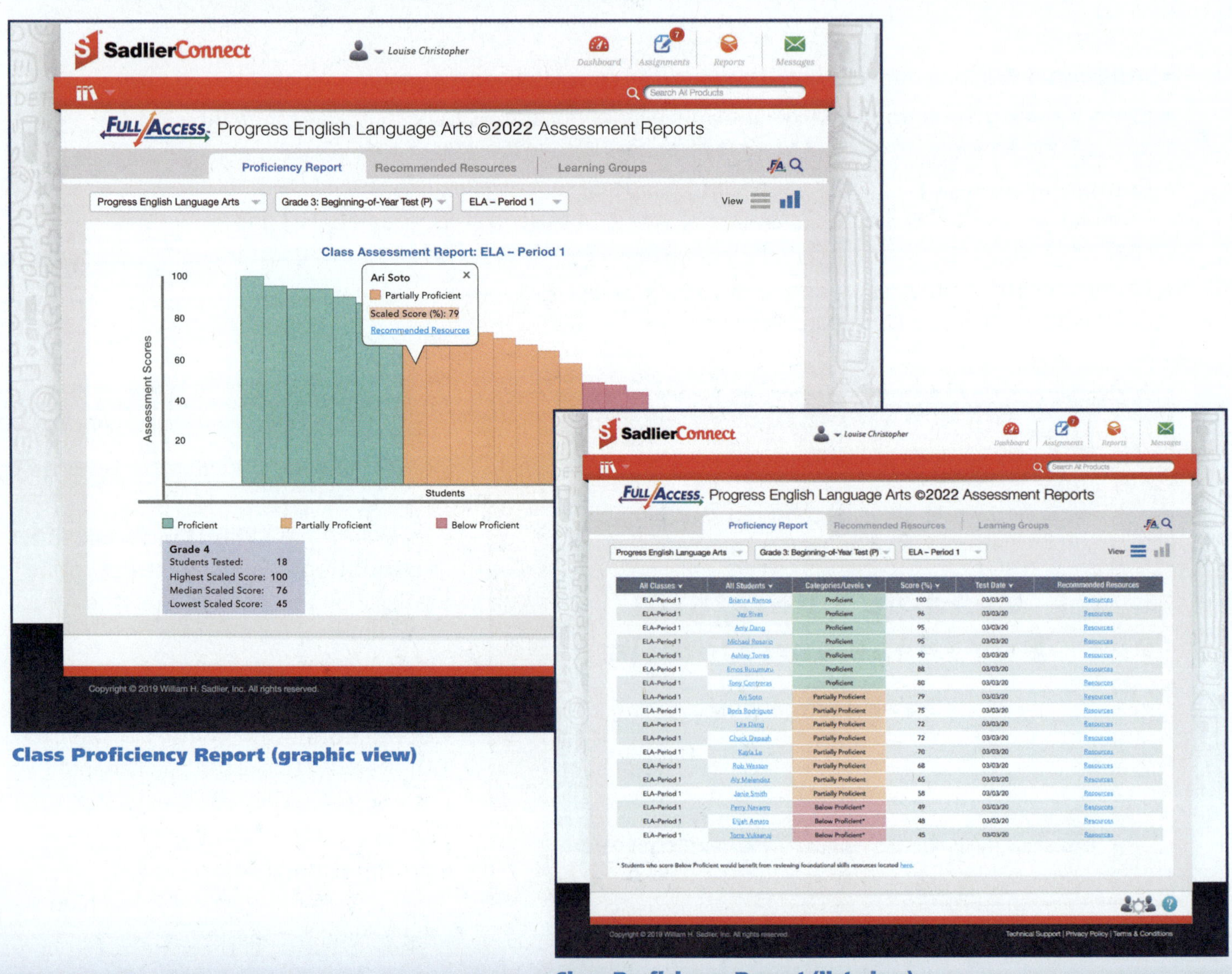


| All Classes | All Students | Categories/Levels | Score (%) | Test Date | Recommended Resources |
|---|---|---|---|---|---|
| ELA-Period 1 | Brianna Ramos | Proficient | 100 | 03/03/20 | Resources |
| ELA-Period 1 | Jay Rivas | Proficient | 96 | 03/03/20 | Resources |
| ELA-Period 1 | Amy Dang | Proficient | 95 | 03/03/20 | Resources |
| ELA-Period 1 | Michael Rosario | Proficient | 95 | 03/03/20 | Resources |
| ELA-Period 1 | Ashley Torres | Proficient | 90 | 03/03/20 | Resources |
| ELA-Period 1 | Emos Busumuru | Proficient | 88 | 03/03/20 | Resources |
| ELA-Period 1 | Tony Contreras | Proficient | 80 | 03/03/20 | Resources |
| ELA-Period 1 | Ari Soto | Partially Proficient | 79 | 03/03/20 | Resources |
| ELA-Period 1 | Boris Rodriguez | Partially Proficient | 75 | 03/03/20 | Resources |
| ELA-Period 1 | Lira Dang | Partially Proficient | 72 | 03/03/20 | Resources |
| ELA-Period 1 | Chuck Depaah | Partially Proficient | 72 | 03/03/20 | Resources |
| ELA-Period 1 | Kayla Le | Partially Proficient | 70 | 03/03/20 | Resources |
| ELA-Period 1 | Rob Weston | Partially Proficient | 68 | 03/03/20 | Resources |
| ELA-Period 1 | Aly Melendez | Partially Proficient | 65 | 03/03/20 | Resources |
| ELA-Period 1 | Janie Smith | Partially Proficient | 58 | 03/03/20 | Resources |
| ELA-Period 1 | Perry Navarro | Below Proficient* | 49 | 03/03/20 | Resources |
| ELA-Period 1 | Elijah Amato | Below Proficient* | 48 | 03/03/20 | Resources |
| ELA-Period 1 | Torre Vuksanaj | Below Proficient* | 45 | 03/03/20 | Resources |

**Class Proficiency Report (graphic view)**

**Class Proficiency Report (list view)**

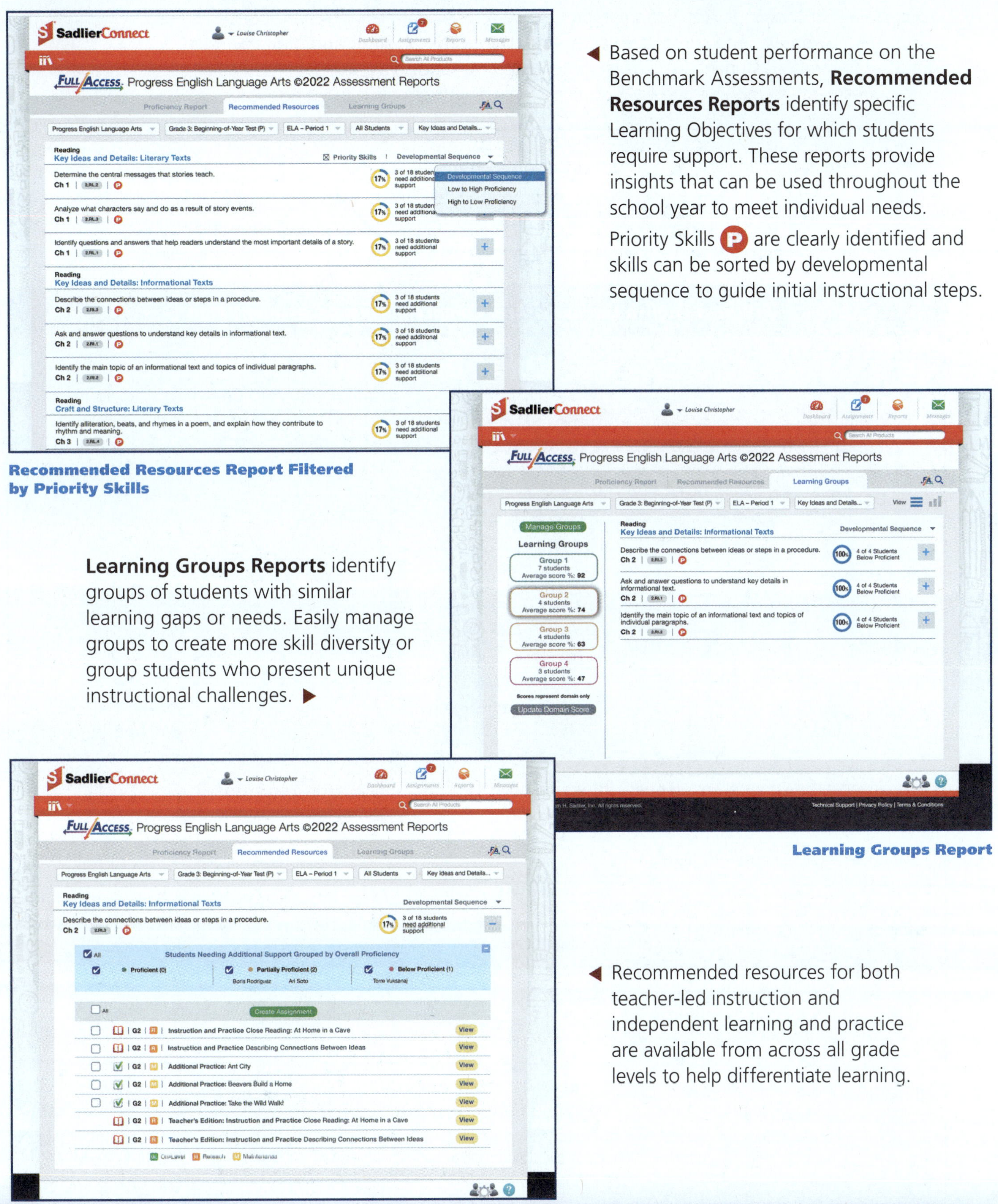

Based on student performance on the Benchmark Assessments, **Recommended Resources Reports** identify specific Learning Objectives for which students require support. These reports provide insights that can be used throughout the school year to meet individual needs.

Priority Skills P are clearly identified and skills can be sorted by developmental sequence to guide initial instructional steps.

**Recommended Resources Report Filtered by Priority Skills**

**Learning Groups Reports** identify groups of students with similar learning gaps or needs. Easily manage groups to create more skill diversity or group students who present unique instructional challenges.

**Learning Groups Report**

Recommended resources for both teacher-led instruction and independent learning and practice are available from across all grade levels to help differentiate learning.

**Recommended Resources**

# Assessment Options

*Progress English Language Arts* has a comprehensive assessment plan which includes diagnostic, formative, and summative assessment options—in print and digital formats—to measure students' skill development. Teachers may choose from among these assessments to monitor and track students' mastery throughout the school year.

**Assess before** each chapter to identify gaps and accelerate pacing when appropriate.

**Assess during** each chapter to adjust instruction thus meeting students' immediate needs.

**Assess after** each chapter to determine levels of skill mastery and determine the next step in the instructional process.

***Progress English Language Arts* Comprehensive Assessment Plan***

| Assessment Type | Assessment | What Is Assessed | Frequency | Where Found |
|---|---|---|---|---|
| Diagnostic | Beginning-of-Year (Prerequisite Skills) | previous grade-level reading standards | once per grade level | Full Access (optional purchase) |
| Diagnostic | Beginning-of-Year (Growth) | grade-level reading standards | once per grade level | Full Access (optional purchase) |
| Diagnostic | Mid-Year Test (Growth) | grade-level learning objectives | once per grade level | Full Access (optional purchase) |
| Diagnostic | Benchmark 1 | grade-level reading standards | once per grade level | Progress Monitor (optional purchase) |
| Diagnostic | Benchmark 2 | grade-level learning objectives | once per grade level | Progress Monitor (optional purchase) |
| Formative | Comprehension Check | lesson objective | each Reading lesson | Online Digital Resource |
| Formative | Chapter Review | chapter learning objectives | every chapter | Student Worktext |
| Summative | Chapter Test | chapter learning objectives | every chapter | Online Digital Resource |
| Summative | Cumulative Comprehension Checks | lesson objectives for chapters 1–3; 4–6 | at the end of chapters 1–3 and 4–6 | Online Digital Resource |
| Summative | End-of-Year Test (Growth) | grade-level learning objectives | once per grade level | Full Access (optional purchase) |
| Summative | Benchmark 3 | grade-level learning objectives | once per grade level | Progress Monitor (optional purchase) |

* Additional Reading and Language Assessments are also available with the purchase of Full Access.

*Progress English Language Arts* contains many formative and summative assessment opportunities to help teachers gather evidence of students' progress toward mastering grade-level skills and concepts and prepare for the state-standardized assessments.

## Integrated, Ongoing Assessment Opportunities

**Lesson Observational Diagnostics** appear at point-of-use within lessons, reminding teachers to observe student response to instruction, and offer a reteaching prescription. ▶

**Assess and Respond**

**If** students have difficulty answering the questions in the Comprehension Check . . .

**Then** have pairs of students review the story and create a list of the inferences they made as they read. Students should identify the clues they used to make their inferences.

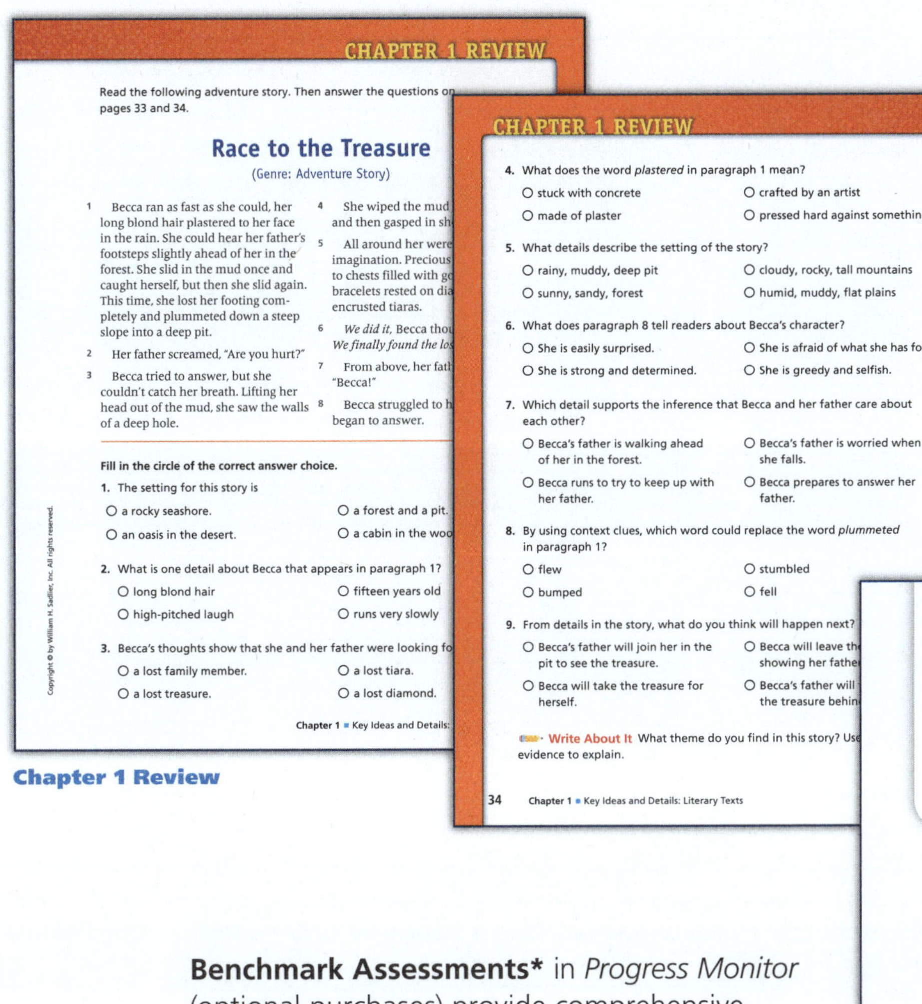

CHAPTER 1 REVIEW

Read the following adventure story. Then answer the questions on pages 33 and 34.

**Race to the Treasure**

(Genre: Adventure Story)

1 Becca ran as fast as she could, her long blond hair plastered to her face in the rain. She could hear her father's footsteps slightly ahead of her in the forest. She slid in the mud once and caught herself, but then she slid again. This time, she lost her footing completely and plummeted down a steep slope into a deep pit.

2 Her father screamed, "Are you hurt?"

3 Becca tried to answer, but she couldn't catch her breath. Lifting her head out of the mud, she saw the walls of a deep hole.

4 She wiped the mud and then gasped in sh

5 All around her were imagination. Precious to chests filled with g bracelets rested on di encrusted tiaras.

6 *We did it*, Becca tho *We finally found the lo*

7 From above, her fath "Becca!"

8 Becca struggled to h began to answer.

**Fill in the circle of the correct answer choice.**

1. The setting for this story is
   - ○ a rocky seashore.
   - ○ a forest and a pit.
   - ○ an oasis in the desert.
   - ○ a cabin in the wo
2. What is one detail about Becca that appears in paragraph 1?
   - ○ long blond hair
   - ○ fifteen years old
   - ○ high-pitched laugh
   - ○ runs very slowly
3. Becca's thoughts show that she and her father were looking fo
   - ○ a lost family member.
   - ○ a lost tiara.
   - ○ a lost treasure.
   - ○ a lost diamond.

Copyright © by William H. Sadlier, Inc. All rights reserved.

Chapter 1 ■ Key Ideas and Details:

CHAPTER 1 REVIEW

4. What does the word *plastered* in paragraph 1 mean?
   - ○ stuck with concrete
   - ○ crafted by an artist
   - ○ made of plaster
   - ○ pressed hard against something
5. What details describe the setting of the story?
   - ○ rainy, muddy, deep pit
   - ○ cloudy, rocky, tall mountains
   - ○ sunny, sandy, forest
   - ○ humid, muddy, flat plains
6. What does paragraph 8 tell readers about Becca's character?
   - ○ She is easily surprised.
   - ○ She is afraid of what she has found.
   - ○ She is strong and determined.
   - ○ She is greedy and selfish.
7. Which detail supports the inference that Becca and her father care about each other?
   - ○ Becca's father is walking ahead of her in the forest.
   - ○ Becca's father is worried when she falls.
   - ○ Becca runs to try to keep up with her father.
   - ○ Becca prepares to answer her father.
8. By using context clues, which word could replace the word *plummeted* in paragraph 1?
   - ○ flew
   - ○ stumbled
   - ○ bumped
   - ○ fell
9. From details in the story, what do you think will happen next?
   - ○ Becca's father will join her in the pit to see the treasure.
   - ○ Becca will leave th showing her fathe
   - ○ Becca will take the treasure for herself.
   - ○ Becca's father will the treasure behin

Write About It What theme do you find in this story? Us evidence to explain.

34 Chapter 1 ■ Key Ideas and Details: Literary Texts

**Chapter 1 Review**

◀ **Chapter Reviews** are provided with each chapter and offer an opportunity for students to encounter standardized test practice for the skills that have been taught within the chapter.

6 As her career went on, people stopped reading Hurston's stories. Some people thought she should write about race issues or politics, not about everyday life in the rural South. Soon those people's opinions took over. By Hurston's death in 1960, publishers had stopped printing her books.

7 However, public opinion did not stay the same. Other African American writers found Hurston's work. They recognized the value and beauty in her stories. They wanted to read about regular people. Since this rediscovery, Hurston has been considered one of the best writers of her time. Hurston's collections and fiction continue to thrill readers, just like the African American folktales that inspired her stories.

6. Part A What is the meaning of the word ***patron*** in paragraph 3?
   - A a person from Harlem who creates art
   - B a rich person who supports an artist or writer
   - C a person who buys and sells art
   - D a person who starts an artistic movement

   Part B Which statement from the passage best explains how Hurston used the money from her patron?
   - A "These people were called patrons."
   - B "Hurston easily found a patron for her research."
   - C "With that money, Hurston used what she learned in college to study different African American communities."
   - D "They taught in the schools."
7. Which of these statements best describes how the sentences in paragraph 4 are related?
   - A The paragraph compares the folktales Hurston collected in the South to folktales people told in the North.
   - B The paragraph describes what causes Hurston to write down the folktales and explains the effects of recording them.
   - C The paragraph describes the steps Hurston took to record the folktales she heard in the South.
   - D The first sentence indicates the topic, folktales, and the other sentences give more details about the topic.

Copyright © by William H. Sadlier, Inc. All rights reserved.

Benchmark 1 • Section A 7

**Progress Monitor**

**Benchmark Assessments*** in *Progress Monitor* (optional purchases) provide comprehensive assessments that can be administered periodically throughout the school year to evaluate students' knowledge and skill level relative to grade-level English Language Arts skills and concepts. ▶

*Items are mapped to CCSS.

# Notes

CHAPTER 1

Key Ideas and Details

Literary Texts

**Focus on Reading** Literary texts include fables, folktales, and myths. In order to understand these stories, you can ask and answer questions as you read, discover the central message of a text, and describe the characters.

**Think About Theme** Think about the people we call heroes. There are many ways to be heroic. You might outsmart a bigger rival or defeat an opponent in competition. In this chapter, you will learn about a few heroes from different parts of the world.

**Let's Get on Our Way!** As a reader, you can learn a lot from exploring the key ideas and details presented in literary texts.

These are the skills you will build in this chapter. Before you begin, check the boxes on the left of any items you can do well now. At the end of the chapter, you will return to this page to use the check boxes on the right to show what you have learned.

- ☐ Ask and answer questions to help me understand a story. ☐
- ☐ Retell important details to help determine a story's message. ☐
- ☐ Describe the characters and how their actions affect the story. ☐
- ☐ Use context clues in a sentence to learn the exact meaning of unknown words. ☐



Chapter 1 ■ Key Ideas and Details: Literary Texts

**Student Page 9**

## Progress Check

The Progress Check is a self-assessment feature that students can use to gauge their own progress. Research shows that when students take accountability for their own learning, their motivation increases.

Before students begin work on Chapter 1, have them check the boxes next to any item that they feel they can do well. It is fine if they don't check any of the boxes. Tell them that they will have an opportunity to learn about and practice all of these items while studying the chapter. Let them know that near the end of the chapter they will have a chance to reconsider how well they can do each item on this list.

Before students begin the Chapter 1 Review on page 33, have them revisit this page. You can use this information to work with students on any items they don't understand before they tackle the Review.

## HOME ✦ CONNECT...

The Home Connect feature is a way to keep parents or other adult family members apprised of what their children are learning. The key learning objectives are listed, and some ideas for related activities and discussions are included.

Explain to students that they can share the Home Connect page with their parents or the adult family members in their home. Let students know how much time the class will be spending on this chapter so they can plan their time accordingly at home.

Encourage students and their parents to share their experiences using the suggestions on the Home Connect page. You may wish to make a place to post some of this work.

HOME ✦ CONNECT...

Focused readers **ask and answer questions** as they read. What is the story about? Who are the characters? How does the story turn out? Finding important details to answer questions helps your child understand the meaning of a story. Choose a print or online text your child might enjoy. Read it together, asking each other questions such as "What's going to happen next?"

Knowing the author's **central message or lesson** in a story lets children relate the story to their own life. Choose a print or online folktale about a character you and your child admire. Take turns reading aloud to each other. Then ask questions such as "What can we learn from this character?" and "How would we act in a similar situation?"

Uncovering **characters' traits and motivations** helps young readers understand why things happen in a story. Why did the character do this? Watch a television drama with your child. During breaks, talk about what the characters said and did. Make predictions about the story's outcome based on your observations.

**Conversation Starter:** With your child, brainstorm what might occur if a hero from a myth or folktale were brought to life in the modern world. How would the character's powers or skills be used today? How would modern people react to the character? Sketch pictures of the original hero and how the character's appearance would change.

**IN THIS CHAPTER, YOUR CHILD WILL...**

- Ask questions and answer them, using details from the text, to gain a better understanding of the text as a whole.
- Retell stories, including important details about characters, setting, and events.
- Determine the central message of a text and how the author conveys the message through details.
- Describe characters' traits and motives and explain how their actions move a story along.
- Use context clues to define words that are unknown or that have multiple meanings.
- Compare and contrast three texts with the same theme: a fable, a folktale, and a myth.

**WAYS TO HELP YOUR CHILD**

Help your child enjoy reading. Encourage your child to find and share short texts about interesting topics, and read them aloud to each other. Ask questions about the texts that promote reasoning skills: Why do you think the person did that? What might have been a better thing to do? Challenge your child to offer supporting reasons for any opinions.

ONLINE For more Home Connect activities, continue online at sadlierconnect.com



10 Chapter 1 ■ Key Ideas and Details: Literary Texts

**Student Page 10**

## LEARNING PROGRESSIONS

In this chapter, students will learn how an author of a fictional text conveys a central message or lesson through key ideas and details. In order to learn the skills in this chapter, students will further develop skills learned in second grade. They should be encouraged to retain these skills, as they will continue to build on them in fourth grade.

|  |  |
| --- | --- |
| **Asking and Answering Questions** | • Proficient second-grade students should have ended the school year with an ability to ask and answer such questions as *who, what, where, when, why,* and *how* to show understanding of a text.<br>• As third graders, students should be able to refer explicitly to the text as the basis for their answers to these same types of questions to show understanding of a text.<br>• This skill will prepare them for fourth grade, when they will be expected to refer to details and examples in the text when explaining what the text says explicitly and when drawing inferences from the text. |
| **Determining a Central Message** | • By the end of grade 2, students should be able to recount stories, including fables and folktales, from diverse cultures, and determine their central message, lesson, or moral.<br>• In grade 3, students will build on this skill by explaining how the central message, lesson, or moral is conveyed through key details in stories, including fables, folktales, and myths from diverse cultures.<br>• When students move on to grade 4, they will expand on the use of this skill to determine the theme of a story, drama, or poem from details in the text and to summarize the text. |
| **Describing Characters** | • Grade 2 students should have completed the year able to describe how characters in a story respond to major events and challenges.<br>• In the third grade, students will widen their application of this skill to describe characters in a story (e.g., their traits, motivations, or feelings) and explain how their actions contribute to the sequence of events.<br>• Students will be expected to build on this skill in grade 4 and describe in depth a character, setting, or event in a story or drama, drawing on specific details in the text (e.g., a character's thoughts, words, or actions). |

**Essential Question:**
**How do authors convey a central message or lesson?**

In this chapter, students will focus on key ideas and details in stories to help them ask and answer questions to clarify understanding, determine the message in a story, and describe characters.

## Theme: It Takes a Hero

Students will read literature selections related to the theme of the need for heroes. They will read about heroes in two fables, a folktale, and a myth.

## Curriculum Connection: English/Language Arts

Students will read about two types of heroic characters—characters who are heroes because they save others or themselves, and characters who are heroes because they set a good example.

## Vocabulary Overview

### General Academic Vocabulary

amends 14, decorated 24, expanse 20, feud 26, invade 18, mighty 16, numerous 12, pensive 22, plentiful 28, pompous 27, quarreled 20, rebelling 26, report 13, scarlet 20, so-called 24, spray 12, straggled 28, superior 24, united 17, urgent 18, vengeful 25, woe 15

### Domain-Specific Vocabulary

Acropolis 28, bandit 18, bow 22, captive 22, envoy 14, snare 16, trident 27

## Guided Instruction

**OBJECTIVE**
**Show an understanding of the text by asking questions and citing evidence from the text to answer questions.**

### Genre: Fable

Explain to students that a fable is a type of short story, often first told many years ago. Point out that it usually includes at least one animal as a character and teaches a lesson.

### Set the Purpose

Help students understand the purpose for learning the reading skill by asking *Do you ever not understand what is happening in a story? What do you do to better understand the story?*

### Model and Teach

Read the selection as students follow along in their books.

**CITE EVIDENCE**

**A** *I know that a problem is something that causes trouble for a character.*

*Which characters are mentioned in the title?* (Rabbit, Elephant) *What trouble are the elephants having?* (There has been a drought.)

**B** *The last sentence in paragraph 2 explains what the elephant-king does. Why does he send the swift elephants in eight directions?* (The elephants need to find water.)

## ASKING AND ANSWERING QUESTIONS

### Guided Instruction

**WORDS TO KNOW**
**numerous**
**report**
**spray**

To understand a text, **find details** in the text to help you **answer questions.**

**CITE EVIDENCE**

**A** To understand a story, it helps to **ask and answer questions** such as, *What characters are in the story?* Underline details in the title that answer this question. It also helps to ask, *What is the main problem?* Circle the sentence in paragraph 2 that answers this.

**B** Questioning why characters do things is also important. Underline the sentence in paragraph 2 that explains why the elephant-king does what he does. What other fables or folktales have you read in which one character is the leader?

# How the Rabbit Fooled the Elephant

(Genre: Fable from India)

1 In a part of the forest lived an elephant-king named Four-Tusk. He had **numerous** followers. Much time was spent protecting the herd.

2 Now once there came a twelve-year drought, so that ponds, swamps, and lakes went dry. Then all the elephants said to the lord of the herd: "O King, our little ones are so thirsty. Pray find a method of removing thirst." So he sent in eight directions elephants swift as the wind to search for water.

3 Now those who went east found a lake named Lake of the Moon. It was beautiful with swans, herons, ducks, cranes, and water-creatures. It was surrounded by flowering **sprays** of branches drooping under the weight of various blossoms. Why describe it? It was a part of paradise.

4 When they saw this, they rushed back to report to the elephant-king.

### Words to Know

**General Academic Vocabulary**
**numerous** (*adjective*): many in number
**report** (*noun*): a detailed description or statement
**spray** (*noun*): a tree branch covered in flowers

**Working with Word Meaning** Encourage students to draw a picture of each moment in the story that is described with these words.

# KEY IDEAS AND DETAILS

## Guided Instruction

5 So Four-Tusk, on hearing their **report**, traveled with them to the Lake of the Moon. The lake sparkled in the spring sun. The elephants plunged in. But in doing so they stepped on the rabbits who long before had made their home on the banks of the lake. Now after drinking and bathing, the elephant-king with his followers departed to his own part of the jungle.

6 Then the rabbits held an emergency meeting. "What are we to do now?" they said. "These fellows will come here every day. Let some plan be made at once to prevent their return."

7 A rabbit named Victory, seeing their terror and sorrow, said with sympathy, "Have no fear. They shall not return. I promise it."

8 Victory departed and saw the elephant-king in the act of returning to the lake. Victory thought, "It is impossible for folk like me to come too near. I must seek safe ground before introducing myself."

**Comprehension Check**

What role does Victory play in the story so far?

### CITE EVIDENCE

**C** Ask yourself, *What words does the author use to help me see the action?* Circle the words in paragraph 5 that help you see what is happening.

**D** The story's setting includes *when* it happens. Underline details that tell you when this story happens.

## Support English Language Learners

Students who are learning English may have a difficult time making sense of idiomatic language that is more familiar to native speakers. Explain that an idiom is a phrase that means something other than the meaning of the individual words put together. Then point out these idiomatic phrases: *time was spent* (page 12, paragraph 1), *removing thirst* (page 12, paragraph 2), and *seek safe ground* (page 13, paragraph 8).

Guide students to use context clues in nearby sentences and paragraphs to figure out the meaning of the idioms.

## Guided Instruction

### CITE EVIDENCE

**C** *I know that "action" is what characters do. So, I will look for words that describe—or allow me to see—what the characters are doing.*

*The elephants plunge in. What words help you see what happened to the rabbits when the elephants went to the water?* (stepped on) *What phrase helps you see why the rabbits were there?* (made their home) *What word helps you see what happened after the elephants bathed?* (departed)

**D** *The author established what the setting looks like in the beginning of the story. So, I will look later in the story for a word that relates to time—or when the story happens.*

*What word in paragraph 5 tells you when the story happens?* (spring)

**Comprehension Check**

**Sample Answer:** Victory is a rabbit who sees that the other rabbits are scared of the elephants at their watering hole. Victory promises the other rabbits that he will stop the elephants from returning.

**Answer Explanation:** Students should recognize that the rabbits' main problem is that the elephants are using their watering hole and stepping on the rabbits. Because the rabbits are so much smaller than the elephants, they are scared. Victory seems to be a leader among the rabbits.

## Guided Practice

### Recap Reading Selection

Let students know that they will continue reading the fable about the the rabbit and the elephant. Review what they read about the elephants stepping on the rabbits at the watering hole, and Victory's promise to stop them from returning.

### Read and Practice

Have partners take turns reading the selection as you circulate to provide support. Model practicing asking and answering questions with Cite Evidence callout A. For callout B, circulate and provide partners with scaffolding as needed. You might use the following suggestions to help students who are having difficulty.

#### CITE EVIDENCE

**A** Prompt students to recall that the main action so far has been by a watering hole. Remind students that at the end of the previous page, Victory "departed" to stop the elephants. That is a clue that the setting is about to change. Have students look in paragraph 10 for a description of the new setting. (lonely path)

**B** Help students identify that Victory is telling a story to make it seem like the rabbits have more power and protection than they really have.



## Guided Practice

**WORDS TO KNOW**
**amends**
**envoy**
**woe**

**CITE EVIDENCE**

**A** Ask yourself if the setting has changed. Underline the words in paragraph 10 that show the new setting.

**B** Circle the story that Victory tells to fool the elephant. Think of a time when someone fooled you with a story.

**How the Rabbit Fooled the Elephant** *continued*

9 He climbed on a tall rock-pile before saying, "Is it well with you, lord of the two-tusked breed?"

10 And the elephant-king, hearing this, peered around and said, "Who are you, sir, and what brings you to this lonely path?"

11 "I am an **envoy** in the service of the blessed moon," said the rabbit.

12 "State your business," said the elephant-king, and the rabbit stated it thus.

13 "By command of the moon, I say to you that you have violated the Lake of the Moon. The moon warns you, O King: 'You have slain rabbits who are under my special protection. This is evil. One would think you are the only creature in the world who does not know the rabbit in the moon. Stop, or great disaster will happen to you at my hands.' "

14 Hearing this, the elephant-king began to shake. He said, "Point out to me quickly how I may win the moon's forgiveness."

15 The rabbit said, "Come, sir, alone. I will point it out." So he went by night to the Lake of the Moon, and showed him the moon reflected in the water.

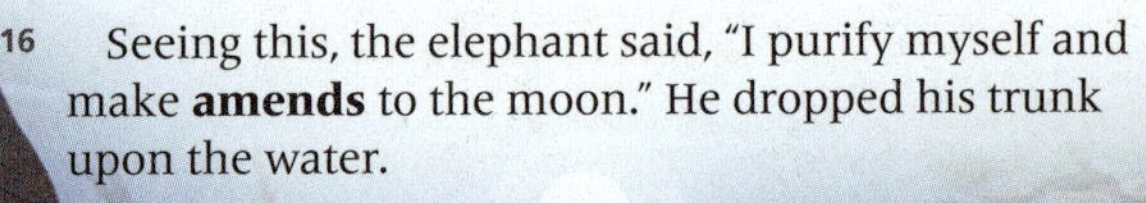

16 Seeing this, the elephant said, "I purify myself and make **amends** to the moon." He dropped his trunk upon the water.





## Words to Know

**General Academic Vocabulary**

**amends** (*noun*): payment for something one has done wrong

**woe** (*noun*): sorrow

**Domain-Specific Vocabulary**

**envoy** (*noun*): a representative of a leader or government sent to another leader or government to be a spokesperson

**Working with Word Meaning** Have partners take turns acting out each phrase (making amends, showing woe, and playing the envoy) for each other.

17 Then Victory started back, looking very upset. He said to the elephant-king, "**Woe**, woe to you, O King! You have doubly angered the moon. You have touched this water!" So the elephant-king, with drooping ears, bowed his head to the earth with deep respect in order to win forgiveness from the blessed moon.

18 And he spoke again to Victory: "My worthy sir, in all other matters, also, beg for me the forgiveness of the blessed moon. I shall never return here." And with these words he went to his own place.

(a retelling from *The Panchatantra*, translated by A.W. Ryder)

**Comprehension Check** MORE ONLINE **sadlierconnect.com**

1. How does Victory fool the elephant-king?
   - **a.** He claims the water in the lake is poisoned.
   - **b.** He says that the long drought will end very soon.
   - **(c.)** He claims to be an envoy of the moon.
   - **d.** He warns that hunters will attack the elephant herd.

2. Which of the following best states the moral, or lesson, of the fable?
   - **(a.)** Cleverness can sometimes defeat size and strength.
   - **b.** Lies are more effective than truth.
   - **c.** Forgiveness is better than revenge.
   - **d.** Look before you leap.

3. Work with a partner. Think of questions you might ask and answer to prove that the moral given is correct. Use details from the story.

Sample answer: Does it seem that the elephants do not care about or notice the rabbits? How can a rabbit fight an elephant? A rabbit may not be as big as an elephant, but he can be smarter.





## Guided Practice

**Comprehension Check**

**Answer Explanations:**

1. Choice C, *He claims to be an envoy of the moon*, is how Victory fools the elephant-king. The text tells how the rabbit warns the elephant to stop, or the moon's envoy will bring disaster.
2. Choice A, *Cleverness can sometimes defeat size and strength*, is the lesson this story teaches.
3. The questions and answers students note may vary but should reflect that the rabbit is little and does not have an obvious way to stop the elephants, so he has to trick the elephant-king to protect the rabbits.

## Peer Collaboration

Follow this procedure for each item: Ask students to think independently about each Comprehension Check question and form their own ideas for answering them. Then have students discuss their responses to the questions with a partner. Encourage students to adjust their ideas about how to answer the questions based on the discussion with their partners. Finally, ask pairs to share their responses to the questions with another pair.

## Foundational Skill: Fluency

Tell students that they can read more fluently if they read with expression. Explain that to read with expression, they should change the pitch and pace of their voices to reflect the mood when reading narration and to convey how a character may be feeling when reading dialogue. Model reading paragraph 13 on page 14 with expression. Try to convey a sense of formality and command when reading Victory's dialogue. After students practice reading another paragraph with expression with a partner, have them record themselves reading the paragraph and then listen to their recording to improve prosodic skills. Additional fluency passages and activities can be found at **sadlierconnect.com** in the *Foundational Skills Handbook*.

## Independent Practice

### Recap Reading Selection

Remind students that they read a fable. Have them recall the two main characters in the fable (the rabbit and the elephant), the moral of the story (cleverness can win over strength), and what the author had the rabbit do to convey the moral (the rabbit fooled the elephant).

### Read and Apply

Have students read the selection independently as you circulate. If you notice students struggling, you can provide support with the suggestions below.

### CITE EVIDENCE

**A** Explain that asking and answering questions help readers understand the text. Help students identify that Swift thinks the man is dangerous, and he warns the other birds.

**B** Help students see that because they have been warned by Swift, the birds are not tricked by the hunter's trap.

ASKING AND ANSWERING QUESTIONS

Independent Practice

**WORDS TO KNOW**

**mighty**
**snare**
**united**

**CITE EVIDENCE**

**A** Circle the words in paragraph 1 that answer the question *How does Swift try to protect the other birds?*

**B** In paragraph 2, why don't the birds fall into the trap? Underline the text that supports your answer.

## The Winning of Friends

(Genre: Fable from India)

1 In the southern country, there was a very tall banyan tree with a **mighty** trunk and branches. In the tree lived a crow named Swift. One morning Swift started across the sky in search of food. But he saw a hunter who lived in the neighborhood. The hunter was approaching the tree to trap birds. Swift thought, "What does he mean to do? Hurt me?" He warned all the other birds.

2 Now the hunter picked a spot, spread a **snare**, scattered grain, and hid. But the birds who lived there remembered Swift's warning. They thought the grains were poison, and did not eat.

3 At this point, a dove-king named Gray-Neck, with many dove followers, was wandering in search of food. He spotted the grains. In spite of Swift's warning, Gray-Neck greedily sought to eat the grains and landed in the great snare. The moment he did so, he and his followers were caught.



16 Chapter 1 ■ Key Ideas and Details: Literary Texts

### Words to Know

**General Academic Vocabulary**

**mighty** (*adjective*): possessing great strength or size
**united** (*adjective*): acting as one

**Domain-Specific Vocabulary**

**snare** (*noun*): a trap set for birds

**Working with Word Meaning** Reinforce the meaning of each word by having students use each word in a sentence unrelated to the fable.

KEY IDEAS AND DETAILS

Independent Practice

4 So the hunter happily lifted his club and ran forward. Then Gray-Neck and his followers were upset. But the dove-king, with much presence of mind, said to the doves, "Have no fear, my friends. We must all agree in purpose, fly up together, and carry the snare away. This is not possible without **united** action. For death comes to those of divided purpose."

(a retelling from *The Panchatantra*, translated by A.W. Ryder)

**Comprehension Check** MORE ONLINE sadlierconnect.com

1. How does the hunter try to trick the birds?
   - **a.** He pretends to be their friend.
   - **b.** He hunts the birds by night.
   - **(c.)** He lures the birds with grain.
   - **d.** He buries the snare in the ground.

2. According to the text, how does Gray-Neck save himself and his followers?
   - **a.** After eating the grain, Gray-Neck and his followers unite to attack the hunter.
   - **(b.)** By telling everyone to fly off together, they will carry away the snare.
   - **c.** By making a deal with Swift, he is able to escape.
   - **d.** Gray-Neck heeds Swift's warning and avoids the grain.

3. Reread the last line of the fable. Why do you think the author wrote this fable? Use information from the text in your answer.

Sample answer: The author wrote this fable to show people that by cooperating with others, they are stronger than if they act alone.





## Extend Thinking: Create

Help students extend their thinking by writing a one- or two-paragraph fable on paper or on a computer. Remind students to include an animal as one of the main characters, convey a moral or lesson, and illustrate their stories.

Before writing, have partners brainstorm morals (for example, bad friends lose friends; a bird in the hand is better than two in the bush; honesty is the best policy) that they could convey in their stories.

Have students present their fables to the class. Listeners should pay attention and ask questions to check their understanding. Speakers should speak clearly, in complete sentences, and at a reasonable rate.

## Independent Practice

**Comprehension Check**

**Answer Explanations:**

**1.** Choice C, *He lures the birds with grain,* tells how the hunter tries to trick the birds.

**2.** Choice B, *By telling everyone to fly off together, they will carry away the snare,* explains how the birds worked together to escape.

**3.** Students' answers may vary but should reflect that the author is emphasizing the importance of working together by showing how it can save lives.

## Critical Comprehension

Use the following questions to help students think more deeply about the text. Students should be prepared to support their answers with evidence from the text.

- *What are three details that show that the birds are clever?* (Swift knew not to trust the hunter; the other birds listened to Swift's warning; Gray-Neck figures out a way to escape.)
- *What do you think would have happened to the birds if Gray-Neck had not told everyone to fly off together?* (He would have come up with another solution.)

**Assess and Respond**

**If** students have difficulty answering the questions in the Comprehension Check…

**Then** work individually with them, providing sentence frames to guide them to the answers. Point to details in the text and ask how they help answer the questions.

## Guided Instruction

**OBJECTIVE**

**Determine and explain the central message, lesson, or moral of a story, using key details from the text.**

### Genre: Folktale

Explain to students that a folktale is a short story first told long ago. It is often based on the life of a real person. It may tell, in an exaggerated way, about an amazing feat the person did.

### Set the Purpose

Help students understand the purpose for learning the reading skill by asking *Why do you think people tell folktales?*

### Model and Teach

Read the selection as students follow along in their books.

### CITE EVIDENCE

**A** *I will look for details that help me understand when and where the folktale takes place.*

*What detail helps us understand the time and place Momotaro lived?* ("a long time ago in Japan")

**B** *The text tells me that Momotaro is a fifteen-year-old boy. What is extraordinary about Momotaro?* (He had a courageous heart and was very wise. He also was "not just any ordinary child.")

**Guided Instruction**

**WORDS TO KNOW**

**bandit**
**invade**
**urgent**

To explain how a folktale **conveys its central message**, you can **retell the key details** of the story.

**CITE EVIDENCE**

**A** In paragraph 1, underline the key details that provide this folktale's **setting**—its time and place. Many stories take place long ago or in faraway places. What is the setting of one of your favorite stories?

**B** To understand the **central message** of the folktale, look for how the author uses **key details** to communicate the central message. Circle the details that tell whom the folktale is about and what this person is like.

## Momotaro

(Genre: Folktale from Japan)

1 A long time ago in Japan, there lived an old man and an old woman who had to work hard to earn their daily rice. They had a son named Momotaro who was fifteen years old. He was taller and stronger than other boys his age. He had a handsome face and a courageous heart; he was also very wise. His parents were pleased and proud when they looked at him because they thought that he was exactly what a hero should be.

2 One day, Momotaro came to his father and made an **urgent** request. "I want to go away," he said. "There is an island in the sea far away from here where a group of dangerous **bandits** lives. I've heard stories about how they **invade** this land, hurt people, and steal all they can find. I will stop them."

3 The old man was surprised, but he knew that his son was strong and fearless; he also knew that his son was not just any ordinary child. He decided to let his son go to the island.

4 Momotaro left in a hurry. On his journey, he began to feel hungry. While he was having his lunch, a dog almost as large as a colt came running out from the high grass.





### Words to Know

**General Academic Vocabulary**

**invade** (*verb*): to enter and occupy a place

**urgent** (*adjective*): requiring immediate action

**Domain-Specific Vocabulary**

**bandit** (*noun*): someone who attacks and steals from others, often as a member of a group; robber, thief

**Working with Word Meaning** Broaden students' understanding of the words by having them create a word web for each word, completing it with synonyms and examples.

## KEY IDEAS AND DETAILS

5 The dog ran straight for Momotaro and showed his teeth, saying: "You are a rude man to pass my field without asking for permission first. If you give me all of your food, I will let you depart from here. Otherwise, I will bite!"

6 "What is that you are saying? Do you know who I am? I am Momotaro," Momotaro said.

7 "What do I hear? The name of Momotaro? Are you really Momotaro? I have heard that you are the strongest man in the village. If you will take someone rude like me as one of your followers, I would be very grateful," the dog said.

8 "I think I can take you with me if you want to go," said Momotaro.

### Guided Instruction

**CITE EVIDENCE**

**C** Folktales often have unrealistic elements. Underline one of the unrealistic elements in paragraph 5.

**D** Folktales often include larger-than-life characters whose special abilities move the story toward its central message. In paragraph 7, circle Momotaro's special ability.

**Comprehension Check**

How is Momotaro's character different from the dog's character?





## Guided Instruction

### CITE EVIDENCE

**C** *I'll look for details that show something that cannot happen in real life.*

*A talking dog is not something that happens in real life. What deal does the dog try to make with Momotaro?* (The dog says if Momotaro gives him all of his food, the dog won't bite Momotaro.)

**D** *I'll look for words that relate to a special ability Momotaro has.*

*What phrase in paragraph 7 helps you understand what makes Momotaro special?* (the strongest man in the village)

**Comprehension Check**

**Sample Answer:** Momotaro is focused on his mission, which will help other people. The dog is only interested in helping himself.

**Answer Explanation:** Students should recognize that Momotaro is working for the good of the people, while the dog is interested only in stealing food to help himself.

### Review: Ask and Answer Questions

Have students come up with questions about the dog's offer in paragraph 7. Prompt students by asking why the dog wants to come with Momotaro.

### Support English Language Learners

Help Mandarin native speakers and other English language learners who speak languages that do not rely heavily on pronouns to make sense of sentences with pronoun references.

Explain that a pronoun is a word that takes the place of a noun. List common pronouns: *I, me, he, him, she, her, they, them, we, us*. Read the third sentence of the story. Explain that "he" refers to, or is taking the place of, "Momotaro," who is mentioned in the second sentence. Have students read the third sentence aloud, replacing "he" with "Momotaro" to reinforce their understanding of how pronouns relate to nouns. Repeat as you continue reading the story with students, providing a gradual release to allow them to identify the noun.

## Guided Practice

### Recap Reading Selection

Have students recall what they have read so far about Momotaro. They should mention that Momotaro is a teenage boy. He is very strong and brave. He is on a mission to stop some bandits from invading and stealing.

### Read and Practice

Have partners take turns reading the selection as you circulate to provide support. Model determining a central message with Cite Evidence callout A. For callout B, circulate and provide partners with scaffolding as needed. You might use the following suggestions to help students who are having difficulty.

#### CITE EVIDENCE

**A** Ask students to look for a detail that describes the monkey's character. ("I admire your courage.") Ask them what that character trait might have to do with the central message of the story.

**B** Help students identify that the dog and the monkey are both on the same mission, but they are "quarreling a lot." This clue may help them anticipate some problems the characters will face. Then ask students if a team that is fighting within can win against others. Prompt them to cite evidence to support their opinions.

## DETERMINING A CENTRAL MESSAGE

### Guided Practice

**WORDS TO KNOW**
**expanse**
**quarreled**
**scarlet**

**CITE EVIDENCE**

**A** One characteristic of folktales is that the characters often represent traits (like wisdom). Circle the trait that the monkey represents.

**B** A story sometimes gives clues about what might happen later in the story. Underline a clue in paragraph 14 about a problem that the group might face later in the story.

**Momotaro** *continued*

9 As they were going along, a monkey came up to Momotaro.

10 "Good morning, Momotaro!" the monkey said. "You are welcome in this part of the country. May I go with you? I know about your journey. Nothing would make me happier than to follow you."

11 "Do you really want to go to Bandit Island and fight with me?"

12 "Yes, sir," replied the monkey.

13 "I admire your courage," said Momotaro. "Come along!"

14 So the monkey joined Momotaro. The dog and the monkey **quarreled** a lot; they were always snapping at each other as they walked.

15 Soon they came to a large, open **expanse**. A bird flew down and landed on the ground just in front of the little party. It was the most beautiful bird Momotaro had ever seen, with colorful feathers on its body and a **scarlet** cap on its head.

16 "May I follow behind the dog and the monkey?" the bird asked.

20 Chapter 1 ■ Key Ideas and Details: Literary Texts



### Words to Know

**General Academic Vocabulary**

**expanse** (*noun*): a large surface or area
**quarreled** (*verb*): angrily disagreed; fought
**scarlet** (*adjective*): of a bright-red color

**Working with Word Meaning** Pair students and have one partner give the definition and the other partner then name the word. Then have partners switch roles. You may want to create flash cards for students.

## Guided Practice



17 Then Momotaro stood and gave this order: "Now everyone must listen to me. If we are going to be an army, we need to have harmony. When we are not at peace amongst ourselves, it is hard to subdue an enemy. From now, all three of you—the dog, the monkey, and the bird—must be friends. It must be like the three of you have the same mind."

### Comprehension Check

1. According to the text, how does Momotaro solve his problem in the story?

   **(a.)** He makes the dog and monkey promise not to fight anymore.

   **b.** He leaves the dog and monkey on Bandit Island.

   **c.** He tells the bird to talk to the dog and monkey.

   **d.** He tells the dog and monkey to apologize to the bird.

2. What prediction is MOST LIKELY accurate based on the information in the story so far?

   **a.** The bird will leave the group and go to Bandit Island alone.

   **b.** The dog and monkey will continue to quarrel with each other.

   **(c.)** The characters will agree to get along with one another.

   **d.** Momotaro will return home rather than go to Bandit Island.

3. What message is the story teaching so far? Cite information from the text to support your answer.

   Sample answer: The story teaches that it is important to work peacefully with a team rather than fighting with your teammates. The evidence from the story that proves this point is that Momotaro tells them that if they don't have peace with one another, it will be hard to subdue an enemy.





### Comprehension Check

**Answer Explanations:**

**1.** Students should have noticed the use of the phrase *gave this order* in paragraph 17 and recognize that choice A, *He makes the dog and monkey promise not to fight anymore,* shows how Momotaro solves the problem.

**2.** Choice C, *The characters will agree to get along with one another,* is the best answer. The text emphasizes that Momotaro is a leader and he is determined to carry out his task.

**3.** Students' responses may vary, but students should note that in order for this small team to beat their enemy, they will have to work together.

### Writearound

Organize students in groups of four. Tell them they are going to summarize the story. Have all students write down this sentence starter on a piece of paper: *Momotaro is on a mission to* ______. Ask students to complete the sentence individually. Then have them pass their papers to the right, read the sentence they receive, and add a sentence to build the summary. Repeat two more times. Then give each group time to review their four summaries, pick their favorite, and revise it.

### Digital Connection: Post to a Website

Point out that Momotaro's story has been told orally and in print for hundreds of years. Explain that today we can use the Internet to share information, such as a story.

Have students write one or two paragraphs to retell a fable or folktale of their choosing or one that you have assigned to them. Then help them post their retellings to the school or class website.

To challenge students, you may wish to have them create a screenplay of their retelling, acting it out with a partner or small group. If possible they can make a video recording of their retelling, and then post it to the website.

## Independent Practice

### Recap Reading Selection

Have a short class discussion about the folktale "Momotaro." Prompt students to recall Momotaro's superhuman skills (very strong and brave), the amazing feat he plans to accomplish with those skills (defeat an island of bandits), and the central message of the story (you can win if you work together peacefully).

### Read and Apply

Have students read the selection independently as you circulate to provide support. If you notice students struggling, you can provide support with the suggestions below.

### CITE EVIDENCE

**A** Students should recognize that in reality no small group can fight "like they were an army of a hundred people." However, in the folktale, this action is the dramatic event that provides a turning point.

**B** The words *bandit chief* should signal to students that this is the evil character in the story. The text also says that the bandit chief and his men had been scaring the villagers for a long time.

Students should explain that Momotaro must be brave in order to beat the bandit chief and win the treasure.

DETERMINING A CENTRAL MESSAGE

Independent Practice

**WORDS TO KNOW**

**bow**
**captive**
**pensive**

**CITE EVIDENCE**

**A** A folktale's central message is often reached by way of a dramatic event. Circle the paragraph that includes the dramatic event of the story.

**B** Another characteristic of folktales is that they have an evil character in them. Who is the evil character in this story? Underline details about him and his followers.

**Momotaro** *continued*

18 They promised not to fight anymore. Then Momotaro got a small ship, and they all got on board and set sail. One day, the four were standing on the **bow** of the ship. They saw some land and got so excited that they were finally close.

19 They saw a large castle facing the sea on top of a steep shore; Momotaro knew that they were looking at Bandit Island. Momotaro was **pensive** as he wondered how he should begin the attack.

20 Momotaro landed and they walked to the top of the castle. They found a little back door in the lowest part of the castle wall.

21 Momotaro, the bird, the dog, and the monkey fought like they were an army of a hundred people and defeated most of the bandits.

22 The bandit chief was the only one left. He knew that Momotaro was stronger than other men, so he came up to Momotaro and threw down his iron bar.

23 "I cannot defeat you," the bandit chief said. "I will give you all the treasure hidden in this castle."

24 Momotaro tied up the bandit chief, then went into the rooms of the castle and set all the prisoners free. He gathered all the stolen treasure he found. Momotaro returned to his home as the winner, and he held the bandit chief as his **captive**.

25 The country made a hero of Momotaro upon his return. They rejoiced because they were free from the bandits who had scared them for a long time. Momotaro's parents were happy to have him back. The treasure allowed them to live happily ever after.

(adapted from *Japanese Fairy Tales*, Yei Theodora Ozaki, 1908)





### Words to Know

**General Academic Vocabulary**
**pensive** (*adjective*): thoughtful, lost in thought

**Domain-Specific Vocabulary**
**bow** (*noun*): the front of a ship
**captive** (*noun*): a person held against his or her will

**Working with Word Meaning** Have students share an example and a nonexample for each word with a partner.

# KEY IDEAS AND DETAILS

## Independent Practice

### Comprehension Check

MORE ONLINE sadlierconnect.com

1. Folktales use exaggeration to tell about the characters. What is an exaggerated detail about Momotaro, the dog, the monkey, and the bird?
   a. The group found an entrance into the castle.
   (b.) The group fought like an army of a hundred people.
   c. The group got onto a small ship.
   d. The group found Bandit Island.

2. Exaggerated details in a folktale are often based on a real problem. What is MOST LIKELY real in the story?
   a. Many bandits could not fight against Momotaro's attack.
   b. The dog, the monkey, and the bird can speak.
   c. The dog and the bird carried the stolen treasure back to Momotaro's country.
   (d.) Bandits were stealing treasure from local people.

3. In a few sentences, retell the story of Momotaro and his army. How do their actions support the folktale's message?

   Sample answer: Momotaro, the dog, the monkey, and the bird entered the castle and attacked quickly. They defeated the bandits easily, and the bandit chief surrendered. Then they freed the prisoners and gathered all of the stolen treasure to bring back to their home. They showed that a team working together can accomplish the impossible.





## Independent Practice

### Comprehension Check

**Answer Explanations:**

1. Students should understand that the exaggerations about Momotaro and the others storming the castle support choice B, *The group fought like an army of a hundred people.*
2. Choice D, *Bandits were stealing treasure from local people*, is something that could happen in real life.
3. Students' responses may vary but should retell the folktale and explain the message that a team working together is powerful.

### Critical Comprehension

Use the following questions to help students think more deeply about the text. Students should be prepared to support their answers with evidence from the text.

- *What do the dog, the bird, and the monkey do to show they are as brave as Momotaro?* (They join with him to defeat the bandits.)
- *Why do you think the four good characters were able to defeat the bandits?* (They worked together for a good cause.)

### Assess and Respond

**If** students have trouble answering the questions in the Comprehension Check

**Then** make sure students understand the questions before rereading the story. Have them paraphrase each paragraph to check comprehension.

### Foundational Skill Review: Inflectional Endings

Review reading words with the inflectional ending *-ed*, reminding students that the *-ed* ending can be pronounced in three different ways—/t/, /d/, and /ed/. Model these three pronunciations using words such as: *dressed* (/t/), *played* (/d/), and *boasted* (/ed/). Then have students identify the inflectional ending sound for these words from the text: *landed* (/ed/), promised (/t/), *wondered* (/d/), *defeated* (/ed/), *tied* (/d/), *gathered* (/d/).

Additional phonics activities can be found in the *Foundational Skills Handbook* at **sadlierconnect.com**.

## Guided Instruction

**OBJECTIVE**

**Describe characters in a story, including how their actions contribute to the sequence of events.**

### Genre: Myth

Explain that a myth is a story that was first told long ago. Myths often explain the natural world, tell a cultural tradition, or show good or heroic behavior. Greek myths feature humans, fantastical creatures, and gods and goddesses.

### Set the Purpose

Activate students' thinking about the reading skill by asking *What words would you use to describe yourself?*

### Model and Teach

Read the selection as students follow along in their books.

### CITE EVIDENCE

**A** *The final sentences in paragraph 1 tell about how the gods interacted with humans.*

*What words show how they felt?* (fascinated, gain their attention)

**B** *Zeus's first line of dialogue is in paragraph 4.*

*How does Zeus describe his family?* (He says his family is "amazing.")

## DESCRIBING CHARACTERS

### Guided Instruction

**WORDS TO KNOW**

**decorated**
**so-called**
**superior**
**vengeful**

Think about details that help you **understand characters** and why they do what they do.

**CITE EVIDENCE**

**A** Each **character** has **feelings, qualities**, or **motivations** that help explain how he or she acts. Underline the words in paragraph 1 that describe some qualities of the Greek gods that tell you about their relationship to humans.

**B** Circle the sentence that explains Zeus's feeling about his family.

# Athena and Poseidon

(Genre: Greek Myth)

1 In ancient Greece, the people went to great lengths to praise their gods and goddesses. They **decorated** their pottery with images of their gods, and built great temples to honor them. These **superior** beings influenced the fate of nations. From their thrones on Mount Olympus they took an interest in the lives of heroes. But they didn't only use their powers to do impossible deeds. They were fascinated by the lives of mortals. No human activity was too small to gain their attention.

2 Twelve gods and goddesses stood apart from all the others. These were the Olympians, **so-called** because they lived on Mount Olympus.

3 From his throne on Mount Olympus, Zeus, greatest of all gods, gazed at his family—the Olympians were the family of Zeus.

4 "This is one amazing family," he said.

5 "We are *so* famous and popular," the Olympians said with pride.





### Words to Know

**General Academic Vocabulary**

**decorated** (*verb*): made beautiful
**so-called** (*adjective*): having to do with a name or term commonly given to something
**superior** (*adjective*): higher in rank or status
**vengeful** (*adjective*): looking to pay back a wrong or injury

**Working with Word Meaning** Have students write a sentence for each word, leaving a blank for the word. Then have them trade papers with a partner and write the correct word to complete their partner's sentences.

24 Chapter 1 ■ Key Ideas and Details: Literary Texts

## Guided Instruction

### KEY IDEAS AND DETAILS

6 "I am very popular, Father," said a woman's voice. It was Athena, daughter of Zeus and the goddess of war, strategy, intelligence, spinning, and weaving.

7 "You, Athena my dear, are my favorite one," he said. "From the moment of your birth, you have been astonishing. We were all surprised when you came into the world dressed in armor. You are popular, my dear. But the people often describe you as fierce, **vengeful,** and rather cruel."

8 "But I am changing, Father. I want to get people interested in arts and crafts. And I think I might like to become the patroness-protector of a great city!"

9 Zeus stroked his long white beard thoughtfully. "A patroness, my dear? That is a big responsibility. However, you do have your mother's wisdom, and your father's strength. Perhaps it could work. I wonder… " Zeus's voice trailed off.

**Comprehension Check**

In what ways does Athena say she is changing? How does her father react to her words?

#### Guided Instruction

**CITE EVIDENCE**

**C** Descriptive words, such as adjectives, help readers understand characters. Underline each adjective in paragraph 7 that describes a character.

**D** A story can only move forward through characters' actions. Circle the action of of Zeus's that lets you know an important decision is about to be made.



25

### CITE EVIDENCE

**C** *As I read, I'll look for a character name. Then I'll look for an adjective that describes him or her. The first character mentioned is Athena. What adjectives describe her?* (favorite, astonishing, dressed in armor, popular, fierce, vengeful, cruel) *What does this tell you about Athena?* (She is interesting and powerful.)

**D** *I'll do the same thing for actions. What action does Zeus do in paragraph 9?* (stroked his long white beard thoughtfully) *What does this tell you about his state of mind?* (He has an idea he is thinking over.)

**Comprehension Check**

**Sample Answer:** Athena says she wants "to get people interested in arts and crafts" and would like to be a "patroness-protector." Zeus is thinking of ways Athena can prove she has changed.

**Answer Explanation:** Students should understand that Athena is a powerful goddess who wants to be recognized for more than her strength and cruelty.

### Listening and Viewing Skills

Reread paragraph 6 as students look at the illustration on page 25. *What is Athena the goddess of?* (war, strategy, intelligence, spinning, and weaving) *Why might those qualities make her a good "patroness-protector"?* (She is strong and intelligent, and interested in creating things.)

### Review: Determining a Central Message

Remind students to identify key details in the text that will help them determine the central message of the story. Ask them to think about how Athena might prove she has changed.

### Support English Language Learners

English language learners who are speakers of Arabic or another language that does not have an equivalent to the verb "to be" may have difficulty unpacking the meaning of sentences that contain *am, is, are, was, were,* and other forms of the verb. For these students, the meaning of "These celestial beings influenced" is easier to determine than the meaning of "These celestial beings were influenced."

Explain that "to be" is a verb that shows a state of existence. Create lists of the present and past tense forms of the verb. Read through the story with students, stopping at each "to be" word. Discuss whether the verb is in the present or past tense and how it affects the meaning of the sentence.

## Guided Practice

### Recap Reading Selection

Have students recall what they have read so far in the myth. They should be able to say that the two main characters so far are Zeus, ruler of the gods, and Athena, his daughter.

### Read and Practice

Have partners take turns reading the selection as you circulate to provide support. Model how to describe characters with Cite Evidence callout A. For callout B, circulate and provide partners with scaffolding as needed. You might use the following suggestions to help students who are having difficulty.

#### CITE EVIDENCE

**A** Point out the sentence "Zeus knew his family was in the habit of rebelling against his rule" in paragraph 10. Then guide students to identify the sentence that shows what happens when the gods argue. (Serious feuds developed.)

**B** Direct students to the phrase "make Poseidon furious" and ask students to identify what happens when Poseidon is furious. (bad things tend to happen)



## Guided Practice

#### WORDS TO KNOW

**feud**
**pompous**
**rebelling**
**trident**

#### CITE EVIDENCE

**A** Circle evidence in paragraph 10 that provides information about the Olympians.

**B** Underline the words in paragraph 11 that describe what might result if Zeus shows Athena any favoritism.

**Athena and Poseidon** *continued*

10 Zeus knew his family was in the habit of **rebelling** against his rule. And when they weren't rebelling against Zeus, they were arguing with each other. Serious **feuds** developed. And one of the worst was between his daughter Athena and the god Poseidon.

11 "If I show Athena too much favor, it's sure to make Poseidon furious," he mused. And when Poseidon was furious, bad things tended to happen.

12 Poseidon was the god of the sea, earthquakes, and horses. He was also Zeus's brother. They had another brother, Hades, who was god of the Underworld. When the three brothers had rebelled against their father, Cronus, they had split his world among themselves. Zeus became god of the sky, Poseidon god of the sea and earth, and Hades took the underworld for himself.

13 Now, Athens was the greatest city in ancient Greece. Its citizens wanted a patron god. Zeus was aware of their plans.

### Words to Know

**General Academic Vocabulary**
**rebelling** (*verb*): acting in opposition to or against
**feud** (*noun*): a long fight or dispute between groups or families
**pompous** (*adjective*): exceedingly proud or self-important

**Domain-Specific Vocabulary**
**trident** (*noun*): a fishing spear with three prongs

**Working with Word Meaning** Challenge students to write a one-paragraph short story about one of the Greek gods, using the words above.

# KEY IDEAS AND DETAILS

## Guided Practice

14 He said, "Athena, if you are so interested in being the patron deity of a city, why not Athens? The city could use a good goddess like you."

15 "What? A girl as patron of a great city such as Athens," roared Poseidon, who had just arrived among his family. "Don't be ridiculous. What the people of Athens want is a powerful god like myself." And the **pompous** god leaned against his **trident**.

16 Zeus sighed and covered his face with his hands. "Here we go again," he said.

### Comprehension Check

**1.** According to the text, the Olympians were

**a.** brave

**b.** loyal

**c.** troublesome

**d.** heroes

**2.** Which is a trait that is NOT supported by the text's description of Zeus?

**a.** fearful

**b.** clever

**c.** affectionate

**d.** thoughtful

**3.** What Olympian trait does the text say Athena and Poseidon illustrate?

Sample answer: The Olympians are rebellious and quarrelsome. They develop feuds among themselves, and "one of the worst was between his daughter Athena and the god Poseidon."





## Discussion Skills

Explain to students that when they share ideas during a class discussion, it is important to follow certain rules, such as speaking one at a time, listening to others with respect and without interrupting, asking questions without being insulting, and not over-talking or monopolizing.

After explaining the rules for respectful discussion, present a series of scenarios to students and then ask whether a scenario reflects the rules. For example: *Ben shares an idea for a creative project. Gina says, "That's boring!"* (does not follow the rules) *Ben shares an idea for a creative project. Gina says, "That could be fun. But what if we did this other idea instead?"* (follows the rules)

## Guided Practice

### Comprehension Check

**Answer Explanations:**

**1.** Choice C, *troublesome*, is correct because paragraph 10 says the gods were always "rebelling" and "arguing."

**2.** Choice A, *fearful*, is the only trait not supported by the text, which describes Zeus as being clever about trying to keep his family happy, affectionate toward his daughter, and thoughtful.

**3.** Students' responses should note how the ancient Greek gods were noted for having arguments among themselves, and Poseidon and Athena have an ongoing feud.

## Grouping Options

Support striving readers in answering these questions, which require a fair amount of inferencing, by pairing them with proficient or advanced readers. Have partners discuss the questions and work together to answer them. Tell partners to be sure that both members of the pair understand each question before attempting to answer it.

## Independent Practice

### Recap Reading Selection

Remind students that they have been reading a Greek myth called "Athena and Poseidon." Ask students what they remember about what they have read so far. Students should recall that the goddess Athena wants to become patroness of a city. Her father, Zeus, thinks she might make a good patroness of Athens. His brother, Poseidon, thinks he himself should be the patron god of the city.

### Read and Apply

Have students read the selection independently as you circulate. If you notice students struggling, you can provide support with the suggestions below.

#### CITE EVIDENCE

**A** Students should recognize that no real person could produce a pool of water by striking the ground.

**B** Have students identify the decision of the judges. (They chose Athena as patroness.) Then have them identify why the judges chose Athena. This should help them recognize that she won the honor fairly by winning the contest.



**Independent Practice**

**WORDS TO KNOW**
**Acropolis**
**plentiful**
**straggled**

**CITE EVIDENCE**

**A** Underline evidence in paragraph 21 that suggests that Poseidon is a supernatural, mythical being.

**B** Box the results of the contest. This result shows the contest was fair. Is fairness important to you and your friends?

**Athena and Poseidon** *continued*

17 "Well, you may be right," said Zeus, uncovering his face. "But why don't we decide with ... a contest!"

18 "Oh yes, a contest, a contest!" The other Olympians nodded and applauded their approval. A contest was always fun to watch and you never knew what was going to happen.

19 So Athena and Poseidon descended to Athens. Behind them, at a safe distance, **straggled** a happy band of gods and goddesses, chattering excitedly among themselves.

20 "Would-be patron gods!" exclaimed Zeus. "Shake hands and show Athens why you should be patron. I want a clean competition here—no cheating!"

21 Poseidon claimed his right to the city by driving his trident into the earth in front of the **Acropolis**. Water flowed from the earth and formed a pool. At first, the Athenian judges were impressed. They thought Poseidon had created a spring. But when they tasted the water, they realized it was full of salt. "The god of the sea is impressive and wonderful!" they said dutifully. "But Greece has **plentiful** salt water. We would like to see what Athena has to offer."

### Words to Know

**General Academic Vocabulary**

**plentiful** (*adjective*): more than enough
**straggled** (*verb*): trailed off from the main group

**Domain-Specific Vocabulary**

**Acropolis** (*noun*): the fortified section of an ancient city

**Working with Word Meaning** Have students use a thesaurus to find one synonym and one antonym for one of the words. Then have them share their synonyms and antonyms with a partner, who will state which word each synonym and antonym relates to.

KEY IDEAS AND DETAILS

Independent Practice

22 Athena replied to this challenge by planting an olive tree—her own invention. The people observed the olive fruit. The judges tasted it. One exclaimed, "These will be delicious in some of that salty water from Poseidon!"

23 Another judge squeezed an olive and observed the thick golden oil that seeped out. "I just cannot wait to mix this oil with herbs and dip some fresh bread in it!" she remarked.

24 Because her gift was judged greater than Poseidon's, Athena became patroness-protector of the city named in her honor, Athens.

**Comprehension Check** MORE ONLINE sadlierconnect.com

1. Which is NOT a reason the judges had for choosing Athena?
   - **a.** The city already had a lot of salt water.
   - **b.** The olives were delicious.
   - **c.** The olives produced a tasty oil.
   - **(d.)** The judges thought Poseidon had cheated.

2. What information does the passage provide that explains why the water from Poseidon's trident was salty?
   - **a.** Poseidon didn't really want to be patron of Athens.
   - **b.** Zeus made it salty so that Athena would win.
   - **c.** Poseidon thought the people needed more salt water.
   - **(d.)** Poseidon is god of the sea, which is made of salt water.

3. In what ways are the gods similar to and different from humans?

   Sample answer: The gods are all members of a family that has its ups and downs, just like a human family. They hold a contest to make a decision, like people might, but they use supernatural powers in the competition.





## Speaking and Listening Presentation

Ask students to create presentations on fables, folktales, or myths. Have students from diverse backgrounds interview each other about stories from their cultures. After gathering information, students should take turns presenting to the class. Presenters should:

- state their topics and present appropriate facts with descriptive details.
- use formal language suitable for an academic presentation, including precise words for effect.
- speak clearly, in complete sentences, and at a reasonable rate.
- answer questions in complete sentences.

Students should listen attentively and ask questions.

## Independent Practice

**Comprehension Check**

**Answer Explanations:**

**1.** Students should recognize that all options other than choice D, *The judges thought Poseidon had cheated,* are supported by details in the text.

**2.** Students should recall that in paragraph 21 the judges call Poseidon "the god of the sea," so choice D is correct.

**3.** Students' responses should explain that the gods have superhuman powers, but their emotions and relationships are similar to those of humans.

## Critical Comprehension

Use the following questions to help students think more deeply about the text. Students should be prepared to support their answers with evidence from the text.

- *What details signal that Athena will win the contest?* (The judges find her gift tasty and useful.)
- *What was one result of naming Athena patroness?* (The city is named in her honor.)

**Assess and Respond**

**If** students have trouble answering the questions in the Comprehension Check...

**Then** model scanning the text, looking for details that relate to the first question. Guide students to use the details to answer the question. Repeat for the remaining questions.

## Connect Across Texts: *4 points*
## Review Reading Selections

Lead the class in summarizing each of the reading selections by providing summary sentence starters.

## Compare and Contrast Texts

Review the directions on page 30 with students. Have them write characters' names in each column of the T-Chart.

**T-Chart Rubric**

| | |
|---|---|
| 4 | Student identifies two characters and records four or more common and unique characteristics in their proper places. |
| 3 | Student identifies two characters and records at least three common and unique characteristics in their proper places. |
| 2 | Student identifies two characters and records at least three characteristics but may have trouble categorizing them. |
| 1 | Student identifies two characters and records at least one common or unique characteristic. |
| 0 | Student did not complete the assignment or demonstrate understanding of selections. |

## CONNECT ACROSS TEXTS

### Compare and Contrast Texts

In this chapter, you read about the Rabbit and the Elephant, a hunter and Gray-Neck, Momotaro, and Athena and Poseidon. Think about the characters in these stories. Then choose any two characters and compare and contrast them, using the T-Chart below. List key details and other evidence from the texts to show similarities and differences. Be prepared to discuss your ideas with the class.

| Similarities | Differences |
|---|---|
| The Rabbit and Momotaro: brave; clever; heroic; want to protect their land | The Rabbit: tricks the elephant-king into leaving the lake, works alone<br>Momotaro: uses force to defeat the bandits, has help from others |





## Extend Thinking: Compare and Contrast

Have students make a Venn diagram to compare and contrast the adventures of two of the heroes in this chapter. Students should look at important facts about the adventures, including how and where they occur, and what effects they have on the communities. Students should consider the most important details pertaining to each event. Students should note information on where the events differ, as well as the areas where they are alike. Have the students present their ideas to each other in small groups.

## CONNECT ACROSS TEXTS

### Connect to the Essential Question

***How do authors convey a central message or lesson?*** In small groups or as a class, discuss the Essential Question. Think about what you have learned about asking and answering questions, identifying details and determining the central message of a text, and describing characters. Use evidence from the chapter texts to answer the question.

Authors convey a central message through details. In "How the Rabbit Fooled the Elephant," the message that cleverness can defeat strength is conveyed through the rabbit's quick thinking when faced with a stronger enemy. "Athena and Poseidon" has a similar message, which is conveyed through Athena's useful gift over Poseidon's gift. Both "The Winning of Friends" and "Momotaro" convey the central message by showing how people can escape danger by working together.

### Connect to the Theme

***It Takes a Hero*** Think about the characters in each of the stories you read. Which characters would you consider to be heroes? What does it mean to be a hero? Support your answer with details from the text.

Rabbit is a hero because he protects the other rabbits from the elephants. Swift is a hero because he warns the other birds about the hunter. Momotaro is a hero because he defeats the bandits who have been invading and stealing from the local people. Athena is a hero because she defies the odds and wins in a contest. Heroes look out for others or defy the odds, but not all heroes have superpowers.



**To strengthen your response, reread parts of the texts that support your answers. Add to your answers any additional details you find.**



## Assess and Respond (pages 30–31)

| If | Then |
|---|---|
| Students scored 0–2 points, they are **Developing** their understanding of the skills. | Provide students with reading support and more intensive modeling of skills. |
| Students scored 3–5 points, they are **Improving** their understanding of the skills. | Use students' scores to target areas that are weak and review those specific skills. |
| Students scored 6–8 points, they are **Proficient** in their understanding of the skills. | Have these students move on. They are ready for more formal assessment. |

## Support Essential Question Discussion

Have students reread the Essential Question. Challenge them to finish this sentence: *One way an author can convey a central message or lesson is to…*

If students have difficulty responding, prompt them by asking how characters' actions and characteristics can reveal a central message.

## Theme Wrap-Up

Lead students in a group discussion on the theme of *It Takes a Hero*. Talk about the ways in which the heroes take on challenges, find solutions, and help the communities they are part of.

## Short-Answer Questions: *2 points each*

**Connect to the Essential Question Rubric**

| | |
|---|---|
| 2 | Students are able to identify how authors convey a central message or lesson in a text. |
| 1 | Students are able to identify some ways that authors convey a central message or lesson in a text. |
| 0 | Students are not able to identify ways that authors convey a central message or lesson in a text. |

**Connect to the Theme Rubric**

| | |
|---|---|
| 2 | Students correctly identify the characteristics of a hero and what it means to be a hero. |
| 1 | Students identify some characteristics of a hero but do not expand on what it means to be a hero. |
| 0 | Students are not able to identify any characteristics of a hero or what it means to be a hero. |

**OBJECTIVES**

**Use context to determine the meaning of unfamiliar words and phrases.**

## Guided Instruction

Review the Guided Instruction section on page 32 with students. Be sure they understand that a context clue is a word or phrase that appears in the same sentence or a nearby sentence and that provides a clue to the meaning of the unknown or multiple-meaning word. By recognizing context clues, they can clarify meaning on their own and develop their vocabulary.

## Guided Practice

If students are having difficulty, have them say each sentence aloud, replacing the word from the chart with the first definition, and then repeating with the second definition to identify the correct meaning. You might also have them do this exercise with a partner.

## Independent Practice

If students are having trouble determining the correct meaning of the words in italics, have them say each sentence aloud, replacing the word with each dictionary definition until they identify the correct one. Have them underline clues in the sentence that confirm this meaning.

## Apply to Reading

Have students return to "How the Rabbit Fooled the Elephant" to circle multiple-meaning words and underline their context clues. Students may find *sprays* (page 12, paragraph 3), *part* (page 12, paragraph 3), and *spring* (page 13, paragraph 5).

# LANGUAGE

## Context Clues

**bound 1.** *(adj.)* going or ready to go: She is **bound** for home.
**2.** *(n.)* a leap or jump: They crossed the field in leaps and **bounds**.

**Guided Instruction** **Context clues** can help you understand the meanings of unknown and multiple-meaning words. After using context clues, you can check the meanings in a dictionary.

Read this sentence: *I'm bound to get some apples there.* Context clues in the text indicate that this sentence uses meaning 1 of *bound*.

Look at the chart to find other examples of multiple-meaning words.

| | |
|---|---|
| **track** | 1. *(n.)* a course for running<br>2. *(v.)* to follow the tracks of |
| **scour** | 1. *(v.)* to clean by rubbing<br>2. *(v.)* to move quickly while searching |

**Guided Practice** Write the number of the meaning of the word from the chart above that appears in each sentence.

2 **1.** The hunter learned to *track* animals in the forest.

1 **2.** Bring your sneakers if you're going to the *track*.

1 **3.** Will you *scour* this sticky pot with this kitchen sponge?

2 **4.** I'll *scour* the city until I find her.

**Independent Practice** Write the correct meaning of the word in italics. Use context clues and a dictionary to help you.

How long do you think the game will *last*?

___

The shoemaker used his tools to *bore* a hole in leather.

___





## Support English Language Learners

Recognizing a multiple-meaning word requires prior knowledge. Students who are learning English may not recognize that a word has more than one meaning. Help students develop a strong bank of multiple-meaning words by providing definitions for several multiple-meaning words in "How the Rabbit Fooled the Elephant." Then have students work with partners to identify context clues to the meaning of each word as it is used in the text. For example: *bank(s)* (page 13, paragraph 5); definition 1: a place to keep money; definition 2: land next to a body of water; context clue: "the lake."

## CHAPTER 1 REVIEW

Read the following passage in which you can apply skills for asking and answering questions, identifying details and determining the central message, and understanding characters. Then answer the questions on pages 33 and 34.

### The Daydreamer

(Genre: Folktale)

1 A poor farmer was walking through his fields, when he saw a rabbit hopping a few feet ahead.

2 "What a stroke of luck!" he shouted. "I'll catch that rabbit. I'll sell it at the market for ten dollars. I'll buy a fat pig. It will have piglets. The piglets will grow to be big as their mother. Soon I'll be rich!

3 "I'll hire a housekeeper and cook. I'll get married. My wife will have two sons. They will plow the fields. I'll sit on the porch and supervise.

4 "'Hey boys,' I'll holler. 'Don't work yourselves too hard! You know you were born stinking rich!'"

5 The farmer bellowed these last words so loud that the rabbit was frightened and fled. So his riches, his wife, and his children were lost.

**Fill in the circle of the correct answer choice.**

**1.** Because the farmer is daydreaming, the rabbit

- ○ is caught
- ○ is sold
- ● escapes
- ○ bellows

**2.** *Bellowed* is closest in meaning to

- ○ daydreamed
- ○ whispered
- ○ listened
- ● shouted

**3.** The farmer's wife

- ○ cooks and cleans
- ○ has two sons
- ● does not exist
- ○ scolds him





### Self-Assessment: Progress Check

Have students revisit the Progress Check on page 9 and respond to the questions again. Ask them to compare their Before and After responses.

You may wish to have students rate their own answers on a scale of 0–2 rather than simply checking (or not checking) the box. Instruct them to write a 0 if they feel they don't understand the given skill at all, a 1 if they feel they have some understanding, and a 2 if they feel they have a solid grasp of the skill.

## Chapter Summary

At this point, students have had instruction and practice in reading fables, folktales, and myths, with a focus on heroism. Students have also learned different strategies for asking and answering questions, determining the central message of a text, and describing characters. Students have practiced working with concepts across texts, and practiced using context clues to determine the meaning of unknown and multiple-meaning words. They should be well-prepared for the review section.

## Introduce the Review

Explain to students that they will read a new passage that is related to the chapter's theme and the selections they have already read. Instruct students to read the passage carefully and then answer the questions on pages 33 and 34.

### Answer Explanations

Scoring: Items 1–9 on pages 33–34 are worth 1 point each. See the rubric for guidance on scoring the Write About It question on page 34.

**1.** The text describes how the farmer wastes time daydreaming, rather than acting quickly to catch the rabbit. So, the answer is the third choice, *escapes*.

**2.** The text states that the farmer "bellowed" so loudly that "the rabbit was frightened and fled." So, *bellowed* is closest in meaning to the fourth choice, *shouted*.

**3.** The text describes how the farmer dreams about getting married, so the farmer's wife *does not exist*. The third choice is correct.

### Answer Explanations

**4.** It was *foolish* of the farmer to waste time rather than acting quickly to catch the rabbit. The fourth choice is correct.

**5.** Students should realize that the farmer is happy about the unexpected event, and that "a fortunate event" is the best answer.

**6.** The boys will do the work, and the father will supervise from the porch. Context clues should show students that "to be in charge of" is the best answer.

**7.** Since the farmer thinks the rabbit will bring him money, "many riches" is the best answer.

**8.** Because the farmer dreams about easy ways to make money, and fails, "Hard work will pay off" is the correct answer.

**9.** Instead of working to earn money, the farmer spends his time dreaming of it. He is lazy.

### Write About It Rubric

| | |
|---|---|
| 2 | Determines the central message/ lesson, and explains how it is conveyed through story events. |
| 1 | Determines the central message/ lesson, but does not explain how it is conveyed through story events. |
| 0 | Does not determine the central message/lesson. |

## CHAPTER 1 REVIEW

**4.** The farmer is best described as

- ○ hard-working
- ○ angry
- ○ capable
- ● foolish

**5.** What is the meaning of the phrase *stroke of luck* in paragraph 2?

- ○ an unhappy accident
- ○ a careful plan
- ● a fortunate event
- ○ a wish come true

**6.** What is the meaning of the word *supervise* in paragraph 3?

- ○ to help out with
- ● to be in charge of
- ○ to stay away from
- ○ to ignore

**7.** What did the farmer think the rabbit would bring him?

- ● many riches
- ○ good luck
- ○ one pig
- ○ more rabbits

**8.** What is the central message of this story?

- ○ Daydreaming is effective.
- ○ Lucky people can succeed.
- ○ Daydreaming is enjoyable.
- ● Hard work will pay off.

**9.** What is one trait of the farmer as shown by his actions?

- ● lazy
- ○ hard-working
- ○ serious
- ○ talented

**Write About It** What lesson should the farmer learn based on story events?

Sample answer: He should learn that if he worked as hard as he dreamed, he might get the things he wants.





### Analyze Student Scores

| | |
|---|---|
| 9–11 pts Strong | Student has a good grasp of the skills and concepts taught in this chapter. Point out any mistakes the student has made and explain the correct answers if necessary. |
| 4–8 pts Progressing | Student is struggling with some skills or concepts. Identify the specific skills that are problematic to target a review of instruction. |
| 0–3 pts Emerging | Student is having serious problems understanding the skills and concepts taught in this chapter. Student may need to redo the work with a higher level of support. |

# Key Ideas and Details: Informational Texts

CHAPTER 2

CHAPTER 2

## Key Ideas and Details
## Informational Texts

**Focus on Reading** Informational texts present key ideas and support them using details. In order to understand a text's main idea, you need to ask and answer questions to determine important details and to understand the relationships between ideas in the text.

**Think About Theme** Woven into our modern world are threads from the past. True stories of amazing discoveries of ancient civilizations tell us that people have always created art and invented things. The discoveries have something to tell us.

**Let's Get on Our Way!** As a reader, you can learn a lot from understanding key ideas and details presented by authors of informational texts.

These are the skills you will build in this chapter. Before you begin, check the boxes on the left of any items you can do well now. At the end of the chapter, you will return to this page to use the check boxes on the right to show what you have learned.

Progress Check **Can I?**

| Before Chapter 2 | | After Chapter 2 |
|---|---|---|
| ☐ | Ask and answer questions about a text to better understand it. | ☐ |
| ☐ | Retell a text's important details to show understanding. | ☐ |
| ☐ | Summarize the main idea of a text. | ☐ |
| ☐ | Describe how events or ideas in a text are related. | ☐ |
| ☐ | Explain how certain words are used to describe real life. | ☐ |





**Student Page 35**

## Progress Check

The Progress Check is a self-assessment feature that students can use to gauge their own progress. Research shows that when students take accountability for their own learning, their motivation increases.

Before students begin work on Chapter 2, have them check the boxes next to any item that they feel they can do well. Explain that it is fine if they don't check any of the boxes. They will have an opportunity to learn about and practice all of these items while studying the chapter. Let them know that near the end of the chapter they will have a chance to reconsider how well they can do each item on this list.

Before students begin the Chapter 2 Review on page 59, have them revisit this page. You can use this information to work with students on any items they don't understand before they tackle the Review.

## HOME CONNECT...

The Home Connect feature is a way to keep parents or other adult family members apprised of what their children are learning. The key learning objectives are listed, and some ideas for related activities and discussions are included.

Explain to students that they can share the Home Connect page with their parents or other adult family members in their home. Let students know how much time the class will be spending on this chapter so they can plan their time accordingly at home.

Encourage students and their parents to share their experiences using the suggestions on the Home Connect page. You may wish to make a place to post some of this work.

## HOME CONNECT...

It is easy to **ask and answer questions** about a nonfiction text because it is full of details. Sometimes, asking yourself about what you have read is the only way to keep the information straight in your head. Choose a print or online news report on a topic of interest to your child. Use the article's title and subheadings to preview the subject and **main idea**. Read it together, asking and answering questions about **interesting details**. Pause at certain points to have your child summarize the information. Discuss the main idea of the text when you are done reading.

Authors of nonfiction texts use wording that **describes how a series of historical events or ideas are related.** In this chapter, your child will learn about several important archaeological discoveries. Have your child describe events in his or her life that led to some kind of understanding or discovery. How did he or she come to play a certain sport, learn a new skill, or meet someone new? Talk together using language that connects different events.

**On the Go:** The texts in this chapter focus on scientific research on ancient objects. With your child, think of ways that research skills might be used closer to your time and place. You might try to find out more about your ancestors, for example. Or, perhaps there is an old monument or landmark near your home. Finding out who built it and why can open up your town's history. A visit to a local historical society can add a hands-on element to any Internet research that you do.

**IN THIS CHAPTER, YOUR CHILD WILL...**

- Ask questions and answer them to gain a better understanding of an informational text.
- Determine the main idea of a text, and explain how details in the text support the main idea.
- Describe relationships between events or ideas in a text using words and phrases that show time order, sequence, and cause and effect.
- Connect the meaning of words to real-life situations.
- Compare and contrast three texts on the same theme: a magazine article, an historical text, and a science magazine article.

**WAYS TO HELP YOUR CHILD**

Help your child connect "school" reading with everyday reading. Pick a topic from your child's schoolwork as a jumping off point. Use keywords from the topic to fuel an Internet search for similar, age-appropriate articles. Ask your child to tell you the most interesting facts from the articles. Follow up with your own search for additional information, either online or in print. Suggest that your child find out more about the subject and then teach you something new.

ONLINE For more Home Connect activities, continue online at sadlierconnect.com





**Student Page 36**

## LEARNING PROGRESSIONS

In this chapter, students will learn how an author of an informational text conveys a main idea and supports it with details. In order to learn the skills in this chapter, students will further develop skills learned in second grade. They should be encouraged to retain these skills, as they will continue to build on them in fourth grade.

| Asking and Answering Questions | • Grade 2 students should have completed the school year able to ask and answer questions such as who, what, where, when, why, and how to demonstrate understanding of key details in the text.<br>• As third graders, students will build on this skill by referring explicitly to the text as the basis for their answers to these same kinds of questions in order to demonstrate understanding of the text.<br>• In grade 4, students will be expected to refer to details and examples in the text when explaining what the text says explicitly and when drawing inferences. |
|---|---|
| Determining Main Idea and Key Details | • By the end of grade 2, students should be able to identify the main topic of a multi-paragraph text as well as the focus of specific paragraphs within the text.<br>• In grade 3, students will widen their application of this skill to determine the main idea of a text and recount the key details and explain how they support the main idea.<br>• When students move on to grade 4, they will continue to practice determining the main idea and explaining how it is supported by key details, as well as learn to summarize the text. |
| Describing Relationships Between Ideas | • Proficient second-grade students should have ended the school year able to describe the connection between a series of historical events, scientific ideas or concepts, or steps in technical procedures in a text.<br>• Throughout grade 3, students' use of this skill will become more sophisticated as they learn to describe these same connections, or relationships, using language that pertains to time, sequence, and cause/effect.<br>• Students will be expected to apply this skill at a more complex level in grade 4 by explaining events, procedures, ideas, or concepts in a historical, scientific, or technical text, including what happened and why, based on specific information in the text. |

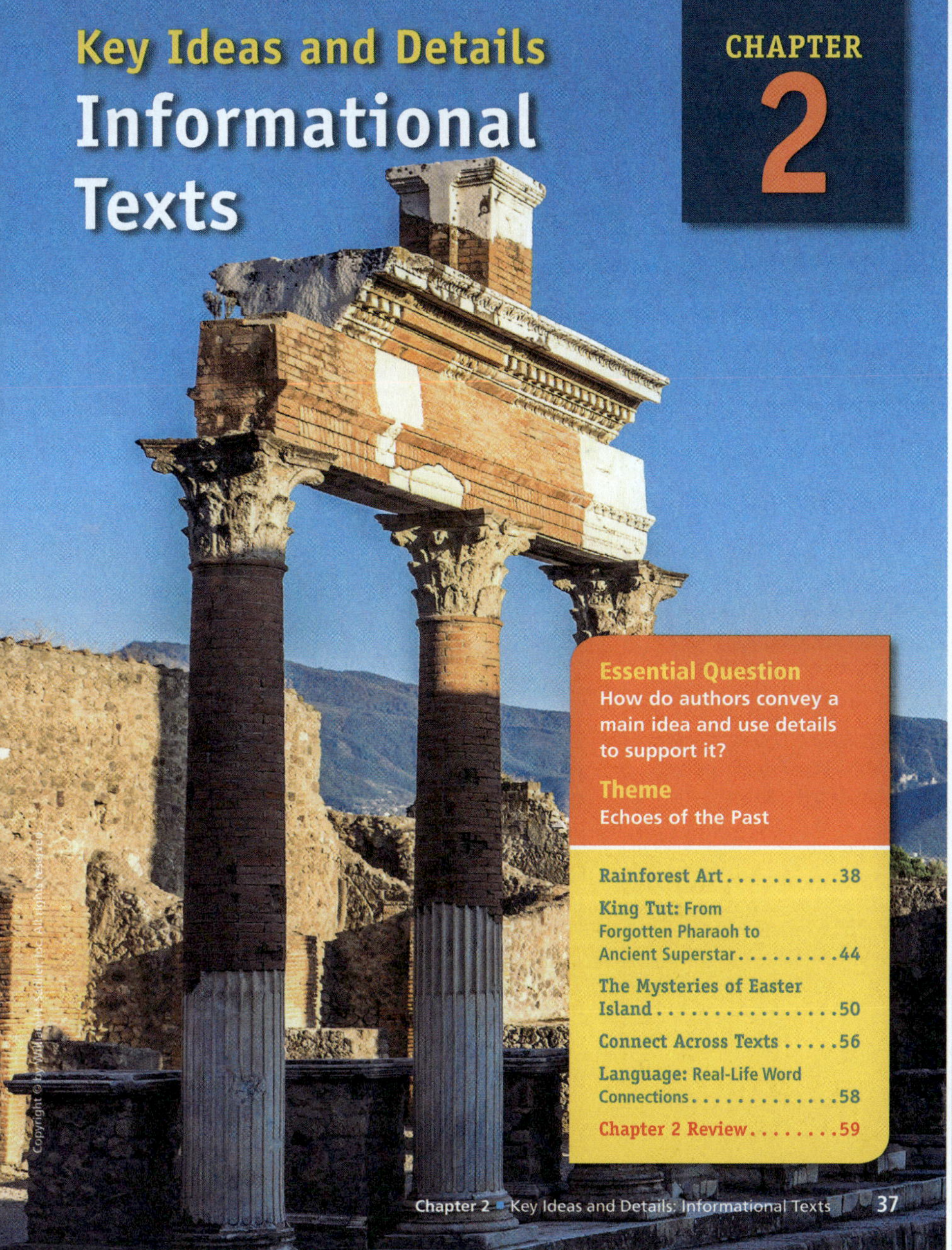


**Essential Question:**
**How do authors convey a main idea and use details to support it?**

In this chapter, students will learn about how to identify and make connections between the main idea and key details of an informational text, specifically by asking and answering questions and describing relationships between ideas.

## Theme: Echoes of the Past

Students will read informational texts related to the theme of human history, or our collective past. They will read about amazing discoveries, such as one of the largest collections of prehistoric rock art ever found, the three-year search for King Tut's tomb, and the mysteries of Easter Island.

## Curriculum Connection: Social Studies

Students will learn about the settlers of the Amazon River Basin, ancient Egypt, and the inhabitants of Rapa Nui (Easter Island), as well as how scientists, archaeologists, and explorers study the past.

## Vocabulary Overview

### General Academic Vocabulary

architecture 47, chamber 45, custom 45, craze 46, dazzled 48, degree 42, expansion 40, fractured 48, inhabitant 40, intact 46, interior 52, livelihood 54, massive 54, monument 51, motive 42, notable 52, rodent 40, ruins 45, safeguard 54, similar 42, society 50, technology 48, ton 50, tropical 38, worshipping 42

### Domain-Specific Vocabulary

archaeologist 50, extinct 39, megalith 52, prehistoric 38, quarry 52, rainforest 38, sarcophagus 46, tomb 44

## Guided Instruction

**OBJECTIVE**
**Show an understanding of an informational text by asking questions and citing evidence from the text to answer questions.**

### Genre: Magazine Article

Explain to students that a magazine article is a type of informational text that appears in a print or digital magazine.

### Set the Purpose

Help students understand the purpose for learning the reading skill by asking *What text have you read recently that you did not understand? What did you do to better understand it?*

### Model and Teach

Read the selection as students follow along in their books.

### CITE EVIDENCE

**A** *I know that I need to look for details in the text to know what this article is about.*

*What is the setting in paragraph 1?* (the Amazon River Basin in South America) *If I read paragraph 2, I can find out what happened there.* (Explorers discovered one of the largest collections of prehistoric rock art.)

**B** *Paragraph 3 explains when this discovery occurred. Why was there a problem getting the news out about this event?* (there was a civil war in Colombia)

ASKING AND ANSWERING QUESTIONS

Guided Instruction

**WORDS TO KNOW**
**extinct**
**prehistoric**
**rainforest**
**tropical**

To **understand a text,** use details from the text to **ask and answer questions.**

**CITE EVIDENCE**

**A** To understand a text, it helps to ask and answer questions such as *What is the text about?* Underline details in paragraph 2 that answer this question.

**B** It also helps to ask *When did it happen?* Circle details in paragraph 3 that answer this question.

## Rainforest Art

(Genre: Magazine Article)

### Discovery in the Amazon River Basin

1 The Amazon River Basin is in northern South America. This huge region covers 2.7 million square miles. The Amazon River flows through the basin. This region is home to the largest **rainforest** in the world. Millions of different kinds of living things can be found here.

2 Explorers recently made a great discovery in this **tropical** region. They found one of the largest collections of **prehistoric** rock art ever discovered. Some of this art can be dated back to 10,600 BCE. The collection includes many paintings of humans and animals. One grouping stretches for eight miles near the Guayabero River in Colombia.

3 The British and Colombian researchers could not explore the area before 2016 due to a civil war in Colombia. In 2017–2018, they made many finds. But the news did not become public until late 2020.



38 Chapter 2 ■ Key Ideas and Details: Informational Texts

### Words to Know

**General Academic Vocabulary**
**tropical** (*adjective*): of or occurring in the tropics; hot and humid

**Domain-Specific Vocabulary**
**extinct** (*adjective*): no longer living or existing
**prehistoric** (*adjective*): taking place before the time of recorded history
**rainforest** (*noun*): a tropical forest that receives lots of rain and has very tall trees

**Working with Word Meaning** Have partners make flash cards for the vocabulary words—with the word on one side and the definition on the other side—and then take turns using the flash cards to quiz each other.

## KEY IDEAS AND DETAILS

### What Was Found?

4 The researchers found thousands of rock art paintings. The art depicts a variety of subjects. Many of the images show animals that are still found in the area. These include monkeys and snakes. There are also images of fish and birds. The pictures are very realistic.

5 There are also many paintings of animals that no longer exist. These **extinct** creatures include Ice Age horses, a giant sloth, and a mastodon. The mastodon is related to elephants.

6 Why did these animals die out? We can't be sure. Possible causes include over-hunting, change in climate, and loss of habitat, or suitable surroundings.

7 There are also many paintings of geometric designs. Strangely, many of the images are located high up on the rock wall. They are so high that researchers have used drones to examine them. The artists must have used ladders or scaffolds. It is interesting that the paintings include pictures of wooden towers.

**Comprehension Check**

Where were the newly discovered paintings found? Why was the discovery so important? Use details from the text as a basis for your answer.

### Guided Instruction

**CITE EVIDENCE**

**C** In most informational texts, it helps to ask *What happened?* Box the words in paragraph 4 that answer this question.

**D** Texts that tell facts will also explain *why* something happened. Underline the details in paragraph 6 that tell why the animals died off. How can studying the reasons something in the past happened help scientists today?

## Guided Instruction

### CITE EVIDENCE

**C** *I am looking for clues to find out what happened. I know that they found prehistoric rock art. I'm going to keep reading to find out what it looked like.*

*Which words tell you what the researchers found?* (art, a variety of subjects, animals that are still found in the area)

**D** *Why is the cause in a cause-and-effect relationship. The effect is the animals dying off. So I'll look for a word that signals the cause for this event.*

*What word signals why they died off?* (causes) *How many causes does the text list?* (three) *How might knowing about these causes help scientists protect other animals?* (They can watch to see if these same events threaten to make other animals extinct today.)

**Comprehension Check**

**Sample Answer:** The newly discovered paintings were found on rock walls in the Amazon River Basin in South America. The discovery was important because they were from a time long ago, some dating back to 10,600 BCE. Many paintings depict animals that are no longer around because they have died off.

**Answer Explanation:** Students should notice that the text explains that many of these animals are extinct, so the only way to see them are on the rock walls. Students should recognize that this discovery can help scientists prevent the animals we see today from having the same fate.

## Support English Language Learners

Help English language learners become familiar with *r*-controlled vowels. Explain that when *r* follows a vowel in a word, the *r* changes the way the vowel sounds. Display an example: *cat*, *cape*, *car*. Discuss how the *a* keeps its normal short or long sound in the first two words, but the *r* in the third word changes it. Explain that *a* only makes this sound when followed by *r*. Model pronunciation for the following *r*-controlled words in paragraph 1, and then ask students to repeat each word after you: *River*, *northern*, *covers*, *largest*, *rainforest*, *world*.

Discuss how the *r* changes the vowel sound in each word. Have students find and pronounce *r*-controlled words in the second paragraph.

## Guided Practice

### Recap Reading Selection

Let students know that they will continue reading the article about the prehistoric rock art. Review what they read about how the rock art was discovered and what might have caused the prehistoric animals to become extinct.

### Read and Practice

Have partners take turns reading the selection as you circulate to provide support. Model practicing asking and answering questions with Cite Evidence callout A. For callout B, circulate and provide partners with scaffolding as needed. You might use the following suggestions to help students who are having difficulty.

#### CITE EVIDENCE

**A** Discuss with students the differences between the people studying the art and the people who made the art. Explain that researchers, experts, and scholars study the paintings in order to find out how people lived, what they ate, and why they made the art. Have students look at paragraph 8 for a description of a social activity the artists may have taken part in.

**B** Remind students that animals are featured in many of the paintings and that they played an important role in the lives of the people who created the artwork. Guide students to see that the animals as well as the fruits that the people ate were crucial to their survival.

## ASKING AND ANSWERING QUESTIONS

### Guided Practice

#### WORDS TO KNOW

**expansion**
**inhabitant**
**rodent**

#### CITE EVIDENCE

**A** Check your understanding by asking yourself, *Who are the people studying this art?* Underline words that show who is studying this discovery.

**B** In paragraph 12, circle the sentences that explain what the art tells us about the people's diet. Ask yourself, *Why would the author choose to include that information?*

**Rainforest Art** *continued*

8 Besides the animals, the paintings also feature humans. Some of these images hint that making art was a social activity. Others suggest that the creators of the paintings had a sense of humor. One image features a row of figures holding hands while dancing. A researcher thinks they might be turtle-shaped men! Another image shows a man wearing a strange mask with a beak.

#### The Artists

9 What do we know about the artists of the rock paintings? And what can the paintings teach us about their creators?

10 Experts believe that the creators of the rock art were early **inhabitants** of the area. Scholars of prehistory suppose that the Americas were settled by people who migrated eastward from Asia. They crossed the Bering Land Bridge starting about 25,000 years ago. The bridge linked what is today northeast Asia and North America.

11 Other settlers pushed southward to South America. The creators of the rock art made their home in the Amazon River Basin. They were part of a major wave of human **expansion** on the planet.

12 The paintings tell us about the people in that region. They had an extremely varied diet. They ate fruits, alligators, and frogs. They also ate **rodents** like the small paca and the very large capybara. They fished in the nearby river.





### Words to Know

**General Academic Vocabulary**

**expansion** (*noun*): the act or process of becoming bigger or making something bigger
**inhabitant** (*noun*): a person or animal that lives in a place
**rodent** (*noun*): a small mammal (such as a mouse, rat, squirrel, or beaver) with sharp front teeth used for gnawing

**Working with Word Meaning** Ask students to imagine a social activity that may have taken place during prehistoric times. Have them make a drawing. Encourage students to use the word *inhabitants* and share their drawings with a partner.

**Comprehension Check**

1. In paragraph 12, all of the following are mentioned as part of the humans' diet EXCEPT
   - **a.** fruits
   - **b.** alligators
   - **(c.)** sheep
   - **d.** capybaras

2. Which of the following statements is BEST supported by the text?
   - **a.** The artists themselves crossed the Bering Land Bridge.
   - **(b.)** The creators of the paintings were part of a great wave of human expansion on Earth.
   - **c.** The vast majority of the paintings were made by a single artist.
   - **d.** No two paintings in the collection are exactly alike.

3. Work with a partner. Explain why the team of explorers could not get access to the area for a long time.

Sample answer: The area was blocked for a long time because of a civil war in Colombia. A war would have made the area dangerous to enter and study.





## Foundational Skills: Fluency

Explain that students can read more fluently if they read with proper phrasing, which means they pause after appropriately grouped words, sometimes signaled by a comma. Demonstrate this concept by reading paragraph 1 with poor phrasing (*The Amazon / River / Basin is / in / northern South / America.*) or by running all the words together. Then reread paragraph 1 with proper phrasing: *The Amazon River Basin / is in northern South America.* Allow students to practice reading another paragraph with proper phrasing. Next, have them record themselves reading the same paragraph and then listen to the recording to improve prosodic skills. Additional fluency passages and activities can be found at **sadlierconnect.com** in the *Foundational Skills Handbook*.

## Guided Practice

**Comprehension Check**

**Answer Explanations:**

**1.** Choice C is correct because the article states that humans at that time ate fruit, alligators, and capybaras. There is no indication that they ate sheep.

**2.** Choice B is correct. Paragraph 11 says that the creators of the rock art were "part of a major wave of human expansion on the planet."

**3.** Students' responses may vary, but they should note that the text says the news of the researchers' findings did not become public until late 2020 because of a civil war in Colombia.

## Peer Collaboration

Have students confirm their answer choices for Comprehension Check 1 and 2 on page 41 by turning to a partner and discussing why each answer option they did not select can be ruled out. For Comprehension Check 2, suggest that students discuss how the wording in the incorrect choices differs from the wording in the text. Encourage students to revise their answer choices based on their discussions with their partners. Then ask pairs to report their answers to the whole group.

## Independent Practice

### Recap Reading Selection

Remind students that they have been reading a magazine article. Have them recall the topic of the article (recently discovered prehistoric rock art) and why this discovery is important (the art tells about a time long ago, what animals were alive, and how humans lived).

### Read and Apply

Have students read the selection independently as you circulate to provide support. If you notice students struggling, you can provide support with the suggestions below.

### CITE EVIDENCE

**A** Guide students to understand that experts study rock art to find out how people lived during prehistoric times. Help students identify the detail that "humans had a special relationship with forest animals" and depended on them "to a great degree for their survival and safety" to connect the many animals in the paintings and the humans' need to stay alive. In addition, the humans recognized the power that the animals had to injure or kill hunters.

**B** Help students see that the rock art will be studied for years to come. Prompt students to pose a question about the paintings.

ASKING AND ANSWERING QUESTIONS

**Independent Practice**

**WORDS TO KNOW**
**degree**
**motive**
**similar**
**worshipping**

**CITE EVIDENCE**

**A** Ask yourself, *Why would the prehistoric paintings feature so many animals?* Circle the detail in paragraph 14 that answers this question.

**B** Underline the detail that tells about what will happen with the paintings in the future. What questions about the paintings would you like to ask an expert?

**Rainforest Art** *continued*

#### Why Make Art?

13 The artists' **motives** for creating the rock paintings are unclear. Experts have argued in favor of several theories. Such arguments explain other prehistoric paintings as well. These include artworks found in France and Spain.

14 One leading theory is that humans had a special relationship with forest animals. This relationship reflected the fact that some animals could injure or even kill hunters. Meanwhile, people depended to a great **degree** on hunting for their survival and safety. A **similar** relationship is found in many cultures that depend on animals for food and clothing material.

15 One of the leaders of the research team commented, "It is interesting that many of these large animals appear surrounded by small men with their arms raised, almost **worshipping** these animals."

16 As of the end of 2020, the rock art site in Colombia is so new that it has not even been named yet. One thing is certain, though. The artworks are so beautiful and wide-ranging that experts will be studying them for years to come.





### Words to Know

**General Academic Vocabulary**

**degree** (*noun*): an amount or intensity
**motive** (*noun*): something that causes a person to take a certain action
**similar** (*adjective*): almost the same
**worshipping** (*verb*): participating in a ceremony to show deep respect to someone or something

**Working with Word Meaning** Show pictures that relate to two or more words and have partners discuss which word goes with which picture.

# KEY IDEAS AND DETAILS

## Independent Practice

### Comprehension Check

1. According to paragraph 13, where else has prehistoric art been discovered?
   a. England and Germany
   (b.) France and Spain
   c. Russia and China
   d. Italy and Greece

2. In paragraph 15, the detail about pictures of the small men raising their arms before the animals tells the reader that
   a. the people were afraid of the animals
   b. the people were not used to seeing animals
   (c.) animals were important to the people
   d. animals were friends with the people

3. Work with a partner. Discuss your reactions to the photos in the article. What questions would you ask a researcher studying this rock art?

Answers will vary.





## Foundational Skill Review: Consonant Digraphs

Review words with the consonant digraphs *ch*, *sh*, and *th*. Display <u>ch</u>ain, <u>sh</u>ake, and <u>th</u>em, and underline the digraph as you say each word. Point out that the two letters in each digraph combine to form a new sound. Explain that the digraph can appear at the beginning, middle, or end of a word. Then have students identify *ch* words in paragraph 6 (*change*) on page 39 and paragraph 9 (*teach*) on page 40; *sh* words in paragraph 8 (*shaped*) and paragraph 11 *(pushed)* on page 40; and *th* words in paragraph 1 (*the, this, through*) on page 38 and paragraph 4 (*thousands, that, these, there*) on page 39.

## Independent Practice

### Comprehension Check

**Answer Explanations:**

**1.** Choice B, *France and Spain*, tells where else prehistoric art has been discovered.

**2.** "Small men with their arms raised" appeared to be worshipping the animals, so choice C is correct.

**3.** Students' answers will vary but should reflect content they see in the photos. Students might also have questions about the job of a researcher.

## Critical Comprehension

Use the following questions to help students think more deeply about the text. Students should be prepared to support their answers with evidence from the text.

- *Do you think the rock art should be studied or left alone?* (Answers will vary, but students may say that people studying or viewing the rock art should take steps to make sure it is not damaged.)
- *What details help you understand that the discovery of the rock art in the Amazon River Basin was exciting to the science community?* (the discovery was mentioned in the news; experts have developed theories about the artists' motives; experts will be studying the art for many years to come)

### Assess and Respond

**If** students have difficulty answering the questions in the Comprehension Check,

**Then** work individually with them, helping them check each answer option against the text to help them rule out wrong options before selecting the correct choice.

## Guided Instruction

**OBJECTIVE**

**Determine and explain the main idea of a text, using key details from the text.**

### Genre: Historical Text

Explain to students that an historical text is a type of informational text that tells about an event from the past, or something related to history.

### Set the Purpose

Help students understand the purpose for learning the reading skill by asking *Why do you think authors write about events that took place in the past?*

### Model and Teach

Read the selection as students follow along in their books.

**CITE EVIDENCE**

**A** *I know that titles are usually the first part of a text and are often in larger letters. Which words in the title help you understand whom the text is about?* (King Tut) *The next part of the title is called the subtitle. What idea does this subtitle tell about?* (King Tut went from being forgotten to being extremely famous.)

**B** *The subtitle is "From Forgotten Pharaoh to Ancient Superstar." In paragraph 1, I see sentences telling that King Tut was not thought of as important during his lifetime, and that much later, his situation would change and he would become world famous.*

DETERMINING MAIN IDEA AND KEY DETAILS

Guided Instruction

**WORDS TO KNOW**

**chamber**
**custom**
**ruins**
**tomb**

Look for the **main idea** of a text. Find **key details** and explain how they **support the main idea**.

**CITE EVIDENCE**

**A** In an informational text, **details** in the title can point toward the **main idea**. In the title, draw a circle around six words that tell the main focus of this text.

**B** The author usually tells the reader the main idea early in the text. In paragraph 1, underline three sentences that tell the main idea. How do these sentences work with the words you circled in the title?

# King Tut

## From Forgotten Pharaoh to Ancient Superstar

(Genre: Historical Text)

1 During his lifetime, Tutankhamun was not an important pharaoh. He ruled ancient Egypt for only a short time and died at a young age. More than 3,000 years after his death, however, the young king came out of the shadows. Against all odds, his **tomb**, his treasures, and his remains were found. Before long, he would become the world's most famous pharaoh. And he would become known simply as "King Tut."

### A Fantastic Find

2 From 1922 to 1925, an English scientist named Howard Carter spent three years unearthing Tut's tomb. The job was a tough one, for a number of reasons. To begin with, it was surprising that the tomb was found at all. Carter was searching in a part of Egypt known as the Valley of the Kings. Many pharaohs had been buried there.

44 Chapter 2 ■ Key Ideas and Details: Informational Texts

## Words to Know

**General Academic Vocabulary**

**chamber** (*noun*): a room

**custom** (*noun*): the usual way of doing something

**ruins** (*noun*): parts of a building or other structure that remain after a destructive event

**Domain-Specific Vocabulary**

**tomb** (*noun*): a room, usually underground, that is used as a grave

**Working with Word Meaning** Ask students to write one sentence, unrelated to the information in the text, for each word.

## Guided Instruction

But robbers had already found most of the tombs. They knew that Egyptian **custom** was to bury pharaohs with treasures for use in the afterlife. So they broke in and carried the treasures away.

3 On November 4, 1922, Carter stumbled upon Tut's tomb while checking other **ruins**. At first, the only part that was visible was the top of a rock stairway. After workers cleared it step by step, they found something thrilling. It was a sealed door that had royal signs with Tut's name.

4 Carter made a small hole in the door. He then used a flashlight to look inside. Behind the door was a passage filled with rocks. They were there as a result of flooding over the ages. Carter was sure he had found a major tomb.

5 Three weeks later, Carter and his team entered the tomb. They opened the door and cleared the rocks. They then reached a second door, sealed like the first. Again, Carter made a hole to look inside. A teammate asked Carter if he could see anything. "Yes, wonderful things!" Carter replied.

### Wonderful Things

6 The objects in the tomb were wonderful and original. The walls were painted with scenes from the king's life. There were couches and chairs. There were statues of gods and a gold chariot. And there was another doorway. It led to a burial **chamber**.

**Comprehension Check**

Which details from the text help the reader understand why King Tut was forgotten before the discovery of his tomb?

Howard Carter

**CITE EVIDENCE**

**C** In paragraph 3, the author includes a sentence that expresses a feeling. Circle the sentence. How does this detail about a feeling support the main idea?

**D** In this section, the author gives a step-by-step account of the discovery of the tomb. In paragraphs 4 and 5, underline the sentences that tell about this discovery. How do these details support the main idea?





## Support English Language Learners

Help English language learners build and connect to background knowledge before they read this text so that they can focus their energy on comprehending the ideas the author presents rather than on trying to make sense of unfamiliar ideas and references.

Be sure English language learners recognize this text is about a discovery of something that has been buried for a long time, just like the prehistoric rock art they read about on pages 38–43. Show pictures of archaeological digs to help students understand what Howard Carter was doing. Show pictures of entrances to tombs in the Valley of the Kings, as well as of the elaborate interiors of tombs. Use language from the text to talk about the images you show, pointing to words in the text as you say them.

## Guided Instruction

### CITE EVIDENCE

**C** *As I read, I'll look for a sentence that conveys a feeling.*

*I see a sentence that say the workers who were clearing the steps found something "thrilling." How does this feeling connect to the main idea?* (It suggests that what they find is important and will help make King Tut famous.)

**D** *I see that the author goes into detail to tell about how Carter got into the tomb.*

*How do these details in paragraphs 4 and 5 support the main idea?* (They help to emphasize how serious and important the discovery was. Also, Carter says that he can see "wonderful things.")

**Comprehension Check**

**Sample Answer:** The text says he was not an important pharaoh. Also, he ruled only for a short time and died at a young age. In addition, his tomb was well hidden.

**Answer Explanation:** King Tut ruled a long time ago for only a short time, before books and videos, so people could not easily record and save information for future generations.

### Review: Asking and Answering Questions

Remind students to ask and answer questions to better understand the text. Prompt them to look for details in the text that help them understand why we know so much about King Tut now, even though he was forgotten after his rule.

## Guided Practice

### Recap Reading Selection

Have students recall what they have read so far about King Tut and his tomb. They should mention that King Tut ruled ancient Egypt but was forgotten about because he died young and ruled only for a short time.

### Read and Practice

Have partners take turns reading the selection as you circulate to provide support. Model determining the main idea and key details with Cite Evidence callout A. For callout B, circulate and provide partners with scaffolding as needed. You might use the following suggestions to help students who are having difficulty.

### CITE EVIDENCE

**A** Help students recognize the importance of finding Tut's tomb and his treasures intact. Explain that robbers had stolen the treasures from the other tombs, but King Tut's tomb still had its contents. This allowed scientists and historians to study and learn from actual objects and not just from writings and paintings.

**B** Help students see that everyday people also gained from the discovery of Tut's tomb. If scientists and historians were lacking in information about ancient Egypt, regular people knew even less. This news led to "Tut-mania." Prompt students to recognize that these details help support the idea why the tomb discovery led to Tut being a "worldwide smash."

DETERMINING MAIN IDEA AND KEY DETAILS

Guided Practice

**WORDS TO KNOW**
**architecture**
**craze**
**intact**
**sarcophagus**

**CITE EVIDENCE**

**A** The author states that scientists and historians were "stunned" by the importance of the objects that Carter found. Underline the details in paragraph 8 that explain why the objects were so important.

**B** In paragraph 9, the author names another group, apart from scientists and historians, who were excited by Carter's find. Circle the words that tell *who.* How does this information support the main idea?

**King Tut:** From Forgotten Pharaoh to Ancient Superstar *continued*

7 Inside the chamber was the **sarcophagus**—a human-shaped outer coffin. Carter opened the top. He found a set of three beautifully decorated gold coffins, one inside another. Here was the final resting place of King Tut, whose mummy wore a dazzling mask of solid gold.

#### A Worldwide Smash

8 Carter spent years cleaning and studying the contents of Tut's tomb. He then sent each piece to a museum in Cairo, the capital of Egypt. There, the objects were studied by scientists and historians, who were stunned by their importance. Before Tut's, no Egyptian royal tomb had been found **intact**. Experts knew about ancient Egypt mostly from writings and paintings—not from actual objects.

9 The experts were not the only ones who were amazed by Tut and his treasures. Carter's discovery made headlines. Photographs, drawings, and descriptions of the objects spread around the world. As a result of the news, normal, everyday people felt carried off to another time and place. All the excitement led to a **craze** sometimes called "Tut-mania."

46 Chapter 2 ■ Key Ideas and Details: Informational Texts

### Words to Know

**General Academic Vocabulary**
**architecture** (*noun*): a style of building
**craze** (*noun*): something that is very popular for a short time
**intact** (*adjective*): unbroken, not damaged

**Domain-Specific Vocabulary**
**sarcophagus** (*noun*): a stone coffin

**Working with Word Meaning** Challenge students to draw a picture that includes items they can label with two or more vocabulary words.

KEY IDEAS AND DETAILS

Guided Practice

10 Egyptian style and culture began to dominate fashion, design, and **architecture**. In the 1920s and 1930s, there were songs and movies with Egyptian themes. President Hoover named his dog King Tut.

### The Return of King Tut

11 Fast-forward about fifty years. In 1976, a museum exhibit called "Treasures of Tutankhamun" launched a tour of the United States. The show traveled to major cities. It was the first time any of Tut's treasures were on view in the U.S.

**Comprehension Check**

1. Which detail describes the excitement that followed Carter's find?
   - a. There was a sarcophagus in the burial chamber.
   - b. Tut's mummy wore a solid gold mask.
   - c. Carter sent the objects to Cairo.
   - (d.) News of Carter's discovery set off a craze called "Tut-mania."
2. The text implies that during "Tut-mania," an American might own
   - (a.) a chair decorated with the designs of ancient Egypt
   - b. a solid gold table
   - c. a photograph of Howard Carter making the discovery
   - d. a real mummy
3. Work with a partner. Describe the effect that Carter's discovery had on everyday people. In what way were their feelings similar to those of experts on ancient Egypt?

   Sample answer: Everyday people were very excited to learn about the discovery. It made them want to surround themselves with styles of ancient Egypt. Experts were also excited to learn more about Egypt.





## Digital Connection: Online Research

Help students add to the knowledge they have gained from reading this text by reading an online article about King Tut or ancient Egypt on a reliable site. Then display a search engine on the whiteboard and model how to use keywords to find a text online. (You should preselect a text.) Then read the online text together. Guide students as they use the lesson skills to identify the main idea and key details of the text. Discuss with students how the information in the online article confirms and adds to what they already know. Point out that the Internet is a good resource for learning more about a topic provided that the sites they read from are credible. Discuss what makes a site credible.

## Guided Practice

**Comprehension Check**

**Answer Explanations:**

1. Choice D is correct because it is supported by evidence in paragraph 9.
2. Choice A is correct. Paragraph 10 provides details about how Egyptian style caught on, including in fashion and design.
3. Partners' responses will vary, but students should note that both everyday people and experts were excited by the discovery and wanted to learn more about Egypt.

## Numbered Heads Together

Organize students in groups of four, and have them number off from one to four. Then say *At what point after uncovering a rock stairway did Carter know that he was digging up King Tut's tomb? You have two minutes to find and discuss the answer.* (when they found the door that had royal signs with Tut's name) After the time is up, have students with the number three stand up and share the answer their group decided on. Affirm correct responses and guide students who give incorrect responses as they reexamine the text. Ask follow-up questions such as *Do you think Carter would have kept digging if there were no signs on the door?*

## Independent Practice

### Recap Reading Selection

Have a short class discussion about the last section of "King Tut" that students read. Students should mention that King Tut's tomb was an important discovery because it had not been robbed, and thus contained its original treasures.

### Read and Apply

Have students read the selection independently as you circulate to provide support. If you notice students struggling, you can provide support with the suggestions below.

### CITE EVIDENCE

**A** Students should recognize as time passed and technology progressed, more information was revealed. In the museum exhibit from the 1970s, people learned how Carter entered the tomb and the order in which the objects were found. In the twenty-first century, technology and modern science made it possible to learn new, important information about Tut's life.

**B** Help students recognize that the last sentence in paragraph 16 connects to the idea expressed in the title. Students should explain how King Tut went from "forgotten pharaoh to ancient superstar." Students should also recognize why museums are important and that they educate everyday people and historians about people and lands that were once mysterious and unknown.



**Independent Practice**

**WORDS TO KNOW**
**dazzled**
**fractured**
**technology**

**CITE EVIDENCE**

**A** In paragraphs 12 and 13, the author describes two more time periods when people felt excitement about King Tut. Circle the phrases that tell what these time periods were.

**B** In the text's final section, the author restates the main idea. Underline the sentence in paragraph 16 that restates the main idea. What important details from paragraph 15 support the idea that Tut's fame will last into the future?

**King Tut:** From Forgotten Pharaoh to Ancient Superstar *continued*

12 The 1970s exhibit included 55 objects. One of them was the mummy's solid gold mask. Visitors saw how Howard Carter entered the dark tomb. And they learned the order in which the objects were found. Across the country, millions of people waited in long lines to enter. The show set off another wave of Tut-mania, as people were **dazzled** by the richness, beauty, and mystery of what they saw.

#### Twenty-first Century Tut

13 The late 1900s and early 2000s were a time of great progress in **technology**. New kinds of tests were run on King Tut. They revealed important new information about his life.

14 For example, the tests showed that King Tut suffered from malaria. This is a serious illness spread through mosquito bites. Also, the mummy showed evidence of a **fractured** leg. There had always been many questions about how Tut died. The tests did not provide final answers. However, many articles and television shows covered the mummy's meeting with modern science. And so a new wave of interest in King Tut began.

15 In the early 2000s, an even more important event occurred in the timeline of King Tut. Egyptian experts began planning and building the Grand Egyptian Museum. The beautiful, modern museum will be one of the largest in the world. It will hold and display thousands of objects. Among them—and almost certain to be the most popular—are the treasures from King Tut's tomb.





### Words to Know

**General Academic Vocabulary**
**dazzled** (*verb*): to be impressed
**fractured** (*adjective*): broken or cracked
**technology** (*noun*): electronic or digital products and systems

**Working with Word Meaning** Ask students to write a paragraph, using the vocabulary words. Have partners share their writing.

KEY IDEAS AND DETAILS

Independent Practice

16 Meanwhile, it has been decided that the king's mummy will remain at rest in the tomb in which it was buried. And we can assume it is more likely than ever that King Tut will hold on to his place as the world's most famous pharaoh.

**Comprehension Check** MORE ONLINE sadlierconnect.com

1. In the late 1900s and early 2000s, new kinds of scientific tests were performed on Tut's mummy. What was one result of these tests?
   a. The cause of Tut's death was discovered.
   b. Tut was found to be old, not young, when he died.
   c. A new museum exhibit was created.
   (d.) People's interest in Tut grew once again.

2. Why did the author include information about the new Grand Egyptian Museum?
   a. It will be one of the world's largest museums.
   b. It will hold and display thousands of objects.
   (c.) It will hold and display King Tut's treasures.
   d. King Tut's mummy will be kept there.

3. In your own words, what is the main idea of this text? What are some important details that support the main idea?

Sample answer: After the discovery of his tomb in 1922, King Tut went from being a forgotten pharaoh to being the world's most famous pharaoh. The discovery helped experts learn much more about ancient Egypt. News stories and exhibits about Tut also caused interest and excitement for everyday people.





## Extend Thinking: Develop a Logical Argument

Help students extend their thinking by having them compare the discovery of the prehistoric rock art (pages 38–43) to the discovery of King Tut's tomb, and then develop a logical argument about which discovery was more important.

Ask students to consider as they develop their argument why each discovery was amazing and what each discovery helped scientists learn.

Have students present their argument to the class. Listeners should pay attention and ask questions to check their understanding. Speakers should speak clearly, in complete sentences, and at a reasonable rate.

## Independent Practice

**Comprehension Check**

**Answer Explanations:**

1. Choice D is correct. A new wave of interest in King Tut began as a result of the scientific tests.
2. Choice C is correct. Treasures from Tut's tomb will be among the objects displayed at the new musuem.
3. Students' responses may vary but should convey that the main idea is that the discovery of Tut's tomb made a forgotten pharaoh into the world's most famous pharaoh. The discovery allowed experts to learn more about ancient Egypt and caused huge interest from everyday people.

## Critical Comprehension

Use the following questions to help students think more deeply about the text. Students should be prepared to support their answers with evidence from the text.

- *What detail, other than that King Tut was forgotten, helps you understand why robbers did not break into Tut's tomb?* (The entryway was covered by stones and dirt.)
- *What can you infer about King Tut from the difficulty of finding his tomb and detail of his treasures?* (Possible answer: Although he ruled only for a short time, he was still royal. His tomb was hidden and sealed behind three doors. He had gold chariots, masks, etc. buried with him.)

**Assess and Respond**

**If** students have trouble answering the questions in the Comprehension Check…

**Then** reread the text with students. Have them paraphrase each section to check comprehension.

## Guided Instruction

**OBJECTIVE**

**Describe the relationship between ideas, using language related to time, sequence, and cause/effect.**

### Genre: Science Magazine Article

Tell students that a science magazine article is a type of informational text about a scientific topic that appears in a print or digital magazine.

### Set the Purpose

Activate students' thinking about the reading skill by asking *What words would you use to tell someone about what you did this past week?*

### Model and Teach

Read the selection as students follow along in their books.

### CITE EVIDENCE

**A** *I know a date can include a month, day, and year. Some dates list only the month and the year when the day is not known.*

*What date is given in the second paragraph?* (April 1722) *What time-related word is used to tell when Easter Island got its name?* (after) *I'll keep reading to see what happened after April 1722.* (Chile claimed possession of Easter Island.)

**B** *I'll look for time-related words or phrases that signal when other events happened.*

*What words or phrases tell you when other events took place?* (Since the time; first; between 400 and 1500 CE; at least 500 years old; Today)

DESCRIBING RELATIONSHIPS BETWEEN IDEAS

Guided Instruction

**WORDS TO KNOW**

**archaeologist**
**monument**
**society**
**ton**

Look for **language** that helps you **recognize the sequence of historical events.**

**CITE EVIDENCE**

**A** Authors use dates and other **time-related words** to let the reader know the **order of events**. Circle the date in paragraph 2 when explorers landed on Easter Island. In the same paragraph, underline text describing an event that happened after this date.

**B** In paragraphs 3 and 4, draw a box around other words that indicate the time of events. Why are these words so important to the reader?

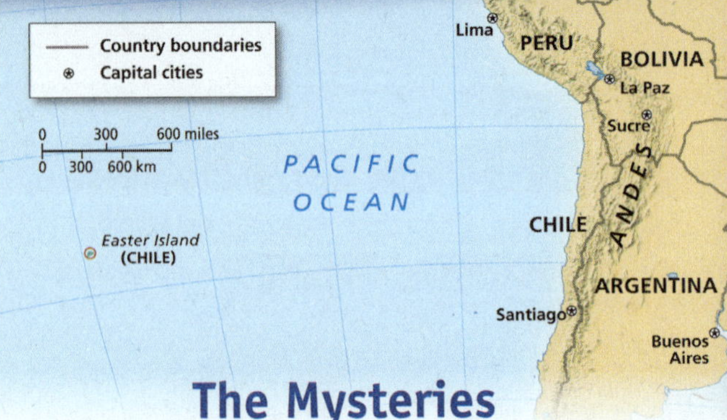


## The Mysteries of Easter Island

(Genre: Science Magazine Article)

1 Easter Island lies in the southern Pacific Ocean. It is a territory of Chile. The island is located more than 2,000 miles west of the mainland of South America.

2 The island got its name from Dutch explorers after they landed there on Easter Sunday in April 1722. The land is called "Rapa Nui." Rapa Nui is also the language of those who live on the island. In 1888, Chile claimed possession of Easter Island. It is the easternmost island of the group known as Polynesia.

3 Since the time the Dutch first landed on Easter Island, it's been known for its giant stone statues. There are about 1,000 of these sculptures. They stand at an average height of 13 feet and weigh about 14 **tons**. Many people who have studied the statues agree that they were built sometime between 400 and 1500 CE. That means they are at least 500 years old. **Archaeologists** have several different ideas about the reasons the statues were built and the role they played in **society**.



50 Chapter 2 ■ Key Ideas and Details: Informational Texts

### Words to Know

**General Academic Vocabulary**

**monument** (*noun*): something made in memory of a person or event
**society** (*noun*): a group of people who share values, traditions, and laws
**ton** (*noun*): a measure of weight equal to 2,000 pounds

**Domain-Specific Vocabulary**

**archaeologist** (*noun*): someone who studies past human life by analyzing objects such as pottery, tools, and statues left by ancient peoples

**Working with Word Meaning** Have students write a sentence for each word, leaving a blank where the word should be. Then have them trade sentences with a partner and complete their partner's sentences.

# KEY IDEAS AND DETAILS

4 Some think they were built to be **monuments** to honor ancestors of the people on the island. Others believe they represent fertility due to the rich soil in the region where the statues were built. Today the mysteries of Easter Island remain. Were the statues built to honor leaders, or to please the ancestors? Were they connected to warfare or to the island's economy? How were they moved from one location to another?

5 In the Rapa Nui language, these stone figures are called "moai." Most of them sit on a base, which is called an "ahu." Ahus are often thought to be the base of a grave, where the body of the person featured in stone was buried.*

**Comprehension Check**

Look at the map at the top of page 50. Why might the island's existence have been unknown to Europeans until 1722?

## Guided Instruction

**CITE EVIDENCE**

**C** Authors often include text that helps the reader to make a connection to the past. In paragraph 4, underline text that tells why the statues may have been built.

**D** Language showing the relationship between ideas can help the reader understand a sequence of events. Place a star next to the text that gives a clue about what happened after someone died on Easter Island. What is a possible reason moai were built for people who passed away?

## Support English Language Learners

Students who are learning English may not recognize some of the proper nouns and will likely have trouble keeping track of what they signify.

Say and define these proper nouns for students, pointing to the words as they appear in the text, and asking students to repeat them after you: *Easter Island*, *Pacific Ocean*, *Chile*, *South America*, *Dutch*, *Rapa Nui*, and *Polynesia*. Then guide students as they draw a simple map of South America, marking Chile, Easter Island, and the Pacific Ocean. Tell students to refer to their maps as needed, to help them clarify information as they read.

## Guided Instruction

### CITE EVIDENCE

**C** *I know that an ancestor is someone who lived before someone else in the same family.*

*How are the statues connected to the island's ancestors?* (They may have been built to honor the ancestors of people on the island.)

**D** *I know that when someone dies, there is usually a marker or grave stone to tell a little about them (such as name, birth date, and the date they passed).*

*What is a possible reason moai were built for people who passed away?* (to represent the person who passed, to pay respect)

**Comprehension Check**

**Sample Answer:** Before there were airplanes, it was difficult to get to faraway places. It would take a long time to explore by boat, and the islands are located far away from other places. Until recently, there was no technology to communicate with each other about the island and its people and location.

**Answer Explanation:** Students should use time-related words to discuss the differences between exploration then and now.

### Listening and Viewing Skills

Reread paragraph 4 as students listen and look at the photograph on page 51. *How does the photograph help you understand why the moai are mysterious?* (There is no information to go with the statues.)

### Review: Determining Main Idea and Key Details

Remind students that the title of a text can hint at the main idea of the text. Have students think about the title and ask them to look for details that relate to the title.

## Guided Practice

### Recap Reading Selection

Let students know that they will continue reading about the moai of Easter Island. Review some of the theories about why the moai were built and the fact that it remains a mystery.

### Read and Practice

Have partners take turns reading the selection as you circulate to provide support. Model practicing describing relationships between ideas with Cite Evidence callout A. For callout B, circulate and provide partners with scaffolding as needed. You might use the following suggestions to help students who are having difficulty.

#### CITE EVIDENCE

**A** Remind students that a cause is why something happens. Explain that the cause is usually stated right before or right after the statement that describes the effect. This should help students identify that the cause is "Many of the megaliths have not been uncovered completely" so "much of the actual statue remains underground."

**B** Explain to students why the carvers needed material that was easy to carve and used the toki. Help them see that because Easter Island was so far from other countries, they did not have the most current tools to use. The location of the island also affected how they paid for the moai. Students should infer that the people on the island used what they had to trade because they did not have currency at that time.



## Guided Practice

#### WORDS TO KNOW

**interior**
**megalith**
**notable**
**quarry**

#### CITE EVIDENCE

**A** Underline the cause that led to some statues being called "heads."

**B** Circle the words in paragraph 9 that tell you why the carvers made their monuments with tuff. Why is this detail important?

**The Mysteries of Easter Island** *continued*

6 Due to their enormous size, the statues are sometimes called **megaliths**. This word means "big stones." Many of the megaliths have not been uncovered completely. Thus, some of the statues are mistakenly called "heads." In these cases, much of the actual statue remains underground.

7 The moai vary widely in height. Most of them are taller than humans. The average height is 13 feet, but some moai reach more than 40 feet. The heaviest of them is estimated to weigh 86 tons. Among their many **notable** features is that almost all face the **interior** of the island, with their backs to the ocean. Their facial features make clear that they are all carved to represent individual people. No two moai are exactly alike.

8 Some researchers believe that the moai were first created soon after people arrived on the island, around 1200 CE. Moai construction seems to have reached a peak in the period 1400–1650 CE. No moai seem to have been built after European contact with the island in the eighteenth century.

9 Researchers have found that there was a central **quarry** at which most of the moai were made. This was the volcanic crater of Rano

### Words to Know

**General Academic Vocabulary**

**interior** (*noun*): an inner part; inside
**notable** (*adjective*): special or remarkable

**Domain-Specific Vocabulary**

**megalith** (*noun*): a very large stone used in ancient cultures as a monument or part of a building
**quarry** (*noun*): an open pit used for digging up stone, slate, or limestone

**Working with Word Meaning** Ask students to create a word web for each vocabulary word, noting an example, a synonym, an antonym, or other association for each word.

## Guided Practice

### KEY IDEAS AND DETAILS

Guided Practice

Raraku. It had large quantities of tuff, or compressed volcanic ash. This material was easy to carve, which was important, since the people carved the material with stone tools. Most of their tools were simple chisels, called "toki." One group of carvers made the markings on the statues. People would pay for a moai in trade.

**Comprehension Check**

1. During what period were the megaliths most likely built on Easter Island?
   - **a.** 400–1500 CE
   - **b.** 600–1600 CE
   - **c.** 1300–1700 CE
   - **d.** 1700–1900 CE

2. Before building the moai, the people had to get material from
   - **a.** the Europeans
   - **b.** the volcanic crater, Rano Raraku
   - **c.** sand from the Pacific Ocean
   - **d.** other people, through trade

3. Many things about Easter Island and the moai continue to be mysteries, while others are now known. Name two results of the research on the building of the moai. Cite evidence.

Sample answer: People now know more about the moai because of research. Paragraph 9 says that the moai were built from volcanic ash taken from the volcanic crater, Rano Raraku. It also says that the people used the toki, a stone chisel, to carve the moai.





**Comprehension Check**

**Answer Explanations:**

**1.** The text says the moai were most likely built shortly after people arrived on the island in 1200 CE and peaked between 1400 and 1650 CE. Choice C covers that time frame.

**2.** Choice B is correct because the moai were built using materials from the volcanic crater since it was easy to carve.

**3.** Students should write about what they just read: that researchers now know that the moai were built from volcanic ash and the people used a stone chisel to form the moai.

### Team Jigsaw

Put students in groups of three. Assign paragraphs 1–3 to one student in each group, paragraphs 4–6 to another student in each group, and paragraphs 7–9 to the third student in each group. Ask students to independently reread their assigned sections and draw their own moai. Encourage students to be creative with their statues. Then have students put their illustrations together and discuss the details they used to make their moai.

### Discussion Skills: Building on Ideas

Explain to students that in a class discussion it is important to be respectful. Give examples of ways to be respectful, such as not interrupting others, making positive comments, and giving credit to other people when you get an idea from something they say. At the same time, they should feel confident to add to another student's ideas.

Provide students with these sentence starters:

*I think you make a good point, but I'd like to add that ...*

*I agree, but I also think that ...*

*I see where you are coming from, but I think ...*

## Independent Practice

### Recap Reading Selection

Prompt students to share what they have learned from reading the article. Students should mention that, to this day, many things about the moai are still a mystery, including how they were made, why they were made, and how they were transported.

### Read and Apply

Have students read the selection independently as you circulate to provide support. If you notice students struggling, you can provide support with the suggestions below.

#### CITE EVIDENCE

**A** Tell students that why is the reason for something happening. The effect is the result of that thing happening. Help students identify that the effect of using wooden rollers to move the moai from the quarry was "the decline in the numbers of thick, straight trees on the island."

**B** Remind students that time-related words let readers know the order of events. Help them to understand that *after* shows that something came before and then something happened later as a result. Students should see that one theory is the locals believed that the moai were symbols of growth and agriculture; thus, because crops need water to grow, they believed that building the moai, which safeguard crops, close to fresh water would ensure that "annual harvests would be plentiful."

DESCRIBING RELATIONSHIPS BETWEEN IDEAS

Independent Practice

#### WORDS TO KNOW

**livelihood**
**massive**
**safeguard**

#### CITE EVIDENCE

**A** In paragraph 11, underline the sentence that tells the effects of using wooden rollers to move the moai from the quarry.

**B** Circle information in paragraph 13 that tells what some people believed would happen to their crops after building the moai. Why was it important to have the moai located close to fresh water?

**The Mysteries of Easter Island** *continued*

10 On top of some statues is a red hatlike shape called a "pukao." It was made to represent a topknot of hair worn by high-ranking men. Leaders never cut their hair because they believed that it had "mana," or special power. A small number of moai are decorated on their backs with petroglyphs, or rock art. This art seems to relate to aspects of Easter Island agriculture, such as soil fertility and crop choice.

11 Researchers have developed two major theories about how the people managed to transport these **massive** statues across different parts of the island. Some say that the statues were moved upright from the quarry on wooden rollers. The use of these rollers caused the decline in the numbers of thick, straight trees on the island.

12 Others believe that the statues were moved upright by rocking them back and forth. This method would require more time and extra labor. But it would fit the stories told by the islanders that the statues "walked" to their destination.

13 The purpose of these towering idols and how they came to be still fascinate researchers today. Perhaps some were built for the spirits of those who passed away to watch over the people and bring good fortune through the moai. Moai were created to honor famous leaders and keep their memories alive. Some think the moai were meant to **safeguard** crops. Planting and harvesting were the islanders' **livelihood**. The moai could have been symbols of growth and agriculture, ensuring that the annual harvests would be plentiful.



54 Chapter 2 ■ Key Ideas and Details: Informational Texts

### Words to Know

**General Academic Vocabulary**

**livelihood** (*noun*): the ways one supports oneself to live
**massive** (*adjective*): very large and heavy
**safeguard** (*verb*): to protect

**Working with Word Meaning** Challenge students to draw a picture of a monument they are familiar with and discuss it with a partner, using one or more of the words.

KEY IDEAS AND DETAILS

Independent Practice

14 The fact that many sites of the moai are near sources of fresh water seems to be evidence for the second theory. This discovery supports the idea that the moai were linked to agriculture and, thus, to survival.

**Comprehension Check** MORE ONLINE **sadlierconnect.com**

1. One idea suggests that the cause of the stories of statues "walking" to their destinations is
   - a. the rollers used to transport the statues
   - (b.) the rocking method people used to move the statues
   - c. the stories told by the petroglyphs on the statues
   - d. the lack of other methods to move the statues

2. According to the text, leaders had a topknot of hair, which resulted in
   - a. a special skill
   - b. good fortune
   - c. the use red hats to show rank among the people
   - (d.) statues with pukaos to represent men of high rank

3. What might have caused the people to build moai near sources of fresh water? Use text from the article in your answer.

Sample answer: Fresh water is necessary for growing foods. The article says the people may have looked to the moai to "safeguard crops" and ensure "that the annual harvests would be plentiful."





## Speaking and Listening Presentation

Have students create a presentation on one of the texts in this chapter. If you have students from diverse geographic or cultural backgrounds, have students interview each other about whether any of the stories in the chapter are from countries they are familiar with. After gathering information, students should take turns presenting to the class. Presenters should:

- state their topic; choose words for effect.
- present appropriate facts elaborated with relevant descriptive details.
- use formal language suitable for an academic presentation.
- speak clearly, in complete sentences, and at a reasonable rate.

## Independent Practice

**Comprehension Check**

**Answer Explanations:**

1. Choice B, *the rocking method people used to move the statues,* is the only option supported by details in the text.
2. According to the text, high-ranking men wore the topknot represented by the *pukao*. Therefore, choice D is correct.
3. Students' responses may vary but should explain that fresh water is necessary to grow food and some people believed that the moai would cause crops to be plentiful.

## Critical Comprehension

Use the following questions to help students think more deeply about the text. Students should be prepared to support their answers with evidence from the text.

- *Do you think the moai would have looked different if the carvers had tools other than the simple chisel?* (Yes, they would have been able to use materials other than volcanic ash.)
- *Was the Easter Island civilization advanced? How do you know?* (No. They had simple tools and used chickens, sweet potatoes, bananas, and mats to trade.)

**Assess and Respond**

**If** students have trouble answering the questions in the Comprehension Check...

**Then** review how to eliminate incorrect answers by checking them against the text.

## Connect Across Texts: *4 points* Review Reading Selections

Assign pairs of students one of the texts to summarize. Encourage students to build on each other's ideas. Repeat for the remaining two texts.

## Compare and Contrast Texts

Review the directions on page 56 with students. Instruct students to write the two events they have chosen in the outer parts of each circle.

**Venn Diagram Rubric**

| | |
|---|---|
| 4 | Student has identified two events and recorded four or more key details and pieces of evidence in their proper places. |
| 3 | Student has identified two events and recorded at least three key details and pieces of evidence in their proper places. |
| 2 | Student has identified two events and recorded at least three key details and pieces of evidence but may have had trouble categorizing them properly. |
| 1 | Student has identified two events and recorded at least one key detail or piece of evidence. |
| 0 | Student did not complete assignment or demonstrated no understanding of selections. |

## CONNECT ACROSS TEXTS

### Compare and Contrast Texts

In this chapter, you read about the discoveries of rock art paintings in the rainforest, King Tut's tomb, and Easter Island. Choose two of these events and compare and contrast them using the Venn diagram below. List key details and other evidence from the texts to show similarities and differences. Be prepared to discuss your ideas with the class.

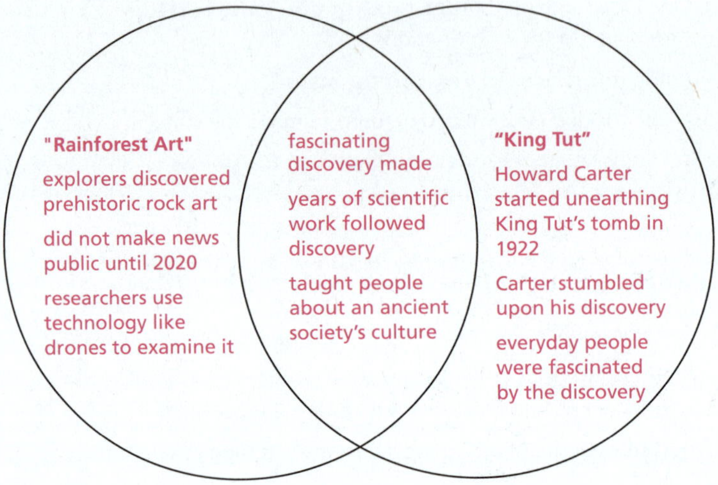

## Extend Thinking: Hypothesize

Assign one of the chapter texts to each student. Tell students to reread their text, making notes about how the discovery described in it was made. Then tell them to suppose that the person or people who made the discovery had never made the discovery. Ask them to form a hypothesis about whether someone else would have made the discovery later, or if the discovery would have likely remained unknown. Have students write one paragraph explaining their hypothesis, supporting it with evidence from the text. Then have students present their hypotheses to the class.

## CONNECT ACROSS TEXTS

### Connect to the Essential Question

***How do authors convey a main idea and use details to support it?*** In small groups or as a class, discuss the Essential Question. Think about what you have learned about asking and answering questions, determining main idea, and recognizing relationships in a text. Use evidence from the chapter texts to answer the question.

Authors convey a main idea by using evidence and describing relationships between ideas. In "Rainforest Art," the author gives facts to tell what explorers found and what the art teaches us about the people who made it. In "King Tut," the author explains how Carter made his discovery and what it meant to researchers and to regular people. In "The Mysteries of Easter Island," the author presents ideas to explain different theories about the origins of the moai.

### Connect to the Theme

***Echoes of the Past*** In this chapter, you read texts about discoveries that uncovered people from the past. Why is it important to learn about the past? Support your answers with details from the text.

Learning about the past can help us understand different cultures that came before us, as well as our world today. The rainforest art is "over 10,000 years old." It helps us understand what was important to the people who made it. The discovery of King Tut's tomb showed what Egyptian culture was like at the time. The article on the Easter Island statues presents different theories on how and why people built them.



**To strengthen your response, reread parts of the texts that support your answers. Add to your answers any additional details you find.**



### Assess and Respond (pages 56–57)

| If | Then |
|---|---|
| Students scored 0–4 points, they are **Developing** their understanding of the skills. | Provide students with reading support and more intensive modeling of skills. |
| Students scored 5–7 points, they are **Improving** their understanding of the skills. | Use students' scores to target areas that are weak and review those specific skills. |
| Students scored 8–10 points, they are **Proficient** in their understanding of the skills. | Have these students move on. They are ready for more formal assessment. |

### Support Essential Question Discussion

Have students reread the Essential Question. Challenge them to finish this sentence. *Authors convey a main idea and use details to support it by...*

If students have difficulty responding, remind them of the skills they learned in the chapter.

### Theme Wrap-Up

Lead students in a group discussion on the theme *Echoes of the Past*. Talk about the ways in which researchers study our collective past and how the past affects the present.

### Short-Answer Questions: *2 points each*

**Connect to the Essential Question Rubric**

| | |
|---|---|
| 2 | Students are able to show ways authors convey a main idea and use details to support it. |
| 1 | Students are able to identify some ways that authors convey a main idea and use details to support it. |
| 0 | Students are not able to explain any ways that authors convey a main idea or use supporting details. |

**Connect to the Theme Rubric**

| | |
|---|---|
| 2 | Students are able to identify why researchers study our collective past and explain how the past affects us in the present. |
| 1 | Students identify some reasons why researchers study our collective past and explain how the past affects us in the present. |
| 0 | Students cannot identify any reasons why researchers study our collective past or explain how the past affects us in the present. |

**OBJECTIVE**
**Understand how words in texts connect to real life.**

## Guided Instruction

Review the Guided Instruction section on page 58 with students. Be sure they understand that "real life" means their own world or life, not a world or life that they have read about. Discuss how paying attention to words used in texts can help them develop a more accurate vocabulary for describing their own experiences.

## Guided Practice

If students are having difficulty, have them make a list of six or seven experiences they have recently had. Have them review their lists to see if they can use either of the words in the table to describe any of the experiences. You might also have them do this exercise with a partner.

## Independent Practice

If students are having trouble writing sentences, then discuss events and experiences in their own lives that relate to the two words until students have made a real-life connection to each word.

## Apply to Reading

Have students return to "Rainforest Art" (pages 38–43) and circle three challenging words to which they can make a real-life connection. Then have them write a sentence for each word, describing a real-life experience. They may make a real-life connection to *discovery* (paragraph 2), *variety* (paragraph 4), and *humor* (paragraph 8).

# LANGUAGE

### Real-Life Word Connections

**Guided Instruction** Identify **real-life word connections** with your own life. Describing your own experiences can help you practice new words, phrases, and meanings.

The team that explored King Tut's tomb found "something thrilling." In the example below, a student has used the same phrase to describe a personal experience.

*I had to wait until after dinner to open my presents on my last birthday. Sitting at the table, I hoped something thrilling would be in one of the boxes.*

| | |
|---|---|
| original | (*adj.*) independent and creative in thought or action |
| assume | (*v.*) to suppose something true without knowing the facts |

Look at the chart to find definitions of two words from "King Tut." Use the definitions to complete the exercise below.

**Guided Practice** Use each word in the table to describe two real-life experiences.

1. Sample answer: My dancing at the party was original.
2. Sample answer: My grandmother dresses differently. She is original.
3. Sample answer: I assumed it would be sunny yesterday and got wet.
4. Sample answer: My friends assume they know the real me.

**Independent Practice** Make real-life connections using these words from "King Tut" below. If necessary, use a dictionary to determine word meanings.

culture
Sample answer: My friend Spiro grew up in another culture.

dominate
Sample answer: I wish I could dominate a soccer game the way my brother does.





## Support English Language Learners

In order for English language learners to make real-life connections to vocabulary, they must have a clear and deep understanding of the words. Review the definition of *original* and *assume*. Then provide sets of example sentences for each word, with the first sentence in each set reflecting a real-life connection, and the second sentence not reflecting a connection. **Real-life connection:** *I assume I will get better if I take this medication.* **No real-life connection:** *The doctor assumed her patient was taking her medication.* Point to the use of *I* in the first sentence and explain how the sentence describes your own experience. Discuss how the second one does not.

# CHAPTER 2 REVIEW

Read the following passage. Pay attention to the important details and the relationship between ideas to help you understand the text. Then answer the questions on pages 59 and 60.

## Vikings in North America

(Genre: Textbook Article)

1 Columbus was not the first person to discover the Americas. The first inhabitants of North America migrated from Asia over 16,000 years ago. There is also evidence that Vikings reached the mainland about 500 years before Columbus's journey.

2 Stories of Vikings finding North America were centuries old. Without evidence, these claims remained just legends. In 1960, however, a Norwegian explorer discovered the remains of a Viking village in northeastern Canada. The site was excavated. Items found at the site show that Vikings lived there. Items included a stone used to sharpen metal objects, an oil lamp, and a bronze pin. These items were specific to Viking culture. The discovery proved there was truth in the old Viking legends.

**Fill in the circle of the correct answer choice.**

1. Vikings came to North America
   - ○ before anyone else
   - ● 500 years before Columbus
   - ○ only in legends
   - ○ at the same time as Columbus

2. The last sentence in the article suggests that legends
   - ○ can never be trusted
   - ● sometimes contains truths
   - ○ do not inform about history
   - ○ are for entertainment only

3. In paragraph 2, *show* means
   - ○ a TV program or play
   - ○ to put on display
   - ● to provide evidence
   - ○ to teach or instruct





### Self-Assessment: Progress Check

Have students revisit the Progress Check on page 35 and respond to the questions again. Ask them to compare their Before and After responses.

You may wish to have students rate their answers on a scale of 0–2 rather than simply checking (or not checking) the box. Instruct them to write a 0 if they feel they do not understand the given skill at all, a 1 if they feel they have some understanding, and a 2 if they feel they have a solid grasp of the skill.

## Chapter Summary

At this point, students have had instruction and practice in reading informational texts, with a focus on learning about important discoveries related to human history. Students have also learned to ask and answer questions to deepen their understanding of the text, to determine the main idea and key details of a text, and to describe relationships between ideas. Students have practiced working with concepts across texts and practiced making real-life connections to unfamiliar words. They should be well prepared for the review section.

## Introduce the Review

Explain to students that they will read a new passage that is related to the chapter's theme and the selections they have already read. Instruct students to read the passage carefully and then answer the questions on pages 59 and 60.

### Answer Explanations

Scoring: Items 1–9 on pages 59–60 are worth 1 point each. See the rubric for guidance on scoring the Write About It question on page 60.

**1.** The text explicitly states that "the Vikings reached the mainland about 500 years before Columbus's journey," so the second choice, "500 years before Columbus" is correct.

**2.** The text states that the "discovery proved there was truth" to the legends, so "sometimes contains truth" is correct.

**3.** The text states that "studies of these items show that Vikings lived at the site." So *show* means "to provide evidence," the third choice. The sentence makes sense if you say it with "provided evidence" instead of *show*.

## Answer Explanations

**4.** Only "metalwork" is mentioned, so the first choice is correct.

**5.** The text says the first inhabitants of North America migrated from Asia, so "a trip to a different country" is the correct answer.

**6.** It is believed that the Vikings reached the Americas 500 years before Columbus, so the third choice is correct.

**7.** Workshops that were found helped prove that Vikings were in mainland North America long ago since the items were unknown to Native Americans at that time.

**8.** The text states that the village was excavated after a Norwegian explorer discovered the remains of a Viking village, so the first choice is correct.

**9.** The first inhabitants of the Americas were immigrants from Asia, so the first choice is correct.

## Write About It Rubric

| Score | Description |
|---|---|
| 2 | Student notes the article says that Vikings used boats and that it does not provide evidence of sailing ships. |
| 1 | Student notes the article says that Vikings used boats or that it does not provide evidence of sailing ships. |
| 0 | Student does not note the article says that Vikings used boats or that it does not provide evidence of sailing ships. |

## CHAPTER 2 REVIEW

**4.** Which technology did the Vikings use 1,000 years ago?

- ● metalwork
- ○ electricity
- ○ steam engines
- ○ mass production

**5.** Review *journey* in paragraph 1. The best example of a journey is

- ● a trip to a different country
- ○ a visit to the doctor's office
- ○ a walk around the block
- ○ an afternoon at the playground

**6.** The main idea of "Vikings in North America" is that

- ○ Columbus did not discover the Americas
- ● Vikings reached the Americas 500 years before Columbus
- ○ Vikings didn't find the Americas
- ○ Vikings used metal tools

**7.** The items in the village help prove that Vikings were in North America

- ○ because they were not found anywhere else in the world
- ● because they were known to be specific to Viking culture
- ○ because they were old
- ○ because they were Norwegian

**8.** Directly after the explorer discovered the remains of a Viking village

- ● the village was excavated
- ○ people believed the legends
- ○ Viking items were discovered
- ○ Vikings arrived in North America

**9.** Based on the article, who were the first inhabitants of the Americas?

- ● immigrants from Asia
- ○ Columbus
- ○ the Vikings
- ○ immigrants from Norway

**Write About It** What evidence does the article provide indicating that the Vikings had sailing ships?

The article does not provide much evidence. The article says only that they used boats.



60 Chapter 2 ■ Key Ideas and Details: Informational Texts

## Analyze Student Scores

| Score | Description |
|---|---|
| 9–11 pts Strong | Student has a good grasp of the skills and concepts taught in this chapter. Point out any mistakes the student has made and explain the correct answers if necessary. |
| 4–8 pts Progressing | Student is struggling with some skills or concepts. Identify the specific skills that are problematic to target a review of instruction. |
| 0–3 pts Emerging | Student is having serious problems understanding the skills and concepts taught in this chapter. Student may need to redo the work with a higher level of support. |

Craft and Structure
# Literary Texts

CHAPTER 3

**Focus on Reading** Authors of literary texts choose language and structure that will best tell their tales. Plays, stories and poems are all different ways to tell a tale. Sometimes an old story can be made new by telling it in a new way or from a new point of view.

**Think About Theme** What does it mean to be a best friend? How could you prove your friendship? In this chapter, you will read about the different ways people show that they are friends.

**Let's Get on Our Way!** In this chapter, you will learn how language, point of view, and text structure are all parts of an author's craft.

These are the skills you will build in this chapter. Before you begin, check the boxes on the left of any items you can do well now. At the end of the chapter, you will return to this page to use the check boxes on the right to show what you have learned.

After Chapter 3

- ☐ Understand literal and nonliteral language. ☐
- ☐ Recognize the different parts of a drama. ☐
- ☐ Distinguish my point of view from those of the narrator and characters. ☐





**Student Page 61**

## Progress Check

The Progress Check is a self-assessment feature that students can use to gauge their own progress. Research shows that when students take accountability for their own learning, their motivation increases.

Before students begin work on Chapter 3, have them check the boxes next to any item that they feel they can do well. Explain that it is fine if they don't check any of the boxes. They will have an opportunity to learn about and practice all of these items while studying the chapter. Let them know that near the end of the chapter they will have a chance to reconsider how well they can do each item on this list.

Before students begin the Chapter 3 Review on page 85, have them revisit this page. You can use this information to work with students on any items they don't understand before they tackle the Review.

## HOME ✦ CONNECT...

The Home Connect feature is a way to keep parents or other adult family members apprised of what their children are learning. The key learning objectives are listed, and some ideas for related activities and discussions are included.

Explain to students that they can share the Home Connect page with their parents or other adult family members in their homes. Let students know how much time the class will be spending on this chapter so they can plan their time accordingly at home.

Encourage students and their parents to share their experiences using the suggestions on the Home Connect page. You may wish to make a place to post some of this work.

### HOME ✦ CONNECT...

Creative writers use **nonliteral** phrases to create images in a reader's mind. The **literal**, or actual, meaning of the words might be different from what the author is really trying to say. Help your child see the difference. In a children's story or poem, highlight a phrase that is not meant literally. Talk with your child about what it means. Have your child find other examples.

Good readers can talk about the parts of stories, poems, and plays. To help your child understand the **parts of a drama**, find a children's play online or in the library. Read it together, and talk about what happens in each scene. Discuss how scenes in a play are like chapters in a book.

In stories, a narrator or character often feels strongly about something. Readers learn to understand those **points of view** and distinguish them from their own. Read together a children's story or play with a strong point of view. Ask your child about the narrator or character's feelings. Discuss whether you both share these feelings.

**Conversation Starter:** With your child, talk about a favorite story. Ask your child:

- *Can you name examples of figurative language or idioms in the story? What are they?*
- *If you turned the story into a play, how many scenes would there be? What would happen in each scene?*
- *How would you describe the main character's point of view? Do you agree with that point of view?*

**IN THIS CHAPTER, YOUR CHILD WILL...**

- Figure out the meanings of unfamiliar words in texts.
- Distinguish literal language from figurative words and phrases, such as idioms.
- Understand parts of a drama, including scenes, setting, character list, and stage directions.
- Understand the point of view of a narrator or character in a story and distinguish it from his or her own point of view.
- Compare and contrast three texts with the same theme: realistic fiction, drama, and a narrative poem.

**WAYS TO HELP YOUR CHILD**

Help your child understand how writers use language to spur readers' imaginations. Read stories and poems together, and point out lines and phrases that you particularly enjoy. Encourage your child to find examples of favorites, too. You might also listen for oral language that creates images on the internet, radio, or television.

ONLINE
For more Home Connect activities, continue online at sadlierconnect.com





**Student Page 62**

## LEARNING PROGRESSIONS

In this chapter, students will learn how the craft and structure of a literary text contribute to their understanding of it. In order to learn the skills in this chapter, students will further develop skills learned in second grade. They should be encouraged to retain these skills, as they will continue to build on them in fourth grade.

| Distinguishing Literal/ Nonliteral Language | • By the end of grade 2, students should have been able to describe how words and phrases add rhythm and meaning in a story, poem, or song.<br>• In grade 3, students will build on this skill by not only describing how words supply meaning, but also determining the meaning of words and phrases and distinguishing literal from nonliteral language.<br>• When students move on to grade 4, they will be asked to determine the meaning of more complex words and phrases, including those that refer to specific characters found in mythology. |
|---|---|
| Understanding Parts of a Drama | • Proficient second-grade students should have ended the school year knowing how to discuss the beginning and end of a story.<br>• As third graders, they should be able to refer to specific parts of stories, dramas, and poems, using appropriate terms such as chapter, scene, and stanza. By the end of third grade, students should master the ability to describe how parts of works build on earlier sections.<br>• These skills will prepare them for fourth grade, when they will explain the differences between poems, drama, and prose and refer to their structural elements. |
| Distinguishing Points of View | • By the end of second grade, students should have been able to acknowledge differences in the points of view of characters.<br>• As third graders, students must take this concrete knowledge of characters' points of view and distinguish it from their own points of view.<br>• This ability to distinguish points of view will become even more complex in fourth grade, when they will learn to compare and contrast the differences between first- and third-person narration. |

Craft and Structure

Literary Texts

CHAPTER 3

**Essential Question**
How do authors craft stories?

**Theme**
Best Friends







## Essential Question:
How do authors craft stories?

In this chapter, students will learn about the craft and structure of literary texts, specifically how authors use vocabulary, text structure, and point of view to tell stories in different genres.

### Theme: Best Friends

Students will read selections related to the theme of best friends. They will read about friends sharing an exciting secret, the start of a new friendship, and loyalty.

### Curriculum Connection: English/Language Arts

Students will learn about the theme of friendship in literature.

## Vocabulary Overview

### General Academic Vocabulary

artificial 71, betray 78, bouquet 71, burden 71, chirped 68, cordially 72, curious 66, desert 80, dreary 76, dropped in 64, embrace 78, experiment 65, faithful 75, fate 80, firmness 65, inspect 64, inspiring 76, perplexed 73, poring 74, precious 81, rambling 72, remark 68, solemn 68, splendid 68, squinting 74, suspicious 77

### Domain-Specific Vocabulary

ivied 66, lad 66, orphanage 71, steed 78, treason 76

## Guided Instruction

**OBJECTIVE**

**Use vocabulary strategies to determine the meaning of words and phrases, distinguishing literal from nonliteral language.**

### Genre: Realistic Fiction

Explain to students that realistic fiction tells a story that comes from an author's imagination. The characters might seem believable and true to life, but they do not really exist.

### Set the Purpose

Help students understand the purpose for learning the reading skill by asking *Do you think words can have different meanings? What do you do to figure out the meaning?*

### Model and Teach

Read the selection as students follow along in their books.

### CITE EVIDENCE

**A** *I'm looking for a phrase in paragraph 1 that means something different from the literal meaning. The literal meaning of* saucers *is "dishes." I don't think the character's eyes really look like saucers. They're just large and round because he is thinking.*

*How does the phrase* eyes as big as saucers *help you picture how Colin looks?* (His eyes are large, round, and wide open.)

## DISTINGUISHING LITERAL/NONLITERAL LANGUAGE

### Guided Instruction

**WORDS TO KNOW**

**dropped in**
**experiment**
**firmness**
**inspect**

**Nonliteral language** gives different meanings to **words and phrases** from those of **literal language**.

**CITE EVIDENCE**

**A** Writers may use **literal words** that say exactly what they mean. Or they may use **nonliteral, figurative words** that mean something other than what the words say. Circle the nonliteral phrase in paragraph 1. What is the literal meaning of the phrase? What does the phrase mean here?

# The Secret Garden

(Genre: Fiction)

*This adapted excerpt is from a book by Frances Hodgson Burnett, published in 1911. Colin is a young boy who has long been ill. Mary is his cousin, who has recently arrived to live with her uncle's family. Dickon is a neighbor boy whose family works for Colin's father.*

1 "What big eyes you've got, Colin," said Mary. "When you are thinking they get as big as saucers. What are you thinking about now?"

2 "I am thinking about what it will look like," he answered.

3 "The garden?" asked Mary.

4 "The springtime," he said. "I've really never seen it before. I scarcely ever went out and when I did go I never looked at it."

5 Later the nurse made Colin ready. She noticed he sat up and made efforts to get ready, and he talked and laughed with Mary all the time.

6 "This is one of his good days, sir," she said to Dr. Craven, who **dropped in** to **inspect** him. "He's in such good spirits that it makes him stronger."





### Words to Know

**General Academic Vocabulary**

**dropped in** (*verb*): stopped in; visited
**experiment** (*noun*): a test done to find something out
**firmness** (*noun*): the quality of showing certainty
**inspect** (*verb*): to take a close look at

**Working with Word Meaning** Encourage students to rephrase the definitions, putting them in their own words.

64 Chapter 3 ■ Craft and Structure: Literary Texts

# CRAFT AND STRUCTURE

## Guided Instruction

7 "I'll call later in the afternoon," said Dr. Craven. "I must see how this **experiment** going out agrees with him. I wish that he would let you go with him."

8 "I'd rather give up the case this moment, sir, than even stay here while it's suggested," answered the nurse with sudden **firmness**.

9 "We'll try the experiment. Dickon's a lad I'd trust with a new-born child," said the doctor.

10 The largest footman gathered his strength and carried Colin to his wheeled chair outside.

11 Dickon pushed the wheeled chair slowly. Mistress Mary walked beside it. Colin leaned back and lifted his face to the sky. The small snowy clouds seemed like white birds floating below its crystal blueness. The wind swept in soft big breaths and was strange with a wild clear scented sweetness.

12 "What is that scent the puffs of wind bring?"

13 "It's gorse on the moor that's blooming," answered Dickon. "Eh! The bees are at it wonderful today."

**Comprehension Check**

Reread paragraph 11. Find the phrase "soft big breaths." What does the narrator mean?

### CITE EVIDENCE

**B** Idioms are figurative language phrases that are usually used in informal writing and speech. Circle the idiom in paragraph 10. What does this idiom mean?

**C** Find and box the figurative language used to describe the clouds in paragraph 11. What do the clouds look like?

**D** Context clues can help you figure out literal meanings of unfamiliar words. Look for hints in surrounding words to help you understand a word. Circle the word *gorse* in paragraph 13. Then underline the nearby word that helps you figure out its meaning.

## Support English Language Learners

Students who are learning English will have a more difficult time with nonliteral language than native speakers. Idioms and other figurative language vary among languages, so generally there is no way to adequately translate these phrases.

As students read the passage, have them make a list of nonliteral phrases. Give students practice with the phrases by asking them to use each one as they add it to their lists. For example, ask them to use the phrase *gathered his (or her) strength* in a sentence.

## Guided Instruction

### CITE EVIDENCE

**B** *The text says that the largest footman "gathered his strength" and then carried Colin downstairs in his wheelchair. Strength isn't really something you can gather, like you could gather books or boxes.*

*What does this idiom mean about what the footman did?* (He got ready to perform an action that would take physical strength.)

**C** *Similes are figurative language phrases that begin with* like *or* as. *I see the phrase* like white birds, *meaning that the clouds stood out and moved gracefully in the sky.*

*How does the phrase make you feel about the sky?* (It is beautiful and uplifting.)

**D** *I want to look around the word* gorse *for clues about what it means.*

*Which word tells you what the gorse is doing?* (blooming) *What does this tell you the gorse is?* (a kind of flower or plant)

**Comprehension Check**

**Sample Answer:** The narrator uses the phrase *soft big breaths* to say that the wind is warm and gentle.

**Answer Explanation:** Students should realize that the phrase *soft big breaths* has a nonliteral meaning. The wind does not actually breathe, like a living thing, but to the narrator, it seems as if it does.

## Listening and Viewing Skills

Read the beginning of paragraph 11 aloud to students and instruct them to look at the picture on page 65. Ask students to identify the characters in the picture and tell what they think the characters are feeling.

## Guided Practice

### Recap Reading Selection

Let students know that they will read more about Colin and Mary's outdoor adventure. Review what they read about these characters and their friendship.

### Read and Practice

Have partners take turns reading the selection as you circulate to provide support. Model practicing interpreting a nonliteral phrase with Cite Evidence callout A. For callout B, circulate and provide partners with scaffolding as needed. You might use the following suggestions to help students who are having difficulty.

### CITE EVIDENCE

**A** Help students see that *caught sight* is a nonliteral phrase. Nothing is being physically caught; rather, the phrase means "seen." Point out to students that *sight* is related to *see*.

**B** Point out that *on pins and needles* is also a nonliteral phrase. Mary is not actually standing on pins and needles; rather, she is excited and nervous about being in the garden. The writer might use this expression to make the writing more interesting and allow the reader to get a better sense of the emotions.

## DISTINGUISHING LITERAL/NONLITERAL LANGUAGE

### Guided Practice

#### WORDS TO KNOW

**curious**
**ivied**
**lad**

#### CITE EVIDENCE

**A** Reread paragraph 14. Underline the phrase *caught sight*. What does it mean?

**B** Reread paragraph 15. Circle the idiom that means "excited and nervous." Why did the author use this expression?

**The Secret Garden** *continued*

14 Not a human creature was to be caught sight of in the paths they took. In fact every gardener or gardener's **lad** had been disappeared like a puff of smoke. But they wound in and out among the shrubbery and out and round the fountain beds, following their carefully planned route for the mere mysterious pleasure of it. But when at last they turned into the Long Walk by the **ivied** walls the excited sense of an approaching thrill made them, for some **curious** reason they could not have explained, begin to be as silent as a picture.

15 "This is it," breathed Mary, on pins and needles. "This is where I used to walk up and down and wonder and wonder."

16 "Is it?" cried Colin, and his eyes began to search the ivy with eager curiousness. "But I can see nothing," he whispered. "There is no door."

17 "That's what I thought," said Mary.

18 Then there was a breathless silence and the chair wheeled on.

19 "That is the garden where Ben Weatherstaff works," said Mary.

20 "Is it?" said Colin.

21 A few yards more and Mary whispered again.

### Words to Know

**General Academic Vocabulary**
**curious** (*adjective*): odd; strange

**Domain-Specific Vocabulary**
**ivied** (*adjective*): covered with ivy, a vine with dark-green leaves
**lad** (*noun*): an old-fashioned word for *boy*

**Working with Word Meaning** Encourage students to make up an original sentence for each word.

# CRAFT AND STRUCTURE

## Guided Practice

22 "This is where the robin flew over the wall," she said, recounting an earlier conversation, in which Mary had told him of the robin.

23 "Is it?" cried Colin. "Oh! I wish he'd come again!"

### Comprehension Check

1. Circle the letter that shows a nonliteral phrase in the story.
   - a. *not a human creature*
   - b. *like a puff of smoke*
   - c. *among the shrubbery*
   - d. *carefully planned route*

2. Circle the letter that tells what the phrase *silent as a picture* means in paragraph 14.
   - a. They are not moving.
   - b. They are making very little noise.
   - c. The garden is pretty as a picture.
   - d. They are having their picture taken.

3. Work with a partner. Reread paragraph 18. Discuss the phrase *breathless silence*. What does the phrase mean here? Why does the narrator use this description?

The phrase means "very quiet." The phrase shows that the children are excited and it seems as if the world around them shares their excitement.





## Guided Practice

### Comprehension Check

**Answer Explanations:**

1. Choice B, *like a puff of smoke*, is a nonliteral phrase. The gardener's lad is not really a puff of smoke; rather, he seems to disappear into the air as one of these would.
2. Choice B, *They are making very little noise*, explains the nonliteral phrase *silent as a picture*. A picture is something that is incapable of making sounds, like the excited children at this moment.
3. Students should understand that the "breathless silence" results from the children's excitement. The children are so thrilled by the garden that they can barely speak and are almost, but not literally, holding their breath. Students should understand that if they read everything literally, they may misunderstand the meaning of a text or miss out on the emotions behind the words.

### Peer Collaboration

You might have students work in pairs so that peers can support each other in responding to callouts A and B on page 66 and Comprehension Check 1 and 2 on page 67.

Ask students to finalize their answers and then share them with a partner. Students should then make changes to their answers based on the discussion with their partners. Finally, ask pairs to report their answers to the whole group.

### Digital Connection: Online Reference Resources

Let students know that they can use an online dictionary or thesaurus to determine the difference between literal and nonliteral language. These resources can help students clarify the meaning of words and phrases.

Challenge students to write two short paragraphs. One should use only literal language. The other should use only figurative language. Students can then compare their writing to see the differences.

## Independent Practice

### Recap Reading Selection

Remind students that they have been reading about Colin, a boy in a wheelchair, and Mary, his cousin. Have them recall the major events in the story so far: Colin has been in poor health and is making a special visit to the garden. Mary, who appears to know some exciting secrets about the garden, accompanies him.

### Read and Apply

Have students read the selection independently as you circulate. If you notice students struggling, you can provide support with the suggestions that follow.

#### CITE EVIDENCE

**A** Help students see that *as if through a haze* is a figurative phrase that suggests an image of a blur. It means that Colin is trying to see the exact spot in the garden Mary is pointing out but is not sure exactly where to look.

**B** The figurative phrase *hanging green curtain* helps show why the door was not visible. When Mary takes hold of the ivy that makes up the "curtain," a normally hidden, secret door becomes visible. Apparently, this door leads to a secret garden within the larger garden outside the house.



## Independent Practice

**The Secret Garden** *continued*

#### WORDS TO KNOW

**chirped**
**remark**
**solemn**
**splendid**

#### CITE EVIDENCE

**A** Reread paragraph 25. Underline the figurative language that suggests an image in the sentence.

**B** Reread paragraph 27. Circle the figurative language that helps you understand why the key was not visible. How does it help you understand the title of the story?

24 "And that," said Mary with **solemn** delight, pointing under a big lilac bush, "is where he perched on the little heap of earth and showed me the key."

25 Then Colin sat up and looked as if through a haze.

26 "Where? Where? There?" he cried, and his eyes were as big as the wolf's in Red Riding-Hood, when Red Riding-Hood felt called upon to **remark** on them. Dickon stood still. The wheeled chair stopped.

27 "And this," said Mary, stepping on to the bed close to the ivy, "is where I went to talk to him when he **chirped** at me from the top of the wall. And this is the ivy the wind blew back," and she took hold of the hanging green curtain.

28 "Oh! is it—is it!" gasped Colin.

29 "And here is the handle, and here is the door. Dickon push him in—push him in quickly!"

30 And Dickon did it with one strong, steady, **splendid** push. They stepped into the garden like actors onto a stage.

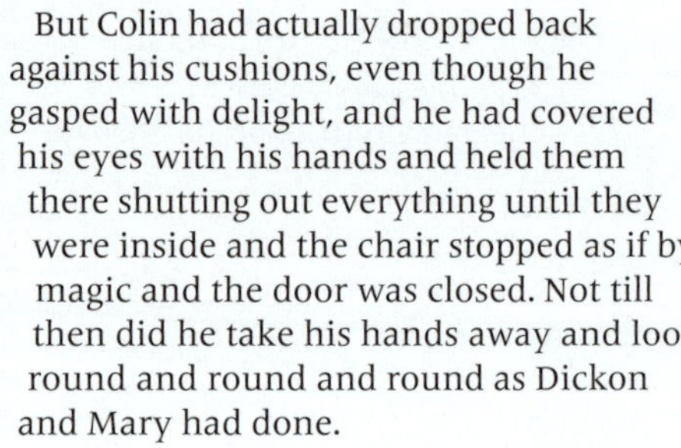

31 But Colin had actually dropped back against his cushions, even though he gasped with delight, and he had covered his eyes with his hands and held them there shutting out everything until they were inside and the chair stopped as if by magic and the door was closed. Not till then did he take his hands away and look round and round and round as Dickon and Mary had done.





### Words to Know

**General Academic Vocabulary**

**chirped** (*verb*): made a high, sharp sound
**remark** (*verb*): to make a statement or comment
**solemn** (*adjective*): serious; formal
**splendid** (*adjective*): impressive; excellent

**Working with Word Meaning** Encourage students to reread the text with the definitions in mind to increase comprehension.

## Independent Practice



Independent Practice

32 And the sun fell warm upon his face like a hand with a magical touch. And in wonder Mary and Dickon stood and stared at him. He looked so strange and different because a pink glow of color had actually crept all over him—ivory face and neck and hands and all.

33 "I shall get well! I shall get well!" he cried out. "Mary! Dickon! You can count on it! And I shall live forever and ever!"

### Comprehension Check

MORE ONLINE sadlierconnect.com

1. What is the meaning of the word *crept* in paragraph 32?

 a. smeared

 b. crawled

 c. walked

 (d.) spread

2. What is the meaning of the idiom *count on it* in paragraph 33?

 a. don't do it

 (b.) be sure of it

 c. be careful with it

 d. keep hold of it

3. Why do you think an author might use idioms and other nonliteral language?

Sample answer: Idioms and other nonliteral language make the emotions in a story seem more real. They make the tone friendlier. When I read nonliteral language it creates pictures in my mind.





### Extend Thinking: Create

Help students extend their thinking by creating artwork that represents their own vision of a secret garden. Supply them with blank sheets of paper, scissors, and glue sticks. Also supply gardening catalogs and other print materials that include colorful photos of plants and gardens and can be cut up. Ask students to review the story to find and list words and phrases to use for inspiration, such as *shrubbery, wall, door, ivy,* and *green curtain.*

To take the project a step further, also supply materials such as fabric and leaves, seeds, and twigs that have been gathered from outdoors. Students can look online to find examples of multimedia collages and then incorporate these materials to make a secret garden collage.

### Comprehension Check

**Answer Explanations:**

1. Choice D, *spread*, gives the literal meaning of the word *crept*, as it is used to tell the way that a pink glow spreads over Colin's skin.
2. Choice B, *be sure of it*, gives the literal meaning of the phrase *count on it*, as it is used by Colin.
3. Have students look back at all of the nonliteral language used throughout the passage and consider how it adds to the reader's experience. Authors use such language to make emotions seem more real and help readers visualize the story better.

## Critical Comprehension

Use the following questions to help students think more deeply about the text. Students should be prepared to support their answers with evidence from the text.

*In what ways is Mary a good friend to Colin?* (She seems to understand him as a person and is eager to share the secret garden with him.)

*Why does the garden have such a powerful effect on Colin?* (He can enjoy the outdoors only rarely; perhaps the garden has special "magic" powers.)

### Assess and Respond

**If** students have difficulty answering the questions in the Comprehension Check…

**Then** have students make a list of the nonliteral words and phrases in the selection and write the meaning of each. Have students reread the selection using the translations to aid comprehension.

## Guided Instruction

**OBJECTIVE**

**Use terms such as *scene* to describe how parts of a drama build on each other.**

### Genre: Drama

Explain to students that a drama is a form of writing that is the basis for a play. It includes notes to the actors called stage directions as well as specific lines, called dialogue, for each character to say. A drama is written for the purpose of the actors acting it out.

### Set the Purpose

To activate students' prior knowledge about the reading skill, ask *How is reading a play different from reading a story?*

### Model and Teach

Read the selection as students follow along in their books.

### CITE EVIDENCE

**A** *I know that a play has a list of characters at the beginning, so I will look at the top of the page.*

*Who are the characters?* (Marilla Cuthbert, Mrs. Rachel Lynde, Anne Shirley, Diana Barry, Mrs. Barry)

**B** *The setting is usually mentioned in the stage directions at the beginning of the scene.*

*What is the setting?* (the living room of Marilla Cuthbert's house in the 1870s) *Why is it important to know the setting?* (It shows where and when the action takes place.)

UNDERSTANDING PARTS OF A DRAMA

Guided Instruction

**WORDS TO KNOW**
**artificial**
**bouquet**
**burden**
**orphanage**

Refer to and explain the importance of the parts of a **drama**, including **setting, stage direction,** and **scene.**

**CITE EVIDENCE**

**A** A **drama** has many parts. A list of **characters** tells who is in the play. Circle the characters in this play.

**B** The **setting** tells where and when the play takes place. Underline the setting for Scene 1. Why is the setting important?

## Anne of Green Gables

(Genre: Drama)

CHARACTERS

**Marilla Cuthbert**: Anne's mother figure
**Mrs. Rachel Lynde**: Friend of Marilla
**Anne Shirley**: an 11-year-old girl Marilla adopted
**Diana Barry**: Anne's neighbor and closest friend, though they have not met in Scene 1
**Mrs. Barry**: Diana's mother

### Scene 1

*The living room of Marilla Cuthbert's house in the early 1870s. (Anne walks inside wearing a hat with a flower wreath on it and sees Marilla.)*

1 **MARILLA:** Anne, Mrs. Rachel says you went to town last Sunday with ridiculous roses and buttercups on your hat. What made you do something so silly?

**ANNE:** Well, pink and yellow aren't the best colors on me. . .

70 Chapter 3 ■ Craft and Structure: Literary Texts



### Words to Know

**General Academic Vocabulary**

**artificial** (*adjective*): made by humans; not natural
**bouquet** (*noun*): a bunch, referring to flowers
**burden** (*noun*): something that is hard to bear or put up with

**Domain-Specific Vocabulary**

**orphanage** (*noun*): a place where children who have lost their parents live together and are taken care of

**Working with Word Meaning** Help students remember the vocabulary words by asking them to give an example and nonexample of each word's meaning.

## Guided Instruction

CRAFT AND STRUCTURE

Guided Instruction

**MARILLA:** *(looks serious)* It has nothing to do with what looks good on you. Flowers on your hat, no matter the color, will never look good. You are such a foolish child!

**ANNE:** I don't know why it's more ridiculous to wear flowers on your hat than on your dress. So many little girls in town had **bouquets** pinned on their dresses. What's the difference?

5 **MARILLA:** *(looks stern)* Don't talk back to me, Anne. It was silly of you to do something like that. Please don't do something like that again. Mrs. Rachel said that people were talking about you.

**ANNE:** *(teary)* I'm so sorry. I didn't think you'd mind. I just saw the roses and buttercups and thought they would look perfect on my hat. So many of the other little girls there had **artificial** flowers on their hats. I don't think this is going to work out. I think I'm going to be too much of a **burden** for you, so you should send me back to the **orphanage**. *(Anne starts to cry. Marilla softens and cups Anne's face.)*

**CITE EVIDENCE**

**C** **Stage directions** tell what the characters in a drama are supposed to do. Underline the four stage directions on this page.

**D** Stage directions also give a clue to what the characters are feeling. In paragraph 6, circle the text that tells why Anne starts to cry. How do the stage directions help you better understand the relationship between Anne and Marilla?

**Comprehension Check**

How does the setting help you better understand what's happening in the drama?

71



### CITE EVIDENCE

**C** *I'm looking for stage directions with instructions for the characters. Stage directions are in parentheses and italics.*

*What do the stage directions tell the characters to do?* (look serious, look stern, look teary, start to cry, soften and cup Anne's face)

**D** *Just before Anne starts to cry, she says that she feels like a burden and believes that Marilla should send her back to the orphanage. The stage direction helps show that Anne has strong feelings about both these matters. Anne is afraid of not pleasing Marilla.*

*What does the first stage direction in paragraph 5 help show about Marilla?* (The fact that she looks stern shows that she is displeased with Anne.) *What does the second stage direction show about her?* (The fact that she is affected by Anne's feelings.)

### Comprehension Check

**Sample Answer:** The setting helps me understand what is happening in the drama because I can picture the time period of the action and where the characters are located.

**Answer Explanation:** Students should realize that knowing the setting helps them visualize the characters, their costumes, and the action of the play.

### Support English Language Learners

Students who are learning English may be familiar with roses, but they may not know what buttercups are. Show a picture of these flowers and invite students to tell how they think the flowers got their name. (They are yellow like butter and are shaped like cups.) Work with students to list the names of other flowers and view pictures or describe what they look like. Some possibilities include daffodils, tulips, lillies, bluebells, sunflowers, and daisies.

### Review: Distinguishing Literal/Nonliteral Language

Point out that the phrases *talk back* and *work out* on page 71 are idioms because they have nonliteral meanings. Make sure students understand that *talk back* means "to respond in a rude or challenging manner"; *work out* means "to end in an acceptable or successful way."

## Guided Practice

### Recap Reading Selection

Have students recall what they have learned so far about the characters. They might mention that Anne is the adopted daughter of Marilla and that the two have disagreed about whether it made sense for Anne to put fresh flowers on her hat when she went to town. Let students know that they will now read more about these characters as well as meet new ones.

### Read and Practice

Have partners take turns reading the selection as you circulate to provide support. Model finding scene breaks with Cite Evidence callout A. For callout B, circulate and provide partners with scaffolding as needed. You might use the following suggestions to help students who are having difficulty.

#### CITE EVIDENCE

**A** Point out the subheadings for *Scene 1 continued* and *Scene 2*. Ask students where to place the star to show the end of Scene 1. (next to the stage direction "Anne runs to get another hat") Help students understand that in additional scenes, the action can develop and the setting can change.

**B** Students should see that Anne's last line is spoken to Marilla. And is filled with mixed feelings. She is both hopeful about the possibility of becoming best friends with Diana and uncertain about how Diana's mother will feel about her.

UNDERSTANDING PARTS OF A DRAMA

Guided Practice

**WORDS TO KNOW**
**cordially**
**perplexed**
**rambling**

**CITE EVIDENCE**

**A** **Scenes** are parts of a play. Just like with chapters in a book, each new scene in a play builds on the one before. Put a star next to the end of the scene. Why might a play have more than one scene?

**B** Circle the last line of dialogue from Anne in Scene 1. What do we learn about how she's feeling?

Anne of Green Gables *continued*

### Scene 1 *continued*

**MARILLA:** *(upset at herself for making Anne cry)* Please don't cry. I'm sorry for upsetting you. I promise I don't want to send you back to the orphanage. All I want is for you to behave like other girls and not look so silly. I have some good news that will cheer you up! Diana Barry came home this afternoon. I'm going to her house to see if I can borrow a skirt pattern from Mrs. Barry. You can come with me and get to know Diana.

**ANNE:** *(trembling, her face pale and tense)* Oh, Marilla! What if she doesn't like me?

**MARILLA:** Calm down. I think Diana will like you well enough. But if Mrs. Barry has heard that you go to town with buttercups on your hat, I don't know what she'll think about you. You must be polite and well behaved, and you can't make any of your **rambling** speeches either. Look at you! You're actually trembling.

**ANNE:** Oh, Marilla, you'd be excited too if you were going to meet a girl that you want to be your best friend, but you're worried her mother might not like you. *(Anne runs to get another hat.)* ★

### Scene 2

*The Barry home later that afternoon.*

(*Anne and Marilla stand at the front door when Marilla knocks. Mrs. Barry answers the door. She is tall with black eyes and black hair.*)

**MRS. BARRY:** (***cordially***) Come in, Marilla. This is the little girl you've adopted?

**MARILLA:** Yes, this is Anne Shirley.

72 Chapter 3 ■ Craft and Structure: Literary Texts



### Words to Know

**General Academic Vocabulary**
**cordially** (*adverb*): in a friendly manner
**perplexed** (*adjective*): puzzled; confused
**rambling** (*adjective*): long and wordy

**Working with Word Meaning** Help students work with words in context by having them write sentences with a partner, focusing on the Words to Know.

**ANNE:** (*gasping with excitement*) Spelled with an E.

**MRS. BARRY:** *(looking* ***perplexed*** *as she shakes Anne's hand)* How are you?

**ANNE:** I'm fine physically, but my spirit is a bit rumpled. *(to Marilla in a loud whisper)* Was that okay? Did I say anything wrong?

### Comprehension Check

1. Why is Anne so nervous to meet Mrs. Barry in both scenes?
   - a. She made a negative impression with Mrs. Barry in the past.
   - b. She wants Mrs. Barry to like her so that she can be Diana's friend.
   - c. She knows that Mrs. Barry does not like Marilla.
   - d. She does not want Mrs. Barry to misspell her name.

2. What do the stage directions show about how Mrs. Barry feels when she meets Anne?
   - a. Mrs. Barry is confused about why Anne spells her name when she introduces herself.
   - b. Mrs. Barry is worried about how Marilla is treating Anne.
   - c. Mrs. Barry is excited that Anne tells her how to spell her name.
   - d. Mrs. Barry is upset because she does not think that Anne should be wearing a hat.

3. How does Scene 2 so far build on what happened in Scene 1?

   Sample answer: In Scene 1, Marilla and Anne wanted to meet Mrs. Barry and Diana. In Scene 2, they go to the Barry home and meet Mrs. Barry.





## Foundational Skills: Fluency

The natural-sounding dialogue in this dramatization offers students a good opportunity to practice fluency. Model fluent reading of the opening dialogue between Mrs. Barry and Anne in Scene 2 on pages 72–73. Then have students work as partners to practice fluent reading of the end of Scene 1 on page 72 (or they can choose part of Scene 1 on pages 70–71). Tell students that once they become comfortable with their readings, they should try to incorporate the feelings noted in the stage directions.

Additional fluency passages and activities can be found at **sadlierconnect.com**.

## Guided Practice

### Comprehension Check

**Answer Explanations:**

1. Choice B, *"She wants Mrs. Barry to like her so that she can be Diana's friend*, is correct. Students can determine the answer by locating the lines where Anne says "What if she doesn't like me?" and "...but you're worried that her mother might not like you."
2. Choice A, *Mrs. Barry is confused about why Anne spells her name when she introduces herself*, identifies Mrs. Barry's feelings. The second stage direction for her in Scene 2 indicates that she is "perplexed." *Perplexed* is a synonym for *confused.*
3. Students should consider the events of both scenes. They should understand that the events in Scene 2 continue building on the story from Scene 1, with Marilla and Anne following through with the visit to Mrs. Barry and Diana that they discussed in Scene 1.

## Reciprocal Teaching

Form groups of four and assign one of the following roles to each group member: Summarizer, Questioner, Clarifier, and Predictor. In a group discussion, the Summarizers should say what they have learned so far about characters in the play. Questioners should think of something else to ask about the characters. The Clarifiers should answer the question or say where they could look for the answers, and the Predictors should say what they think they will learn next in relation to the characters. Call on different groups to share their ideas with the class.

## Independent Practice

### Recap Reading Selection

Have a short group discussion about what students have read so far. Ask students if they remember where Scene 2 is set and remind them of the reason Marilla and Anne are there. Have students discuss the major plot points.

### Read and Apply

Have students read the selection independently as you circulate to provide support. As you circulate, provide students with targeted scaffolding as needed.

### CITE EVIDENCE

**A** Students should look at the stage directions under the Scene 3 subheading for information about the setting. They should notice that they are in "the garden in the backyard of the Barry house." Students should understand that they have gone outside so they can spend some time becoming friends, as Diana's mother suggested.

**B** Students should recognize that the three scenes have different settings. The writer breaks the play into three scenes so the action can take place in three different locations. The settings are important to the action and development of the story.



**Independent Practice**

**WORDS TO KNOW**
**faithful**
**poring**
**squinting**

**CITE EVIDENCE**

**A** Put a star next to the information that helps you understand where Diana and Anne are when they are talking.

**B** Circle the first line of dialogue in Scene 3. Why did the writer break the play into three scenes?

**Anne of Green Gables** *continued*

#### Scene 2 *continued*

*(Diana, smiling, rises from the sofa where she is sitting. She is a pretty girl with black eyes and hair like her mother and rosy cheeks.)*

**MRS. BARRY:** This is my daughter, Diana. Diana, can you take Anne out into the garden and show her your flowers? It will be better for you than **squinting** over that book. *(Speaking to Marilla as the girls go outside)* She's always **poring** over a book. I'm glad she has the opportunity to have a friend. Perhaps it will convince her to go outside more.

#### Scene 3

*In the garden in the backyard of the Barry house.*

★ *(Anne and Diana stand in the garden, looking shyly at one another over the flowers.)*

**ANNE:** Diana, do you think you like me a little? Enough to be my best friend?

**DIANA:** *(laughing)* I think so. I'm glad that you're living at Green Gables. No other girls live close to me, and my sisters aren't old enough to play with me.

**ANNE:** Do you swear to be my friend forever?

**DIANA:** *(looking shocked)* It's not a good idea to swear.

**ANNE:** Oh no! Not the swearing I'm asking you to do. There are two different kinds.

**DIANA:** I've only heard of one kind.

**ANNE:** Well, this one isn't bad. It just means to make a solemn promise.

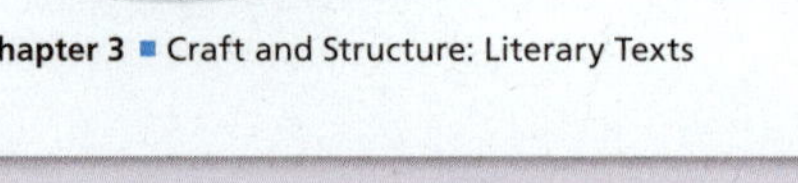





### Words to Know

**General Academic Vocabulary**

**faithful** (*adjective*): loyal and devoted

**poring** (*verb*): studying or looking at carefully

**squinting** (*verb*): looking at with partly closed eyes in order to see more clearly

**Working with Word Meaning** Have students use pantomime or facial expressions to demonstrate the meaning of each word.

**DIANA:** I can do that. How do you do it?

**ANNE:** We have to hold hands. Now imagine the path we're on is running water. I'll say it first: I solemnly swear to be **faithful** to my best friend, Diana Barry, forever and ever. Now you say it.

*(Diana repeats the oath, laughing.)*

**DIANA:** Everyone told me you were different, but I think we're going to get along just fine.

*(The girls laugh as the curtain closes.)*

*–Adapted from the book by L. M. Montgomery, 1908*

**Comprehension Check** MORE ONLINE **sadlierconnect.com**

1. What happens in Scene 3 that Anne was nervous about in Scene 1?
   - **a.** Anne puts bright flowers on her hat.
   - **b.** Marilla talks to Mrs. Barry.
   - **c.** Mrs. Barry argues with Diana.
   - **(d.)** Anne becomes friends with Diana.

2. How is Anne different at the end from how she was in Scene 1?
   - **(a.)** She is relieved.
   - **b.** She is nervous.
   - **c.** She is angry.
   - **d.** She is careful.

3. Why did the writer continue Scene 2 on page 74 rather than begin a new scene?

   Sample answer: Everyone is still at the Barry home, the setting did not change. Because the setting is the same, the scene doesn't change.





## Foundational Skill Review: Consonant Blends

Review consonant blends with students, reminding them that they are two consonants put together. Reinforce to students how they should clearly say the sounds of both letters in the blend. Model how this sounds, exaggerating each specific sound using common words such as *fruit*, *trip*, and *snow*. Explain that students can use this knowledge when they sound out longer or uncommon words, such as these from the passage: *flowers*, *dresses*, *scowl*, and *promise*.

Additional phonics activities can be found at **sadlierconnect.com**.

## Independent Practice

**Comprehension Check**

**Answer Explanations:**

1. To arrive at choice D, students must remember that at the end of Scene 1, Anne tells Marilla that she is worried that Diana won't like her and that she wants Diana to be her best friend.
2. Students can arrive at choice A, *She is relieved*, by looking at the stage directions at the end of the play. Specifically, both Anne and Diana are laughing.
3. Students should understand that scenes are dependent on continuous action and setting rather than page breaks. A new page does not mean a new scene.

## Critical Comprehension

Use the following questions to help students think more deeply about the text. Students should be prepared to support their answers with evidence from the text.

*Based on the dialogue and stage directions, what kind of person is Anne?* (She is independent-minded and spunky, but she is also uncertain and worried about how other people feel about her.)

*How would this play be different as a story?* (Answers will vary, but may include that there would not be as much dialogue and the setting might not change as much.)

**Assess and Respond**

**If** students have difficulty answering the questions in the Comprehension Check…

**Then** assign students roles and have them read the play out loud or act it out.

## Guided Instruction

**OBJECTIVE**
**Differentiate between a personal point of view and the narrator's or character's point of view.**

### Genre: Narrative Poem

Explain to students that a narrative poem is a story told in poem format. It has characters and a plot like a story. It has common elements of poems such as stanzas and rhyme as well.

### Set the Purpose

Help students understand the purpose for learning the reading skill by asking *Have you ever thought about a situation in a different way from the way someone else thought about it? What did that help you understand?*

### Model and Teach

Read the selection as students follow along in their books.

### CITE EVIDENCE

**A** *I know that a pronoun takes the place of a noun. Some pronouns are:* I, me, he, she, we, us *and* you.

*Which pronouns are used in the third line of the poem? (I, you) Whom do these pronouns represent?* (The pronoun *I* represents the narrator; *you* represents the reader.)

**B** *I see that there are three characters in the poem that are mentioned by name.*

*What are their names?* (Damon, Pythias, Dionysius)



Guided Instruction

**WORDS TO KNOW**
**dreary**
**inspiring**
**suspicious**
**treason**

A reader may have a different **point of view** from that of a text's narrator or characters.

**CITE EVIDENCE**

**A** Pronouns can help you figure out to whom a **point of view** belongs. Circle the pronouns in the third line of the poem. Then tell whom these pronouns represent.

**B** How many characters are in this poem so far? Put a star by each character's name.

# Damon and Pythias

(Genre: Narrative Poem)

1 Welcome, dear friends.
Sit back and enjoy,
While I tell you an **inspiring** story.
It's a tale of two youths
Who lived long ago,
And displayed friendship in its true glory.

2 It takes place in a land
That we call ancient Greece,
Or, more exactly, a kingdom within it.
Syracuse was its name,
And it had a cruel king.
His harshness was without limit.

3 Now, Damon was one friend.
He was the finest of young men.
And Pythias was the other.
They had grown up together.
They had played side by side,
And thought of each other as brothers.

4 Dionysius, the king,
Summoned Pythias one day.
And here's what he gave as his reason:
The young man, he'd heard,
Had spoken against him.
The king said that amounted to **treason**!

5 But that wasn't all.
The king called his guards,
And told them to lead Pythias away.
He said, "Take him from here
To a dark, **dreary** cell.
Lock him up there until his dying day!





## Words to Know

**General Academic Vocabulary**
**dreary** (*adjective*): gloomy; bleak
**inspiring** (*adjective*): bringing about good feelings and actions
**suspicious** (*adjective*): distrustful; having doubts

**Domain-Specific Vocabulary**
**treason** (*noun*): the act of betraying or showing disloyalty to one's country

**Working with Word Meaning** Help students develop their understanding of the vocabulary words by working with them to think of an antonym for each.

# CRAFT AND STRUCTURE

## Guided Instruction

6 Young Pythias was brave.
He had indeed spoken out.
This was something he did not deny.
Now he asked only one thing:
"Let me see my parents once more.
I ask only for a chance to say good-bye."

7 Then the king laughed and sneered.
He snorted and said,
With a look in his eye that was cruel,
"If I let you leave here,
You'll never come back.
You really must think me a fool!"

8 At this point, Damon stepped up.
He had come with his friend
To make sure that nothing was wrong.
He could not believe what he'd heard.
He knew he had to help out.
And he knew that he didn't have long.

9 Damon said to the king,
"Let me take his place.
Lock *me* away, not Pythias.
If he doesn't return,
You can keep me locked up."
The king listened, but was **suspicious**.

### CITE EVIDENCE

**C** Circle the lines on this page that show Pythias's feelings about being sent to prison. Also circle the lines that show Damon's feelings about it. In what way are the two friends' feelings similar?

**D** How does the king feel about Damon's offer to take Pythias's place in prison? Underline the word that reveals his point of view.

### Comprehension Check

Based on what you have read so far, how do you think Damon and Pythias feel about friendship? How do you think the king feels about it?





## Support English Language Learners

English language learners may need support in understanding idioms. Point out the idiom "stepped up" in stanza 8. Then point out to students that the expression does not mean that Damon physically took a step in an upward direction. Explain that the expression "stepped up" means that Damon is taking action to accept a responsibility or a challenge. Ask students to share a time they stepped up to do something.

## Guided Instruction

### CITE EVIDENCE

**C** *I'll look for the lines that tell Pythias's feelings about being sentenced to prison. Then I'll look for the lines that tell Damon's feelings about this.*

*How does each friend feel?* (Pythias accepts it and asks only to go say good-bye to his parents first. Damon feels he must do something to help Pythias.)

*In what ways are the two friends' feelings similar?* (The both show a sense of courage and honor.)

**D** *I look at the poem again and see that Damon makes his offer in stanza 9. At the end of that stanza, it says the king was "suspicious."*

*What does the word* suspicious *mean?* (distrustful)

### Comprehension Check

**Sample Answer:** Damon and Pythias think of each other as brothers and Damon offers to take Pythias's place in prison. I think this means that friendship is very important to them. The king is suspicious of Damon's offer. This is because the king does not believe someone would make such a sacrifice for a friend.

**Answer Explanation:** Students should recognize the key details and events that reveal each character's point of view.

### Review: Understanding Parts of a Drama

Bring students' attention to the way that the poem is broken up. Ask students if they remember what these parts of poems are called. (stanzas) See if they can recall the way a drama is broken up and what the parts of a drama are called. (scenes) Ask students to compare stanzas and scenes.

## Guided Practice

### Recap Reading Selection

Have students recall what they have learned so far about Damon and Pythias and their friendship. They should be able to say Pythias has been sentenced to prison by the cruel king Dionysius. And Damon has offered to take Pythias's place while Damon goes off to say good-bye to his parents.

### Read and Practice

Have partners take turns reading the selection as you circulate to provide support. Model distinguishing point of view with Cite Evidence callout A. For callout B, circulate and provide partners with scaffolding as needed. You might use the following suggestions to help students who are having difficulty.

### CITE EVIDENCE

**A** Dionysius accepts Damon's offer because "one way or another," he will have sent someone to prison. Students should understand that this reasoning is a sign of his cruelty and ruthlessness.

**B** Students should understand that Pythias is a loyal friend. Tell students to look for words he says in stanza 11 that show he means to keep his promise to Damon. ("I would never betray a dear friend.")

Ask students to tell about times when they have kept a promise to a friend or a friend has kept a promise to them.

DISTINGUISHING POINTS OF VIEW

Guided Practice

**WORDS TO KNOW**

**betray**
**embrace**
**steed**

**CITE EVIDENCE**

**A** What reason does King Dionysius give for accepting Damon's offer to take his friend's place in prison? Circle the line that tells his reason. What does the king's reason reveal about the kind of character he is?

**B** Underline the promise that Pythias makes in stanza 11. What does this promise reveal about the kind of character he is?

**Damon and Pythias** *continued*

10 At last King Dionysius said, "Fine—
Let's try it your way.
I'll have a prisoner one way or another.
But of this I am sure:
Your friend won't come back.
So you'll stay in prison forever!"

11 At this point, Pythias stepped up.
He said, "Damon, you know
I would never **betray** a dear friend.
Despite what the king says,
I'll be back in three days.
And then you'll see your prison stay end."

12 With this, Pythias went off.
He hadn't much time.
His parents lived in a faraway place.
He turned, waved good-bye,
And then jumped on his horse.
Now began his difficult race.

13 Pythias rode like the wind.
He reached the door of their home
And then he jumped off of his **steed**.
He broke the bad news
And said, "Please be brave.
Perhaps, some day, I'll be freed."

14 When the sun rose the next day,
He gave his mother a kiss,
And his father a farewell **embrace**.
He got back on his horse
And rode as fast as he could.
Pythias knew there was no time to waste.

78 Chapter 3 ■ Craft and Structure: Literary Texts



### Words to Know

**General Academic Vocabulary**

**betray** (*verb*): to be disloyal to
**embrace** (*noun*): a hug

**Domain-Specific Vocabulary**

**steed** (*noun*): a horse that is ridden by a person

**Working with Word Meaning** Ask students to use each word in an original sentence. Challenge students to use the new vocabulary terms in a short story about a heroic action.

# CRAFT AND STRUCTURE

## Guided Practice

15 Sometime later, in Syracuse,
The king visited Damon
And said, "The moment of truth—it draws near.
The evening's upon us,
And it looks like your time's up.
I'm sure that your friend won't appear.

### Comprehension Check

1. Which of these lines from the poem helps show Pythias's point of view?
   a. "When the sun rose the next day."
   b. "He got back on his horse"
   c. "And rode as fast as he could."
   (d.) "Pythias knew there was no time to waste."

2. According to stanzas 10 and 15, what are the king's feelings about Pythias's return?
   a. He wants Pythias to stay away, because Pythias is guilty of treason.
   b. He hopes Pythias will not come back, because Damon deserves to be in prison even more than Pythias does.
   (c.) He believes Pythias does not want to be put in prison, and so he will not return.
   d. He believes Pythias intends to return.

3. Work with a partner. Predict whether or not Pythias will come back in time. Use text evidence to support your point of view.

Sample answer: Pythias will come back in time. He has shown himself to be brave and honorable and has promised to return. Also, we see that he rushes away from his parents' home and seems determined to get back.





## Discussion Skills

Remind students that it is acceptable to agree or disagree with something that someone else has said. Students should always strive to come up with their own reasoned conclusions, but they must be able to support them.

Give students some sentence stems to help scaffold an agreement or disagreement:

- *I agree/disagree with that because…*
- *I agree/disagree because of this evidence from the text…*
- *Based on my personal experience…*
- *Based on my understanding…*
- *What makes you agree/disagree with what I said?*

## Guided Practice

### Comprehension Check

**Answer Explanations:**

1. Choice D, *Pythias knew he had no time to waste,* is correct. The word *knew* provides a clue that this answer reveals his point of view.
2. Choice C, *He believes Pythias does not want to be put in prison, so he will not return*, best describes the king's feelings. This answer is supported by these words spoken by the king: "Your friend won't come back" and "I'm sure your friend won't appear."
3. Text evidence suggests that Pythias will come back. Students should note details such as his promise to return and his riding "as fast as he could" after leaving his parents' home.

### Numbered Heads Together

Another way to engage students in a comprehension review is to give them a chance to discuss their answers with a small group of their peers. Ask students to number off in their teams from one to four. Announce a question, such as *How does Pythias feel when he leaves his parents' home?* or *Does the king share Damon's trust in Pythias?* Then set a time limit. Each group of students should try to decide on an answer. Call a number and ask all students with that number to stand and answer the question. Recognize each response and engage in discussion.

## Independent Practice

### Recap Reading Selection

Remind students that they have been reading about Damon and Pythias's friendship. Ask students to tell you the last thing that happened in the poem. (King Dionysius went to see Damon in prison and told him that it looks like Pythias will not return to serve his sentence.)

### Read and Apply

Have students read the selection independently. As you circulate, provide students with targeted scaffolding as needed.

### CITE EVIDENCE

**A** Students should recall that earlier the king had said he was sure that Pythias would not return. Students should see that his point of view changes when Pythias actually does come back. How does the king demonstrate this change? (He frees both Damon and Pythias.)

**B** Remind students that when authors make comparisons, they express how two things are alike or different. Have them look in stanza 21 for two things the author compares to friendship. (gold, a king) What qualities do these comparisons reveal about friendship? (It is both precious and powerful.) Encourage students to express their own points of view about this idea.

DISTINGUISHING POINTS OF VIEW

Independent Practice

**WORDS TO KNOW**

**desert**
**fate**
**precious**

**CITE EVIDENCE**

**A** Stanza 20 tells about the king's reaction to Pythias's return. Draw a circle around the lines that show how the king's point of view changes as a result of what Pythias has done.

**B** Use of comparisons can show a character's or narrator's point of view. Underline where the narrator compares things to friendship in stanza 21. Do you agree or disagree with these ideas?

**Damon and Pythias** *continued*

16 Damon took a deep breath.
He looked the king in the eye
And said, "I have faith in my friend.
He would not **desert** me.
I know he'll come back
Before the full three days end."

17 "Damon, you fool!"
The king spat out these words.
"You deserve whatever sad **fate** you get.
You should not believe Pythias.
No friend is that true.
You'll see—I'll be proven right yet!"

18 Then came the sound.
The loud sound of hooves
Was heard by the king and the young man.
They turned to the doorway.
They stood still and stared.
They waited to see who would walk in.

19 It was Pythias, of course!
He said, "Damon, I'm back.
My friend, I'm sorry it took me so long!"
And then he looked at the king
And said, "Remember your promise.
Free Damon—he has done nothing wrong."

80 Chapter 3 ■ Craft and Structure: Literary Texts

## Words to Know

**General Academic Vocabulary**

**desert** (*verb*): to leave and not return
**fate** (*noun*): the thing that will happen to a person
**precious** (*adjective*): having great value

**Working with Word Meaning** To help students retain the meaning of the new vocabulary, ask them to restate the definitions in their own words. Then they can try to use each new word in a sentence.

## CRAFT AND STRUCTURE

### Independent Practice

20 At first, the king was amazed.
He knew not what to say.
For he was not expecting this sight.
Then he said, "So it shall be
And Pythias, too, shall go free."
For he knew, in the end, this was right.

21 And so, dear friends,
Think back and take in
That friendship's a wonderful thing.
It can melt a cold heart.
It's more **precious** than gold,
And more powerful than any king.

**Comprehension Check** MORE ONLINE sadlierconnect.com

1. Who had little faith in the power of friendship?
   - **a.** the king
   - **b.** Damon
   - **c.** Pythias
   - **d.** the narrator

2. Which term below best describes the narrator's point of view about Damon and Pythias's actions?
   - **a.** doubting
   - **b.** admiring
   - **c.** conflicted
   - **d.** confused

3. Which character in the poem changes? Explain how his viewpoint is different at the beginning and at the end. Which of these viewpoints do you share?

Sample answer: The king and his viewpoint change. At first, he does not believe in friendship. But once he sees that Pythias keeps his promise to return, he starts to believe in it. I agree with his later viewpoint, because friendship is one of the most important things we can have in life.





## Speaking and Listening Presentation

Have students create a presentation about friendship and its challenges. Have students present to the class. Presenters should:

- state their topic and present appropriate facts and descriptive details.
- use formal language and precise words for effect.
- speak clearly, in complete sentences, and at a reasonable rate.
- answer questions in complete sentences, giving elaboration and detail.
- provide engaging visuals to enhance their presentation.

Listeners should listen attentively and ask questions to better understand the information.

## Independent Practice

**Comprehension Check**

**Answer Explanations:**

1. Choice A, *the king*, is correct because the king doubted Pythias would return to take his friend's place in prison.
2. Choice B, *admiring*, best describes the narrator's point of view. At the beginning of the poem, the narrator says that Damon and Pythias "displayed friendship in its full glory." At the end, the narrator says it is "more precious than gold" and "more powerful than any king."
3. Students should understand that the king's viewpoint changes. Until Pythias's return, he did not have faith in the power of friendship. Students will probably share his changed viewpoint.

### Critical Comprehension

Use the following questions to help students think more deeply about the text. Students should be prepared to support their answers with evidence from the text.

- *What kind of experiences with friendship do you think the narrator has had?* (The narrator has probably had positive experiences.)
- *How would this poem have been different if it were a story or play?* (Sample answers: It would not rhyme. In a play, the characters would speak in dialogue.)

**Assess and Respond**

**If** students have difficulty answering the questions in the Comprehension Check…

**Then** assign students the characters of Damon, Pythias, the king, and the narrator. Have students read their parts of the poem aloud.

## Connect Across Texts: *4 points*
## Review Reading Selections

Put students into groups, giving each the responsibility to summarize one of the three reading selections. Ask volunteers from each group to help the class recall the main events from each selection.

## Compare and Contrast Texts

Review the directions on page 82 with students. Instruct students to write the titles of their chosen selections in the outer parts of each circle.

**Venn Diagram Rubric**

| | |
|---|---|
| 4 | Student has correctly identified the similarities and differences between two texts in the chapter. |
| 3 | Student has correctly identified some of the similarities and differences between two texts in the chapter. |
| 2 | Student has correctly identified either the similarities or the differences between two texts, but not the elements of both. |
| 1 | Student has identified two texts from the chapter, but has not compared or contrasted them. |
| 0 | Student has not identified the selections or included pertinent information. |

# CONNECT ACROSS TEXTS

### Compare and Contrast Texts

In this chapter, you have read stories about friendship. Now, pick out two of the texts you read for this chapter. Using the Venn diagram below, map out what the stories have in common and what is unique about them. Think about the ways friendship is presented in each text. Be prepared to discuss your ideas.

**The Secret Garden**

Mary's friend Colin has been sick, but is having a good day and is excited to see a garden. Mary takes him to the garden and he feels better.

Both friends help each other in tough times and make the other feel good.

**Anne of Green Gables**

Anne and Diana do not know each other at the beginning of the story. Anne is nervous to meet Diana, but Diana is nice to her and says she will be her friend.





### Extend Thinking: Assess

Ask students to consider the friendship presented in each reading selection. *Which friendship do you think is the most rewarding and why?* Instruct students that they should be able to cite evidence from the texts in their arguments. You may wish to have students with different answers provide additional support for their points to sway classmates.

## CONNECT ACROSS TEXTS

### Connect to the Essential Question

***How do authors craft stories?*** In small groups or as a class, discuss the Essential Question. Think about what you have learned about figurative language, sections of a text, and point of view. Use evidence from the chapter texts to answer the question.

Authors craft stories by choosing a structure that best conveys the central message of the story. The drama "Anne of Green Gables" uses scenes, stage directions, and dialogue to show two girls who will be friends "forever and ever." "Damon and Pythias" is a narrative poem about what friends do for each other. and uses different points of view. The author of *The Secret Garden* uses both literal and nonliteral language to bring the characters and story to life.

### Connect to the Theme

***Best Friends*** In this chapter, you read three stories about friendship. What does friendship mean to each of the characters? How do they help their friends? Support your answers with details from the text.

Friendship is very important to all of the characters in the three texts. In *The Secret Garden*, Mary cares about Colin very much and wants to help him feel better. In "Anne of Green Gables," Anne is nervous because she feels out of place, but Diana accepts her and "solemnly swears" to be her friend. Damon and Pythias show the king how strong their friendship is and "the king was amazed.".

**To strengthen your response, reread parts of the texts that support your answers. Add to your answers any additional details you find.**





## Assess and Respond (pages 82–83)

| If | Then |
|---|---|
| Students scored 0–2 points, they are **Developing** their understanding of the skills... | Provide students with reading support and more intensive modeling of the skills. |
| Students scored 3–5 points, they are **Improving** their understanding of the skills... | Use students' scores to target areas that are weak and review those specific skills. |
| Students scored 6–8 points, they are **Proficient** In their understanding of the skills... | Have these students move on. They are ready for the formal assessment. |

## Support Essential Question Discussion

Have students reread the Essential Question. Lead a discussion by prompting them to finish the following: *Authors craft their stories by...*

If students have difficulty responding, remind them of the skills they learned in the chapter.

## Theme Wrap-Up

Lead students in a group discussion on the theme of best friends. Talk about the different friendships presented and how the friends help each other.

## Short-Answer Questions: *2 points each*

### Connect to the Essential Question Rubric

| | |
|---|---|
| 2 | Students are able to correctly identify how authors craft their stories. |
| 1 | Students are able to identify some ways that authors craft their stories. |
| 0 | Students are not able to explain any ways in which authors craft their stories. |

### Connect to the Theme Rubric

| | |
|---|---|
| 2 | Students correctly identify the different friendships and how the friends help each other. |
| 1 | Students identify the different friendships but not how the friends help each other. |
| 0 | Students are not able to identify the different friendships or how the friends help each other. |

**OBJECTIVE**

**Determine the meaning of figurative language, such as idioms.**

## Guided Instruction

Review the Guided Instruction section on page 84 with students. Be sure they understand that an idiom is a type of nonliteral, or figurative, phrase. The nonliteral meaning has little to do with the literal meaning. By understanding the meaning of nonliteral phrases, students can understand the meaning of the text.

## Guided Practice

If students are having trouble, help them to work through the possibilities by reviewing both the literal and nonliteral meanings in the Guided Instruction. Students can use the definitions to help determine which meaning is used in the sentences.

## Independent Practice

If students are having trouble using the idiom *hold on to your hat*, have them first explain what the nonliteral meaning of the phrase is. Then have them use it in a sentence.

## Apply to Reading

Have students return to "Anne of Green Gables" to hunt for phrases that have nonliteral meanings. They will find "talk back" (page 71) and "work out" (page 71).

## LANGUAGE

### Literal and Nonliteral Meanings

**Guided Instruction** **Nonliteral**, or **figurative**, language is language that means something other than what the words say. An idiom is an example of figurative language. Idioms are popular expressions that have been used for a long time. The meaning of an idiom can be much different from the literal meanings of its words. Read this sentence: *Keeping their shortcut a secret would be a piece of cake.* The idiom *that's a piece of cake* means "that is really easy."

| | |
|---|---|
| **bend over backwards** | 1. nonliteral meaning: to do whatever is needed to help<br>2. literal meaning: to completely bend one's back |
| **a green thumb** | 1. nonliteral meaning: someone good at gardening<br>2. literal meaning: someone's thumb is the color green |

Look at the chart to find other examples of nonliteral idiomatic phrases.

**Guided Practice** Determine whether each sentence uses an idiom or not. In the blank before each sentence, write "n" for *nonliteral* or "l" for *literal* meaning.

__l__ **1.** As he painted, he saw that he had a green thumb.

__n__ **2.** Look at her garden; she has a real green thumb.

__n__ **3.** His mom bent over backwards to make his birthday happy.

__l__ **4.** She had to bend over backwards to get under the fence.

**Independent Practice** Using the phrase *hold on to your hat*, write one sentence that contains an idiom, or nonliteral meaning, and one that contains a literal meaning.

________________________________________

________________________________________

________________________________________

________________________________________





## Support English Language Learners

Students whose first language is not English may have difficulty knowing when a phrase is supposed to have a nonliteral meaning. Work with these students to complete the Guided Practice and point out how context can help one determine if the author is using the phrase in a literal or nonliteral way. Students should see if a literal interpretation makes sense in the context of the sentence.

Knowing idioms requires memorization and familiarity with the language, so provide additional example sentences for each idiom.

# CHAPTER 3 REVIEW

Read the following poem in which nonliteral language and a narrator's point of view appear in the stanzas. Then answer the questions on pages 85 and 86.

## Friendship—Yum

(Genre: Poem)

1 What does the word *friendship*
Mean to you?
Is it about being faithful
To friends pure and true?
Does it mean trusting others
With all your might?
Does it mean always agreeing
With never a fight?

2 I think friendship's like chocolate
And fruit combined.
It's delicious and nutritious,
And sometimes it's mine.
Look out for nice friends,
And if a fine one you meet,
Hold on; a great friendship
Is good enough to eat.

**Fill in the circle of the correct answer choice.**

1. Which word in stanza 2 shows the opinion belongs to the narrator?
   - ● I
   - ○ nice
   - ○ delicious
   - ○ you

2. In which lines of the poem does the narrator compare friendship to food?
   - ○ Stanza 1, lines 7 and 8
   - ○ Stanza 2, lines 3 and 4
   - ● Stanza 2 , lines 1 and 2
   - ○ Stanza 2, lines 5 and 6

3. If the poem was instead a drama, what part of a drama would stanza 1 be?
   - ● dialogue
   - ○ characters
   - ○ setting
   - ○ stage directions

4. Which word in stanza 2 hints that figurative language will follow?
   - ○ it's
   - ○ good
   - ○ fine
   - ● like





## Self-Assessment: Progress Check

Have students revisit the Progress Check on page 61 and respond to the questions again. Ask them to compare their Before and After responses.

You may wish to have students rate their answers on a scale of 0–2 rather than simply checking (or not checking) the box. Instruct them to write a 0 if they feel they do not understand the given skill at all, a 1 if they feel they have some understanding, and a 2 if they feel they have a solid grasp of the skill.

## Chapter Summary

At this point, students have had instruction and practice in reading literary text, with a focus on learning about different kinds of friendships. Students have also learned different strategies for determining the meaning of nonliteral language, understanding the parts of dramas and stories, and distinguishing points of view. Students have practiced working with concepts across texts and practiced working with idioms. They should be well-prepared for the review section.

## Introduce the Review

Explain to students that they will read a new passage that is related to the chapter's theme and the selections they have already read. Instruct students to read the passage carefully and then answer the questions on pages 85 and 86.

### Answer Explanations

Scoring: Items 1–9 on pages 85–86 are worth 1 point each. See the rubric for guidance on scoring the Write About It question on page 86.

1. The narrator telling the story in the poem uses the pronoun *I* to express his or her point of view.
2. Stanza 2 compares friendship to chocolate and fruit.
3. The sentences in stanza 1 sound like a person talking. The equivalent in a drama is dialogue.
4. The word *like* suggests a figurative expression will follow.

### Answer Explanations

5. "Friendship's like chocolate" contains the word *like* and is an example of nonliteral language.
6. "Hold on" means that people should keep their good friends.
7. "Following your friends to the end of the earth" is the choice that relates to being faithful, not just close, as friends.
8. The first stanza asks for the reader's point of view and the second stanza states the narrator's point of view.
9. The nonliteral language in the poem adds up to suggest that friendship is important and wonderful.

### Write About It Rubric

| | |
|---|---|
| 2 | Student clearly states point of view and gives logical support. |
| 1 | Student states point of view and gives limited reasons in support. |
| 0 | Student does not state point of view. |

## CHAPTER 3 REVIEW

5. Which phrase from the poem is an example of nonliteral language?
   - ○ Does it mean trusting others
   - ● friendship's like chocolate
   - ○ Does it mean always agreeing
   - ○ sometimes it's mine

6. What does the author mean by the idiom "Hold on"?
   - ● keep your good friends
   - ○ hug your friends tightly
   - ○ wait to meet new friends
   - ○ eat dessert with your friends

7. What figurative or nonliteral phrase describes being faithful to your friends?
   - ○ I will always be on the lookout for good friends.
   - ● Friends follow each other to the ends of the earth.
   - ○ Friends are like two peas in a pod.
   - ○ Good friends are joined at the hip.

8. How does the point of view change from stanza 1 to 2?
   - ○ It starts in third-person point of view and moves to first-person point of view.
   - ○ It describes about the dangers of friendship and then the benefits of friendship.
   - ● It asks for the reader's point of view and then states the narrator's point of view.
   - ○ It describes friendship and then gives advice on how to keep friends.

9. What is the narrator's point of view about friendship?
   - ○ Friendship doesn't last long.
   - ○ Friendship is about having fun.
   - ● Friendship is important.
   - ○ Friends should never fight.

**Write About It** Do you share the narrator's point of view on friendship? Why or why not? Sample answer: I would not compare friendship to food, but I agree it's important to "hold on" to good friends when you find them.





### Analyze Student Scores

| | |
|---|---|
| 9–11 pts Strong | Student has a good grasp of the skills and concepts taught in this chapter. Point out any mistakes the student has made and explain the correct answers if necessary. |
| 4–8 pts Progressing | Student is struggling with some skills or concepts. Identify the specific skills that are problematic to target a review of instruction. |
| 0–3 pts Emerging | Student is having serious problems understanding the skills and concepts taught in this chapter. Student may need to redo the work with a higher level of support. |

# **Craft and Structure:** Informational Texts

CHAPTER 4

Craft and Structure
## Informational Texts
CHAPTER 4

**Focus on Reading** You can learn more about a topic by reading different texts will a similar focus. Look for words and text features that help you understand what you are reading. Reading about a topic from different points of view will also help you learn.

**Think About Theme** Weather is all around us, and sometimes it can be extreme! Read about different types of weather events, what causes them, and what people can do to be prepared.

**Let's Get on Our Way!** You have many tools to help you understand what you read. Writers support readers with craft and structure to help the audience understand their texts.

These are the skills you will build in this chapter. Before you begin, check the boxes on the left of any items you can do well now. At the end of the chapter, you will return to this page to use the check boxes on the right to show what you have learned.

Progress Check

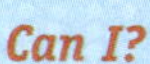

- ☐ Determine the meaning of academic and content area words and phrases. ☐
- ☐ Use text features and search tools to locate information. ☐
- ☐ Distinguish my point of view from the author's point of view. ☐
- ☐ Find the meaning of a new word when a familiar prefix or suffix is added. ☐



Chapter 4 ■ Craft and Structure: Informational Texts

**Student Page 87**

## Progress Check

The Progress Check is a self-assessment feature that students can use to gauge their own progress. Research shows that when students take accountability for their own learning, their motivation increases.

Before students begin work on Chapter 4, have them check the boxes next to any item that they feel they can do well. It is fine if they do not check any of the boxes. Tell them that they will have an opportunity to learn about and practice all of these items while studying the chapter. Let them know that near the end of the chapter they will have a chance to reconsider how well they can do each item on this list.

Before students begin the Chapter 4 Review on page 111, have them revisit this page. You can use this information to work with students on any items they don't understand before they tackle the Review.

## HOME ✦ CONNECT...

The Home Connect feature is a way to keep parents or other adult family members apprised of what their children are learning. The key learning objectives are listed, and some ideas for related activities and discussions are included.

Explain to students that they can share the Home Connect page with their parents or other adult family members in their home. Let students know how much time the class will be spending on this chapter so they can plan their time accordingly at home.

Encourage students and their parents to share their experiences using the suggestions on the Home Connect page. You may wish to make a place to post some of this work.

## HOME ✦ CONNECT...

Newspaper writers and editors are good about providing context clues for tough words in their articles. **Context clues** are words that give readers the help they need to understand the meanings of unfamiliar words. Choose a print or online news article your child might enjoy. Highlight any difficult words defined in context. Then ask your child to help you use context clues to find the meanings of the highlighted words.

**Text features** such as subheads, charts, and sidebars can help children see what is important in an article. Choose an online article with an appealing topic. Before reading, have your child point out subheads and predict what the article will be about. Talk about sidebars, maps, and charts, and discuss why information is shown this way.

Understanding an **author's point of view** about a subject is an important reading skill. Find an editorial in a newspaper or children's magazine. Read it with your child. Have your child state the author's opinion and say whether they agree with the author.

**Activity:** With your child, explore interesting Web links related to extreme weather. Use correct terms for the text features you see on screen, such as *sidebar, heading, caption, hyperlink, boldface type*. Talk about why some of the texts you explore are easier to follow or more appealing than others. List the interesting new facts you learn, and create your own fact sheet on the computer.

**IN THIS CHAPTER, YOUR CHILD WILL...**

- Use clues in a text to figure out the meaning of unfamiliar words and words with multiple meanings.
- Learn how text features such as headings or visuals (charts, photos, hyperlinks, etc.) help readers locate information within the text.
- Identify an author's point of view, or opinion about a topic, and decide whether or not he or she agrees with it.
- Combine the meaning of a base word, such as *agree*, with those of prefixes and suffixes, such as *dis-* and *-able*, to understand word meanings.
- Compare and contrast three texts on the same theme: an explanatory text, a journal article, and an editorial.

**WAYS TO HELP YOUR CHILD**

Show respect for your child's point of view on topics while also helping your child develop the thinking and speaking skills needed to express and support opinions. Whether you are discussing sports, current events, or daily life, ask for your child's point of view. Encourage him or her to offer supporting reasons for it.

ONLINE
For more Home Connect activities, continue online at sadlierconnect.com



88 Chapter 4 ■ Craft and Structure: Informational Texts

**Student Page 88**

## LEARNING PROGRESSIONS

In this chapter, students will learn how the craft and structure of an informational text contribute to their understanding of it. In order to learn the skills in this chapter, students will further develop skills learned in second grade. They should be encouraged to retain these skills, as they will continue to build on them in fourth grade.

### Determining Word Meanings

- By the end of grade 2, students should have been able to determine the meaning of words and phrases in a text relevant to a grade 2 topic or subject area.
- In grade 3, students will learn to determine the meaning of both academic and domain-specific words and phrases relevant to a grade 3 topic or subject area.
- In grade 4, students will be determining the meaning of academic and domain-specific words and phrases relevant to more complex texts.

### Using Text Features

- Proficient second-grade students should have ended the school year knowing how to use various text features to locate key facts or information in a text.
- As third graders, they should be able to use these same text features as well as search tools in order to locate information relevant to a given topic. The ability to distinguish between information that is relevant and information that is irrelevant is one that students should master by the end of third grade.
- This skill will prepare them for fourth grade, when they will learn to use these text features as well as the text itself to describe the overall structure of events, ideas, concepts, or information in a text.

### Distinguishing Points of View

- By the end of second grade, students should have been able to identify the author's purpose in an informational text, including what he or she wants to answer, explain, or describe.
- As third graders, students must take this concrete knowledge of the author's purpose and point of view and distinguish it from their own point of view.
- This ability to distinguish between points of view will become even more complex in fourth grade, when they will learn to compare and contrast firsthand and secondhand accounts of the same event or topic.

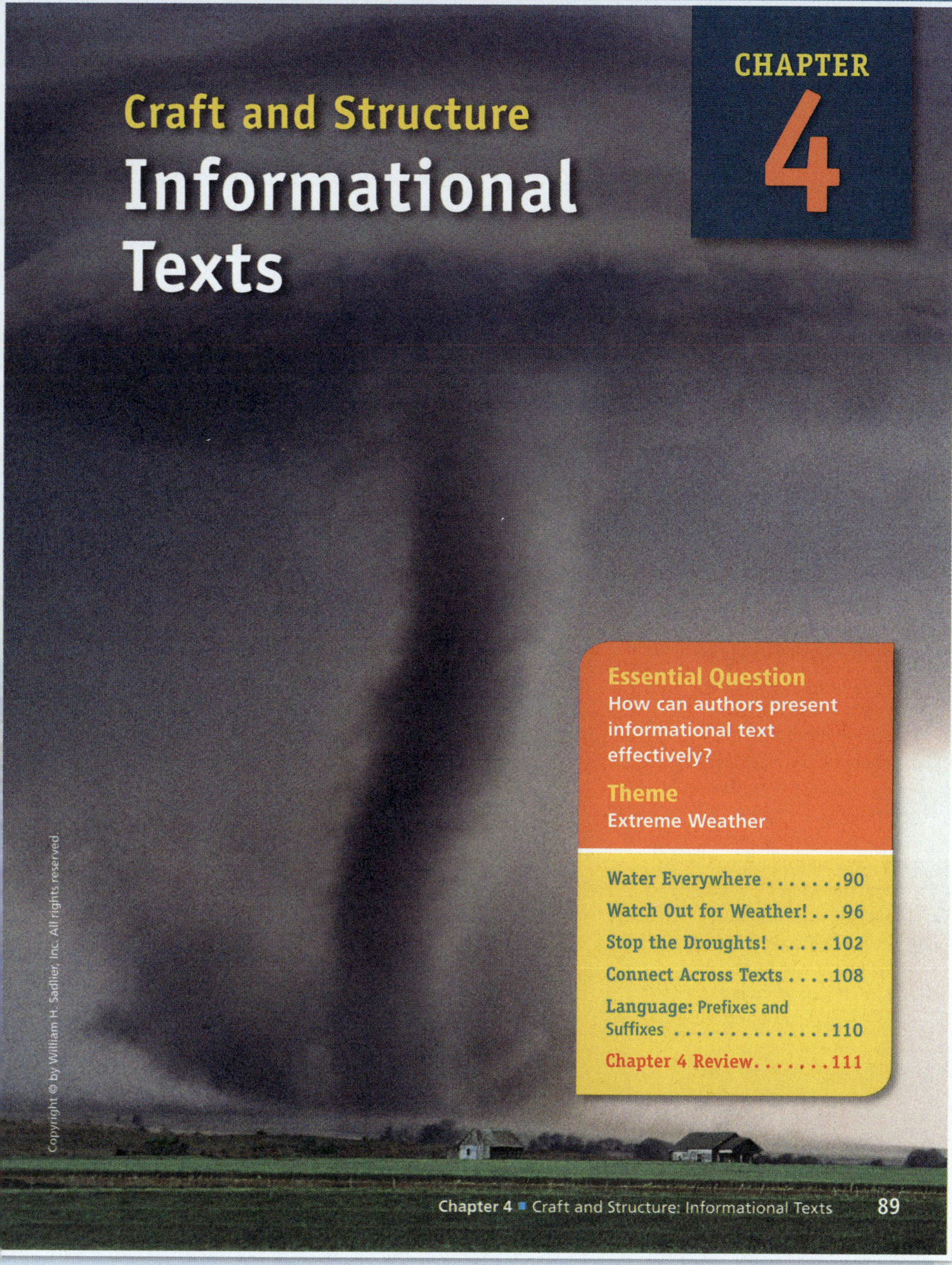


**Essential Question:**
**How can an author present informational text effectively?**

In this chapter, students will learn about the craft and structure of informational text, specifically how authors use vocabulary, text features, and point of view to communicate information and ideas.

## Theme: Extreme Weather

Students will read selections related to the theme of extreme weather. They will read about floods, droughts, and storms—including tornadoes, hurricanes, and blizzards.

## Curriculum Connection: Science

Students will learn about weather patterns and storm systems, the water cycle, and how essential water is for living things.

## Vocabulary Overview

### General Academic Vocabulary

absorb 94, barrier 90, conserving 102, contaminated 94, crew 98, dangerous 100, destroy 97, devastating 104, disaster 92, precious 106, predict 98, severe 100, system 90

### Domain-Specific Vocabulary

adapted 104, atmosphere 96, condense 103, continent 106, debris 92, levee 90, prairie 100, snowmelt 94, vapor 103, wildfire 106

## Guided Instruction

**OBJECTIVE**

**Use vocabulary strategies to determine the meaning of general academic and domain-specific words in text.**

### Genre: Explanatory Text

Explain to students that explanatory text gives the reader information about a topic. Point out that the word *explanatory* is related to the word *explanation.*

### Set the Purpose

Help students understand the purpose for learning the reading skill by asking *Do you ever find a new word while reading? What do you do to figure out the meaning?*

### Model and Teach

Read the selection as students follow along in their books.

### CITE EVIDENCE

**A** *The text says that "water went over the first barrier," and that houses were lifted up by the water. The photograph also shows many houses under water.*

*What does* submerged *mean, based on the clues?* (under water)

**B** *I will look for a word that means the same thing as* halt. *I will put that word in place of* halt *and see if the sentence still makes sense.*

*What synonym for* halt *is in the last sentence of paragraph 3?* (stop) *So what does* halt *mean?* (stop)

DETERMINING WORD MEANINGS

Guided Instruction

**WORDS TO KNOW**
**barrier**
**levee**
**system**

To determine the **meaning of a word,** readers can use context clues located in the same sentence as the word or in nearby sentences.

**CITE EVIDENCE**

**A** **Inference** clues help you figure out the **meaning of an unknown word**. By using the text, readers can infer—or figure out—what a word means. Circle the word *submerged* in paragraph 2. Underline the nearby words that help you figure out its meaning.

**B** **Synonyms** are words that have the same or similar meanings, such as *big/large*. Sometimes synonyms can be context clues. Circle the word *halt* and its synonym in the last sentence of paragraph 3. Why are synonyms often good context clues?

# Water Everywhere

(Genre: Explanatory Text)

1 The worst flood in the United States took place in 1993. It is known as "The Great Flood of 1993." It rained for five months, causing the Mississippi and Missouri rivers to overflow. This extra water resulted in flooding across nine states.

### Too Much Rain

2 **Levees** stand along the sides of the rivers and keep the river water from going into nearby towns. This time, there was too much rain. Water went over the first **barrier** on June 7. Seventy-five towns were soon submerged. Garbage, bridge parts, and lumber floated on the river. The river water even lifted entire houses.

### Floods in the Future

3 We can protect ourselves from floods. Better levees can be built to hold back floodwaters. Rainfall can be measured by taking pictures from space. A flood warning **system** is also important. It can send an alert to people to leave their homes. Human beings can't stop the rain, but we may be able to halt its flow.

90 Chapter 4 ■ Craft and Structure: Informational Texts

## Words to Know

**General Academic Vocabulary**

**barrier** (*noun*): something that gets in the way of or stops something else

**system** (*noun*): a group of things that work together for the same purpose

**Domain-Specific Vocabulary**

**levee** (*noun*): land along a river that is built up higher than the water to prevent flooding

**Working with Word Meaning** Encourage students to rephrase the definitions, putting them in their own words.

## CRAFT AND STRUCTURE

4 Flooding is a big problem in places that are below sea level. The Netherlands is a country in Europe. That country has been dealing with floods for a long time. And people there have some new ideas.

### Fighting Floods

5 In the Netherlands, the Dutch fight floods by letting some water in. As sea levels rise, levees and other barriers do not work as well. So the Dutch government created a flood zone. Floodwaters can spill there. No one is hurt. No property is damaged.

6 In the United States, during Hurricane Katrina in 2005, the levees around New Orleans failed. The city was badly flooded. New levees kept the city mostly dry during Hurricane Isaac in 2012, but other areas were swamped. It may not be possible to protect everyone with levees. The East Coast also experienced massive flooding in 2012 during Hurricane Sandy. Now some people there are wondering if they should create flood zones as people have done in the Netherlands.

#### Guided Instruction

**CITE EVIDENCE**

**C Restatement** occurs when a text restates what a word means—similar to a definition. Sentence 3 in paragraph 5 includes the term *flood zone*. Underline the restatement that helps you figure out the meaning of *flood zone*. How does the restatement help you?

**D Antonyms** are words that are opposite in meaning, like *glad/sad*. Sometimes antonyms can be used as context clues. Circle the word *swamped* and its antonym in paragraph 6.

**Comprehension Check**

How does determining the meaning of *flood zone* help you understand solutions to flooding? Give specific examples.

## Guided Instruction

**CITE EVIDENCE**

**C** *I want to look after the term* flood zone *for some clues that tell what a flood zone is.*

*What sentences restate the meaning of* flood zone? ("Floodwaters can spill there. . . . No property is damaged") *Based on the restatement, what is a* flood zone? (an area where flood waters can flow without damage to people or property)

**D** *I'm looking for a word that is opposite in meaning from* swamped. *The text says that "New levees kept the city mostly dry . . . but other areas were swamped." I think this is a clue, because* dry *and* swamped *are set up as opposites.*

*What word in paragraph 6 is an antonym of* swamped? (dry) *What does* swamped *mean?* (flooded)

**Comprehension Check**

**Sample Answer:** Understanding the meaning of *flood zone* helps me understand the solution the people in the Netherlands have created to deal with their flooding problem.

**Answer Explanation:** Students should realize that the text says that a flood zone is a place where floodwater can go without hurting anyone or damaging any property. It follows that this is a good solution for places that have many floods, because flood zones can keep floodwaters away from places where people live.

### Support English Language Learners

Students who are learning English are going to encounter many more unknown words in this passage than are native speakers. If English language learners speak a Romance first language, i.e., one with roots in Latin such as Spanish or French, they can look for cognates. A cognate is a word in one language that is similar in form and meaning to a word in another language.

For native Spanish speakers, some cognates that students might find include: *important/importante, completely/completamente, disaster/desastre*. Native French speakers might also recognize *debris/débris*.

## Guided Practice

### Recap Reading Selection

Let students know that they will read more about floods. Review what they read about the Great Flood of 1993, Hurricane Katrina, and the idea of using flood zones as a way to keep flooding away from people and property.

### Read and Practice

Have partners take turns reading the selection as you circulate to provide support. Model practicing determining word meanings with Cite Evidence callout A. For callout B, circulate and provide partners with scaffolding as needed. You might use the following suggestions to help students who are having difficulty.

**CITE EVIDENCE**

**A** Point out the clues in the text that can help students determine what *dampness* means. It is something "left behind by water," and it "causes mold to grow." Suggest that this sounds like a bathroom after a shower. This may help them understand that *dampness* means "a slight wetness."

**B** Help students see that *strike* and *hit* are used in the same way in the first two sentences of paragraph 9. *Hit* is a synonym for *strike*, and both words describe the action of a flood on a place.

## DETERMINING WORD MEANINGS

### Guided Practice

**WORDS TO KNOW**
**debris**
**disaster**

**CITE EVIDENCE**

**A** Underline the words in paragraph 7 that help you determine what the word *dampness* means.

**B** Read paragraph 8. Circle the text that helps explain the word *assistance*. In paragraph 9, underline the context clue that helps you figure out what the word *strike* means.

**Water Everywhere** *continued*

#### Flood and Funds

7 Floods are expensive. Floodwater is powerful, lifting buildings off the ground and sending cars sailing. Floodwater is also dirty. When the water drains away from buildings, mud and other **debris** are left behind. The dirty water can ruin furniture, electrical appliances, and other household items. Dampness left behind by water causes mold to grow, and wood and other building materials can be ruined by water. Even a few inches of water can mean thousands of dollars in cleaning and repairs. Many buildings cannot be repaired.

8 A major flood can cost billions of dollars. After Hurricane Sandy, some neighborhoods were completely destroyed. New York City subway tunnels were underwater. That flood was a **disaster**, and many people needed assistance. Government workers rescued those who were stranded. They provided food and water. The government also gave people money to fix their homes and businesses.

#### Finding Solutions

9 Floods can strike almost anywhere. But they tend to hit the same places over and over. Low-lying places near water are at the greatest risk. People build homes where there may be floods. When a flood hits, they may get money from the government to rebuild. Sometimes they rebuild in the same spot.





### Words to Know

**General Academic Vocabulary**
**disaster** (*noun*): a terrible event that destroys things or harms people

**Domain-Specific Vocabulary**
**debris** (*noun*): small scattered pieces left over when something has been destroyed

**Working with Word Meaning** Encourage students to draw images that help them remember these words. In this case, because the words are related, students could draw a single image titled "Disaster" with a label for the debris.

## CRAFT AND STRUCTURE

### Guided Practice

10 Some say these owners should be allowed to rebuild where they want. It's their home. Others say that when government pays, everyone pays. They think the owners should not be allowed to rebuild in the same place. What do you think?

**Comprehension Check**

1. Circle the letter next to the word that helps you figure out the meaning of *appliances* in paragraph 7.

   a. dirty

   b. ruin

   c. furniture

   (d.) electrical

2. Circle the letter next to the word that is a synonym of *provided* in paragraph 8.

   a. rescued

   b. stranded

   (c.) gave

   d. fix

3. Work with a partner to determine the meanings of unknown words on pages 92–93. Why is it important to know what the words mean in order to understand information in the passage?

   Sample answer: It's important to know what words in the text mean so that the reader won't miss any details and will completely understand the topic.





## Foundational Skills: Fluency

Explain to students that they can read more fluently if they pay attention to punctuation marks—for example, pausing at periods and raising intonation at question marks. Model fluent reading for the section "Finding Solutions" on page 92 in the Student Book.

Give students a chance to practice fluent reading with a partner. They may also want to record themselves reading the selection so that they can play it back and listen to their own phrasing for improving prosodic skills. Additional fluency passages and activities can be found at **sadlierconnect.com**.

## Guided Practice

**Comprehension Check**

**Answer Explanations:**

**1.** Choice D, *electrical*, is a clue to the meaning of *appliances* because it is the adjective that describes the noun.

**2.** Choice C, *gave*, is a synonym for *provided*. The text would also make sense if you used *gave* in place of *provided* in sentence 5.

**3.** Have students use context clues to determine the meanings of the boldface words on page 152. They can use inferencing, synonyms, antonyms, or restatements. Students should understand that if they do not know what a word in the passage means, they might miss an important piece of information.

## Peer Collaboration

You might have students work in pairs so that peers can support each other in responding to callouts A and B on page 92 and Comprehension Check questions 1 and 2 on page 93.

Ask students to finalize their answers and then share them with a partner. Students should then make changes to their answers based on the discussion with their partner. Finally, ask pairs to report their answers to the whole group.

## Independent Practice

### Recap Reading Selection

Remind students that they have been reading about floods and flooding. Have them recall the kind of damage that floods do (ruining things and leaving them dirty and moldy) and a possible solution (creating a flood zone, so the water can go someplace that will not cause damage).

### Read and Apply

Have students read the selection independently as you circulate. If you notice students struggling, you can provide support with the suggestions that follow.

#### CITE EVIDENCE

**A** Help students see that the word *safe* is the opposite of the word *treacherous*, so *treacherous* clearly means something like "dangerous."

**B** The word *leave* is a synonym for *evacuate*. Students can check this by using the word *leave* twice: "If you are asked to *leave*, *leave* as quickly as you can." Since this substitution does make sense, the two words are synonyms.

Students should see that the synonyms and antonyms on the page help the reader understand the text better by giving clues to the meanings of unknown words.



**Independent Practice**

**WORDS TO KNOW**
**absorb**
**contaminated**
**snowmelt**

**CITE EVIDENCE**

**A** Circle an antonym that helps you determine the meaning of the word *treacherous* in the first sentence of paragraph 13.

**B** In paragraph 13, bullet point 3, underline a synonym for *evacuate*. How did these synonyms and antonyms help you understand this section on flood safety?

**Water Everywhere** *continued*

### What Causes Floods?

11 Floods are caused by storms and heavy rain. But other conditions cause flooding as well. Melting snow can turn into gallons of water. **Snowmelt** can flow downhill and fill rivers and streams. When they get too full, they overflow. Wildfires can also lead to flooding. Fire burns away the trees and other plants that **absorb** water. Without plants to soak up the water, floodwaters take longer to go down.

12 Finally, dam failures also cause floods. Dams control the flow of rivers. They can create lakes that we use for fun or to supply us with drinking water. Dams can also turn the flow of water into a source of electrical power. But if a dam fails, all that water rushes out, crushing everything in its path. The floodwater from a dam break is like a tidal wave because the water moves with great force. A dam failure was the cause of the tragic Johnstown flood in Pennsylvania. It happened in 1889 after heavy rains. More than 2,200 people died.

### Flood Safety

13 Floods can be treacherous. Take steps to stay safe.

- Listen to the weather forecast if you are at risk. A flood watch means a flood is possible. A flood warning means flooding has begun.
- Unplug electrical appliances.
- If you are asked to evacuate, leave as quickly as you can. Keep a bag packed with essential items that you can grab fast.
- Do not try to walk through moving water. It can knock you down. And floodwater can be **contaminated** with waste.





### Words to Know

**General Academic Vocabulary**
**absorb** (*verb*): to soak in or soak up
**contaminated** (*adjective*): unclean or harmful

**Domain-Specific Vocabulary**
**snowmelt** (*noun*): the water created when snow melts

**Working with Word Meaning** Help students remember the vocabulary words by asking them to give an example and nonexample of each word's meaning.

# CRAFT AND STRUCTURE

## Independent Practice

14 After a flood you may need to boil water to make it safe to drink. Be sure electrical appliances are completely dry before you use them. Watch out for snakes or other creatures that might have floated into your home. Floods are the most common natural disaster. So stay safe!

### Comprehension Check

MORE ONLINE sadlierconnect.com

1. Circle the letter next to the word in paragraph 13 that helps you figure out the meaning of the word *contaminated*.

   a. float

   (b.) waste

   c. water

   d. flood

2. Circle the letter next to the words in paragraph 11 that help you determine the meaning of the word *overflow*.

   (a.) get too full

   b. gallons of water

   c. flow downhill

   d. fill rivers and streams

3. The section "What Causes Floods?" discusses the conditions that bring about flooding. What context clues tell you the meaning of *conditions* in paragraph 11? How does knowing the meaning of the word help you understand this section?

   Sample answer: "Floods are caused by storms and heavy rain" followed by "other" and "cause flooding as well" help me understand that *conditions* means "things that cause something else." The meaning helps me understand the things that cause flooding.





## Extend Thinking: Create

Help students extend their thinking by doing a short creative project. Have groups of students make a public service advertisement for a public solution to flooding. They could advocate for flood zones, more levees, or other, more fanciful solutions that they imagine.

Students should create a visual to represent the flood-control solution and then present their solution to the rest of the class.

Speakers should speak clearly, in complete sentences, and at a reasonable rate. Listeners should pay attention and ask questions to check their understanding.

## Independent Practice

### Comprehension Check

**Answer Explanations:**

1. Choice B, *waste*, should help students figure out that *contaminated* means "unclean."
2. Choice A, the phrase *get too full*, shows the cause of overflow and gives a clue to that word's meaning.
3. The first sentence in paragraph 11 says that "floods are caused by storms and heavy rain," and the second sentence says that "other conditions cause flooding as well." This means that storms and heavy rain are also conditions, which leads to the conclusion that *conditions* are things or situations that can cause flooding.

## Critical Comprehension

Use the following questions to help students think more deeply about the text. Students should be prepared to support their answers with evidence from the text.

- *Why are some parts of the U.S. at greater risk of flooding than others?* (Areas close to or below sea level or near the coastlines are at greater risk.)
- *How can people lower their chances of losing their home to a flood?* (ask the local government to put more flood-control measures in place; build their homes away from low-lying areas; build their homes on posts)

### Assess and Respond

**If** students have difficulty answering the questions in the Comprehension Check...

**Then** create a reading group to review the selections, summarizing each section as you go and modeling the skills that had been practiced independently.

## Guided Instruction

**OBJECTIVE**
**Use text features and search tools to locate information in a text.**

### Genre: Journal Article

A journal article is a form of writing that explains a topic. It often includes photographs and other features that offer additional information to the reader. A journal article might appear in print or online.

### Set the Purpose

To activate students' prior knowledge about the reading skill, ask *What does it mean if you see words in an article that look different from other words? Why might some text be in a box?*

### Model and Teach

Read the selection as students follow along in their books.

#### CITE EVIDENCE

**A** *I know that a hyperlink might be set in a different color or with underlining to show that it can be clicked on.*

*What is the hyperlink in paragraph 1?* (www.weather.gov) *What word in the link tells you what kind of information is on this site?* (weather)

**B** *I will look for a subhead on a line by itself. What is the subhead on this page?* (Twirling Tornadoes) *Based on the subhead, what do you predict you will learn about in this section of the passage?* (tornadoes)

USING TEXT FEATURES

Guided Instruction

**WORDS TO KNOW**
**atmosphere**
**destroy**

**Text features** and **search tools** help readers locate **information.**

**CITE EVIDENCE**

**A** A **hyperlink** is a search tool that is used to find **information** on the Internet. The words in the link tell what information can be found there when you click on it. Circle the hyperlink in paragraph 1. Underline the word that tells what information you might find when you click on it.

**B** A **subhead** is a title within a selection. This text feature introduces a specific part of a reading passage. Subheads are included on a separate line above the part of the passage they introduce. Put a star next to the subhead on this page. What might you learn in this section?

## Watch Out for Weather!

(Genre: Journal Article)

1 Tornadoes, hurricanes, and blizzards are all extreme weather events. They are often called natural disasters. Scientists at the National Weather Service (**www.weather.gov**) watch and study weather. They warn people when a dangerous storm is on its way. Each year, the National Weather Service sends out 50,000 warnings for extreme weather events. The warnings give people time to prepare for storms and protect themselves.

### Twirling Tornadoes ★

2 *Twister, funnel,* and *whirlwind* are all nicknames for one dangerous weather event: a tornado. Tornadoes develop from thunderstorms. Before a tornado appears, warm air near the ground meets cold air higher in the **atmosphere.** The two masses of air push against each other in a circular motion. Then they form a funnel of water droplets. If the funnel touches the ground, the storm is a tornado. Winds inside a tornado may reach 200 miles per hour. The funnel picks up dust and dirt in its path. It can even uproot trees and pick up cars. One big tornado picked up a train. It carried the train in the air for 80 feet. All the passengers were still inside!





### Words to Know

**General Academic Vocabulary**
**destroy** (*verb*): to completely break or ruin something, leaving nothing but scattered pieces

**Domain-Specific Vocabulary**
**atmosphere** (*noun*): the layer of air that surrounds a planet

**Working with Word Meaning** Have students make flash cards of the two words. The word and a picture that represents the word should be on one side of the card. On the other side should be a word they associate with the vocabulary word and a sentence using the word. Have students use the cards to help them remember the meanings of the words.

# CRAFT AND STRUCTURE

## Guided Instruction

3 Tornado funnels can be a mile wide. Most of them do not stay on the ground for long. Still, they do a lot of damage. Tornadoes can **destroy** everything in their paths. Hospitals, schools, and homes may be completely ruined. Because they twist and turn as they race across the ground, tornadoes may destroy one house and leave the next one untouched.

4 Sometimes a tornado travels over water. It forms a waterspout. It picks up water and fish along the way. Some fish have been carried hundreds of miles in water spouts.

**TORNADO ALERT!**

People may be injured or killed by objects tossed by the funnel. That is why it is important to know what to do when a tornado approaches.

- Stay inside.
- Go to the basement or ground floor.
- ★ Stay away from windows.
- Get under a table or stairs that can protect you from falling objects.

**Comprehension Check**

How does each text feature in this passage improve your understanding of tornadoes?

**CITE EVIDENCE**

**C** A **sidebar** is a text feature that provides extra information about the topic of an article. Circle the "Tornado Alert!" sidebar.

**D** A **bulleted list** is a text feature that organizes information. A bullet is a small circle. Each bullet introduces a fact or piece of information. Put a star next to a bulleted piece of information about staying safe during a tornado. What else do you learn from this list?





## Digital Connection: Hyperlinks

Let students know that when they are reading an article online it may sometimes be difficult to identify a hyperlink. However, if they put their cursor over a hyperlink, the cursor will change from an arrow into a pointing finger.

Challenge students to go to the National Weather Service Website, by typing in the address in the hyperlink on page 96 (www.weather.gov). Have them look for another hyperlink at that site and click through. Ask students to a make a list or a branch diagram of the web pages they visited and what they learned on each one.

## Guided Instruction

### CITE EVIDENCE

**C** *I know that a sidebar is not part of the main text. I will look for something that seems to be set apart from the text.*

*What is the title of the sidebar on this page?* (Tornado Alert!) *What do you predict this sidebar will be about?* (knowing what to do in case of a tornado)

**D** *Bullets are small circles or dots, so I will look for a list with dots in front of them. Where is the bulleted list on the page?* (in the sidebar) *How many safety tips are in the list?* (four)

### Comprehension Check

**Sample Answer:** The hyperlink gives me more information about weather. The subhead helps me find the part of the article that is just about tornadoes. The sidebar gives me extra information about what to do in case of a tornado.

**Answer Explanation:** Students should understand that the various text features help the reader locate more information about the topic of the article.

### Listening and Viewing Skills

Reread paragraph 4 as students listen and look at the photograph. *What is the funnel of a tornado over water made of?* (water) *What else can get picked up when a tornado goes over water?* (fish, and possibly other things that are in the water)

### Review: Determine Word Meanings

Have students use the vocabulary strategies they learned earlier in the chapter to determine the meaning of an unfamiliar word. You might suggest the word *develop* (used with its synonym *appear*) in paragraph 2 on page 96.

## Guided Practice

### Recap Reading Selection

Have students recall what they have learned so far about tornadoes. They should understand that these are destructive storm clouds that rotate and reach down to the ground. Let students know that in this section they will read about hurricanes, another kind of storm.

### Read and Practice

Have partners take turns reading the selection as you circulate to provide support. Model finding text features with Cite Evidence callout A. For callout B, circulate and provide partners with scaffolding as needed. You might use the following to help students who are having difficulty.

#### CITE EVIDENCE

**A** By this point, students should be able to tell the difference between sidebar text and the article's main text. Guide students to look at the green sidebar labeled "Hurricane Facts." Ask them what kind of text feature appears in the sidebar. (a bulleted list)

**B** Remind students that a subhead is a text feature authors can use to organize information. Have students scan pages 98–99 for the subhead that mentions famous hurricanes.

**C** Help students think about what information might be located at the web page. Guide students to understand that the link will provide readers with additional information the author does not have room to provide.

## USING TEXT FEATURES

### Guided Practice

**WORDS TO KNOW**

**crew**
**predict**

**CITE EVIDENCE**

**A** Circle the text feature that gives you facts about hurricanes.

**B** Put a star next to the text feature that tells you that you will be reading about famous hurricanes.

**C** Underline the hyperlink. Why does the author include it?

**Watch Out for Weather!** *continued*

### Horrible Hurricanes

5 A hurricane can be as dangerous as a tornado. A hurricane is a storm that brings strong winds and heavy rain. Hurricanes begin as tropical storms near Earth's equator. They form over warm ocean waters. As the water becomes warmer, the winds become faster. Once wind speeds reach 75 miles per hour, the storm is a hurricane. The winds spin in a closed circle.

**HURRICANE FACTS**

- Hurricanes in the Pacific Ocean are usually called typhoons.
- Hurricanes in the Indian Ocean are usually called cyclones.
- When the eye of a hurricane passes overhead, the weather is sunny, calm, and quiet.
- Most hurricanes travel about 10–20 miles per hour.

### Too Much Wind

6 Scientists on the ground need to get information about a storm. Hurricane hunters fly right into storms to get the facts. They bravely go into the storm's eye through fierce winds. The eye is the hurricane's calmest part. There the plane's **crew** drops instruments into the air. The instruments check wind speed and temperature. Scientists on the ground study the information and use it to **predict** how serious the storm will be. It's also important to try to figure out in what direction the storm will travel. Scientists can't stop a hurricane. But they can warn people who might be in the path of a natural disaster. To see a video about hurricane hunters, visit https://oceantoday.noaa.gov/hurricanehunters/.

### Words to Know

**General Academic Vocabulary**

**crew** (*noun*): a team of people who work together, especially on board a ship or an airplane

**predict** (*verb*): to make an informed guess about something that has not happened yet

**Working with Word Meaning** Encourage students to use new vocabulary words in speaking and in writing. Ask students to use the words in discussions when appropriate. You might use a signal, such as finger snapping, to recognize when someone uses a vocabulary word.

### Famous Hurricanes ★

7 The Galveston hurricane hit Texas in 1900. Its highest winds reached 140 miles per hour. Hugo hit the Atlantic Coast in 1989. Its highest winds reached 160 miles per hour. Andrew hit Florida in 1992. Its highest winds reached 165 miles per hour. Katrina hit and destroyed much of New Orleans in 2005. Its highest winds reached 170 miles per hour.

#### Comprehension Check

1. Circle the letter next to the sentence that is NOT included in a sidebar text feature.
   - a. Hurricanes in the Indian Ocean are usually called cyclones.
   - b. Most hurricanes travel about 10–20 miles per hour.
   - c. When the eye of a hurricane passes overhead, the weather is sunny, calm, and quiet.
   - (d.) The Galveston hurricane hit Texas in 1900.

2. Circle the letter next to the text feature that a reader would use to see a video about hurricane hunters.
   - a. Too Much Wind
   - b. Hurricane Facts
   - (c.) https://oceantoday.noaa.gov/hurricanehunters/
   - d. Famous Hurricanes

3. With a partner, read and discuss the "Hurricane Facts" sidebar on page 98. Why does the author include this text feature? How does it help you understand "Horrible Hurricanes"?

   Sample answer: The sidebar adds extra important facts. It helps me understand the essay because it gives me more information.





## Supporting English Language Learners

Build background information for English language learners by telling them that larger hurricanes and tropical storms are given human names. *Hugo*, *Andrew*, and *Katrina* are all names given to storms. Over the course of a hurricane season, the storms are named in alphabetical order. If storms have names, people who work in weather-related fields can more easily talk about and distinguish them.

As students read the last paragraph on page 99, they should be able to read more fluently and with less confusion because they know that the proper names are the names of hurricanes, not people.

## Guided Practice

### Comprehension Check

**Answer Explanations:**

1. Choice D, the only fact about the Galveston hurricane, was not mentioned in the sidebar.
2. Students can see that the words *hurricane hunters* are in the hyperlink. Therefore, choice C is correct. They can also revisit the text at the bottom of page 98.
3. Students should understand that the sidebar gives additional information that is helpful for learning more about hurricanes.

## Reciprocal Teaching

Form groups of four, and assign one of the following roles to each group member: Summarizer, Questioner, Clarifier, and Predictor. In a group discussion, the Summarizers should say what they have learned so far about the topic of hurricanes. The Questioners should think of at least two questions to ask about the topic. The Clarifiers should answer those questions or identify where the answers could be found. The Predictors should say what they think they will learn about the topic in the next section. Call on different groups to share their ideas with the class.

## Independent Practice

### Recap Reading Selection

Have a short group discussion about what students have learned so far about tornadoes and hurricanes. Ask students if they remember how tornadoes and hurricanes form. (Tornadoes form when cold and warm air meet; hurricanes form when warm ocean water causes wind speed to increase.) Let them know they are next going to read about another kind of storm called a blizzard. Depending on where they live or have lived, students may not be familiar with this type of storm.

### Read and Apply

Have students read the selection independently as you circulate to provide support. As you circulate, provide students with targeted scaffolding as needed.

#### CITE EVIDENCE

**A** Remind students to scan the text for the words *Great Lakes*. Once they find the words, have them identify the subhead under which the information appears.

**B** Have students scan pages 100–101 for text features. If necessary, remind students what a bulleted list is. Guide them to identify the bulleted text in the sidebar on page 101.



## Independent Practice

**WORDS TO KNOW**

**dangerous**
**prairie**
**severe**

**CITE EVIDENCE**

**A** Under which subhead would you find information about blizzards in the Great Lakes area? Find that information and underline it.

**B** Underline the sentence in the text feature that states a fact about ground blizzards. What kind of text feature is inside the sidebar?

**Watch Out for Weather!** *continued*

### What Is a Blizzard?

8 A blizzard is usually any serious snowstorm with strong winds of at least 35 miles per hour. To count as a blizzard, there has to be a lot of wind. While blizzards often mean lots of snow, there are no rules about how low the temperature has to be or how much snow must fall—if any—for a storm to be called a blizzard. **Severe** blizzards make it impossible to see buildings or trees just a few yards away.

9 Blizzards can be very **dangerous**. Since it is so hard to see outside, it is dangerous to travel. People can even get lost walking around their own backyard. Also, being out in cold temperatures and strong winds can cause frostbite, or frozen fingers and toes. Before weather could be predicted, blizzards could happen with almost no warning, such as when temperatures were warm. For an example, go to the link about the "Children's Blizzard" that happened in the late 1800s. **(https://www.farmersalmanac.com schoolhouse-blizzard-23397)**

### Where and Why Do Blizzards Happen?

10 In North America, blizzards appear most in the **prairie** states, the Great Lakes, the northeastern United States, and Canada. Blizzards over the prairie happen when cold, dry northern air hits warm, wet southern air. In the Northeast, blizzards usually come from hurricanes moving down from the northern Atlantic Ocean. The poor Great Lakes area! It gets hit by both types of storms. This land is also affected by heavy lake snow and wind, which create even more chance of blizzards.





## Words to Know

**General Academic Vocabulary**

**dangerous** (*adjective*): able to cause harm

**severe** (*adjective*): harsh and strong

**Domain-Specific Vocabulary**

**prairie** (*noun*): a large, flat grassland area

**Working with Word Meaning** Have students write a weather forecast using the vocabulary words. Invite student volunteers to read their forecasts aloud.

# CRAFT AND STRUCTURE

## Independent Practice

### How to Prepare for a Blizzard

11 First, pay attention to the weather forecasts. Next, make sure you have flashlights, batteries, food, water, first aid supplies, and a backup heater in your home. Most importantly, stay inside!

**BLIZZARD FACTS**

- Some unusual blizzards bring no precipitation, or snow.
- Strong winds can pick up ground snow to create a "ground blizzard."
- The strength of a blizzard's wind is more important than the snowfall.

**Comprehension Check**

MORE ONLINE **sadlierconnect.com**

1. If you click the link mentioned in paragraph 9, you would expect to find information about
   - (a.) a blizzard that happened without warning.
   - b. children who played in the snow.
   - c. the importance of having flashlights, batteries, and food.
   - d. how farmers prepare for blizzards.

2. Circle the letter next to the sentence that is included in the sidebar.
   - a. What is a blizzard?
   - (b.) Some unusual blizzards bring no precipitation, or snow.
   - c. Where and why do blizzards happen?
   - d. Blizzards can be very dangerous.

3. Review the text features on pages 100–101. What did each text feature help you understand about blizzards? Cite text evidence to support your answer.

   Sample answer: The text features help me because they organize the passage and let me know what information is coming next, like "what" comes before "where" and "why." The facts give me information, like some blizzards have no snowfall.





## Foundational Skill Review: *R*-controlled Vowels

Review *r* controlled vowels with students by reminding them how the letter *r* after a vowel changes the sound of that vowel. Model how this sounds, using small words such as *car, her, stir, or,* and *fur.* Explain that students can use this knowledge when they sound out longer words, such as *blizzard, southern, temperature, dangerous, forecasts, batteries,* and *importantly.*

Additional phonics activities can be found in the *Foundational Skills Handbook* at **sadlierconnect.com**.

## Independent Practice

### Comprehension Check

**Answer Explanations:**

1. Based on the details in paragraph 9, students should understand that the link will give more information about the Children's Blizzard, which happened suddenly and without warning. Therefore, choice A is correct.
2. The sentence identified in choice B appears in the sidebar.
3. Students should identify subheads, sidebars, and hyperlinks. Students should understand text features help readers find information in a text.

### Critical Comprehension

Use the following questions to help students think more deeply about the text. Students should be prepared to support their answers with evidence from the text.

- *What safety precautions are common to the types of weather discussed in the article?* (Stay inside and keep emergency supplies handy.)
- *What do you think the author's purpose might have been in writing this article?* (to provide safety information to readers)

**Assess and Respond**

**If** students have trouble answering the questions in the Comprehension Check...

**Then** ask them some comprehension questions about the article to determine whether they understood what they read. If not, you may wish to form a reading group to support them.

## Guided Instruction

**OBJECTIVE**
**Distinguish personal and author's point of view.**

### Genre: Editorial

Explain that an author uses an editorial to take a position on an issue. In this editorial, the author expresses a point of view, or opinion, about the problem of droughts and what people can do about them.

### Set the Purpose

To activate students' thinking about the reading skill, ask *How has someone successfully persuaded you to think or do something?*

### Model and Teach

Read the selection as students follow along in their books.

**CITE EVIDENCE**

**A** *I am going to look in the first paragraph for words, such as* should *or* must. *These words are often used to express a point of view, or opinion.*

*What sentence in paragraph 1 states a point of view?* (the last sentence) *How do you know this is a point of view and not a fact?* (The ideas cannot be proven true or false, as facts can.)

**B** *I am going to look for facts that support the author's point of view that people must change their behavior. What text in paragraph 1 can be checked to see if it is true or false?* (the first three sentences)

## DISTINGUISHING POINTS OF VIEW

### Guided Instruction

**WORDS TO KNOW**
**condense**
**conserving**
**vapor**

The author's **point of view** is the author's opinion on a topic. The reader can agree or disagree with this point of view.

**CITE EVIDENCE**

**A** In an editorial, the author's **point of view** is directly and clearly stated. Underline the sentence in paragraph 1 that states the author's point of view.

**B** The purpose of an editorial is to persuade the reader to share the author's point of view. To do this, the author gives evidence to support the opinion. Circle each fact in paragraph 1 that supports the author's point of view.

# Stop the Droughts!

(Genre: Editorial)

1 Our state is currently in the middle of the third worst drought in history. Our land is drying up. Plants and animals are dying. People must change their behavior so that we can end this crisis soon.

2 Droughts happen when the earth is very dry. Because we depend on the water cycle to keep the earth wet, it's a problem when there is not enough rain. Things get worse when high temperatures dry out the land fast. Plants can't grow, and animals don't have enough to eat or drink. Without them, people have no food.

3 People can help lessen the effects of droughts by **conserving** water. We must always try to save water. Doing this before a problem arrives can help an area when it is hit by a drought. Here are a few things we can do to conserve water:

- Take shorter showers.
- Water lawns less often.
- Don't let faucets drip or run.

102 Chapter 4 ■ Craft and Structure: Informational Texts

### Words to Know

**General Academic Vocabulary**
**conserving** (*verb*): saving, or using carefully

**Domain-Specific Vocabulary**
**condense** (*verb*): to turn a gas into a liquid by cooling it
**vapor** (*noun*): the gaseous, invisible form of a liquid

**Working with Word Meaning** Help students retain the meaning of words they learn by asking them to think of examples and nonexamples for each word. Invite student volunteers to share them with the class.

# CRAFT AND STRUCTURE

4 It's essential to prepare for a drought. It's even more important to help keep droughts from coming in the first place. Earth is getting warmer. Cars and smokestacks burn fossil fuels, such as coal and oil. These fuels cause air pollution. The pollution traps heat in the atmosphere, affecting global climate.

5 We should care about global warming because higher temperatures help cause drought. In the water cycle, the sun causes water to evaporate into an invisible gas called water **vapor**. Cooler temperatures cause the vapor to **condense** and form rain. In an unusually hot area, the clouds take the water away. The water condenses and falls where the air is cooler. That is why droughts are worse in hotter areas.

## Rules for Saving Water

6 Water conservation is more important than ever in places with low rainfall. The American Southwest has been suffering from major droughts for years. Many places have water restrictions that affect how often people can water gardens or fill their swimming pools.

7 Restrictions help save water for more important things, such as for drinking! Water conservation saves water for growing crops.

### Comprehension Check

What two weather-related reasons does the author give for drought? What is the author's point of view about the responsibility that people have to limit the effects of droughts? Cite text evidence in your answer.

### Guided Instruction

**CITE EVIDENCE**

**C** Often, an editorial asks the reader to take action. Underline the two sentences in paragraph 4 that tell the reader what he or she should do.

**D** Sometimes an author states opinions related to the main opinion. Circle the sentence that tells how the author feels about global warming. What information supports this point of view?

**Water Cycle**

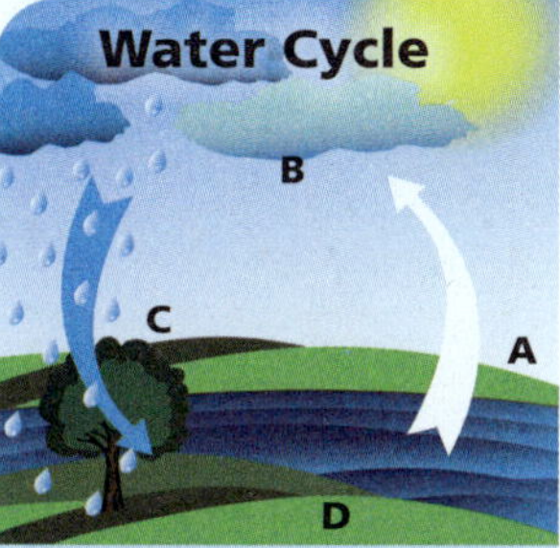


**A** Evaporation—Sun turns water into steam.

**B** Condensation—Steam turns into liquid.

**C** Precipitation—Rain or snow falls.

**D** Collection—Water gathers in the ground or ocean.





## Guided Instruction

### CITE EVIDENCE

**C** *I know that when authors are trying to persuade readers to take action, they often use phrases such as "it is necessary to," "it is important to," and "people must." I will look in paragraph 4 for phrases like these.*

*What action is the author asking readers to take?* (to prepare for a drought; to keep droughts from occurring in the first place)

**D** *I will look for some of the words that I know authors use when giving an opinion or point of view.*

*What word in paragraph 5 gives a clue that the author is giving his point of view, or opinion?* (should)

### Comprehension Check

**Sample Answer:** The author says that drought is caused by lack of rain and high temperatures. People need to conserve water and to help lessen the effects of drought.

**Answer Explanation:** Students should understand that the author's point of view is that people need to take action against global warming and conserve water so we can have enough water to drink, use, and grow food.

## Review: Using Text Features

Bring students' attention to the Water Cycle diagram on page 103. Ask students to identify the type of text feature (a sidebar) and its purpose (to illustrate the water cycle). Challenge students to tell you the best time to stop and read this text feature (before or after "Rules for Saving Water").

## Support English Language Learners

Help English language learners with the spelling pattern *gh*. Review the sounds this letter combination can make—an *f* sound and no sound. Point out the selection words *enough* and *drought* as examples. Work with students to fill in a two-column chart with words in which the *gh* sounds like *f* (*cough*, *tough*, *rough*, *laugh*, *paragraph*) and those in which the *gh* is silent (*thought*, *bought*, *caught*, *fought*, *daughter*, *taught*, *night*, *fight*, *sight*, *right*, *light*, *high*).

## Guided Practice

### Recap Reading Selection

Have students recall what they have learned so far about droughts. They should be able to say that droughts happen when not enough rain falls in a place. They should be able to say that higher temperatures can worsen the effects of droughts. Students should also remember that people can help during a drought by using less water.

### Read and Practice

Have partners take turns reading the selection as you circulate to provide support. Model practicing distinguishing points of view with Cite Evidence callout A. For callout B, circulate and provide partners with scaffolding as needed. You might use the following to help students who are having difficulty.

#### CITE EVIDENCE

**A** Point out the last three sentences of paragraph 8. Ask students, *According to the author, why should someone care about drought if that person is not living in an area affected by drought?* (The price of food goes up for everyone.)

**B** Students should realize that causing thousands of deaths is devastating, as are famine and the loss of crops around the world.



Guided Practice



**WORDS TO KNOW**

**adapted**
**devastating**

**CITE EVIDENCE**

**A** What does the author think you should care about in paragraph 8? Circle that piece of information.

**B** Put a star next to the evidence that the author gives in paragraph 9 to show that droughts are devastating. Explain to a partner why you do or do not share the author's point of view.

### Drought and Famine Hurt Us All

8 Severe droughts are happening around the world. During a severe drought, the rainfall for the year remains less than average. If this goes on for years, reservoirs begin to dry up. Reservoirs are natural or human-made lakes that hold our drinking water. The plants and farm animals can die from thirst when this happens. There may not be a drought where you are, but you can be still affected. Drought can kill crops. Then the price of food goes up for everyone.

9 In places like East Africa, droughts can be **devastating**. The drought there has caused thousands of people to ★ die. In places with a lot of poverty, people cannot afford to pay higher food prices. So they eat less or go hungry. When this happens to many people at once, it is called a famine. Droughts are affecting crops around the world. So other countries have less to share to help people affected by famine.

10 Another place that is experiencing drought is the Amazon rainforest. The rainforests in Brazil are going through a "megadrought." That means that before they could recover from the last drought, another drought struck. The living things in the rainforest have **adapted** to a wet environment. They suffer when it is too dry. Many of the plants and animals are not found anyplace else. And this is bad news for us. Some of the plants in the Amazon are used to make important medicines.





### Words to Know

**General Academic Vocabulary**

**devastating** (*adjective*): terrible in a way that causes a great deal of damage

**Domain-Specific Vocabulary**

**adapted** (*verb*): changed in a way that makes it easier to survive in a certain place

**Working with Word Meaning** Challenge students to use the new vocabulary terms in a short story about an animal that survives by changing in a new environment.

# CRAFT AND STRUCTURE

## Guided Practice

11 So even if there is plenty of rain where you live, there are still a lot of reasons to be concerned. Your source of food may depend on rain in other parts of the country or the world. Many thousands of lives depend on rain. Plants and animals that don't live anyplace else depend on it. Conserving water is an important issue we should all care about!

### Comprehension Check

1. Circle the letter next to the word that best describes how the author feels about droughts.
   a. hopeful
   b. angry
   (c.) worried
   d. sad

2. Circle the letter next to the reason that the author gives for thinking you might not care about droughts.
   a. You think food is too expensive.
   (b.) You do not live in an area with drought.
   c. You have never been to Africa.
   d. You think the rainforests have enough rain.

3. The author gives many reasons to care about droughts. With a partner, discuss which reasons you think are best at making you share his point of view. Why are these reasons so effective?

Sample answer: Droughts are killing many people through famine. The Amazon rainforest is in trouble. These are effective reasons because they show that droughts are a serious problem that we need to do something about.





## Discussion Skills

Remind students that when they are having discussions, they should listen carefully to each other's ideas and try to add on to them. This makes discussions more interesting and productive rather than each participant only introducing new ideas.

Give students some sentence stems to help scaffold a discussion that builds on ideas.

- *What you said makes me wonder if . . .*
- *That comment makes me think that . . .*
- *That thought reminds me of . . .*

## Guided Practice

### Comprehension Check

**Answer Explanations:**

1. Choice C, *worried*, is the best answer because the author is writing about a serious problem and calling the reader to action.
2. Choice B is supported by text in paragraph 8: "There may not be a drought where you are, but you can still be affected."
3. Students should articulate at least two reasons and explain why they were effective. Students should suggest that the author's discussion of famine, crop failure, water shortages, and the deaths of plants and animals are all reasons for everyone to care about drought.

### Turn and Talk

Another way to engage students in a comprehension review is to give them a chance to discuss their answers with a peer. Have students take turns sharing their answers with a partner. Then give them a chance to change or add to their answers based on anything they learned in the discussion. You might wish to have students record the ideas they heard from their partner in order to effectively practice listening skills.

## Independent Practice

### Recap Reading Selection

Remind students that they have been reading about droughts. Ask students to summarize what they have learned so far. They should recall that droughts can cause famines in places where crops fail and people cannot afford to buy more expensive food.

### Read and Apply

Have students read the selection independently as you circulate to provide support. As you circulate, provide students with targeted scaffolding as needed.

### CITE EVIDENCE

**A** Guide students to see that the last sentence of paragraph 12 states what the author thinks is the worst part about droughts: "droughts will happen more often."

**B** Students should understand after reading paragraph 13 that water is not always present in adequate amounts where it is needed most. Help them understand that the author recommends conserving water and using less energy as a way of lessening the effects of droughts.

DISTINGUISHING POINTS OF VIEW

Independent Practice

**WORDS TO KNOW**
continent
precious
wildfire

**CITE EVIDENCE**

**A** What does the author think is the worst thing about droughts? Put a star next to that sentence in paragraph 12.

**B** If there is the same amount of water in the world, why is the author worried? Underline the reason in paragraph 13. How does the author feel we should deal with droughts?

**Stop the Droughts!** *continued*

12 Drought is a problem that is happening around the world. Every **continent** is affected by it. In some places, people have to live with water restrictions. They can't water their lawns or wash their cars. In other places, food crops are dying because droughts are drying out the land. Droughts are causing famines and **wildfires**. The worst part is that★ scientists say droughts will happen more often.

13 The world has always had the same amount of water in it. The water we have evaporates into the sky and comes back down as rain. The water in your glass might be the same water that the dinosaurs drank. The problem is that the water isn't always where we need it. We need it in the places that people live and in places where food is grown. If some are wasting water, others may not have enough. So we have to be careful with our water supplies, conserve them, and keep them clean for ourselves and for all other living things on this planet. And because droughts are happening more often, we all need to pitch in and save our most **precious** resource.

14 By now, maybe you are serious about helping. Do you turn off the faucet while you brush your teeth? That could save gallons. Do you run tap water until it gets cold when you want a drink? That's a lot of clean water down the drain. Instead, fill a pitcher and put it in the refrigerator. Time yourself when you take a shower. The quicker you are, the more water you will save. But that's not all. We also need to use less energy to keep the planet from getting even hotter. Turn off the lights when you leave the room. Ride a bike. It's everyone's job to help the environment.



106 Chapter 4 ■ Craft and Structure: Informational Texts

## Words to Know

**General Academic Vocabulary**

**precious** (*adjective*): having great value

**Domain-Specific Vocabulary**

**continent** (*noun*): one of the seven large landmasses of the globe (North America, South America, Europe, Africa, Asia, Australia, Antarctica)

**wildfire** (*noun*): a fire that burns out of control, usually in forests and grasslands

**Working with Word Meaning** To help students retain the meanings of the new vocabulary, ask them to restate the definitions in their own words.

## CRAFT AND STRUCTURE

### Independent Practice

15 Remember, you can still be affected by a drought even if you live in an area with lots of rain. Remember also that by saving water at your home, you could be helping people who are experiencing drought somewhere else. Think of how amazing if would be if, through your actions, you could help people all over the world.

**Comprehension Check** MORE ONLINE **sadlierconnect.com**

1. Circle the letter next to a problem caused by droughts.

   a. famine

   b. wildfires

   c. restrictions

   (d.) all of the above

2. Circle the letter next to the BEST summary of the author's point of view.

   a. We should help the victims of famine and send them food.

   b. We should turn off the water when we brush our teeth.

   (c.) We should care about droughts and help deal with them.

   d. We should learn more about the history of water.

3. What should people be doing about droughts, in this author's point of view? List as many of the author's specific recommendations as you can.

   Sample answer: Conserve water by taking shorter showers; turn off the tap while brushing teeth; water lawns less often; don't run water waiting for it to get cold; care about droughts all over the world; conserve energy by turning off lights or riding a bike.





## Speaking and Listening Presentation

Have students create a presentation on an extreme weather topic in this chapter. Have students interview each other about the event they or their families experienced. Students should take turns presenting to the class. Presenters should:

- state their topic clearly, and present appropriate facts.
- use formal language, and choose words for effect.
- speak clearly, in complete sentences, and at a reasonable rate.

Elicit responses from students of different cultural backgrounds. Listeners should listen attentively and ask questions.

## Independent Practice

**Comprehension Check**

**Answer Explanations:**

1. Students should know that droughts cause famine, wildfires, and restrictions. Choice D is correct.
2. Choice C, *We should care about droughts and help deal with them*, is the best answer because it explains the main idea of the text.
3. The author's recommendations for dealing with droughts include turning water off while brushing teeth, using the refrigerator for cold water instead of running the tap, taking shorter showers, turning off chargers and lights, and riding a bike.

## Critical Comprehension

Use the following questions to help students think more deeply about the text. Students should be prepared to support their answers with evidence from the text.

- *Would the author have written this editorial if he or she had not experienced a drought? Why or why not?* (The author says that people who have not lived with drought tend not to care about it. He or she likely lives in a place with drought.)
- *What is the connection between drought and conserving water?* (People should conserve water so that they have enough during a drought.)

**Assess and Respond**

**If** students have difficulty answering the Comprehension Check…

**Then** ask them to tell you where they had the most difficulty: reading the text, finding information, or understanding questions. Provide assistance according to students' responses.

## Connect Across Texts: *4 points*
## Review Reading Selections

Put students into groups, giving each the responsibility to summarize one of the reading selections.

## Compare and Contrast Texts

Review the directions on page 108 with students. Instruct students to write the titles of their chosen selections in the outer parts of each circle.

**Venn Diagram Rubric**

| | |
|---|---|
| 4 | Student has identified two selections and recorded four or more characteristics in their proper places. |
| 3 | Student has identified two selections and recorded at least three characteristics in their proper places. |
| 2 | Student has identified two selections and recorded at least three characteristics but may have had trouble categorizing them properly. |
| 1 | Student has identified two selections and recorded at least one characteristic. |
| 0 | Student did not complete assignment or demonstrated no understanding of selections. |

## CONNECT ACROSS TEXTS

### Compare and Contrast Texts

In this chapter, you read about floods, tornadoes, hurricanes, blizzards, and droughts. Think about what you learned from these texts. Then choose two of the texts and compare and contrast them using the Venn diagram below. List key details and important points from the texts to show the similarities and differences between them. Be prepared to discuss your ideas with your class.

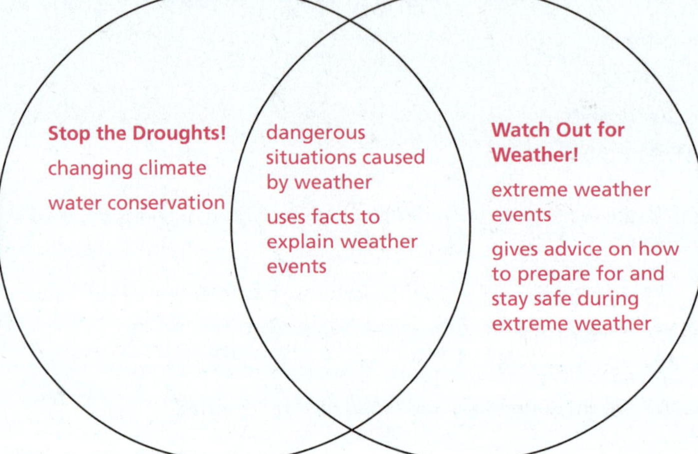






### Extend Thinking: Critical Response

Invite students to further examine the effects of drought. Point out that the text in the chapter called "Stop the Droughts!" explains that droughts can happen almost anywhere. Have students chose a region of the world to investigate when droughts have occurred there. When did the drought or droughts happen? What were the effects? How did the region help people affected by drought? Then have students share their findings with a partner.

## CONNECT ACROSS TEXTS

### Connect to the Essential Question

***How can authors present informational text effectively?*** In small groups or as a class, discuss the Essential Question. Think about what you have learned about word meanings, text features, and point of view. Use evidence from the chapter texts to answer the question.

Sample answer: Authors present informational text effectively by providing clues for word meaning, using text features to organize and explain information, and sharing their points of view to influence others. For example, all three texts use synonyms or restatements to help with comprehension. "Watch Out for Weather!" uses subheads and sidebars to organize information. And "Stop the Droughts!" uses a first-person point of view and "we" to influence readers.

### Connect to the Theme

***Extreme Weather*** In this chapter, you learned about various forms of extreme weather, what causes them, and the dangers they can present. Why is it important to know about these types of extreme weather? Support your answer with details from the texts.

Sample answer: It is important to learn about extreme weather events to help prevent them or to know how to stay safe in one. For example, there are ways to fight floods or lessen the effects of droughts. But, they can still happen, and so the texts explain it is important to stay safe. The texts also discuss staying safe during a tornado, hurricane, or blizzard.



**To strengthen your response, reread parts of the texts that support your answers. Add to your answers any additional details you find.**



## Assess and Respond (pages 108–109)

| If | Then |
|---|---|
| Students scored 0–2 points, they are **Developing** their understanding of the skills... | Provide students with reading support and more intensive modeling of skills. |
| Students scored 3–5 points, they are **Improving** their understanding of the skills... | Use students' scores to target areas that are weak, and review those specific skills. |
| Students scored 6–8 points, they are **Proficient** in their understanding of the skills... | Have these students move on. They are ready for the formal assessment. |

## Support Essential Question Discussion

Have students reread the Essential Question. Challenge them to finish this sentence. *Authors present informational text effectively when they . . .* If students have difficulty responding, prompt them by asking how context clues, text features, and support for the author's point of view help them understand informational text

## Theme Wrap-Up

Lead students in a group discussion on the theme of extreme weather. Talk about the different types of weather and the effects the weather has on people and Earth.

## Short-Answer Questions: *2 points each*

### Connect to the Essential Question Rubric

| | |
|---|---|
| 2 | Students are able to explain how authors present informational text effectively. |
| 1 | Students are able to explain some ways authors present informational text effectively. |
| 0 | Students do not identify ways in which authors present informational text effectively. |

### Connect to the Theme Rubric

| | |
|---|---|
| 2 | Students correctly identify different types of extreme weather discussed in the chapter, and the effects they have on people and Earth. |
| 1 | Students identify some types of extreme weather discussed in the chapter, and the effects they have on people and Earth. |
| 0 | Students are not able to identify types of extreme weather discussed in the chapter, or the effects they have on people and Earth. |

**OBJECTIVE**
**Determine the meanings of words with prefixes and suffixes.**

## Guided Instruction

Review the Guided Instruction section on page 110 with students. Be sure they understand that suffixes and prefixes are word parts that might be added to the beginning or to the end of a base word. Suffixes are added to the end, and prefixes are added to the beginning. By understanding the meaning of the base word and the suffix or prefix, they can understand the meaning of the new word.

## Guided Practice

If students are having trouble, help them work through the possibilities by trying the different suffix and prefix options in each blank and focusing on the meaning needed in the sentence. You might also have them do this exercise in small groups.

## Independent Practice

If students are having trouble writing new sentences using the words, have them check the meaning of the words in a dictionary.

## Apply to Reading

Have students return to "Water Everywhere" to go on a word hunt for words that contain these suffixes and prefixes: *pre-, re-, dis-, un-, -ful, -less.* They may find *powerful* (page 92, paragraph 7) and *rebuild* page 93, paragraph 9).

# LANGUAGE

### Prefixes and Suffixes

**Guided Instruction** **Prefixes** and **suffixes** are word parts that are added to a base word to change its meaning. A prefix is added to the beginning of a base word. A suffix is added to the end of a base word. The new word's meaning is connected to the base word's meaning.

Read this sentence: *The Dust Bowl was set off by a very long drought and unusually high temperatures.* In this sentence, the word *unusually* has a prefix in it. The prefix *un-* has been added to the beginning of the base word *usually*. The word's meaning has changed from *usually* (or "normally") to *unusually* ("not usually").

The chart shows common prefixes and suffixes and their meaning.

| **Prefix** | pre- | dis- | un- |
|---|---|---|---|
| **Meaning** | before | opposite of | not |
| **Suffix** | -er | -ful | -less |
| **Meaning** | one who | full of | without |

**Guided Practice** Add a prefix or suffix from the chart to change the base word's meaning so that each sentence below makes sense.

1. When the lights go out, having candles is very use __ful__.
2. Mia did not want to __dis__ obey her parents.
3. The factory smoke made an __un__ pleasant smell.

**Independent Practice** Each word below contains a prefix or a suffix. Write a separate sentence using each word.

**powerful** **rebuilt**

Sample answer: Powerful spring storms in the plains often include tornadoes.

Sample answer: After a tornado, a neighborhood may need to be rebuilt.

________________________________________

110 Chapter 4 ■ Craft and Structure: Informational Texts



## Support English Language Learners

Students whose first language is not English may have difficulty knowing what affixes make sense with various English words. Work with these students to complete the Guided Practice. Students should substitute each affix into the blank in the sentence and see if the resulting word

- sounds like a word they have heard in English.
- makes sense in the context of the sentence.

For each item, only one affix will complete the word to make sense in the sentence. Understanding suffix and prefix words often relies on memorization, so provide additional example sentences to go with each affix.

# CHAPTER 4 REVIEW

Read the following passage in which vocabulary words, text features, and the author's point of view appear. Then answer the questions on pages 111 and 112.

## Lightning Strikes!

(Genre: Magazine Article)

### Stay Safe

1 Lightning kills more people than hurricanes or tornadoes. If a storm is near, stay inside. If you are outside, try to find shelter. If you can't get inside a building, stay away from tall trees and open fields. If you want to learn more about lightning, try **https://www.weather.gov/safety/lightning.**

### Zapped

2 How many people are hit by lightning each year? Even experts are unsure. People can be killed by lightning strikes, but most survive. Those hit by lightning often have strange problems that doctors cannot explain. Symptoms include headaches, forgetfulness, and trouble sleeping. A survivors' group meets to share stories. It's good to meet others who understand.

**Fill in the circle of the correct answer choice.**

1. What phrase in paragraph 1 is a clue to the meaning of *shelter*?
   - ○ "it is unsafe"
   - ○ "tall trees and open fields"
   - ○ "during a storm"
   - ● "inside a building"

2. Another word for *symptoms* used in paragraph 2, line 4 is
   - ○ explain
   - ● problems
   - ○ strange
   - ○ strikes

3. The word *strange* in paragraph 2 means
   - ● not well understood
   - ○ cannot be cured
   - ○ not very serious
   - ○ made-up or fake





## Self-Assessment: Progress Check

Have students revisit the Progress Check on page 87 and respond to the questions again. Ask them to compare their Before and After responses.

You may wish to have students rate their answers on a scale of 0–2 rather than simply checking (or not checking) the box. Instruct them to write a zero if they feel they do not understand the given skill at all, a 1 if they feel they have some understanding, and a 2 if they feel they have a solid grasp of the skill.

## Chapter Summary

At this point, students have had instruction and practice in reading informational text, with a focus on learning about floods, storms, and droughts. Students have also learned different strategies for determining word meanings from textual clues, learned about text features, and learned to recognize the author's point of view. Students have practiced working with concepts across texts, and practiced working with suffixes and prefixes. They should be well prepared for the review section.

## Introduce the Review

Explain to students that they will read a new passage that is related to the chapter's theme and the selections they have already read. Instruct students to read the passage carefully and then answer the questions on pages 111 and 112.

### Answer Explanations

Scoring: Items 1–9 on pages 111–112 are worth 1 point each. See the rubric for guidance on scoring the Write About It question on page 112.

1. The text urges the reader to find shelter in a storm and then says, "If you can't get inside a building . . ." So the answer is the fourth choice, *inside a building*.
2. The text says that the symptoms include "headaches, forgetfulness, and trouble sleeping." These are problems that the survivors have, so the answer is the third choice, *problems*.
3. The word *strange* refers to something doctors can't explain, so the best answer is "not well understood."

### Answer Explanations

**4.** *Survivors* refers to people who lived after being struck by lightning, so the answer is "people who lived."

**5.** "Stay Safe" is the only subhead from the passage in the answer choices.

**6.** The hyperlink is located at the end of the first paragraph. "Sentence 5" is the correct answer.

**7.** The hyperlink includes the words "safety" and "lightning," so "how to stay safe" Is the correct answer.

**8.** The prefix *un-* means "not," so "not sure" is the correct meaning of *unsure*.

**9.** The author says, "It's good to meet others who understand," so the author's point of view is that the meeting is a good idea.

### Write About It Rubric

| | |
|---|---|
| 2 | Student states an opinion and gives logical reasons in support. |
| 1 | Student states an opinion and gives limited reasons in support. |
| 0 | Student does not state an opinion and/or does not give any reasons in support. |

## CHAPTER 4 REVIEW

**4.** In the last paragraph, *survivors* means

- ● people who lived
- ○ lightning that strikes
- ○ doctors who examine
- ○ groups that meet

**5.** Which phrase is a subhead in the passage?

- ○ Lightning Strikes!
- ○ Lightning kills more people . . . .
- ● Stay Safe
- ○ No one knows how many . . . .

**6.** The hyperlink given in the passage is in paragraph 1 in

- ○ sentence 1
- ○ sentence 4
- ○ sentence 3
- ● sentence 5

**7.** What information do you expect to learn by using the hyperlink?

- ○ what causes lightning
- ○ how often lightning occurs
- ● how to stay safe
- ○ how many people are struck

**8.** What is the meaning of *unsure* in paragraph 2?

- ○ one who is sure
- ● not sure
- ○ very sure
- ○ feeling sure

**9.** The author's point of view about the lightning survivors meeting is that

- ○ it is a bad idea.
- ● it is a good idea.
- ○ it is not necessary.
- ○ it is not helpful.

**Write About It** Do you agree with the author's point of view about the meeting of lightning survivors? Give reasons for your answer.

Sample answer: I agree because it helps to talk to people who know what you've gone through because they have, too.





### Analyze Student Scores

| | |
|---|---|
| **9–11 pts Strong** | Student has a good grasp of the skills and concepts taught in this chapter. Point out any mistakes the student has made, and explain the correct answers if necessary. |
| **4–8 pts Progressing** | Student is struggling with some skills or concepts. Identify the specific skills that are problematic to target a review of instruction. |
| **0–3 pts Emerging** | Student is having serious problems understanding the skills and concepts taught in this chapter. Student may need to redo the work with a higher level of support. |

# Integration of Knowledge and Ideas: Literary Texts

CHAPTER 5

Integration of Knowledge and Ideas

## Literary Texts

CHAPTER 5

**Focus on Reading** The characters in this chapter find themselves in new situations. Think about how the illustrations help you, and compare the stories.

**Think About Theme** Searching for answers may take you away on an adventure or it may mean you search inside yourself. You will read about both.

**Let's Get on Our Way!** You can search for answers in the text. You may find an answer by comparing multiple texts.

These are the skills you will build in this chapter. Before you begin, check the boxes on the left of any items you can do well now. At the end of the chapter, you will return to this page to use the check boxes on the right to show what you have learned.

Can I?

After Chapter 5

| Before | | After |
|---|---|---|
| ☐ | Explain how illustrations help you understand a story. | ☐ |
| ☐ | Compare and contrast the themes of stories with the same characters. | ☐ |
| ☐ | Compare and contrast the plots of stories with the same characters. | ☐ |
| ☐ | Compare and contrast the settings of stories with the same characters. | ☐ |
| ☐ | Use word roots to help find the meanings of words. | ☐ |



Chapter 5 ■ Integration of Knowledge and Ideas: Literary Texts

**Student Page 113**

## Progress Check

The Progress Check is a self-assessment feature that students can use to gauge their own progress. Research shows that when students take accountability for their own learning, their motivation increases.

Before students begin work in Chapter 5, have them check the boxes next to any item that they feel they can do well. Explain that it is fine if they don't check any of the boxes. They will have an opportunity to learn about and practice all of these items while studying the chapter. Let them know that near the end of the chapter they will have a chance to reconsider how well they can do each item on this list.

Before students begin the Chapter 5 Review on page 131, have them revisit this page. You can use this information to work with students on any items they don't understand before they tackle the Review.

## HOME ✦ CONNECT...

The Home Connect feature is a way to keep parents or other adult family members apprised of what their children are learning. The key learning objectives are listed, and some ideas for related activities and discussions are included.

Explain to students that they can share the Home Connect page with their parents or other adult family members in their home. Let students know how much time the class will be spending on this chapter so they can plan their time accordingly at home.

Encourage students and their parents to share their experiences using the suggestions on the Home Connect. You may wish to make a place to post some of this work.

### HOME ✦ CONNECT...

When students are able to combine what they read with what they see in **illustrations**, they are better able to understand the **characters, setting,** and **mood** of a text. As you are reading a story with illustrations, begin by having your child look at the illustrations and tell you what he or she is seeing. Then, read the text. Finally, ask your child about what he or she has seen and read and how the two go together.

Students enjoy reading a series of stories that feature the same characters. When characters are familiar, readers become interested in what will happen next in each story. In this chapter, your child will read two stories featuring the same brother and sister duo. Being able to **compare and contrast** each one of these stories is an important skill. As your child reads, ask him or her to pay attention to the details and themes in each story that are the same across texts and to look for ways in which each story is different.

**Activity:** With your child, use descriptions in a text to create illustrations. First, do a web search on well-known illustrators, and look at some of the illustrations they have created. Then, read a favorite text-only story to your child, and work together to create illustrations to go along with the words.

**IN THIS CHAPTER, YOUR CHILD WILL...**

- Use illustrations to help better understand the meaning of the words in a story.
- Learn how to compare and contrast the settings, plots, and themes of texts featuring the same characters.
- Use a known word (for example, *medium*) to help define a lesser-known word with the same root (such as *medieval*).
- Compare and contrast different texts featuring the same main characters: a mystery story and an adventure story.

**WAYS TO HELP YOUR CHILD**

The ability to compare and contrast situations, characters, and events is an extremely important skill. Help your child develop this skill by asking him or her leading questions, when appropriate. Read two different stories together, back-to-back, and ask your child to tell you how the stories are the same and how they are different. Have your child compare his or her two favorite movies or contrast one favorite sports team with another. Build the concept of comparing and contrasting into everyday conversations.

ONLINE

For more Home Connect activities, continue online at sadlierconnect.com



114 Chapter 5 ■ Integration of Knowledge and Ideas: Literary Texts

**Student Page 114**

## LEARNING PROGRESSIONS

In this chapter, students will learn how readers can make connections using the elements of literature. In order to learn the skills in this chapter, students will further develop skills learned in second grade. They should be encouraged to retain these skills, as they will continue to build on them in fourth grade.

| Connecting Illustrations and Text | |
|---|---|
| | • Second-grade students should have finished the year with the ability to use information from illustrations to build comprehension in literature.<br>• In third grade, students will continue to develop their skills in connecting specific elements of a text with the accompanying illustration.<br>• In grade 4, students will be using this knowledge to make connections between a specific text and a visual or oral presentation of that text. |

| Comparing and Contrasting Stories | |
|---|---|
| | • Proficient second graders should have learned how to compare and contrast two or more versions of the same story.<br>• In third grade, students will learn how to compare and contrast two stories written by the same author that feature the same or similar characters.<br>• This will prepare students for the task of comparing similar themes and events across texts they will encounter in fourth grade. |

CHAPTER 5

Integration of Knowledge and Ideas

Literary Texts

Essential Question
What connections can readers make?

Theme
Searching for Answers







**Essential Question:**
**What connections can readers make?**

In this chapter, students will learn how illustrations in a story can help convey subtle ideas related to character, setting, and plot. Students will also make connections by comparing these elements of fiction across two different texts featuring the same characters.

## Theme: Searching for Answers

Students will read selections based on two recurring main characters. They will read mystery and adventure stories in which the recurring characters work together to solve puzzles and unravel new ideas.

## Curriculum Connection: Language Arts

Students will read stories in which a brother and sister use their curiosity and powers of observation to solve mysteries and discover new things.

## Vocabulary Overview

### General Academic Vocabulary

abnormal 118, admiring 126, evidence 120, exploration 122, expression 116, healthy 120, investigate 118, observation 124, review 120

### Domain-Specific Vocabulary

cactus 117, endangered 124, environment 124, hammock 123, outskirts 123, vein 126, wildlife 126

## Guided Instruction

**OBJECTIVE**
**Use illustrations to help understand a story.**

### Genre: Mystery

Explain to students that a mystery story involves some kind of hidden question that the main characters have to answer.

### Set the Purpose

Help students understand the purpose for learning the reading skill by asking *Did you know that illustrations can be as important to a story as the words you read? What do you think you can learn about a story by looking closely at its illustrations?*

### Model and Teach

Read the selection as students follow along in their books.

**CITE EVIDENCE**

**A** *I see that there are three characters in the illustration that look like they are playing basketball.*

*Can you find the names of those three characters in paragraph 1?* (Sofia, Tino, and Ella)

**B** *When you identify the setting, you are looking for images and words that tell you where and when a story takes place. I see palm trees, cacti, and a basketball court in the illustration.*

*Where might you see palm trees and cacti?* (in a warm climate, the desert)

CONNECTING ILLUSTRATIONS AND TEXT

Guided Instruction

**WORDS TO KNOW**
**cactus**
**expression**

**Illustrations** are pictures of the characters, setting, and events in a story.

**CITE EVIDENCE**

**A** **Illustrations** can help you picture a story's action. Look at the illustration below. In the story, underline the names of the **characters** in the illustration.

**B** The **setting** is where a story takes place. In the illustration, circle any images that tell you about the setting. Where does the story take place?

## The Case of the Missing Fruit

(Genre: Mystery)

1 It was after lunch on Saturday, and Sofia and Tino were playing basketball. Their big sister, Ella, was home from college, and she was watching the children play while their parents were at work. Sofia was beating Tino by six points, and Tino was getting frustrated.

2 Sofia, on the other hand, was enjoying the game a little *too* much. "Hey, Tino, why did the chicken cross the road? To beat you at basketball!"

3 Tino started to get upset, and then he looked at Sofia's face. He had to laugh at her silly **expression**.

4 "Good one. But should you be clowning around when you are only winning by six points?"

5 "I don't know, hermano. Should I be?"

6 Before they could finish their game, a shout rang out from down the block.

7 "What was that?" Tino asked.

116 Chapter 5 ■ Integration of Knowledge and Ideas: Literary Texts



### Words to Know

**General Academic Vocabulary**
**expression** (*noun*): the look on a person's face

**Domain-Specific Vocabulary**
**cactus** (*noun*): a flowering plant able to live in dry regions, with fleshy stems and branches that bear scales or prickles instead of leaves

**Working with Word Meaning** Encourage students to pay attention to context clues when they encounter new words.

# INTEGRATION OF KNOWLEDGE AND IDEAS

8 "I don't know," said Sofia, "but it sounded like it came from Mrs. Moreno's house."

9 Suddenly, another shout pierced the air. The two children and Ella ran toward the sound.

10 When the children arrived at Mrs. Moreno's, she was standing in her backyard, wearing thick gloves, and carrying a metal bucket.

11 "Mrs. Moreno," Ella asked, "are you all right?"

12 "Oh, *niños*, children, I didn't mean to frighten you."

13 "What happened?" asked Sofia.

14 "I came out to pick the fruit from my prickly pear **cactus** plants. It's time for me to make my prickly pear jam for the Labor Day picnic. When I got here, all of the cacti were bare!"

15 Tino and Sofia gave each other a look. They knew they had to help Mrs. Moreno.

16 "When was the last time you noticed the fruit?" Tino asked.

17 "I came outside this morning, and saw that the prickly pear fruit was ready to harvest. After that, I had to run some errands. Then, I came home, made an early lunch, and took a short nap."

18 "Has anyone asked about your prickly pears lately?" Sofia asked.

### Comprehension Check

Illustrations can show you the mood of the characters in a story. Look at the picture of Mrs. Moreno. What is her mood? How can you tell?

## Guided Instruction

### CITE EVIDENCE

**C** Illustrations let you see new characters in a story. Look at the picture of Mrs. Moreno. Then, box the words in the story that match the picture.

**D** Illustrations can help the reader visualize unfamiliar things in a story. Circle in the text what Mrs. Moreno is looking at. Have you seen a prickly pear cactus before?

## Support English Language Learners

Illustrations can be a key element in helping English language learners understand more subtle elements of a story, such as mood and expression. With students who are learning English, introduce stories by using a modified version of the Picture Word Inductive Model. Before reading a text, have them brainstorm words to describe the illustrations that accompany the story. Have the students put those words into categories; for instance, "Setting" or "Characters." Then have students look for words that match their brainstorming session within the text itself.

## Guided Instruction

### CITE EVIDENCE

**C** *In paragraph 10, I see details about how Mrs. Moreno looks. The story talks about what Mrs. Moreno is wearing, what she is doing, and where she is standing.*

*Can you find the words that match the picture?* ("standing in her backyard, wearing thick gloves, and carrying a metal bucket")

**D** *I'm looking for the words on this page that describe Mrs. Moreno's prickly pear cactus. Look carefully in paragraph 14.*

*What does the text tell you about the cactus?* (It bears fruit that can be made into jam; the fruit is missing.)

### Comprehension Check

**Sample Answer:** In the picture, Mrs. Moreno looks like she is upset or worried. Her eyes look sad, and her hand is pointing at the cactus as if she doesn't understand what has happened.

**Answer Explanation:** Students should look for details in the illustration that help them understand Mrs. Moreno's mood. Direct students to look carefully at her facial expression as well as the way she is standing. Also, guide them to look carefully at where she is standing and what she is doing.

## Guided Practice

### Recap Reading Selection

Remind students that they have been reading a mystery story. Have students recall details about what has happened in the story so far. (Tino, Sofia, and their sister Ella are trying to solve a mystery about Mrs. Moreno's missing cactus fruit.) Have students make a prediction about what will happen next in the story.

### Read and Practice

Have partners take turns reading the selection as you circulate to provide support. Model analyzing illustrations with Cite Evidence callout A. For callout B, circulate and provide partners with scaffolding as needed. You might use the following suggestions to help students who are having difficulty.

### CITE EVIDENCE

**A** Remind students to pay close attention to the characters in the illustration to help follow the mystery. Remind them that even a character's clothing can help illustrate details in the story.

**B** Tell students that they should look carefully at the illustration and compare it to the last sentence in paragraph 19. Have students identify what is included in the illustration that is not mentioned in the text. (an empty bird feeder and birdseed)

## CONNECTING ILLUSTRATIONS AND TEXT

### Guided Practice

**WORDS TO KNOW**
**abnormal**
**investigate**

**CITE EVIDENCE**

**A** Look carefully at the illustration. It shows one of the visitors Mrs. Moreno is describing in paragraph 19. Underline the sentences that match the illustration.

**B** Compare the illustration to the words in paragraph 19. What do you notice about the setting in the illustration that is not described in the story?

**The Case of the Missing Fruit** *continued*

19 Mrs. Moreno answered Sofia, "Yesterday, Mr. Layton was walking his dog, and he stopped to tell me how good my plants were looking. This morning, Lisa Wu came over with some homemade bread from her mother. She made sure to tell me that she couldn't wait to try some jam soon. Then, Mr. Abbott from the pet store arrived. He told me he had never seen such vibrant red fruit!"

20 Tino could tell that Sofia's brain was working.

21 "I think we can find out what happened to the prickly pear fruit, but we need to **investigate**. Ella, would you mind driving us a few places?" she asked.

22 Ella answered, "Let's go solve a mystery!"

23 The first place they stopped was Lisa Wu's house. Lisa was in the front yard, watching her little brothers.

24 "Hey guys!" Lisa smiled at her visitors.

25 Tino spoke first. "We were wondering if you noticed anything **abnormal** at Mrs. Moreno's house this morning?"

26 Lisa thought for a minute. "Not that I can think of. Is something wrong?"

27 "All of the fruits from her prickly pear plants have been picked." Tino said.

28 "Oh no!" Lisa cried. "I have been looking forward to that jam all week!"

29 The next stop was Mr. Layton's house. No one was outside when Ella stopped, so the children rang the front doorbell. Mr. Layton came to the door.

30 "Hello, kids. How's it going?"





### Words to Know

**General Academic Vocabulary**

**abnormal** (*adjective*): different than the expected

**investigate** (*verb*): examine the facts to answer a question or solve a mystery

**Working with Word Meaning** Help students work with words in context by having them write sentences with their partner, focusing on the Words to Know.

## INTEGRATION OF KNOWLEDGE AND IDEAS

### Guided Practice

31 "Hi, Mr. Layton," Sofia said, "we have a question for you. When you were at Mrs. Moreno's house yesterday, did you notice anything strange?"

32 "Not at all," said Mr. Layton, "unless you count the fact that her prickly pear cactus plants always grow better than anything else in the neighborhood!"

**Comprehension Check**

1. Use the illustration to help you determine the meaning of the word *vibrant* in paragraph 19.
   - **a.** sweet
   - **(b.)** bright
   - **c.** dark
   - **d.** pale

2. Based on both the description of the setting in the story and the illustrations, where do you think this story takes place?
   - **a.** in the mountains
   - **b.** at the ocean
   - **c.** in a forest
   - **(d.)** in the desert

3. Work with a partner. Think about how you would draw an illustration of the characters and setting in paragraphs 29–32. What would your illustration look like?

   Sample answer: My illustration would show the four kids with Mr. Layton at the door of his house. Mr. Layton would be a man with gray hair, and his mouth would be open as if he was talking.





## Guided Practice

**Comprehension Check**

**Answer Explanations:**

1. Choice B, *bright*, is the correct answer, based on the illustration. In the picture, the prickly pear flowers are bright red.
2. Choice D, *in the desert*, is correct. The illustrations show palm trees and cacti. Also, the text of the story describes Mrs. Moreno's prickly pear cactus, which grows naturally in the desert.
3. Have students think about how they would draw Mr. Layton. Remind them to think about how he would look, what he would be doing, and which characters would be with him.

## Peer Collaboration

Have students think about each Comprehension Check question independently, coming up with their own ideas on how to respond. Then have students discuss their responses with a partner. Students should consider each other's ideas and formulate one response for the pair. Have the partners share their response with the whole group.

## Foundational Skills: Fluency

Explain to students that they can read more fluently if they use expression when reading dialogue. Model fluent reading for paragraphs 24–28 on page 118 in the Student Book. Explain that reading dialogue with expression means understanding how different characters may be feeling, such as curious and surprised, in this example.

Give students a chance to practice reading dialogue with expression with a partner. They may also want to record themselves reading the selection so that they can play it back and listen to their own use of expression in dialogue. Additional fluency passages and activities can be found at **sadlierconnect.com** in the *Foundational Skills Handbook*.

## Independent Practice

### Recap Reading Selection

Remind students that they have been reading about how Tino and Sofia are trying to solve Mrs. Moreno's mystery. Have students recall details from the last section of the story. (They learned who visited Mrs. Moreno.) Have students make predictions about the end of the story, based on the illustrations.

### Read and Apply

Have students read the selection independently as you circulate. If you notice students struggling, you can provide support with the suggestions that follow.

#### CITE EVIDENCE

**A** Help students connect the setting of the illustration with Sofia's explanation of the mystery to Mrs. Moreno. Tell students that in the illustration, Sofia (and later Tino) is explaining what happened to her cactus fruit. Sofia mentions that the fruits were on the cactus when Mr. Abbott filled the empty bird feeder.

**B** Help students find clues to solve the mystery by using both the text and the illustrations. Have them read carefully in paragraph 45 and then identify those details in the illustration. If necessary, direct students to the location of the bird feeder next to the cacti.

## CONNECTING ILLUSTRATIONS AND TEXT

### Independent Practice

**WORDS TO KNOW**

**evidence**
**healthy**
**review**

**CITE EVIDENCE**

**A** Put a box around Sofia's dialogue that is connected to what she is saying in the illustration.

**B** Circle the item in the **illustration** that is related to Mr. Abbot's delivery.

**The Case of the Missing Fruit** *continued*

33 Sofia smiled, politely. "Thanks, Mr. Layton, that's all we needed to know."

34 The last stop was Mr. Abbott's pet store.

35 "Hey kids! What brings you this way?"

36 "We're helping out Mrs. Moreno," said Sofia. "You made a delivery to her house this morning. Can you tell us what it was?"

37 "Sure, I just dropped by to bring her some seed for her bird feeder."

38 Sofia smiled. "Did you just *deliver* the seed, Mr. Abbott, or did you also put it in the feeder?"

39 "Well, I always fill her bird feeder for her as well. The birds have been migrating, and they're hungry."

40 "Thanks for your help, Mr. Abbott!"

41 Once the children were back in Ella's car, Sofia made an announcement. "I know who stole the prickly pear fruits! I'll tell you when we get to Mrs. Moreno's."

42 When they arrived, Mrs. Moreno was sitting on her front porch.

43 "Mrs. Moreno," Sofia said, "I think I know who stole your prickly pear fruit!"

44 "*Niña*, child, have you really solved the mystery? Who did this terrible thing?"

45 "First let's **review** the **evidence**: Mr. Layton noticed how **healthy** your cactus plants were looking. Lisa Wu's mom sent homemade bread, because she knew the fruits were ready to pick. And Mr. Abbott said how red the fruits were, as he filled your bird feeder."





### Words to Know

**General Academic Vocabulary**

**evidence** (*noun*): the facts that help answer a question
**healthy** (*adjective*): growing well; not sick
**review** (*verb*): to go over something again

**Working with Word Meaning** Help students remember the meanings of the words by having them give definitions for the vocabulary, rephrasing the meanings using their own words.

Independent Practice

46 Before Sofia could finish, Tino gave a triumphant shout. "Of course! It wasn't a person who stole your cactus fruits, Mrs. Moreno. It was birds. The food Mr. Abbott put in your feeder attracted them to your yard, but they liked your beautiful red fruits even more. A perfect treat!"

47 Mrs. Moreno looked shocked, and then she began laughing. "I guess the case of the missing fruit has been solved!"

**Comprehension Check**

MORE ONLINE sadlierconnect.com

1. How would you describe the mood of the characters in the illustration on page 120?

   a. sad

   b. bored, uninterested

   (c.) excited, happy

   d. scared

2. Why is the filled bird feeder important to understanding how the fruit disappeared?

   (a.) It attracted birds to the cactus fruit nearby.

   b. It was not present when the cactus fruit disappeared.

   c. Mrs. Moreno did not want birdseed in her feeder.

   d. Mr. Abbott saw the cactus fruit when he filled the bird feeder.

3. If you paid close attention to the story and the illustrations, there were clues given to help you solve the mystery. What were those clues, both in the text and in the illustrations?

   Sample answer: Mrs. Moreno talked about Mr. Abbott making a delivery, and he said he delivered birdseed. In the illustrations, Mrs. Moreno has a bird feeder right next to her prickly pear cactus.





## Discussion Skills

During discussion, prompt students to support or disagree with what another student has said. This helps extend a discussion and generate new ideas.

Have students respond to one another by asking:

- *Do you agree or disagree and why?*
- *Is this always true?*
- *Can you think of any examples that would not work?*

## Independent Practice

**Comprehension Check**

**Answer Explanations:**

**1.** Choice C, *excited, happy,* is correct based on the characters' facial expressions in the illustration on page 120 and the excitement of solving the mystery described in the text.

**2.** Choice A is correct. The location of the bird feeder next to the cactus helps solve the mystery.

**3.** In the story, Mrs. Moreno mentions that Mr. Abbott was making a delivery. Once the kids determine that Mr. Abbott was delivering birdseed, and they see where Mrs. Moreno's bird feeder is located, they are able to solve the mystery.

## Critical Comprehension

Use the following questions to help students think more deeply about the text. Students should be prepared to support their answers with evidence from the text.

- *What actions do Tino and Sofia take to help them solve the mystery?* (gather evidence, interview people, look at the scene of the mystery)
- *How would this story have been different if the setting were in the mountains?* (The trees would not be palm trees; there would not be any cactus, but birds might have stolen a different fruit or nuts from a tree.)

**Assess and Respond**

**If** students have difficulty answering the questions in the Comprehension Check…

**Then** have students work in pairs to answer the questions, having them brainstorm ideas, referencing the text for answers where necessary.

## Guided Instruction

**OBJECTIVE**

**Compare and contrast two stories featuring the same characters.**

### Genre: Adventure Story

Explain to students that an adventure story introduces characters to exciting new experiences. It includes action and sometimes risk as characters are challenged by nature.

### Set the Purpose

Help students understand the purpose for learning the reading skill by asking *Have you ever read two books that are similar? Maybe they have the same characters, or the same setting. Maybe they even tell the same story, but in two different ways. How were those stories the same? How were they different?*

### Model and Teach

Read the selection as students follow along in their books.

### CITE EVIDENCE

**A** *Remember that the setting describes when and where a story takes place.*

*What are details in paragraph 3 that describe the setting of the story?* (Sonoran Desert, outside the city of Tucson, Arizona)

**B** *The main characters in this story are the same as the main characters in the last story.*

*What are the names of the two new characters in paragraph 4?* (Mamá and Papá)

COMPARING AND CONTRASTING STORIES

Guided Instruction

**WORDS TO KNOW**

**exploration**
**hammock**
**outskirts**

**Comparing** two stories is looking at how they are the same. **Contrasting** two stories is looking at how they are different.

**CITE EVIDENCE**

**A** The first story took place in a neighborhood. Underline descriptions of the **setting** in this story.

**B** The first story featured many different **characters**. In this story, there are only four characters. Circle their names. What kind of adventure do you predict for the characters?

## A Camping Adventure

(Genre: Adventure Story)

1 Tino finished rolling his sleeping bag and attached it to his backpack. "Hey, Sofia, I'm ready to go," he called.

2 "Just give me one minute," his twin sister answered back.

3 Tino, Sofia, and their parents were leaving on an overnight camping trip in the Sonoran Desert, just outside of the city of Tucson, Arizona. They had come to Tucson for spring break. They had already visited many interesting places, including an old western movie set and a World War II airplane museum. Yesterday, the family decided that a camping trip would be the perfect way to end their week of fun and **exploration**.

4 Sofia grabbed her first-aid kit and shoved it into her backpack. "Last item! Let's go down to the hotel lobby and find Mamá and Papá!"



122 Chapter 5 ■ Integration of Knowledge and Ideas: Literary Texts

### Words to Know

**General Academic Vocabulary**

**exploration** (*noun*): learning about a new place by travelling through it

**Domain-Specific Vocabulary**

**hammock** (*noun*): an outdoor hanging bed made of rope
**outskirts** (*noun*): the outer parts of a city

**Working with Word Meaning** Help students remember word meanings by having them draw a picture of one of the words above, and then use that word in a sentence.

5 They arrived at the Gilbert Ray campground right before lunch. They were given a campsite on the **outskirts** of the campground. They spent 30 minutes setting up camp: a large tent with three rooms, a fire pit, camp chairs, and a **hammock** stretched between two ironwood trees.

6 Sofia wanted to unroll their sleeping bags and get the cabin ready for the evening. Tino stopped her.

7 "What are you doing, sis?"

8 "I thought I would surprise everyone and make their beds for them for tonight."

9 "Well, they would get a surprise, all right."

10 "What do you mean?"

11 "Did you forget about scorpions?" answered Tino. "An unrolled sleeping bag is the perfect place for a scorpion to crawl in during the day. Imagine sliding into your sleeping bag tonight with one!"

12 "Ahh!" Sofia cried. "I can't believe I forgot that. Thanks for reminding me!"

13 "Any time, hermana!"

14 After lunch, Sofia, Tino, and their parents decided it was the perfect time for a nap. In the Sonoran Desert, it's best to sleep or relax during the heat of the day. Many of the animals do the same, in order to conserve their energy.

**Guided Instruction**

**CITE EVIDENCE**

**C** The first story was a **mystery** story, while this story is an **adventure** story. Box the paragraph that makes you think of an adventure story.

**D** In the first story, Sofia is in charge of solving the problem. Underline the name of the person who solves the problem in paragraph 11. Which problem is more serious?

**Comprehension Check**

Based on what you have read so far, how is this story the same as "The Case of the Missing Fruit"? How is it different?





## Guided Instruction

### CITE EVIDENCE

**C** *We learned that characters in an adventure story have exciting new experiences in nature.*

*What is Sofia and Tino's new experience in nature in paragraph 11?* (learning how to deal with scorpions)

**D** *In paragraph 11, we learn that an unrolled sleeping bag is the perfect place for a scorpion to crawl into.*

*Who reminds Sofia about what scorpions like to do?* (Tino) *Do you think finding a scorpion in your sleeping bag is a more serious problem than finding missing fruit?* (Yes)

**Comprehension Check**

**Sample Answer:** In a mystery story, the characters have to solve a problem by using evidence. In an adventure story, the characters have exciting new experiences. Both stories can have mystery and adventure, and a problem to solve.

**Answer Explanation:** Mysteries often involve some element of adventure, but adventure stories don't always have a mystery or problem to solve.

### Listening and Viewing Skills

Reread paragraph 3 as students listen and look at the accompanying illustration on page 122. *Where are Tino and Sofia going camping?* (in the desert) *Who is going with them?* (their parents)

### Review: Connecting Illustrations and Text

Have students look at the illustration on page 123 as you read paragraph 11 aloud. *How does the illustration reflect what's happening in the text?* (Tino is worried about scorpions in the sleeping bag.)

### Digital Connection: Using Online Resources

Tell students that, even though this story is a work of fiction, the Sonoran Desert is a real desert in the Southwest. Have students visit the Sonoran Desert pages on the National Park Service website. Help students locate information about the climate and wildlife in the Sonoran Desert.

Have students compare and contrast the illustrations in the text with the photographs on the National Park Service website. Ask students how illustrations differ from photographs. Have students identify ways the two are the same. Ask students which kinds of images they prefer: illustrations or photographs.

## Guided Practice

### Recap Reading Selection

Have a short group discussion about the first section of the story. Ask students to recall what has happened in the story so far. (Sofia and Tino are camping in the Sonoran Desert with their parents.) Ask what new information students have learned about camping in the desert. (Watch out for scorpions; save energy during the hottest part of the day.)

### Read and Practice

Have partners take turns reading the selection as you circulate to provide support. Model identifying contrasting details with Cite Evidence callout A. For callout B, circulate and provide partners with scaffolding as needed. You might use the following suggestions to help students who are having difficulty.

**CITE EVIDENCE**

**A** Have students recall that the important animals in the first story were the birds that ate Mrs. Moreno's cacti. Help student identify *coyotes* as the animal featured in this story by asking what animal tracks Tino discovers.

**B** Remind students that, in the first story, Tino and Sofia were investigating a mystery about cacti. Students should identify the endangered plant Sofia finds, and her father identifies, in this story. (Kearney's Blue Star)

COMPARING AND CONTRASTING STORIES

Guided Practice

**WORDS TO KNOW**

**endangered**
**environment**
**observation**

**CITE EVIDENCE**

**A** Circle the animal that is featured among the setting in paragraphs 19 and 20. The first story also has an important animal. **Compare** the important animal from the setting of each story.

**B** Underline the plant that is featured in the setting in paragraph 18. How is it different from the plant in the first story?

**A Camping Adventure** *continued*

15 Once the temperature had dropped, Sofia asked her parents if they could all take a hike. "There are some desert plants I want to see, and I'm hoping to get a picture of some coyote tracks."

16 They decided to take one of the many small trails that intersected with their campground. The plan was to stop along the way to take pictures and explore the natural wonders of the desert.

17 Right away, Sofia noticed some interesting plants. "Take a look at these flowers, Papá. Can you look them up in your guidebook?"

18 Her father looked through his guidebook. "Wow, Sofia, that's a really rare plant. It's called the Kearney's Blue Star, and it's on the **endangered** species list. Make sure you get some good pictures, but don't touch it. We want to leave the **environment** just like we found it." Their father then reminded them of the old hikers' motto: *Take nothing but pictures, leave nothing but footprints.*

19 Tino was the next one to make a discovery. He stopped on the trail when he saw some animal tracks on the ground. "Look over here! Do you think these are coyote tracks?"

20 "Great powers of **observation**, Tino," said Papá. "Those are coyote tracks, for sure."

124 Chapter 5 ■ Integration of Knowledge and Ideas: Literary Texts



### Words to Know

**General Academic Vocabulary**

**observation** (*noun*): the act of paying close attention to details

**Domain-Specific Vocabulary**

**endangered** (*adjective*): describing a species that may die out, or become extinct

**environment** (*noun*): the landscape and surroundings

**Working with Word Meaning** Encourage students to find synonyms for each of the Words to Know. For instance, instead of *environment*, they might say *landscape*.

# INTEGRATION OF KNOWLEDGE AND IDEAS

Guided Practice

21 They hiked for a little while longer, and were just about to turn back for camp, when Tino spotted a small cave about ten feet off the trail.

22 "Mamá, Papá, can we go explore that cave?"

**Comprehension Check**

1. Choose the statement that best describes the settings of the first two stories.
   a. The first story mainly takes place in a pet store. This story mainly takes place in Tucson, Arizona.
   b. The first story mainly takes place in the desert. This story mainly takes place in a campground.
   (c.) The first story mainly takes place in a neighborhood. This story mainly takes place in the desert.
   d. The first story mainly takes place in Mrs. Moreno's yard. This story mainly takes place in Tino and Sofia's tent.

2. There are two new characters introduced in this story. Who are they?
   a. Abuela and Mr. Abbott
   (b.) Mamá and Papá
   c. Kearney's Blue Star and coyote
   d. Leo and Mr. Layton

3. Work with a partner. Name three ways that this story is different from the first story. Base your answer on details from both stories.
   Sample answer: In this story, the setting is different, there are different characters, and Tino and Sofia are not solving a mystery.





## Support English Language Learners

Support English language learners by assigning them a reading buddy with stronger reading skills. Have them take turns reading the selection with their reading buddies, and then summarizing each paragraph after it has been read. Have the students pay close attention to the illustrations that accompany the story. Instruct each partner to describe the illustrations to each other before they read, and then read to see if the text matches what they are seeing.

## Guided Practice

**Comprehension Check**

**Answer Explanations:**

1. Choice C, *The first story mainly takes place in a neighborhood. This story mainly takes place in the desert,* is correct. The first story takes place in the children's own neighborhood; this one is set in the Sonoran Desert during their family vacation.
2. Choice B, *Mamá and Papá*, is correct because they are the only new characters in the story.
3. The three main elements that differ between the stories are characters, setting, and genre. Tino and Sofia are on an adventure and not solving a mystery.

## Reciprocal Teaching

Form groups of four and assign one of the following roles to each group member: Summarizer, Questioner, Clarifier, and Predictor. In a group discussion, the Summarizers should say what they have learned so far about the story, the Questioners should think of something else to ask about the story, the Clarifiers should answer the question or say where they could look for the answers, and the Predictors should say what they think they will learn next in the story. Call on different groups to share their ideas with the class.

## Independent Practice

### Recap Reading Selection

Remind students that they have been reading about the adventure Tino and Sofia are having in the Sonoran Desert. Have students recall details from the story specific to the setting. (desert, cacti, coyotes, endangered species, cave) Ask students what they think Tino and Sofia will find in the cave.

### Read and Apply

Have students read the selection independently as you circulate. If you notice students struggling, you can provide support with the suggestions that follow.

**CITE EVIDENCE**

**A** Have students match the text in paragraph 27 to the illustration. Students should recognize that both the appearance of the cave wall and the missing cacti fruit in the previous story are plot elements based on natural events.

**B** Remind students that the theme of a story is the main message the author is communicating. Have them think about how the message would be different in an adventure story than it would be in a mystery.



## Independent Practice

**WORDS TO KNOW**

**admiring**
**vein**
**wildlife**

**CITE EVIDENCE**

**A** The plots of this story and the last story both focus on nature. Circle the narrator's description of a natural event.

**B** In paragraph 33, underline the sentences that describe a **theme**, or main idea, of this story. What was the main idea of the first story?

**A Camping Adventure** *continued*

23 Papá considered for a moment. "The cave doesn't look big enough for any **wildlife**, so it's probably safe. But, I would like to check it out first."

24 They hiked over to the cave, and Papá looked inside with his flashlight. It wasn't what he expected. The cave was a large room, big enough for people to stand up. Papá went in first, and the family followed.

25 Papá moved his flashlight around the walls. Suddenly, Sofia gasped. "Papá, shine the flashlight back in that corner."

26 As he moved his light to the back of the room, Tino said, "Wow!" while Mama caught her breath. Papa just looked on in wonder.

27 At the back of the cave was one of the most beautiful rock walls any of them had ever seen. It was covered in sparkling shades of green, blue, and red. A small stream of water curled down the wall, highlighting a colored path as it flowed.

28 "What is it, Papá?" Sofia asked.

29 "I'm not completely certain," her father said, "but I think we may have discovered a rare copper **vein**. When the chemicals in the water mix with the chemicals in the rock, it creates colors on the wall."

30 The family members stood quietly, **admiring** the beauty of the cave. After a few minutes, Mamá reminded them that it was time to leave.

31 "This is spectacular," she said quietly, "but we do need to get back to camp before dark."





### Words to Know

**General Academic Vocabulary**
**admiring** (*verb*): looking at something with enjoyment

**Domain-Specific Vocabulary**
**vein** (*noun*): a line of metal running through a rock bed
**wildlife** (*noun*): animals and plants

**Working with Word Meaning** Help students reinforce word meanings by having them write each word in an original sentence.

## INTEGRATION OF KNOWLEDGE AND IDEAS

**Independent Practice**

32 As they left the cave to head back into the desert, Tino turned to his sister. "I don't know about you, Sofia, but I feel like we saved the best part of our spring break trip for last."

33 Sofia smiled. "I'm with you, *hermano*. That was the most amazing thing I have ever seen. What a cool adventure!"

**Comprehension Check** MORE ONLINE **sadlierconnect.com**

1. Based on your understanding of the setting, what is the meaning of the phrase "copper vein" in paragraph 29?
   a. a streak of copper in the rock wall
   b. the way chemicals react
   c. how blood flows through the body
   d. a copper picture in the cave

2. Based on both stories, which character would you describe as intelligent, with a love for the outdoors?
   a. Papá
   b. Sofia
   c. Mrs. Moreno
   d. Mr. Layton

3. Compare and contrast the themes of the first two stories. How are the themes the same? How are they different? Cite text evidence.
   Sample answer: In each story, Tino and Sofia search for answers. In the first story, they find an answer to solve a mystery. In this story, they explore nature and make discoveries. They find answers to nature's secrets.





## Foundational Skill Review: Vowel Diphthongs

Review vowel diphthongs with students, reminding them that they are two letters combined to make one sound. Model how these letter combinations look and sound, using words from the text, such as *caught* and *out*. Have students find other words with vowel diphthongs in the text. (for example, *enough*, *around*, *beauty*)

Additional phonics activities can be found in the *Foundational Skills Handbook* at **sadlierconnect.com**.

## Independent Practice

**Comprehension Check**

**Answer Explanations:**

**1.** The correct choice is A, *a streak of copper in the rock wall*. Students can use the text descriptions in paragraphs 27 and 29 and the illustration to determine the answer.

**2.** Choice B, *Sofia*, is the best answer because she is the only character that appears in both stories and seems to know a great deal about nature.

**3.** The stories are similar in that they each contain an element of mystery. The characters make discoveries and find answers. They differ in central theme: helping neighbors and looking at facts versus respect for nature and appreciating new experiences.

## Critical Comprehension

Use the following questions to help students think more deeply about the text. Students should be prepared to support their answers with evidence from the text.

- *How can we keep endangered species and other natural wonders from disappearing?* (Answers will vary, but may include respecting natural environments and leaving nature as it is found.)
- *What are some of the safety precautions you should take on a hike?* (plenty of water, snacks, sun protection, a compass or map)

**Assess and Respond**

**If** students have difficulty answering the Comprehension Check questions…

**Then** have them think about what it would be like to hike in the desert. Ask them what they should do if they come upon plants and wildlife on a hike. Have them reread the "Hiker's Motto" in the text.

## Connect Across Texts: *4 points*

## Review Reading Selections

Have students work in groups of four to identify similarities and differences in the stories. Each student should have one topic to cover: characters, setting, events, or theme. Have each student share with the rest of the group.

## Compare and Contrast Texts

Review the directions on page 128, and instruct students to write the titles of the selections in the chart.

**T-Chart Rubric**

| | |
|---|---|
| 4 | Student has correctly identified the similarities and differences between the two texts. |
| 3 | Student has correctly identified some of the similarities and differences in the two texts. |
| 2 | Student has correctly identified either the similarities, or the differences, between two texts, but not elements of both. |
| 1 | Student has identified the two texts, but has not compared or contrasted them. |
| 0 | Student has not identified the selections, or included what they learned. |

## CONNECT ACROSS TEXTS

### Compare and Contrast Texts

In this chapter, you read stories that featured the same characters in different situations. Think about how these stories are the same, and how they are different. Then compare and contrast the texts using the T-Chart below. List important details about setting, characters, and theme to show how the texts are similar or different. Be prepared to discuss your ideas with the class.

| Similarities | Differences |
|---|---|
| "The Case of the Missing Fruit" and "A Camping Adventure":<br><br>-include Sofia and Tino as characters<br><br>-makes discoveries about nature | "The Case of the Missing Fruit":<br><br>-sister Ella is a character<br><br>-solve a mystery<br><br>"A Camping Adventure":<br><br>-parents are characters<br><br>-discover a secret cave in adventure story |





## Extend Thinking: Create

Help students extend their thinking by creating a short graphic novel based on a short story. Provide students with a variety of well-known short stories, folk tales, myths, and fairy tales from which to choose. Then have students use illustrations to tell the story. They can use a collage or a computer program if they do not wish to draw. Remind them to focus on the illustrations rather than using text.

After creating their graphic novels, have students present their work. Students should describe their graphic novels to the class, speaking clearly and highlighting appropriate events in the story.

## CONNECT ACROSS TEXTS

### Connect to the Essential Question

***What connections can readers make?*** In small groups or as a class, discuss the Essential Question. Think about what you have learned about making connections between illustrations and texts, and about how you can compare and contrast setting, theme, and characters in different stories. Use evidence from the chapter texts.

Sample answer: Readers can connect ideas within a story as well as between stories with similar characters or events. Connecting the text and illustrations in "The Case of the Missing Fruit" helped me understand what a prickly pear cactus looks like, and that Mr. Abbott was carrying birdseed when he arrived at the house. I connected information about Sofia and Tino in both stories, such as they get along well and are eager to learn about nature.

### Connect to the Theme

***Searching for Answers*** Sofia and Tino looked for answers to a mystery. Why did they search for answers? How did they go about it? Support your answer with details from the texts.

Sample answer: In "The Case of the Missing Fruit," Sofia and Tino searched for answers to solve a mystery. They asked questions and interviewed people. They realized the fruit wasn't stolen but that birds had eaten it. In "A Camping Adventure," they discovered and explored. They found a beautiful rock wall. Both Sofia and Tino liked searching for answers about nature's secrets.



**To strengthen your response, reread parts of the texts that support your answers. Add to your answers any additional details you find.**



## Assess and Respond (pages 128–129)

| If | Then |
|---|---|
| Students scored 0–2 points, they are **Developing** their understanding of the skills... | Provide students with reading support and more intensive modeling of skills. |
| Students scored 3–5 points, they are **Improving** their understanding of the skills... | Use students' scores to target areas that are weak and review those specific skills. |
| Students scored 6–8 points, they are **Proficient** in their understanding of the skills... | Have these students move on. They are ready for the formal assessment. |

## Support Essential Question Discussion

Have students reread the Essential Question. Challenge them to finish this sentence: *When I read two stories, I can make connections between...*

If students have difficulty responding, prompt them by asking what elements of literature, including characters, setting, events, and theme, help build interest in a story.

## Theme Wrap-Up

Lead students in a group discussion on the theme of *Searching for Answers*. Talk about the ways in which the recurring main characters work together to solve puzzles and unravel new ideas.

## Short-Answer Questions: *2 points each*

**Connect to the Essential Question Rubric**

| Score | Description |
|---|---|
| 2 | Students are able to make connections between elements of literature in similar stories. |
| 1 | Students identify some ways of connecting elements of literature in similar stories. |
| 0 | Students are not able to make connections between elements of literature in similar stories. |

**Connect to the Theme Rubric**

| Score | Description |
|---|---|
| 2 | Students are able to identify the ways in which the recurring main characters work together to solve puzzles and unravel new ideas. |
| 1 | Students identify some ways in which the recurring main characters work together to solve puzzles and unravel new ideas. |
| 0 | Students cannot identify any ways in which the recurring main characters work together to solve puzzles and unravel new ideas. |

**OBJECTIVE**
**Use root words to determine word meanings.**

## Guided Instruction

Review the Guided Instruction section on page 130 with students. Be sure they understand that root words provide the basic meaning behind a word. Looking at root words can help a reader decipher the meaning of a word by breaking it down into smaller pieces.

## Guided Practice

If students are having trouble, have them break the words into small pieces, and then try to match those pieces to the roots listed on the word chart in the text. You might also have them do this exercise in small groups.

## Independent Practice

If students are having trouble defining the indicated words, review the meanings of the roots in the boxes. Point out that students should think about how each word is used in the sentence.

## Apply to Reading

Have students return to page 120 of "The Case of the Missing Fruit" to find a word that contains one of the word roots listed in the chart. They should identify *migrating* in paragraph 39. Have the students use the word root chart to define the word and use it correctly in a sentence.

# LANGUAGE

### Roots

**Guided Instruction** Looking at the **root** of a word and comparing it to a familiar word with the same root can help you understand a word's meaning.

| Root | port | cause or cus | vent | vac |
|---|---|---|---|---|
| Meaning | carry | reason | come | empty |

| Root | civ | fac | migra | vert |
|---|---|---|---|---|
| Meaning | citizen | do, make | wander | turn |

**Guided Practice** Identify the root of each word below.

1. fact: fac
2. immigrant: migra
3. report: port

**Independent Practice** Identify the root, and its meaning, in each of the words in **bold** below. Then in the sentence that follows, use what you have learned to write the meaning of the bold word with the same root. Use a dictionary if necessary.

1. "Tino," Abuela said, "thank you for this **adventure**."
   Root/meaning: vent/come
   The people at the comic book **convention** came from all over the world.
   Word meaning: a meeting where people come together
2. "I gave up and moved back to **civilization**."
   Root/meaning: civ/citizen
   The volunteers who cleaned up the park were very **civic** minded.
   Word meaning: relating to the duties of a citizen





## Support English Language Learners

Allowing English language learners the opportunity to physically manipulate the word roots will aid them in comprehension of difficult vocabulary. Write the following words on a separate sheet of paper: *immigrant*, *report*, *adventure*, *civilization*. Model cutting the words up into their individual pieces for the students, leaving the word roots intact. Then have the students physically put the words back together, defining the roots as they do. Finally, have the students write a sentence for each word.

## CHAPTER 5 REVIEW

Read the following mystery story. Think about how this story is the same as the previous stories in this chapter and how it is different. Then answer the questions on pages 131 and 132.

### The Missing Pencil Sharpener

(Genre: Mystery)

1 Sofia and Tino were in their home classroom. Ms. Johnson, their teacher, stood in front of the class with two students. She said she had a mystery challenge, and she'd asked two volunteers to be suspects. The class had to figure out which volunteer "stole" a pencil sharpener from the room.

2 Sofia raised her hand and asked one suspect where he was when the sharpener was taken. The boy said he was outside. Tino put the question to the other student. This student said she was in the cafeteria.

3 Sofia closely inspected both students and then said, "The boy did it. His excuse is not true. It's raining, and his shoes are clean. If he'd been outside, they would be muddy and wet!"

4 Ms. Johnson laughed. "I should have known you two would win my mystery challenge!"

---

**Fill in the circle of the correct answer choice.**

1. What is the setting of this story?

| | |
|---|---|
| ○ the desert | ● a classroom |
| ○ a neighborhood | ○ the pet store |

2. What new character appears in paragraph 1?

| | |
|---|---|
| ● Ms. Johnson | ○ Abuela |
| ○ Mr. Abbott | ○ April |

3. Which story has a theme most like "The Missing Pencil Sharpener"?

| | |
|---|---|
| ○ "A Camping Adventure" | ● "The Case of the Missing Fruit" |
| ○ All of the above. | ○ None of the above. |





## Self-Assessment: Progress Check

Have students revisit the Progress Check on page 113 and respond to the questions again. Ask them to compare their Before and After responses.

You may wish to have students rate their answers on a scale of 0–2 rather than simply checking (or not checking) the box. Instruct them to write a *0* if feel they don't understand the given skill at all, a *1* if they feel they have some understanding, and a *2* if they feel they have a solid grasp of the skill.

## Chapter Summary

At this point, students have had instruction and practice in reading literature, with a focus on connecting texts to illustrations and comparing and contrasting different elements in stories that feature recurring characters. Students have practiced working with concepts across texts, and practiced using different strategies for determining word meanings from word roots. They should be well-prepared for the review section.

## Introduce the Review

Explain to students that they will read a new passage that is related to the chapter's theme and the selections they have already read. Instruct students to read the passage carefully and then answer the questions that start on page 131.

### Answer Explanations

Scoring: Items 1–9 on pages 131–132 are worth 1 point each. See the rubric for guidance on scoring the Write About It question on page 132.

1. The text describes Sofia and Tino's home classroom, so the third choice, *a classroom*, is correct.
2. Sofia and Tino are recurring characters, so the first choice, *Ms. Johnson*, is correct.
3. This story is a mystery, so the third choice, *"The Case of the Missing Fruit,"* is correct.

### Answer Explanations

**4.** There are only two recurring characters in this chapter, so *Tino and Sofia* is correct.

**5.** The root of the word *excuse* is *cus*. The second choice is correct.

**6.** Sofia and Tino solve a mystery, that of who took the missing sharpener, so the first choice is correct.

**7.** Sofia figures out the solution to the mystery in both "The Case of the Missing Fruit" and "The Missing Pencil Sharpener."

**8.** Ms. Johnson and Mrs. Moreno both have a problem they want Tino and Sofia to solve, so the third choice is correct.

**9.** Sofia noticed that the boy's shoes were wet, which led her to solve the mystery, so it would help to show rain outside the window.

### Write About It Rubric

| | |
|---|---|
| 2 | Student accurately describes setting details and characters as they appear in the story. |
| 1 | Student describes either setting details or characters as they appear in the story. |
| 0 | Student does not describe setting details or characters as they appear in the story. |

## CHAPTER 5 REVIEW

4. Which characters appear in all of the stories in this chapter?
   - ○ Sofia and Abuela
   - ● Tino and Sofia
   - ○ Mamá and Papá
   - ○ Ella and April

5. Which word in paragraph 3 has the root *cus*?
   - ○ inspected
   - ● excuse
   - ○ clean
   - ○ outside

6. What is the genre of this story?
   - ● mystery
   - ○ adventure story
   - ○ folktale
   - ○ fairy tale

7. The solution in "The Case of the Missing Fruit" and in this story is
   - ○ announced by Tino
   - ○ announced by Ms. Johnson
   - ○ announced by Mrs. Moreno
   - ● announced by Sofia

8. Ms. Johnson is similar to Mrs. Moreno in "The Case . . . Missing Fruit"
   - ○ because both are teachers
   - ○ because they are neighbors
   - ● because they have a mystery
   - ○ because they grow fruit

9. Which picture of the setting would help you understand the story?
   - ● One showing rain outside
   - ○ One showing kids at desks
   - ○ One showing a teacher
   - ○ One showing a pencil sharpener

**Write About It** How would you illustrate "The Missing Pencil Sharpener"?
Sample answer: The teacher stands at the front of the room; Tino and Sofia have their hands raised; a boy and a girl stand next to the teacher.





### Analyze Student Scores

| | |
|---|---|
| **9–11 pts Strong** | Student has a good grasp of the skills and concepts taught in this chapter. Point out any mistakes the student has made and explain the correct answers if necessary. |
| **4–8 pts Progressing** | Student is struggling with some skills or concepts. Identify the specific skills that are problematic to target a review of instruction. |
| **0–3 pts Emerging** | Student is having serious problems understanding the skills and concepts taught in this chapter. Student may need to redo the work with a higher level of support. |

# Integration of Knowledge and Ideas: Informational Texts

CHAPTER 6

## Integration of Knowledge and Ideas
## Informational Texts

CHAPTER 6

**Focus on Reading** In informational texts, visuals such as charts and diagrams work together with the text to provide information. By paying attention to visuals and text structure, and by comparing and contrasting texts, you can get the most of out informational texts.

**Think About Theme** We are all part of the solar system, but how often do you think about what that means? The texts in this chapter will take you beyond the bounds of planet Earth and into space.

**Let's Get on Our Way!** As you read the texts in this chapter, pay attention to the different ways authors present information on similar topics or themes.

These are the skills you will build in this chapter. Before you begin, check the boxes on the left of any items you can do well now. At the end of the chapter, you will return to this page to use the check boxes on the right to show what you have learned.

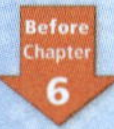


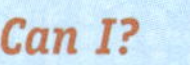


*Can I?*

| Before Chapter 6 | Progress Check Can I? | After Chapter 6 |
|---|---|---|
| ☐ | Connect photos and other visual information to an informational text. | ☐ |
| ☐ | Understand the structure, such as causes and effects and sequence of events, of an informational text. | ☐ |
| ☐ | Compare and contrast important information in two informational texts. | ☐ |
| ☐ | Understand differences of meaning among related words. | ☐ |





**Student Page 133**

## Progress Check

The Progress Check is a self-assessment feature that students can use to gauge their own progress. Research shows that when students take accountability for their own learning, it increases their motivation.

Before students begin work on Chapter 6, have them check the boxes next to any item that they feel they can do well. Explain that it is fine if they don't check any of the boxes. They will have an opportunity to learn about and practice all of these items while studying the chapter. Let them know that near the end of the chapter they will have a chance to reconsider how well they can do each item on this list.

Before students begin the Chapter 6 Review on page 157, have them revisit this page. You can use this information to work with students on any items they don't understand before they tackle the Review.

## HOME ✦ CONNECT...

The Home Connect feature is a way to keep parents or other adult family members apprised of what their children are learning. The key learning objectives are listed, and some ideas for related activities and discussions are included.

Explain to students that they can share the Home Connect page with their parents or the adult family members in their homes. Let students know how much time the class will be spending on this chapter so they can plan their time accordingly at home.

Encourage students and their parents to share their experiences using the suggestions on the Home Connect page. You may wish to make a place to post some of this work.

## HOME ✦ CONNECT...

It is important for readers to learn how to connect **visual information** (such as photographs, illustrations, graphs, and charts) **and text** to understand what they read. Find a magazine article that includes a number of images. Share it with your child, and discuss how the images add to the text.

Cause and effect is a type of **text structure** that nonfiction authors use to organize their writing. Talk with your child about a recent news event. Discuss the reasons why it happened and what occurred (the cause and effect). Work together with your child to create a two-column chart that lists causes and effects related to the event.

This chapter includes a magazine article and an editorial about the same topic: the dwarf planet Pluto. It can be helpful to **compare and contrast texts** about the same subject to better understand a topic. Find a newspaper story and a newspaper editorial on the same subject. Share the two articles with your child. Discuss how they are alike and how they are different.

**Activity:** Work together with your child to search for articles about the universe and space exploration on the Internet. Narrow the topic as you choose links to explore. Use correct terms for the images you see on screen, such as *photograph, illustration, graph,* etc. Discuss why some of the articles are easier to follow or more appealing than others. List interesting facts, and create your own fact sheet about space.

**IN THIS CHAPTER, YOUR CHILD WILL...**

- Connect photographs, illustrations, and other examples of visual information to text.
- Describe text structure—how information and ideas are related—in an informational text.
- Identify causes and effects and sequences of events in a text.
- Compare and contrast the most important points in two texts on the same topic.
- Understand different meanings among related words.
- Compare and contrast texts on the same theme: a technical text, a magazine article, and an editorial.

**WAYS TO HELP YOUR CHILD**

Demonstrate a positive attitude toward reading and learning. Find articles to read with your child. Before you read, pose questions about the topic. You should ask questions you hope the article will address. Encourage your child to ask questions, too. Create a list that includes your questions and those of your child. Then as you read through the article together, search for the answers.

ONLINE
For more Home Connect activities, continue online at sadlierconnect.com





**Student Page 134**

## LEARNING PROGRESSIONS

In this chapter, students will learn how the integration of knowledge and ideas in an informational text contributes to their understanding of it. In order to learn the skills in this chapter, students will further develop skills learned in second grade. They should be encouraged to retain these skills, as they will continue to build on them in the fourth grade.

### Connecting Visual Information and Text

- In second grade, students should have learned how images contribute to and clarify their understanding of a text.
- In grade 3, students will extend their knowledge of how to integrate information learned from words and images to gain understanding of a text.
- In fourth grade, students will be examining more advanced images, such as charts, graphs, and time lines, and exploring how these images increase their understanding of a text.

### Describing Text Structures

- By the end of grade 2, students should have been able to determine how reasons support points an author makes in a text.
- In third grade, students will explore how sequence and cause/effect make logical connections between sentences and paragraphs in a text.
- This will prepare them for fourth grade, in which they will more deeply explore how authors use evidence to support their points in a text.

### Comparing and Contrasting Texts

- Proficient second graders should have ended the school year understanding how to compare and contrast two texts on the same topic.
- In third grade, students will look at the most important points and key details as they compare and contrast two texts on the same topic.
- This will prepare them for grade 4, in which they will integrate information from two texts on the same topic and write about that topic knowledgeably.

**Essential Question:**
**How can authors use text structure to connect ideas and information?**

In this chapter, students will learn about the integration of knowledge and ideas in informational text, specifically how to connect visual information to ideas, analyze text structures, and compare and contrast ideas in two texts on the same topic.

## Theme: The Solar System

Students will read selections related to the theme of the solar system. They will read about how to make a telescope and about the history of Pluto and whether or not it is a planet.

## Curriculum Connection: Science

Students will learn about the solar system and how scientists have made discoveries and decisions about our planets and other objects in the solar system.

## Vocabulary Overview

### General Academic Vocabulary

astronomer 136, calculation 143, category 148, classification 142, comet 140, excess 138, interior 149, judging 150, mnemonic 147, solar system 136, tilted 152, universe 144

### Domain-Specific Vocabulary

asteroid 146, centimeter 138, constellation 140, core 152, crater 140, diameter 150, dwarf planet 146, ellipse 148, gravitational pull 143, gravity 144, orbit 143, reflecting telescope 136, refracting telescope 136

## Guided Instruction

**OBJECTIVE**
**Use illustrations and words to understand the concepts and events in a text.**

### Genre: Technical Text

Tell students that technical texts explain a concept or how to do something. How-to articles often include a series of steps.

### Set the Purpose

Help students understand the purpose for learning the reading skill by asking *Why do you look at illustrations, such as maps or pictures, when you read an informational text?*

### Model and Teach

Read the selection as students follow along in their books.

**CITE EVIDENCE**

**A** *I read that refracting telescopes use lenses and reflecting telescopes use mirrors. I'll look at the labels on the telescope in the image to figure out what it uses.*

*Based on this clue, what type of telescope is in the picture?* (a refracting telescope)

**B** *We figured out that the image shows a refracting telescope. That's described in paragraph 3.*

*Which paragraph describes the reflecting telescope?* (paragraph 4)



**Guided Instruction**

**WORDS TO KNOW**
**astronomer**
**reflecting telescope**
**refracting telescope**
**solar system**

Informational text often includes photos, charts, diagrams, or other kinds of **visual information**. These images help support the text.

**CITE EVIDENCE**

**A** Technical text provides information through **images** and written information. Circle the paragraph that describes the image on this page.

**B** Place a box around the paragraph that describes a telescope that is not shown as an image.

# How to Make a Telescope

(Genre: Technical Text)

1 Hello, budding **astronomers**! Do you want to study objects in the **solar system**? This manual provides all the information you need to build your own telescope. When you are done, you will be able to see the stars and the planets. You might even spot a comet or two!

2 Before you begin, it is important to know how telescopes work. A telescope is a tool that makes distant objects look close.

3 This manual explains how to build a **refracting telescope**, which is made with lenses. You will use two magnifying glasses as your lenses. A refracting telescope shows objects upside down.

4 A refracting telescope is different from a **reflecting telescope**, which is made with mirrors. The world's first telescopes were the refracting kind. Today, most telescopes are the reflecting kind. These are more complicated and harder to build on your own.

5 Follow these instructions to put your refracting telescope together. First, make sure you have everything you will need.

**Refracting Telescope**

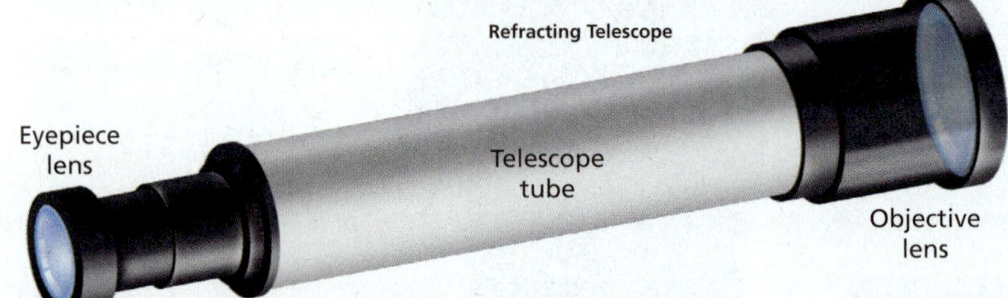






## Words to Know

**General Academic Vocabulary**

**astronomer** (*noun*): a scientist who studies the stars, planets, and other objects in space

**solar system** (*noun*): the planets and other space objects that orbit around the sun

**Domain-Specific Vocabulary**

**reflecting telescope** (*noun*): a telescope that uses mirrors to let users see distant objects

**refracting telescope** (*noun*): a telescope that uses lenses to let users see distant objects

**Working with Word Meaning** Help students understand the meanings of these words by leading an Internet image search for each word.

# INTEGRATION OF KNOWLEDGE AND IDEAS

6 Gather the following items:

- Two magnifying glasses, one big and one small
- A long cardboard tube
- A roll of masking tape
- A black marker
- A piece of newspaper
- A pair of scissors
- Measuring tape
- A friend to lend a hand

7 Now, assemble your telescope.

8 **Step 1:** First, take the newspaper and place it on a table or other flat surface. Hold the big magnifying glass over the paper so the printing appears blurry, or hard to read.

9 **Step 2:** Take the small magnifying glass into your other hand. Hold it between your eyes and the big magnifying glass. Move the small magnifying glass forward and back. Stop when you see the newspaper come into focus in the large magnifying glass. The printing will appear both larger and upside down.

## Comprehension Check

How does the list on this page relate to the image on the page? Include evidence from the text in your answer.

## Guided Instruction

### CITE EVIDENCE

**C** The **illustrations** in a text connect to the words, helping the reader to see key details. Draw a box around the lenses in the text and in the Figure A image.

**D** Illustrations can also help by showing the reader the steps in a process. Circle the text that tells you in what order the telescope assembly occurs. How does seeing the items help you understand the circled text?

**Figure A**

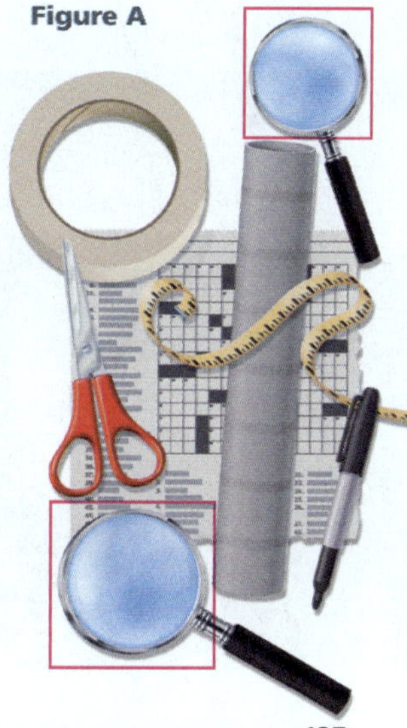





## Support English Language Learners

Help struggling students develop their vocabulary by matching each item on the list at the top of page 137 with the image in the lower right. Students can circle each item and draw a line to the corresponding point in the list. Then have students work with a partner to rephrase Steps 1 and 2 in their own words.

## Guided Instruction

### CITE EVIDENCE

**C** *I'll read through the text first and then look at the image. I don't see the label* lenses, *so I'll have to figure out which are the lenses in the image. I know from the image on page 136 that there are two lenses that are different sizes.*

*Based on this clue, what do you think the lenses are?* (the magnifying glasses)

**D** *Illustrations should work together with the text to give you information. I'll look for words that tell me how to put the telescope together. I'll look for order words, such as* first, *and direction words, such as* take *and* hold.

*Which step or steps use order words and direction words to tell you how to put the telescope together?* (Steps 1 and 2)

## Comprehension Check

**Sample Answer:** The image shows all the items on the list, except the friend. It illustrates the supplies that I must gather to make the telescope.

**Answer Explanation:** Students should be able to integrate the information from the text with that in the image by recognizing that the image illustrates the items in the list, except for the friend. This is the group of supplies that readers would need to build a refracting telescope.

## Guided Practice

### Recap Reading Selection

Remind students that they have discussed two types of telescopes: reflecting and refracting. Ask them to summarize the differences and say which one this text is explaining how to build. Finally, ask them to list some of the supplies that are needed to build the telescope.

### Read and Practice

Have partners take turns reading the selection as you circulate to provide support. For callout A, circulate and provide partners with scaffolding as needed. Model connecting images and text with Cite Evidence callout B. You might use the following suggestions to help students who are having difficulty.

### CITE EVIDENCE

**A** Guide students to read through the text first. Then tell them to look back at each step and scan for the words *cut* and *slot*.

**B** Explain that Step 4 describes how to cut a slot in the tube. Guide students to identify the image (Figure B) that shows a student cutting a tube with scissors.

CONNECTING VISUAL INFORMATION AND TEXT

Guided Practice

**WORDS TO KNOW**

**centimeter**
**excess**

**CITE EVIDENCE**

**A** Circle the step that explains how to cut a slot into the tube and what the slot is for.

**B** Draw a box around the letter of the figure that illustrates Step 4. In your own words, what does that illustration show?

**How to Make a Telescope** *continued*

10 **Step 3:** Hold the two magnifying glasses steady, making sure to keep the newspaper in focus in the larger lens. Ask your friend to use the measuring tape to find the distance between the two magnifying glasses, and have him or her write down that number.

11 **Step 4:** Next, measure a distance of 1 inch (2.5 **centimeters**) from one end of the cardboard tube. Draw a line with the black marker, and use the scissors to cut a slot into the tube on the line you marked. Do not cut all the way through the tube. The slot should only be large enough to hold the big magnifying glass.

Figure B

Figure C

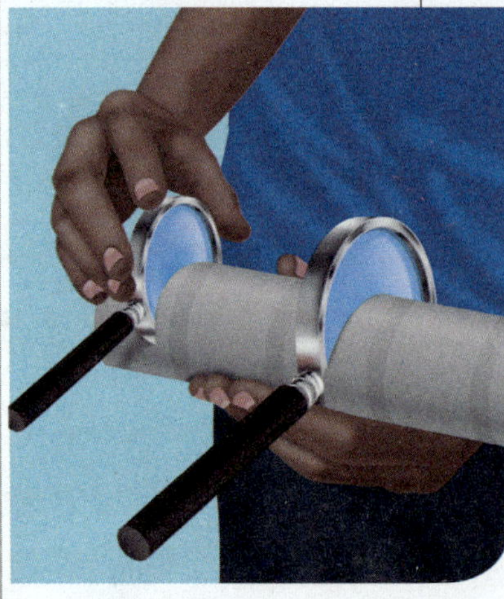

12 **Step 5:** Now, measure the distance your friend wrote down from the slot on the tube. Draw a line with the marker, and cut another slot in the tube. This one should only be large enough to hold the small magnifying glass.

13 **Step 6:** Put the two magnifying glasses into their slots. Remember, the big one goes in the front and the small one goes in the back. Use the masking tape to hold the two lenses in place.

14 **Step 7:** Next, measure about 1 inch beyond the small magnifying glass. Draw a line with the marker. The rest is **excess** tube. Cut it off.



138 Chapter 6 ■ Integration of Knowledge and Ideas: Informational Texts

### Words to Know

**General Academic Vocabulary**
**excess** (*adjective*): extra, not needed

**Domain-Specific Vocabulary**
**centimeter** (*noun*): a small unit of measurement

**Working with Word Meaning** Help students learn these word meanings by asking them to write a sentence using each word.

15 **Step 8:** Finally, test the telescope by looking at the piece of newspaper with it. You may need to adjust the distance between the two magnifying glasses to get the best quality.

**Comprehension Check**

1. What kind of image is Figure C?
   - a. a chart
   - b. a graph
   - (c.) an illustration
   - d. a photograph

2. What does Figure C show?
   - a. It shows how to cut off the excess part of the tube.
   - (b.) It shows how to put the magnifying lenses into place.
   - c. It shows how to test the telescope to get the best quality.
   - d. It shows how to measure 1 inch along the cardboard tube.

3. Work with a partner to discuss how Figure C connects to the text. What does the image show that the text does not say? How does Figure C help the reader?

Sample answer: Figure C helps explain Step 6 in the text. It shows how to put the magnifying lenses into place. The image also shows about how far apart the slots should be, which is not directly stated in the text. It helps the reader follow the instructions to add the lenses to the telescope.





## Foundational Skills: Fluency Practice

Explain to students that when they are following a series of steps like these, often one partner will read the step aloud while the other follows the procedure described. The one reading should pause after each sentence to make sure that their partner has understood and has been able to complete the action. At the end of each step, both partners should pause and read back over the step to make sure that the entire step has been completed. Additional fluency passages and activities can be found at **sadlierconnect.com**.

## Guided Practice

**Comprehension Check**

**Answer Explanations:**

1. Choice C, *an illustration*, is correct. Students should be able to identify Figure C as an illustration, not a chart, graph, or photograph.
2. Choice B, *It shows how to put the magnifying lenses into place*, is correct. Students can check the answer by looking carefully at Figure C.
3. Help students understand that they will need to integrate information from both the text and the illustration in order to get the full picture of what to do. Prompt them to reread the steps and then compare them to the illustration before they answer the question.

## Peer Collaboration

Follow this procedure for each item: Ask students to think about how they would respond to the question or item. Then have them turn to a partner and discuss their response. Students should be prepared to make changes to their own answer based on the discussion with their partner. Finally, ask pairs to report their answers to the whole group.

## Independent Practice

### Recap Reading Selection

Work with the class to summarize each step they read in the previous section. Encourage students to refer back to the text as necessary to recall each step.

### Read and Apply

Have students read the selection independently as you circulate to provide support. If you notice students struggling, you can provide support with the suggestions that follow.

#### CITE EVIDENCE

**A** Students should identify the label "Constellations" at the beginning of paragraph 19 and find the information in this paragraph.

**B** Students should review paragraph 19. They should then look at the images on the page in order to select the caption of the one (the Big Dipper) that illustrates the information conveyed in the paragraph.

CONNECTING VISUAL INFORMATION AND TEXT

**Independent Practice**

**WORDS TO KNOW**
**comet**
**constellation**
**crater**

**CITE EVIDENCE**

**A** Underline the paragraph that explains what a constellation is and names the two best-known constellations.

**B** Which image on this page helps you understand the information in paragraph 19? Draw a box around the label that explains what the image is.

**How to Make a Telescope** *continued*

16 Wait for a clear night to try out your telescope. Stare at the sky through the end with the two lenses. Any objects you see will appear upside down. That is how they looked to the astronomers who built the first telescopes.

17 Here are some things to observe with your new telescope.

18 **The Moon:** The moon is the largest object in the night sky. You can use your telescope to get a better look at **craters** on the moon's surface.

19 **Constellations:** A **constellation** is a collection of stars that forms a pattern. Two of the most well-known constellations are the Big Dipper and Orion.

20 **Planets:** There are seven other planets in the solar system. It is possible to see up to five of them in the sky at night: Mercury, Venus, Mars, Jupiter, and Saturn.

21 **Comets:** A **comet** is a huge ball of ice and dust, streaking across the sky. Comets are often named after the first person who reports seeing them, which is a good reason to look for them!

A comet

The Big Dipper



140 Chapter 6 ■ Integration of Knowledge and Ideas: Informational Texts

### Words to Know

**General Academic Vocabulary**
**comet** (*noun*): an icy space object that sometimes develops a tail

**Domain-Specific Vocabulary**
**constellation** (*noun*): a group of stars that forms a picture
**crater** (*noun*): a hole made by an impact of something

**Working with Word Meaning** Help students understand these word meanings by asking them to draw an illustration of each word.

INTEGRATION OF KNOWLEDGE AND IDEAS

Independent Practice

22 **Objects on Earth:** You can also use your telescope to view faraway objects right here on Earth. It is also great for bird watching or for studying landscapes in the distance. You might learn just as much about life on our planet as you do about outer space.

23 Keep a journal of the objects you see in your telescope. Record your observations, or draw illustrations of everything you see. It is another way to enjoy your homemade telescope!

**Comprehension Check** MORE ONLINE **sadlierconnect.com**

1. Circle the answer that completes the following sentence. The image of the Big Dipper shows you what _______ looks like.
   - **(a.)** a constellation
   - **b.** a comet
   - **c.** Orion
   - **d.** the moon's craters

2. Which text connects to what you see in the image of the comet?
   - **a.** Comets are named after the first person who finds them.
   - **b.** Keep a journal of the objects you see in your telescope.
   - **c.** There are seven other planets in the solar system.
   - **(d.)** A comet is a huge ball of ice and dust, streaking across the sky.

3. What does the image of the comet show that the text does not say? Why was the image included?

   Sample answer: The text in paragraph 21 explains what a comet is. The photograph shows what a comet looks like. The image helps the reader understand what you can see with a telescope.





## Extend Thinking: Analyze and Compare

This article tells readers how to make a refracting telescope. Ask students to research how the more complicated reflecting telescopes are made. They should examine how these telescopes are made and why they have become the more common type of telescope used today. Then they should discuss whether or not they could make one on their own as simply as they could make a refracting telescope.

## Independent Practice

**Comprehension Check**

**Answer Explanations:**

**1.** Choice A, *a constellation*, is correct. According to paragraph 19, the Big Dipper is a constellation.

**2.** Choice D is the correct answer. It is the best and most accurate description of the image of the comet.

**3.** Students should compare the information in the text with the image. Both describe a comet, but the image shows the comet's tail and helps the reader see what a comet looks like.

## Critical Comprehension

Use the following questions to help students think more deeply about the text. Students should be prepared to support their answers with evidence from the text.

- *How does this text change your ideas about telescopes?* (Students may be surprised that a telescope could be made with such simple materials.)
- *Could you have understood this text in the same way without the images?* (Most students will say no, that they needed the illustrations to understand how things look.)

**Assess and Respond**

**If** students have difficulty answering the questions in the Comprehension Check,

**Then** lead a reading group to review the selection, summarizing each section and modeling the skills that had been practiced independently.

## Guided Instruction

**OBJECTIVE**
**Understand the use of cause/effect and sequence in a text.**

### Genre: Magazine Article

Remind students that magazine articles can be about a variety of subjects. They often are written in an objective tone and give an overview of an issue.

### Set the Purpose

Help students understand the purpose for learning the reading skill by asking *Have you ever thought about how an essay is structured? How do you think a problem/solution essay might present its information?*

### Model and Teach

Read the selection as students follow along in their books.

**CITE EVIDENCE**

**A** *I see that the first sentence reads "The year was 1930." That sounds like the opening of a movie trailer! I'll expect to find out what happened in 1930 next. What happened in 1930?* (Astronomers discovered a new object in space.)

**B** *Authors can use clue words, such as* first, second, *or* third *to indicate a sequence of events. They also use dates. I see dates that tell when Uranus and Neptune were discovered. Which was discovered first?* (Uranus)

DESCRIBING TEXT STRUCTURES

Guided Instruction

**WORDS TO KNOW**
**calculation**
**classification**
**gravitational pull**
**orbit**

**Text structure** is the way a text is organized. Different texts can have different structures.

**CITE EVIDENCE**

**A** **Sequence** is one type of text structure. Sequence tells when things happened. In paragraph 1, underline an event that happened in 1930. Box an event that happened after.

**B** Sequence explains the **order of events in a series**. It tells which one happened first, which happened second, and so on. Circle the sentence that describes the discoveries of Uranus and Neptune. Which of these two planets was discovered first?

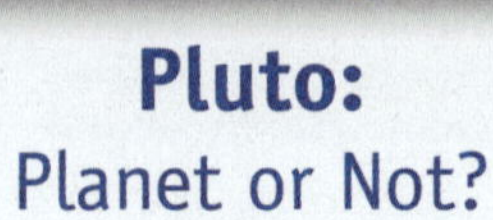

# Pluto:
## Planet or Not?
(Genre: Magazine Article)

1 The year was 1930. Astronomers in Arizona had discovered an unknown object in space. What was it? They were not sure. However, it seemed to behave like a planet, so it must be a planet. They declared it was the ninth planet in our solar system. It became known as Pluto.

2 For decades, that **classification** remained in place. But in 2006, everything changed. Scientists were no longer sure what to call Pluto. Was it a planet or not? Here is the strange story of the former planet Pluto.

### The Search for "Planet X"

3 For years, students were taught the solar system contained nine planets: Mercury, Venus, Earth, Mars, Jupiter, Saturn, Uranus, Neptune, and Pluto. The last three planets were discovered across centuries as astronomers used increasingly sophisticated tools to study space. Uranus was discovered in 1781, and Neptune was found in 1846.



142 Chapter 6 ■ Integration of Knowledge and Ideas: Informational Texts

### Words to Know

**General Academic Vocabulary**
**calculation** (*noun*): figuring something out, often by using math
**classification** (*noun*): the action of placing something in a group

**Domain-Specific Vocabulary**
**gravitational pull** (*noun*): the effect one object's gravity has on another
**orbit** (*noun*): the path an object in space takes around a planet, moon, or the sun

**Working with Word Meaning** Help students learn these word meanings by having them play a simple game of charades.

## INTEGRATION OF KNOWLEDGE AND IDEAS

Guided Instruction

4 About 50 years after Neptune's discovery, an astronomer named Percival Lowell suspected there might be a ninth planet in the solar system. So, in 1905, he decided to search for it. He called it "Planet X." Lowell spent more than a decade searching for this planet, but he could not find it.

### The Discovery of Pluto

5 In 1929, an astronomer named Clyde Tombaugh was working at an observatory that Percival Lowell had founded in Arizona. He wondered if Percival Lowell might be right about a ninth planet in the solar system. So, he took up the search. He started with Lowell's **calculations** and then expanded his search.

6 The following year, Tombaugh's search uncovered a tiny, distant planet on the far edges of the solar system. It appeared no bigger than a bit of dust in a photograph. Could this be it? One clue was the **gravitational pull** of the unknown object, which affected the **orbits** of Neptune and Uranus.

**CITE EVIDENCE**

**C Cause and effect** is another type of text structure. A cause is the reason something happens, and the effect is what happened. Paragraph 4 uses this structure. Circle the effect of Lowell's suspicions in paragraph 4.

**D** Underline the sentence that tells what Tombaugh did when he first took up the search for Lowell's "Planet X." Why did Tombaugh expand his search?

**Comprehension Check**

Clyde Tombaugh decided to continue Percival Lowell's search. What was the effect? Include evidence from the text in your answer.

Percival Lowell





## Extend Thinking: Investigate

Ask students to find and research another astronomer and his or her contribution to our current understanding of the solar system or universe. Tell them to prepare a brief presentation for the class about what they learned. Encourage students to include at least one visual that supports their presentation. Students should make sure they speak clearly and use academic language in their presentation.

## Guided Instruction

### CITE EVIDENCE

**C** *I'll read paragraph 4 to look for any causes it describes. I see that Lowell thought there might be a ninth planet and decided to look for it. These are both causes. The effect will come next. What is it?* (He spent more than a decade searching for the planet.)

**D** *I see the sentence "So, he took up the search." I think the sentence after that will tell me how he started. It actually begins with "He started"!*

*What did Tombaugh do first?* (He started with Lowell's calculations.) *What did he do next, and why?* (Tombaugh expanded his search because Lowell never found anything.)

**Comprehension Check**

**Sample Answer:** The effect of Tombaugh continuing the search was the discovery of Pluto. The heading "The Discovery of Pluto" and the text "Tombaugh's search uncovered a tiny, distant planet" make this clear.

**Answer Explanation:** Some students may be confused because the text does not directly state that Tombaugh discovered Pluto. Students will have to put together the text that reads "Tombaugh's search uncovered a tiny, distant planet" with the heading "The Discovery of Pluto" and the information in the first paragraph about when Pluto was discovered to figure out the effect of Tombaugh's search.

### Review: Connecting Visual Information and Text

In a magazine article, images don't always explain information the way they do in a technical text, but they can still help readers understand the topic. Have students consider what they can learn about Pluto from the image on page 142.

## Guided Practice

### Recap Reading Selection

Work with students to make a time line of the events described in the first section of the text.

### Read and Practice

Have partners take turns reading the selection as you circulate to provide support. Model identifying the sequence of events with Cite Evidence callout A. For callout B, circulate and provide partners with scaffolding as needed. You might use the following suggestions to help students who are having difficulty.

### CITE EVIDENCE

**A** Guide students to locate the date in paragraph 8, and then find out what happened next. (A ninth planet was found.)

**B** Students may be confused because there are no further dates included in paragraph 8. Remind students that the schoolgirl's idea for the name of the ninth planet and her grandfather's passing on the suggestion occurred after the planet was discovered. In paragraph 9, however, there is a date that serves as a clue to when the events occur.

DESCRIBING TEXT STRUCTURES

Guided Practice

**WORDS TO KNOW**

**gravity**
**universe**

**CITE EVIDENCE**

**A** Clyde Tombaugh did not have to search as long as Percival Lowell did to find "Planet X." Underline the event that happened on March 13, 1930.

**B** Circle two things from paragraph 8 that occurred after March 13, 1930. In paragraph 9, circle the detail that tells you if the paragraph describes events from 1930 or refers to an earlier time.

**Pluto:** Planet or Not? *continued*

7 **Gravity** is a force that acts to draw objects together. The bigger an object is, the greater the object's gravitational pull. Gravity on Earth pulls objects to the ground, which is a good thing. Without Earth's gravitational pull, everything on Earth would float into space! The impact of Pluto's gravitational pull on Neptune and Uranus was great enough to make scientists look for its source.

8 On March 13, 1930, the Lowell Observatory announced the discovery. This object was celebrated as the ninth planet in our part of the **universe**. An 11-year-old schoolgirl from England suggested the name *Pluto*, after the name of a Roman god. Her grandfather was friends with an astronomer and passed on her suggestion.

9 Unfortunately, Percival Lowell, who died in 1916, did not live to see the discovery of his mystery planet. But one reason the name *Pluto* was selected was because the first two letters are Percival Lowell's initials.

### A Dwarf Planet

10 Pluto was called a planet for decades. Astronomers continued to study it. Around 1950, a scientist named Gerard Kuiper used a high-powered telescope to study Pluto. In 1978, other scientists discovered one of Pluto's moons. They named it Charon.

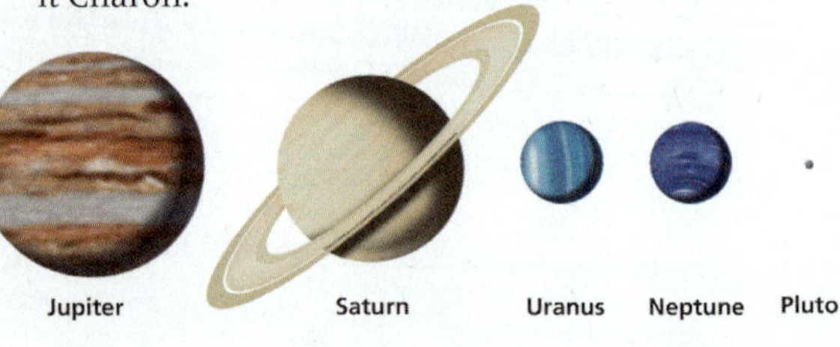




144 Chapter 6 ■ Integration of Knowledge and Ideas: Informational Texts

## Words to Know

**General Academic Vocabulary**

**universe** (*noun*): all the stars and planets; everything that is known to exist

**Domain-Specific Vocabulary**

**gravity** (*noun*): the force that pulls every object toward the center of the Earth or toward other objects

**Working with Word Meaning** Help students learn these word meanings by drawing an illustration of each word.

# INTEGRATION OF KNOWLEDGE AND IDEAS

## Guided Practice

11 Everything changed in 2006 when scientists decided to define the planets. Gravitational strength was a big part of this new definition, and Pluto no longer fit the definition of a planet.

### Comprehension Check

1. What is the effect of Earth's gravity?
   a. It pushes against Pluto.
   (b.) It pulls objects to the ground.
   c. It makes objects float into space.
   d. It helps astronomers find new planets.

2. What information caused Pluto to be called a planet in the first place?
   (a.) Its gravitational pull was great enough.
   b. It was named after a Roman god.
   c. It had a moon called Charon.
   d. It was far out in space.

3. Work with a partner to discuss the events that occurred around 1950 and in 1978. What caused these events? Cite text evidence.

   Sample answer: In the paragraph under "A Dwarf Planet," it says that around 1950, a scientist named Gerard Kuiper studied Pluto with a high-powered telescope. In 1978, other scientists discovered one of Pluto's moons. They named it Charon. Both of these events occurred because scientists decided to study Pluto.





## Foundational Skills Review: Digraph *ch*

Review the use of the digraph *ch* with students, reminding them that the two letters work together to make a single sound. Model how this digraph works in the word *search* that appears in the text. Challenge students to find other words in which this digraph appears. Students will likely point out the word *Charon*, the name of Pluto's moon. Explain that the name, which comes from ancient Greek, is pronounced KA-ren. In this case, the *ch* has a different pronunciation.

Additional phonics activities can be found at **sadlierconnect.com**.

## Guided Practice

### Comprehension Check

**Answer Explanations:**

1. Students should understand that Choice B, *It pulls objects to the ground*, is the effect of Earth's gravity, described in paragraph 7.
2. Choice A, *Its gravitational pull was great enough*, was the reason Pluto was called a planet, as described in paragraph 7.
3. Students should identify the dates 1950 and 1978 in paragraph 10. Both of these events occurred due to scientists' desire to study Pluto and our solar system.

### Reciprocal Teaching

Put students in groups of four, and assign each a role: summarizer, questioner, clarifier, and predictor. Students should then reread the section on pages 144–145.

After they have completed the section, the Summarizer will review what events were described on these pages. The Questioner will ask two or three questions about the topic that the selection has not yet answered. The Clarifier will attempt to answer the questions for the group. Finally, the Predictor will predict what information will be included in the next section of the text. Students should switch roles as they continue with the next section of the text.

## Independent Practice

### Recap Reading Selection

Continue filling in the time line with students. Also, ask students to summarize what gravity is and how Pluto was named.

### Read and Apply

Have students read the selection independently as you circulate. If you notice students struggling, you can provide support with the suggestions that follow.

#### CITE EVIDENCE

**A** Help students find the sentence in paragraph 14 that describes some people's reasoning. Guide students to see that the first sentence of this paragraph shows that some people disagree with calling Pluto a dwarf planet; the next sentence tells why they disagree.

**B** Prompt students to look for time-related clue words that indicate a sequence. You may wish to add these final events to the time line you have been creating. Finally, discuss the mnemonic of the planets' names with students. You may wish to have students look at the illustration of the planets on page 144 as you do so. If students are still confused about why the mnemonic must change, have a student cover up Pluto in the picture.

## DESCRIBING TEXT STRUCTURES

### Independent Practice

#### WORDS TO KNOW

**asteroid**
**dwarf planet**
**mnemonic**

#### CITE EVIDENCE

**A** Underline the text that describes why some people think Pluto should still be called a planet.

**B** Draw a box around words in the first and last sentence in paragraph 16 that point to a sequence of events. Why was a new mnemonic needed?

**Pluto:** Planet or Not? *continued*

12 In 2006, astronomers came up with new measurements for what makes something a planet. They said a planet had to have a certain level of gravity. Pluto did not meet that measurement. Its gravity was not strong enough to pull **asteroids** close or push them away.

13 Instead, Pluto became known as a **dwarf planet**, which is smaller than a regular planet. There are at least two other dwarf planets, Ceres and Eris. In fact, there might be many, many more.

14 Many people question the new classification. After all, Pluto does orbit the sun like the planets of the solar system. Yet size seems to matter the most, and Pluto is simply too small. Plus, it travels around the sun in a strange way. Also, sometimes Pluto passes in and out of Neptune's orbit. No other planets cross orbits with another planet.

#### Pluto Remains a Puzzle

15 Today, Pluto remains a puzzle for many people. Some think it should still be considered a planet. Others consider it to be only a dwarf planet. Still others believe it is somewhere in between. Will Pluto ever be a planet again? Its history shows that anything can happen. After all, 20 years ago, almost no one would have thought that the solar system would *lose* a planet.





### Words to Know

**General Academic Vocabulary**
**mnemonic** (*noun*): a phrase or trick to help one remember something

**Domain-Specific Vocabulary**
**asteroid** (*noun*): a rocky space object
**dwarf planet** (*noun*): a very small planet

**Working with Word Meaning** Help students extend their understanding of these words by giving them examples of mnemonics. Challenge students to work in pairs to come up with their own mnemonic for the names of the planets and share it with the class.

**Independent Practice**

### A Way to Remember

16 After 2006, we looked at Pluto in a new way. We also came up with a new **mnemonic** (nih-MAH-nik). A mnemonic is a phrase that helps you remember something. A mnemonic for the solar system used to be "My Very Educated Mother Just Served Us Nine Pies." The first letter of each word represents a planet. So "My" stood for Mercury, and so on. Now, many students use "My Very Educated Mother Just Served Us Noodles."

**Comprehension Check** MORE ONLINE sadlierconnect.com

1. What happened in 2006 that changed Pluto to a dwarf planet?
   - a. Scientists discovered Neptune.
   - b. Scientists decided Ceres and Eris were dwarf planets.
   - c. Scientists used new measurements to classify planets.
   - d. Pluto failed to orbit the sun.

2. The author seems to suggest that because of its unpredictable past, Pluto could one day
   - a. change in size.
   - b. be named a planet again.
   - c. change places with Neptune.
   - d. drop out of the solar system.

3. Explain the decision astronomers made about Pluto in 2006. What was the cause of this decision? What was the effect?

   Sample answer: In 2006, astronomers decided to call Pluto a dwarf planet. They did this because they believed a planet had to have a certain level of gravity, which Pluto didn't have. People disagreed about this decision.





## Support English Language Learners

Help English language learners pronounce the word *mnemonic*. Point out that the pronunciation of this unusual word appears in parentheses directly after the word where it appears in paragraph 16 on page 147. Say the word aloud several times, and have students repeat after you. Explain that this parenthetical information is intended to help readers pronounce the word it follows and is not meant to be read separately. If time allows, discuss other words in which a letter is not pronounced, such as the words *climb* and *pneumonia*. Remind students that these kinds of words do appear in English, and their pronunciations simply have to be memorized.

## Independent Practice

**Comprehension Check**

**Answer Explanations:**

1. Students should be able to use information in paragraph 12 to see that choice C, *Scientists used new measurements to classify planets*, is correct.
2. The discussion in paragraph 15 should lead students to choice B, *be named a planet again.*
3. Pluto was classified as a dwarf planet in 2006. The cause of this decision was a new definition of the word *planet*, and it led to disagreement and a changed view of the solar system.

## Critical Comprehension

Use the following questions to help students think more deeply about the text. Students should be prepared to support their answers with evidence from the text.

- *Why has the number of planets in our solar system changed over the years?* (New planets were discovered, and a new definition of the word *planet* has been determined.)
- *Based on this article, do you think Pluto should be called a planet?* (Answers will vary.)

**Assess and Respond**

**If** students have difficulty answering the Comprehension Check questions,

**Then** have them tell you where they had the most difficulty—reading the text, finding information, or understanding questions. Provide assistance according to the responses.

## Guided Instruction

**OBJECTIVE**
**Compare and contrast two texts on the same topic.**

### Genre: Editorial

Explain to students that an editorial is an article written to share an opinion or promote an idea.

### Set the Purpose

Help students set the purpose for reading by saying *The previous text, "Pluto: Planet or Not?" provided information about Pluto. Now we're going to compare it to another article that expresses an opinion about whether Pluto should be called a planet.*

### Model and Teach

Read the selection as students follow along in their books.

**CITE EVIDENCE**

**A** *The key details are important information about a topic. I'll look for paragraphs that tell me a lot about Pluto.*

*Which paragraphs do this?* (paragraphs 2 and 3)

**B** *I'll look for scientific details about Pluto that were not in the previous article.*

*Do these details make Pluto seem like a planet?* (Yes. It orbits the sun as do planets.)

COMPARING AND CONTRASTING TEXTS

Guided Instruction

**WORDS TO KNOW**
**category**
**ellipse**
**interior**

To **compare**, you look at how two or more things are alike. To **contrast**, you look at how they are different.

**CITE EVIDENCE**

**A** To **compare** or **contrast** two pieces on the same topic, it is necessary to find the **key details** in each. Box the paragraphs that give key details that describe Pluto.

**B** When comparing, see how details in the pieces are similar; when contrasting, see how they are different. Underline details about Pluto that did not appear in "Pluto: Planet or Not?" Do these details support the idea that Pluto is a planet?

## Pluto Is Our Planet!

(Genre: Editorial)

1 We used to have nine planets: Mercury, Venus, Earth, Mars, Jupiter, Saturn, Uranus, Neptune, and Pluto. Pluto was discovered in 1930 and was a planet until 2006. Then scientists decided that Pluto was only a "dwarf" planet. It does not make sense to add this other **category** of planet. Pluto and the other dwarf planets are planets, too!

2 Pluto is very, very far away from the sun. It is in the Kuiper Belt, an area in space that is full of icy, rocky objects. Pluto is very small. It is only about two-thirds the size of Earth's moon. However, it has at least five moons. One, named Charon, is half as big as Pluto. The other moons are very small.

3 Pluto has a rocky core surrounded by ice. It takes 248 years for Pluto to go around the sun. It moves in an **ellipse**, so sometimes it is nearer to the sun than at other times. When it comes close to the sun, the ice on its surface melts and an atmosphere forms. When it moves farther away, the ice freezes again and the atmosphere disappears.





### Words to Know

**General Academic Vocabulary**
**category** (*noun*): a group of objects that are alike
**interior** (*noun*): the inside of an object

**Domain-Specific Vocabulary**
**ellipse** (*noun*): an oval shape

**Working with Word Meaning** Help students understand the meanings of these words by having them write a paragraph that includes all three words.

## INTEGRATION OF KNOWLEDGE AND IDEAS

4 Pluto is not the only dwarf planet. Another dwarf planet is named Eris. This little world is very similar to Pluto. It, too, has a rocky middle and icy outer surface. It is also about the same size. Eris is even farther from the sun than Pluto. Its orbit around the sun takes 557 years and moves Eris beyond the Kuiper Belt. It only has one known moon.

5 Ceres is yet another dwarf planet. It is in the asteroid belt between Mars and Jupiter. Ceres is only about the size of Texas, but it is more like a planet than an asteroid. It is rocky and nearly round, and it has a lot of water. Its **interior** is in layers like a planet. Astronomers at first called Ceres a planet, too. They then called it an asteroid before deciding it was a dwarf planet.

### Comprehension Check

Compare the details given here about Pluto to those given in "Pluto: Planet or Not?" Which are the same? Which are different? Cite text evidence.

### Guided Instruction

**CITE EVIDENCE**

**C** Look for clue words like *another*, *both*, and *too* that show comparison. Circle the comparison words in paragraph 4.

**D** Underline details that show how the dwarf planets Eris and Ceres are similar to Pluto. Were Eris and Ceres described in "Pluto: Planet or Not?"

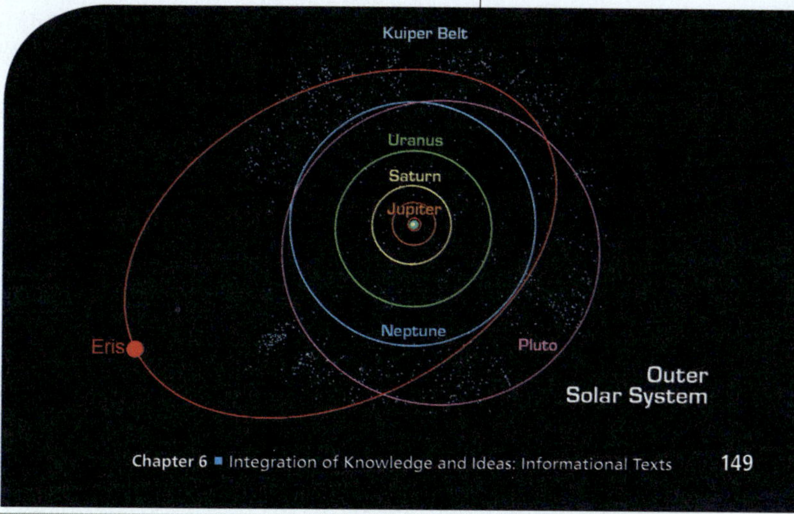






## Support English Language Learners

Help students understand the technical details explained in paragraphs 2 and 3 on page 148. Encourage them to read slowly, making sure they understand each sentence before they move on. It may help for students to illustrate each detail they read about Pluto, especially the elliptical shape of Pluto's orbit and the way its atmosphere forms and then disappears.

## Guided Instruction

### CITE EVIDENCE

**C** *I'll look for those clue words in paragraph 4.*

*What are these words comparing?* (Pluto and the dwarf planet Eris)

**D** *I'll use the clue words I just circled and look for others to help me find the details about other dwarf planets.*

*How are these dwarf planets similar? Were Eris and Ceres discussed in "Pluto: Planet or Not?"* (Eris and Pluto are similar in size and have rocky cores with icy surfaces. They were mentioned but not described.)

### Comprehension Check

**Sample Answer:** These details are a scientific description of Pluto instead of the history of its discovery. Both texts describe Pluto as a small planetlike object that is very far away. This editorial says Pluto has a rocky core surrounded by ice, an atmosphere, and at least five moons.

**Answer Explanation:** Encourage students to refer back to the article "Pluto: Planet or Not?" Students should see that the focus of the two articles is different, but that both contain similar details about Pluto.

## Listening and Viewing Skills

Have students study the image on page 149 while you reread paragraphs 4–5. *Locate Pluto and Eris. What shape is Eris's orbit? Where would Ceres appear in the image?* (Eris has an elliptical orbit. Ceres would appear within Jupiter's orbit.)

## Review: Describing Text Structures

Have students use their knowledge of text structures to determine the cause of Pluto having an atmosphere only some of the time.

## Guided Practice

### Recap Reading Selection

Place students in groups of three. One student should describe Pluto, one Eris, and one Ceres. Encourage students to refer to or create a picture of the solar system and identify where each dwarf planet is located.

### Read and Practice

Have partners take turns reading the selection as you circulate to provide support. Model comparing and contrasting with Cite Evidence callout A. For callout B, circulate and provide partners with scaffolding as needed. You might use the following suggestions to help students who are having difficulty.

#### CITE EVIDENCE

**A** Remind students that contrast clue words include *but*, *unlike*, *instead*, *on the other hand*, *in contrast*, and *on the contrary*. These words let readers know that a description of differences will follow. Students should be able to locate the contrast clue words *On the other hand* at the beginning of paragraph 8.

**B** Help students find the information in paragraph 7 that shows that Pluto and Mercury are similar in size. The similar size of Mercury and Pluto was not described in "Pluto: Planet or Not?"

COMPARING AND CONTRASTING TEXTS

## Guided Practice

**WORDS TO KNOW**
**diameter**
**judging**

**CITE EVIDENCE**

**A** Underline the clue words that show a contrast is being made in paragraph 8.

**B** Circle the name of the planet that is close in size to Pluto. Did the other article discuss the similar size of this planet and Pluto?

**Pluto Is Our Planet!** *continued*

6 Pluto and the other dwarf planets *are* different in some ways. But the dwarf planets are not different enough to be in their own group. In fact, in many ways the dwarf planets are more similar to the interior planets, Mercury, Venus, Earth, and Mars, than these planets are to the outer planets of our solar system.

7 The name *dwarf planet* makes it seem as if these objects are simply too small to be planets. But this is not true. They are small, but the planet Mercury has a **diameter** similar to that of Earth's moon. Pluto is much more similar in size to Mercury than Mercury is to any of the outer planets. Mercury and Venus have no moons. Earth has one, and Mars has only two. These interior planets are small and have only a few moons, just like Pluto.

8 On the other hand, the outer planets, Jupiter, Saturn, Uranus, and Neptune, are all much bigger than Earth. Jupiter is more than ten times bigger, Saturn nine times, and Neptune and Uranus almost four times bigger. All have many moons. Neptune has the fewest with 13. Saturn has at least 53! **Judging** simply by size, it seems that Earth and the inner planets are much more similar to each other and the dwarf planets. Maybe the outer planets should be called "giant planets"!



150 Chapter 6 ■ Integration of Knowledge and Ideas: Informational Texts

## Words to Know

**General Academic Vocabulary**

**judging** (*verb*): forming a conclusion or making a decision

**Domain-Specific Vocabulary**

**diameter** (*noun*): the distance through the middle of a planet or space object

**Working with Word Meaning** Help students become more familiar with these vocabulary words by having them use each one in a sentence of their own.

# INTEGRATION OF KNOWLEDGE AND IDEAS

## Guided Practice

9 Pluto and the other dwarf planets are not big enough to clear asteroids out of their orbits. Instead, they are surrounded by other objects. This is the main difference scientists use to call them "dwarf planets." This difference is not nearly as important as the similarities between Pluto and the planets.

### Comprehension Check

MORE ONLINE sadlierconnect.com

1. What does "Pluto: Planet or Not?" say about dwarf planets that this article does not?
   a. There is only one, Pluto.
   (b.) There might be many, many more.
   c. There are only two, Eris and Ceres.
   d. There are some as big as Mercury.

2. Contrast this article so far to the first one, "Pluto: Planet or Not?" How are they different?
   a. The first is an opinion piece; this one is nonfiction.
   b. The first is fiction; this one is nonfiction.
   c. They are not different; both are opinion pieces.
   (d.) The first is nonfiction; this one is an opinion piece.

3. What key point is the author making in this section? Compare and contrast how this point is discussed here and in "Pluto: Planet or Not?"

   Sample answer: The author points out that Pluto is more similar in size and number of moons to Earth and the interior planets than those planets are to the giant planets. In "Pluto: Planet or Not?" the author does not discuss Pluto's moons or the the differences between the inner and outer planets.





## Discussion Skills

Remind students to apply their own thinking to what others say during a discussion. Tell them to think about whether they agree or disagree with what is said and then add their own comments—with reasons. Students' active participation helps to develop a true discussion instead of just one in which each participant states his or her opinion.

Help students apply their own ideas and reasoning by using these prompts:

- *I mostly agree with what you say, but I think… because ….*
- *I have to disagree with you because….*

## Guided Practice

### Comprehension Check

**Answer Explanations:**

**1.** Students will need time to refer back to "Pluto: Planet or Not?" They should see that choice B, *There might be many, many more*, is correct.

**2.** "Pluto: Planet or Not?" tells about Pluto but does not state an opinion; "Pluto Is Our Planet!" is an editorial with a clearly stated opinion. Therefore, students should recognize that choice D, *The first is nonfiction; this one is an opinion piece,* is the correct answer.

**3.** Guide students to see that this section of the editorial shows how Pluto shares similarities with the inner planets, and that Pluto and all the inner planets are very different from the outer planets. These issues are not discussed in the other article.

### Turn and Talk

Place students in pairs, and ask them to discuss this question: *What categories of planets do we have in our solar system? What size are the planets in each group?* Then ask volunteers to share their ideas with the class.

## Independent Practice

### Recap Reading Selection

Lead students to make three lists: one describing features of the inner planets, one describing features of the outer planets, and one describing features of dwarf planets. Ask students to summarize the differences among these planets.

### Read and Apply

Have students read the selection independently as you circulate. If you notice students struggling, you can provide support with the suggestions that follow.

### CITE EVIDENCE

**A** Remind students that in the previous section you discussed the clue words that signal contrast. Remind them of the clue words that signal comparison: *although*, *also*, *too*, *however*, *similarly*, *likewise*, *as well*, and *both*. Guide them to search for these words in the text.

**B** Help students see that in the callout the word *versus* tells them to look for contrasts between the outer and inner planets. Remind them to look for contrast signal words (*different*) that will show the differences between the two categories.



## Independent Practice

**WORDS TO KNOW**
**core**
**tilted**

**CITE EVIDENCE**

**A** Circle the clue words that signal comparison and contrast on this page.

**B** Underline the details that describe the qualities of the outer versus the inner planets. Did the other article also cover these details?

**Pluto Is Our Planet!** *continued*

10 Pluto is not that different from Earth in how it is formed. Earth and the inner planets Mercury and Mars are mostly made up of rock. Their surfaces are surrounded by an atmosphere, although Mercury has only a very thin one. Pluto also has an atmosphere some of the time. It and the other dwarf planets are rocky, too.

11 However, the outer giants are different. They are not made up mostly of rock. Jupiter has a small, rocky **core** deep inside the planet, but most of it is made of gases like hydrogen and helium. Saturn is very similar to Jupiter, which is made of hydrogen and helium. Spaceships could not land on these planets! Uranus and Neptune are ice giants. Both have thick atmospheres as well. Both are **tilted** strangely to the side and are very, very cold.

12 It is clear that planets have a lot of differences. It is also clear that Pluto is more similar to Earth and the inner planets than the outer planets are. Saying that Pluto is not a planet makes little sense when it is compared to Earth, and Earth to Jupiter or Saturn.

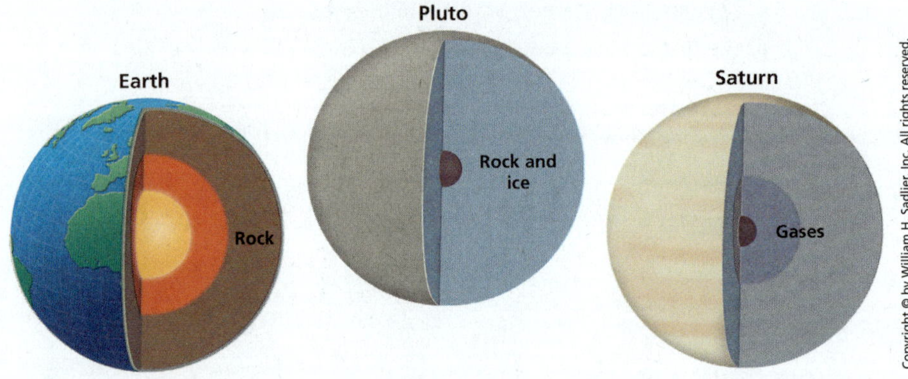






## Words to Know

**General Academic Vocabulary**
**tilted** (*adjective*): at an angle, aslant

**Domain-Specific Vocabulary**
**core** (*noun*): the center of a planet or space object, often surrounded by a surface or atmosphere

**Working with Word Meaning** Help students become more familiar with these words by having them give an example and nonexample for each.

## INTEGRATION OF KNOWLEDGE AND IDEAS

### Independent Practice

13 Pluto deserves to be a planet. It is small, far away, and very cold, but it is still part of our solar system. Our solar system has room for planets as different as Mercury and Jupiter. It has room for Ceres, Eris, and especially for Pluto, too!

**Comprehension Check**  MORE ONLINE **sadlierconnect.com**

1. What does this article tell us about Uranus and Neptune that "Pluto: Planet or Not?" does not?

   **a.** They have rocky cores.

   **b.** They were discovered 65 years apart.

   **(c.)** They are ice giants.

   **d.** They are similar to Jupiter.

2. What does the author of "Pluto: Planet or Not?" tell us about Pluto that this opinion article does not?

   **a.** how Pluto was formed

   **(b.)** how Pluto first became a planet

   **c.** why Pluto was named a dwarf planet

   **d.** why Pluto should be a regular planet again

3. What key point is the author making in this section? Compare and contrast how this point is discussed here and in "Pluto: Planet or Not?"

   Sample answer: The author points out that Pluto is similar to Earth and the interior planets. They are all unlike the gas and ice giant outer planets. The article "Pluto: Planet or Not?" does not compare Pluto directly to other planets in the solar system.





## Speaking and Listening: Presentation

Have students create a presentation on a way that people have extended their understanding of the solar system. After gathering information, students should take turns presenting to the class. Presenters should:

- state their topic, choose words for effect, and present appropriate facts.
- use formal language suitable for an academic presentation.
- speak clearly and answer questions in complete sentences.
- provide engaging visuals to enhance their presentation.

Listeners should listen attentively and ask questions.

## Independent Practice

**Comprehension Check**

**Answer Explanations:**

**1.** Students may need time to refer back to "Pluto: Planet or Not?" in order to determine that choice C, *They are ice giants*, is the correct answer.

**2.** Students may need time to refer back to "Pluto: Planet or Not?" to see that choice B, *how Pluto first became a planet*, is the correct answer.

**3.** Guide students to see that this section compares the composition of Pluto and the inner planets, which is similar, and contrasts it to that of the outer planets. Students may need to refer back to "Pluto: Planet or Not?" to see that it does not discuss this issue.

## Critical Comprehension

Use the following questions to help students think more deeply about the text. Students should be prepared to support their answers with evidence from the text.

- *What types of information did each article give? What was the effect on the reader of the information they gave?* (The first article addressed the history of Pluto's discovery; the second addressed its scientific qualities.)
- *Now that you have read this editorial, do you think Pluto should be a planet? Why? Did your opinion change from the last discussion? Why?* (Answers will vary.)

**Assess and Respond**

**If** students have trouble answering the questions in the Comprehension Check,

**Then** ask them comprehension questions about pages 152–153 to determine whether they understood what they read. If they did not, you may wish to form a reading group to support them.

## Connect Across Texts: *4 points*
## Review Reading Selections

Place students in groups of three. Each student should create a summary of one of the three texts. Then work with the class to summarize each of the texts together.

## Compare and Contrast Texts

Review the directions on page 154 with students. Instruct students to fill in the chart with information about the two texts they are comparing.

**Rubric**

| | |
|---|---|
| 4 | Student has identified multiple similarities and differences between the two texts. |
| 3 | Student has identified some of the similarities and differences between the two texts. |
| 2 | Student has identified at least one similarity and at least one difference between the two texts. |
| 1 | Student has identified some similarities OR differences between the two texts. |
| 0 | Student has not identified the similarities and differences between the two texts. |

## CONNECT ACROSS TEXTS

### Compare and Contrast Texts

In this chapter, you read about how to make a telescope and whether Pluto should be considered a planet. Think about what you learned from the texts and compare and contrast two of them using the T-chart below. List key details and important points from the texts to show the similarities and differences between them. Be prepared to discuss your ideas with the class.

| Similarities | Differences |
|---|---|
| **Pluto: Planet or Not?** and **Pluto Is Our Planet!**<br>how Pluto became a dwarf planet<br>size, gravity, and orbit of Pluto<br>other dwarf planets | **Pluto: Planet or Not?**<br>discovery of Pluto<br>asks whether Pluto should be a planet<br>**Pluto Is Our Planet!**<br>more details of Pluto's characteristics<br>compares Pluto's size, moons, structure, atmosphere to other planets<br>argues should be a planet again |





## Extend Thinking: Create

Ask students to work in pairs to choose a planet other than Pluto or another object in our solar system (such as the moon or a comet) to research. Based on information they found, they should create a visual to present to the class. Suggest that students study the illustrations and diagrams in this chapter for ideas on what their visuals might look like and elements, such as arrows and labels, that they might include.

## CONNECT ACROSS TEXTS

### Connect to the Essential Question

***How can authors use text structure to connect ideas and information?*** In small groups or as a class, discuss the Essential Question. Think about what you have learned about text illustrations, text structures, and comparing and contrasting texts. Use evidence from the chapter texts to answer the question.

Sample answer: Authors use different text structures to best present information. "How to Make a Telescope" uses sequence to explain making a telescope. It also uses visuals to clarify points. "Pluto: Planet or Not?" uses sequence and cause and effect to explain Pluto's discovery and why it is not a planet by some standards. "Pluto Is Our Planet!" uses cause and effect to explain why Pluto is a planet. Comparing and contrasting texts helps the reader form an opinion about Pluto.

### Connect to the Theme

***The Solar System*** In this chapter, you read about planets in the solar system. Why is it important to understand the solar system? Support your answer with details from the text.

Sample answer: The solar system is everything that orbits the sun. Earth is part of the solar system, but so are other masses like Pluto. We can "see the stars and the planets" with tools like telescopes. We can also understand why some objects are considered planets but others are not. People have studied the solar system for centuries. We continue to learn new things that help us understand our world.



**To strengthen your response, reread parts of the texts that support your answers. Add to your answers any additional details you find.**



## Assess and Respond (pages 154–155)

| If | Then |
|---|---|
| Students scored 0–2 points, they are **Developing** their understanding of the skills… | Provide students with reading support and more intensive modeling of skills. |
| Students scored 3–5 points, they are **Improving** their understanding of the skills… | Use students' scores to target areas that are weak, and review those specific skills. |
| Students scored 6–8 points, they are **Proficient** in their understanding of the skills… | Have these students move on. They are ready for the formal assessment. |

## Support Essential Question Discussion

Have students reread the Essential Question. Lead a discussion by prompting them with the following: *I understand the ideas and information authors want to share when…*

Encourage students to think about the skills covered in this chapter as they answer.

## Theme Wrap-Up

Lead students in a group discussion on the theme of the solar system. Discuss how people learned about the solar system and how ideas about it have changed over the years.

## Short-Answer Questions: *2 points each*

### Connect to the Essential Question Rubric

| | |
|---|---|
| 2 | Students are able to correctly identify how authors use text structure to connect ideas and information. |
| 1 | Students are able to identify some ways that authors use text structure to connect ideas and information. |
| 0 | Students are not able to explain any ways in which authors use text structure to connect ideas and information. |

### Connect to the Theme Rubric

| | |
|---|---|
| 2 | Students are able to explain why it is important to understand the solar system and provide support from the text. |
| 1 | Students are able to explain why it is important to understand the solar system but do not provide support from the text. |
| 0 | Students are not able to explain why it is important to understand the solar system and do not provide support from the text. |

**OBJECTIVE**

**Understand shades of meaning in words that describe states of mind or degrees of certainty.**

## Guided Instruction

Review the Guided Instruction section on page 156 with students. Go over the words and their definitions in the chart. Help the class write example sentences using the word *think* and each of its synonyms in the chart.

## Guided Practice

If students are having trouble, encourage them to try filling in the definition from the chart in place of the word in the sentence. They can then determine whether or not the statement reflects a reliance on evidence.

## Independent Practice

If students are having trouble, suggest that they try randomly plugging the boldfaced words into the blanks and then reading aloud the sentences to hear how they sound. If they are still not sure, they can again apply the strategy of replacing the word with its definition until they can match the words *suspect*, *wonder*, and *believe* to the correct sentences.

## Apply to Reading

Have students work in pairs to write a paragraph summarizing the changing ideas humans have held about Pluto, using three of the words from the chart correctly.

# LANGUAGE

## Shades of Meaning

**Guided Instruction** Sometimes words have similar meanings, but they do not mean exactly the same thing. Instead, words have different shades of meaning—like different shades of blue in a box of crayons. Each word describes the same thing in a slightly different way. Compare the synonyms for the word *think* in the chart.

**Guided Practice** Refer to the chart and chapter passages. Answer *yes* or *no* to show if each situation is based on evidence.

| | |
|---|---|
| **suspect** | think based on clues or evidence |
| **wonder** | think about without evidence |
| **believe** | accept without evidence |
| **know; understand** | accept based on evidence |

__yes__ 1. We know that Earth and the other planets move around the sun.

__no__ 2. Percival Lowell believed Pluto had moons.

__yes__ 3. Lowell suspected that there was a ninth planet.

**Independent Practice** Pick the correct synonym to complete each sentence below.

**suspect** **wonder** **believe**

1. Children might __believe__ that the sun moves around Earth.
2. As scientists gathered evidence, they began to __suspect__ that Pluto was not a planet.
3. Ancient people would __wonder__ why stars seemed to move.





## Support English Language Learners

Students who are learning English are less likely to have an intuitive sense of the shades of meaning of the words listed in the chart on this page. Help these students become more familiar with these words by providing several sample sentences for each word and encouraging students to write their own sentences with each word. You may wish to use these prompts:

1. *The clues the detective found led her to* **suspect** ________.
2. *The child shook his birthday present and* **wondered** ________.
3. *She had never been to California, but she* **believed** ________.
4. *After she read the book, she* **knew** ________.

# CHAPTER 6 REVIEW

Read the following passage, which includes illustrations and text features. Then answer the questions on pages 157 and 158.

## Comets

(Genre: Scientific Text)

**Comets** People once believed that comets were signs of something about to happen. Now we know that they are huge balls of frozen gases, like giant, dirty snowballs. As comets near the sun, they heat up. Because the comet gets warmer, some of the ice melts and a long tail forms behind the comet. Astronomer Gerard Kuiper suspected in 1951 that many comets come from a field of objects beyond Neptune. These comets orbit Earth at a distance.

**The Tale of a Tail** The tail of a comet is amazing! It shines like a sword in the sky. No wonder ancient people thought it was an omen. At right, you can see how a comet's tail forms.

**Fill in the circle of the correct answer choice.**

1. Which word in sentence 1 tells you that the people did not know what comets were?
   - ● believed
   - ○ about
   - ○ signs
   - ○ happen

2. Which answer choice could replace *know* in sentence 2 of paragraph 1?
   - ○ suspect
   - ● have evidence to show us
   - ○ believe
   - ○ do not have evidence to show us

3. What is the connection between sentences 3 and 4 in paragraph 1?
   - ○ none
   - ○ steps in a sequence
   - ● cause and effect
   - ○ comparison





### Self-Assessment: Progress Check

Have students revisit the Progress Check on page 133 and respond to the questions again. Ask them to compare their Before and After responses.

You may wish to have students rate their answers on a scale of 0–2 rather than simply checking (or not checking) the box. Instruct them to write a 0 if they feel they do not understand a given skill at all, a 1 if they feel they have some understanding, and a 2 if they feel they have a solid grasp of the skill.

## Chapter Summary

At this point, students have had instruction and practice in reading informational text, with a focus on learning about the solar system. Students have learned how to connect visual information and text, to describe text structures, and to compare and contrast texts on the same topic. Students have practiced working with concepts across texts and examined how shades of meanings contribute to their understanding of words. They should be well prepared for the review session.

### Introduce the Review

Explain to students that they will read a new passage that is related to the chapter's theme and the selections they have already read. Instruct students to read the passage carefully and then answer the questions on pages 157 and 158.

### Answer Explanations

Scoring: Items 1–9 on pages 157–158 are worth 1 point each. See the rubric for guidance on scoring the Write About It question on page 158.

1. Students should understand that the word *believed* shows that people had no evidence.
2. Students should use what they learned from the chart on page 156 to understand that the phrase *have evidence to show us* would best replace the word *know.*
3. *Cause and effect* is the connection between these two sentences.

## Answer Explanations

**4.** Students should refer back to the texts to see that "How to Make a Telescope" also has an image of a comet.

**5.** The cause-and-effect word *because* connects the sentences.

**6.** Nearing the sun is the first step in the formation of a comet's tail.

**7.** Comets start out looking like giant, dirty snowballs.

**8.** The middle illustration on page 157 shows the sun in the distance.

**9.** Only "The Tale of A Tail" includes a description of what a comet's tail looks like—a shining sword in the sky.

## Write About It Rubric

| | |
|---|---|
| 2 | Answer correctly explains sequence of events. |
| 1 | Answer explains some parts of the sequence. |
| 0 | Answer does not explain any parts of the sequence. |

## CHAPTER 6 REVIEW

**4.** Which other text in this chapter has an image of a comet?

- ● "How to Make a Telescope"
- ○ "Pluto Is Our Planet!"
- ○ "Pluto: Planet or Not?"
- ○ none of the texts

**5.** What word connects sentences 3 and 4 in paragraph 1?

- ○ as
- ● because
- ○ near
- ○ gets

**6.** What is the first step in the formation of a comet's tail?

- ○ the comet comes from a field
- ○ the ice starts to melt
- ● the comet gets near the sun
- ○ the comet orbits Earth

**7.** What does a comet look like before it enters our solar system?

- ● like a giant, dirty snowball
- ○ like a ball with a tail
- ○ like a sword in the sky
- ○ like the sun

**8.** According to the illustration, what causes the comet's tail to form?

- ○ frozen gases
- ○ heat from other planets
- ● heat from the sun
- ○ ice

**9.** Only "The Tale of a Tail" includes an explanation of

- ○ how a comet forms
- ○ why comets were omens
- ○ where comets come from
- ● what a comet's tail looks like

**Write About It** Explain the sequence of events in the text.
First, the comet nears the sun, then it heats up and starts to melt, and finally the tail forms behind it.



158 Chapter 6 ■ Integration of Knowledge and Ideas: Informational Texts

## Analyze Student Scores

| | |
|---|---|
| **9–11 pts Strong** | Student has a good grasp of the skills and concepts taught in this chapter. Point out any mistakes the student has made, and explain the correct answers if necessary. |
| **4–8 pts Progressing** | Student is struggling with some skills or concepts. Identify the specific skills that are problematic to target a review of instruction. |
| **0–3 pts Emerging** | Student is having serious problems understanding the skills and concepts taught in this chapter. Student may need to redo the work with a higher level of support. |

CHAPTER 7

Text Types and Purposes

## Write Fictional Narratives

**Focus on Writing** When you write a fictional narrative, you tell a story.

**Think About Theme** Think about a fictional hero whose story you might like to tell.

**Let's Get on Our Way!** The story needs a beginning, a middle, and an end. Use words such as *first* and *then* for clarity.

These are the skills you will build in this chapter. Before you begin, check the boxes on the left of any items you can do well now. At the end of the chapter, you will return to this page to use the check boxes on the right to show what you have learned.

Before Chapter 7 | Progress Check **Can I?**   | After Chapter 7

- ☐ Write a story with imaginary characters and events. ☐
- ☐ Write the story with a beginning, middle, and end. ☐
- ☐ Use dialogue and descriptive details. ☐
- ☐ Use words to make the order of events clear. ☐
- ☐ Choose words and phrases for effect. ☐
- ☐ Write using nouns, including abstract nouns. ☐
- ☐ Write using regular and irregular plural nouns. ☐
- ☐ Write using possessives. ☐
- ☐ Write using correct punctuation in dialogue. ☐





**Student Page 159**

## Progress Check

The Progress Check is a self-assessment feature that students can use to gauge their own progress. Research shows that when students take accountability for their own learning, their motivation increases.

Before students begin work on Chapter 7, have them check the boxes next to any item that they feel they can do well. It is fine if they don't check any of the boxes. Tell them that they will have an opportunity to learn about and practice all of these items while studying the chapter. Let them know that near the end of the chapter they will have a chance to reconsider how well they can do each item on this list.

Before students begin the Chapter 7 Review on page 171, have them revisit this page. You can use this information to work with students on any items they don't understand before they tackle the Review.

## HOME ✦ CONNECT...

The Home Connect feature is a way to keep parents or other adult family members apprised of what their children are learning. The key learning objectives are listed, and some ideas for related activities and discussions are included.

Explain to students that they can share the Home Connect page with their parents or other adult family members in their home. Let students know how much time the class will be spending on this chapter so they can plan their time accordingly at home.

Encourage students and their parents to share their experiences using the suggestions on the Home Connect page. You may wish to make a place to post some of this work.

### HOME ✦ CONNECT...

In this chapter, children will learn about writing **fictional narratives**. A fictional narrative tells about an imagined experience or events. After reading a fictional narrative with your child, ask him or her to retell the story. Point out that the story is told in **sequence** with a beginning, a middle, and an end. Encourage your child's writing imagination by asking what he or she might have changed about a story's events.

Invite your child to share the story that he or she writes for this chapter. Ask questions about the **characters** and **narrators**, and decide together what you learn about the characters through what they say and do.

When writing narratives, writers choose precise words to **describe events** and show **how the characters think, feel, or act**. Encourage your child to concentrate on finding the best, most appropriate words and phrases in his or her writing. Ask your child what different words he or she might use in a passage of **description** or **dialogue** that the two of you read together.

**Activity:** Brainstorm about a character with your child. The character should be fictional but might be based on a real person you both know. Create a time and place for the character. With your child, describe how the character feels about something at a certain point (for example, lonely or excited). Then have your child write a few sentences of dialogue or description to show how the character feels.

**IN THIS CHAPTER, YOUR CHILD WILL...**

- Learn to write a story with imaginary characters and events, using dialogue, descriptive details, and a clear sequence of events.
- Learn to use linking words, such as *first, then,* and *finally* to signal the order of events.
- Learn language skills to use in writing a fictional narrative.
  - Recognize abstract nouns and use them in sentences.
  - Use the correct forms of regular and irregular plural nouns, such as *children* and *women*.
  - Use a possessive to show ownership, such as *Katie's skate*.
  - Write dialogue and use correct punctuation to show who is speaking.

**WAYS TO HELP YOUR CHILD**

Help your child to read like a writer. As your child reads, ask questions about the characters, such as *How does the writer show how the character feels?* or *Why do you think the writer included that event?* Emphasize that the writer thinks carefully about his or her word choice to help the reader understand the characters, actions, and settings.

ONLINE
For more Home Connect activities, continue online at sadlierconnect.com





**Student Page 160**

## LEARNING PROGRESSIONS

In this chapter, students will learn how to develop a fictional narrative with character dialogue. In order to learn the skills necessary to craft a fictional narrative, students will further develop skills learned in second grade. They should be encouraged to retain these skills, as they will continue to build on them in fourth grade.

| Writing Narratives | • By the end of grade 2, students should have been able to write narratives in which they recount a well-elaborated event or short sequence of events.<br>• In grade 3, students will build on this skill by establishing a situation and introducing a narrator and/or characters, and they will be able to organize an event sequence that unfolds naturally.<br>• When students move on to grade 4, they will orient the reader as they establish a situation and introduce a narrator and characters. They will continue to organize an event sequence that unfolds naturally. |
|---|---|
| Including Details | • By the end of grade 2, students should have been able to include details to describe actions, thoughts, and feelings.<br>• Throughout grades 3 and 4, students will build on this skill by using dialogue and descriptions of actions, thoughts, and feelings to develop experiences and events or show the response of characters to situations. |
| Using Temporal Words and Phrases | • By the end of grade 2, students should have been able to use temporal words to signal event order.<br>• In grade 3, students will use not only temporal words, but also phrases, to signal event order.<br>• Throughout grades 3 and 4, students will build on this skill by using a variety of transitional words and phrases to manage the sequence of events. |
| Writing Conclusions | • By the end of grade 2 and throughout grade 3, students should have been able to provide a sense of closure.<br>• This skill prepares students for grade 4, when they will provide a conclusion that follows a narrated experience or event. |

**Essential Question:**
**How do writers develop fictional narratives?**

In this chapter, students will learn that fictional narratives can include dialogue and should have a beginning, middle, and end.

## Theme: It Takes a Hero

Students will continue to explore different types of heroes as they read and analyze a fictional narrative writing model.

## Curriculum Connection: Language Arts

Students will use what they have learned from reading folktales and myths about heroes as they work on their own fictional narrative.

## Connect Reading to Writing

Remind students that they read a fictional narrative entitled "Athena and Poseidon" in Chapter 1 (Student Book pages 24–29). Review the dialogue and details as well as the series of events in that fictional narrative. Tell students they will be reading and writing a fictional narrative in this chapter.

## Writing Handbook

If students need extra practice with writing a fictional narrative, refer them to the *Writing Handbook* at **sadlierconnect.com**. The Writing Handbook gives students detailed instruction on planning, drafting, revising, and editing their writing. They will also find tips on producing, publishing, and presenting their writing.

**OBJECTIVE**

**Write a fictional narrative that includes an event sequence, dialogue and descriptions, sequence words and phrases, and that provides a sense of closure.**

## Introduce: Organizational Structure

Draw students' attention to the fictional narrative outline in the left margin and point out the key elements. Ask students to look for these key elements as you read and analyze the student model together.

## Analyze a Student Model

**EVENT SEQUENCE:** Explain to students that at the beginning of a story, readers find the basic situation and are introduced to the story's characters. Help students find the character names. *I don't find any people's names here, but I know that in some stories, animals are the main characters. The animals must be the main characters here.* (Owl, Rabbit) Assist students in finding the event that sets up the story's situation. *In the first paragraph, Owl signals that "all was safe." I read that trees have fallen. I know that I should look for an event that put the animals in danger. In the second paragraph, I find the event.* (a terrible storm)



# Read a Student Model

Drew is a student in Mr. Tran's 3rd-grade class. He is writing a fictional narrative. He has been asked to use a clear event sequence and to use dialogue and descriptive details. As you read his story, think about how you will organize your fictional narrative.

**CREATING AN ORGANIZATIONAL STRUCTURE**

Drew used an outline to organize his **fictional narrative.** It is divided into three sections: beginning, middle, and end.

Title:
Setting:
Characters:
I. Beginning — Story Events
II. Middle — Story Events
III. End — Conclusion

### What a Mess!

"Hoo-hoo, hoo-hoo!" Owl's voice was the signal that all was safe. Rabbit peeked from under the brush and hopped out into the opening. She jumped over a couple of fallen trees. As she looked around, other animals gathered.

Everyone was talking about the terrible storm that blew through last night. As Rabbit waited for the meeting to begin, she looked at the playground. It was covered with large branches, and trash was scattered everywhere. The broken swings hung limply. Just yesterday, the playground had been filled with laughter and joy. Now, it was a mess.

**EVENT SEQUENCE**

- The beginning of the story gives information about the events and introduces the characters.

***Underline the names of the characters on this page. Circle the event that happened last night.***





### Genre: Fictional Narrative

Tell students that a writer writes a fictional narrative for a purpose: to entertain the reader. To entertain readers, the writer sets up characters and a series of events that unfold naturally. He or she also includes details and descriptions that tell about events and characters, as well as dialogue that brings characters to life. By the time the story ends, the writer has provided a sense of closure.

MORE ONLINE sadlierconnect.com

Soon, Tabby Cat's soft meow got everyone's attention. "Last night was a scary night." Some of the animals shivered thinking about the powerful winds that knocked down many trees. "Luckily," she continued, "we're all safe."

"Then why did you bring us here?" wondered Mouse.

"I've been thinking of the children," Tabby Cat responded. "They will be so sad not to be able to play tomorrow."

The animals enjoyed watching the children run outside each day, eager to climb the monkey bars, swing with their friends, and race down the slides. The animals' bodies sagged with disappointment.

At first, no one said anything. Then, Rabbit softly sighed. "We have to do something to help them."

Next, Mouse looked around. "But what can we do? We are all so small, and the job is so big."

Everyone was quiet after that.

Finally, Brown Dog raised his head. "Well, I can fetch sticks!" He ran and picked up a few sticks, carrying them back.

Tabby Cat purred, "Well that's a start!" Rabbit looked at Tabby Cat and Brown Dog curiously. Then she excitedly hopped away. She picked up a piece of trash and put it with the sticks. Soon, the other animals began to cheer up. Now, they had a plan!

**DIALOGUE**

Dialogue shows thoughts and feelings of characters. Dialogue is surrounded by quotation marks.

***Underline what Tabby Cat says that tells what she thinks about the children.***

**SEQUENCE WORDS**

Use words and phrases to signal event order and make the event sequence clear.

***Circle words that show the sequence of events.***

**DESCRIPTIONS OF ACTIONS, THOUGHTS, FEELINGS**

Use descriptions to show how characters respond to events. Words such as *shivered* and *softly* help show characters' responses.

***Box words in the last paragraph that show how Rabbit responds to Brown Dog's actions.***





## Analyze a Student Model

**DIALOGUE:** Point out that Tabby Cat expresses more than one feeling in her dialogue—fear, gratitude—as she tells about her reaction to the storm. Model identifying Tabby Cat's thoughts about how she believes the children will feel. *In the first and second paragraphs, Tabby Cat mentions her feelings, but she does not mention the children. I will continue reading until I find where she mentions the children specifically.* (They will be so sad not to play tomorrow.)

**SEQUENCE WORDS:** Explain to students that Drew uses sequence words such as *soon* and *then* to show when and in what order the events took place. Have students identify other sequence words in the story. (*At first, Then, Next, Finally, Soon, Now*)

**DESCRIPTIONS OF ACTIONS, THOUGHTS, FEELINGS:** Point out that when Drew writes that Rabbit "softly sighed" in the fifth paragraph, this is describing how Rabbit is responding to Tabby Cat's statement. Ask students to use their own words to tell how they think Rabbit reacts. Then draw students' attention to the last paragraph and ask them to box words that show Rabbit's responses to Brown Dog's actions. (*curiously, excitedly*) If students are struggling, model finding the first word.

## Support English Language Learners

English language learners might have trouble recognizing English sequence words, or words that indicate when and in what order events took place. Review sequence words, such as *soon, later, first, next, then,* and *finally.*

Encourage students to work with a partner to name other sequence words. Then have them take turns using a few of the words to describe a sequence of the day's events.

## Analyze a Student Model

**EVENT SEQUENCE:** Review the ending of the story with students. Point out that the ending should provide a sense of closure. Explain that sometimes in a story, the characters learn a lesson. Ask students to underline the lesson that the animals learn. (Even the biggest jobs can be done when we all work together.)

## Evaluate a Writer's Work

Discuss Drew's fictional narrative with students. Remind them that a story should have a beginning, a middle, and an ending. Ask students to recall the situation at the beginning of the story. (A big storm has damaged the forest.) Discuss what problem the animals are trying to solve in the middle of the story. (The children will be sad because they will not be able to play in the forest.) Review how the characters try to solve the problem. (They work together to clean up the forest.) Ask students whether they found the conclusion of the story satisfying, and have them explain their thinking.

## Model: Organizational Structure

Ask students to think about how Drew might have outlined the story. On a board or projector, post the outline on page 165. Have students help you fill in the outline based on the story. Review the margin notes. Fill in the beginning, middle, and ending. Point out that well-written stories have strong organization, which requires planning and prewriting.

Students will next use the blank outline found in their books to plan their own stories, and then they will draft the story based on their outline.

## WRITE FICTIONAL NARRATIVES

**EVENT SEQUENCE**

The ending completes the story for the reader. It shows how the problem is solved.

***Underline the lesson the animals learn in the end.***

Throughout the night, they worked. Mouse ran back and forth carrying bits of trash to the trash can. Owl and Hawk used their beaks to hang the swing back up. All the animals did what they could.

As the sun rose in the morning, Rabbit looked around once again. "I can't believe it!" she cheered. "The children will be so happy."

Mouse patted Rabbit on the back. "I thought the job was too big, but we did it!"

Tabby Cat smiled. "It's just like I always tell my kittens. Even the biggest jobs can be done when we all work together."

### Review: Asking and Answering Questions

Remind students that when they read the fables "How the Rabbit Fooled the Elephant" and "The Winning of Friends," they asked basic questions about the text and then found answers to their questions within the text.

Encourage students to ask questions about Drew's story (*How do Mouse's feelings change in the story?*), and have them find the answers to the questions within the text. (On page 163, Mouse says, "We are all so small, and the job is so big." This indicates that he thinks the animals cannot clean up the mess. On page 164, Mouse says, "I thought the job was too big, but we did it." This indicates he is proud of their work.)

MORE ONLINE sadlierconnect.com

Use an outline like the one below to organize your own fictional narrative about animal characters. Then write a first draft of your story on a separate sheet of paper. In your draft, be sure to use dialogue and descriptions of characters' thoughts, feelings, and actions to develop your story. Also, use words and phrases that clearly show your story's order of events. Finally, be sure to provide a clear ending. You will use this draft to write your final story draft in the Chapter 7 Review section on page 172.

**Title:** ______________________________

**Setting:** ______________________________

**Characters:** ______________________________

______________________________

I. **Beginning**
   Story Events

   ______________________________

   ______________________________

II. **Middle**
   Story Events

   ______________________________

   ______________________________

III. **End**
   Conclusion

   ______________________________

   ______________________________





## Differentiate Instruction

Some students might have difficulty following the steps for completing the outline. Have students work in pairs to complete their work.

Encourage partners to work together to complete each step of the outline. Have them decide on the characters and the setting for their story. Then ask them to work out what will occur at the beginning and the middle of the story. Remind them that characters in stories usually face a problem that they try to overcome. Review with students that the ending of the story should make the story feel complete. Point out that one way to do this is to have the characters solve the problem that they have faced. Provide support as necessary.

## Create: Organizational Structure

### Brainstorming

Tell students that authors write stories about fictional characters and events that interest them. As a class, brainstorm characters and situations that students find interesting. List these ideas on the board so that students can build on them.

### Planning

Students will use the outline on page 165 to plan their fictional narrative. They should begin by filling in their setting and characters.

- Students should plan and write events for the beginning and middle of the story.
- Remind students that Drew included a lesson at the end of "What a Mess," and that the lesson helped make the story feel complete. Ask students how they will make their story feel complete.

### Drafting a Fictional Narrative

Students should refer to their outline as they draft their fictional narrative on a separate sheet of paper. Be sure students have a title, setting, characters, and a beginning, middle, and end. Remind them to use sequence words.

## Introduce the Writing Process

Remind students that in order to do a good job on a story, they must plan, draft, revise, and edit. These are all steps of the writing process. For more on the writing process, see the *Writing Handbook* at **sadlierconnect.com**.

**Assess and Respond**

**If** students have difficulty turning their outline into a story,

**Then** remind students to use dialogue and details to show how characters respond to events.

**OBJECTIVE**

**Use nouns, including abstract nouns, in writing.**

## Guided Instruction

Ensure that students understand what a noun is. Have them point to examples of persons, places, and things in the classroom and name the nouns. Then explain that abstract nouns name things that cannot be pointed out, such as childhood or feelings. Next have students study the boldface nouns in the examples. Ask them to find the abstract noun in the examples. (*joy*)

## Guided Practice

Have students begin by identifying the underlined noun in the first sentence. (*puppy*) Model how to determine what the noun names. *The underlined noun is* puppy. *A puppy is not a person or a place. It must be a thing.* Then have students write what the noun *store* in the second sentence names (place) and *vet* in the third sentence. (person) Ask students whether any of the underlined nouns is abstract. (no)

## Independent Practice

Have students write a sentence for each of the three abstract nouns. Provide sample sentences as needed.

**Assess and Respond**

**If** students have difficulty using the abstract nouns in sentences,

**Then** provide them with sentence starters. *The best part of my childhood so far is . . .; Friendship is important because . . .; It takes courage to . . .*

# LANGUAGE

## Nouns

**Guided Instruction** A **noun** is a word that names a person, a place, or a thing. An **abstract noun** names something we cannot see or hold, such as *peace* or *talent*.

*I took my **dog** to the **park**.*
*My **brother** brought a **leash** and **water**.*
*A **pet** brings us great **joy**.*

**Guided Practice** Write *person*, *place*, or *thing* to tell what the underlined noun names. If it is an abstract noun, write *abstract*.

1. Drew got a new puppy yesterday. thing
2. He went to the store to get dog food and a leash. place
3. Mom and Drew took the puppy to see a vet. person
4. She needed treatment for one small problem. abstract
5. After the visit, they took the puppy to their house to rest. place

**Independent Practice** Use each abstract noun in a sentence.

1. childhood
   Sample answer: My dog was my best friend during my childhood.
2. friendship
   Sample answer: I formed a friendship with my neighbor.
3. courage
   Sample answer: My dog showed courage when it scared away the fox.





## Differentiate Instruction

Some students may have difficulty in understanding the concept of abstract nouns. Others may not be sure when a noun names a person, place, or thing.

Help these students better understand different types of nouns by having them review *all* of the nouns in the Guided Practice sentences. Instruct them to work in a group to name the nouns that are persons (*Drew*, *He*, *Mom*, *Dad*, *vet*), places (*store*), and things (*dog food*, *leash*, *puppy*). Then ask them to identify any abstract nouns. (*yesterday*)

MORE ONLINE sadlierconnect.com

## Regular and Irregular Plural Nouns

**Guided Instruction** A **plural noun** names more than one person, place, or thing.

| For most nouns, add the letter *s* to the end of the word. | For words ending in *s, ch, sh,* or *x,* add an *es* to the end of the word. | For some nouns that end in a consonant and *y*, change the *y* to an *i* and add *es*. |
|---|---|---|
| *rabbit* *rabbits* | *grass* *grasses*<br>*lunch* *lunches*<br>*box* *boxes* | *bunny* *bunnies* |

Some nouns are irregular plurals. They do not end with the letter *s*. Instead, the spelling of the word is changed, or the word stays the same.

| | | | |
|---|---|---|---|
| ***singular:*** | *man* | *mouse* | *deer* |
| ***plural:*** | *men* | *mice* | *deer* |

**Guided Practice** Write the plural form of each word.

1. puppy ___puppies___
2. fox ___foxes___
3. hamster ___hamsters___
4. goose ___geese___

**Independent Practice** Write the plural form of each word in parentheses to complete each sentence.

1. The ___children___ learned how animals change. (child)
2. Caterpillars change into ___butterflies___. (butterfly)
3. ___Birds___ hatch from eggs. (Bird)





**OBJECTIVE**
**Use regular and irregular plural nouns in writing.**

### Guided Instruction

Make sure that students understand that a plural noun names more than one person, place, or thing. Review the examples of the different ways to form plurals shown in the chart. Explain that when *-es* is added to nouns that end in *-s, -ch, -sh,* or *-x*, another syllable is added. Then point out the irregular plural nouns. Tell students that these words do not follow the usual rules and the plurals must be memorized.

### Guided Practice

Instruct students to write the plural for each of the words. Have students refer to the chart to check the different ways to form plurals. You may wish to tell students that one of the nouns has an irregular plural form that is not listed above. (*geese*)

### Independent Practice

Have students review the different ways to form plural nouns. Then ask them to write the plural form of each noun in parentheses.

**Assess and Respond**

**If** students have difficulty forming plural nouns correctly,

**Then** give students extra practice by repeating the activity in Guided Practice with more examples.

### Support English Language Learners

Forming plural nouns correctly can be difficult for English language learners. Students need to remember not only to add *-s* to form most plural nouns, but also the rule to add *-es* to words ending in *-s, -ch, -sh, or -x,* as well as the rule that for words ending in consonant *-y*, they change the *-y* to an *-i* and add *-es*. Along with these rules, English language learners need to learn which nouns have irregular plurals and don't follow any of these rules.

Write four column heads on the board: + *-s*, + *-es*, Change *-y* to an *-i* and add *-es*, and Irregular. Have students list common singular nouns and discuss under which column the noun belongs. Then demonstrate forming the plural. Make sure to provide other examples of irregular plural nouns, such as *women, teeth, fish,* and *feet*.

**OBJECTIVE**
**Use possessives in writing.**

## Guided Instruction

Be sure students understand that a possessive noun shows when someone or something has or owns something and that most possessives are formed by adding apostrophe *-s*. Remind students that most plural nouns end in *-s* and that for these, possessives are formed by adding only an apostrophe.

## Guided Practice

Have students begin by recognizing who or what has something. (Tran) Then ask students if the noun is a plural that ends in *-s*. (no) Ask students how the possessive should be formed, and tell them to circle the correct response.

## Independent Practice

Have students review how to form a singular possessive and how to form a plural possessive for a word that ends in *-s*. Then instruct students to complete the activity, writing the correct possessive form for each noun in parentheses.

**Assess and Respond**

**If** students have difficulty forming possessives correctly,

**Then** have them review examples of possessives in the student model. (Owl's, Cat's, animals') Discuss with them how each possessive is formed.

# LANGUAGE

## Possessives

**Guided Instruction** **Possessive** nouns show ownership. They show who has or owns something.

*The **horse that Sandeep owns** is at the fair.*
Possessive: ***Sandeep's horse** is at the fair.*

To form a singular possessive, add an apostrophe and the letter *s* to the end of the noun. To form a plural possessive to a word that ends with the letter *s*, add only an apostrophe at the end of the word.

*The **horse's** coat needs brushing.* (singular possessive)
*The **horses'** gate was left open, and they ran out.* (plural possessive)

**Guided Practice** Circle the phrase that is the correct possessive form.

1. the saddle that Tran has — (Tran's saddle) — Trans' saddle
2. the colts who have a mother — the colt's mother — (the colts' mother)
3. the stable of the horse — (the horse's stable) — the horses' stable
4. the spurs the riders have — (the riders' spurs) — the rider's spurs

**Independent Practice** Write the correct possessive form of the noun in parentheses to complete each sentence.

1. The horses ran in the __farmer's__ field each day. (farmer)
2. They ate the __meadow's__ grass. (meadow)
3. They listened for the __boys'__ call to return to the barn. (boys)
4. The __horses'__ lives were safe and enjoyable. (horses)





## Differentiate Instruction

Some students may have difficulty understanding how to form possessives and when possessives should be used.

Help students by providing them with more examples of phrases that can be shortened by forming a possessive. Then have them form the possessive for each underlined word.

- The <u>cows</u> have a barn. — The ____ barn. (cows')
- The <u>cow</u> has a sore leg. — The ____ sore leg. (cow's)
- The <u>barn</u> has a red roof. — The ____ red roof. (barn's)

MORE ONLINE sadlierconnect.com

## Commas and Quotation Marks in Dialogue

**Guided Instruction** **Dialogue** is a conversation written as part of a story.

*Abbey said, **"I would like a pet hamster."***

**Quotation marks** are used to show the person's words. A **comma** is used to separate the other words in the sentence from what the speaker says.

*Mom asked, "Would you take care of the pet?"*

**Guided Practice** Add quotation marks to show each speaker's words.

1. Ryan asked, Do you have any guinea pigs?
   Ryan asked, "Do you have any guinea pigs?"
2. The owner answered, Yes. We have three.
   The owner answered, "Yes. We have three."
3. That brown one sure is cute, Ryan whispered to his mom.
   "That brown one sure is cute," Ryan whispered to his mom.

**Independent Practice** Write the sentence using quotation marks and commas to separate the speaker's words from the rest of the sentence.

1. Ben exclaimed The guinea pig doesn't look like a pig at all!
   Ben exclaimed, "The guinea pig doesn't look like a pig at all!"
2. How big do guinea pigs get? asked Katie.
   "How big do guinea pigs get?" asked Katie.
3. Mrs. Volpe answered Adults are about two pounds.
   Mrs. Volpe answered, "Adults are about two pounds."





**OBJECTIVE**
**Use commas and quotation marks in dialogue.**

### Guided Instruction

Make sure that students understand that in a story, quotation marks are used around the words that someone says.

### Guided Practice

Begin by asking students to identify the speaker's words. (Do you have any guinea pigs?) Then ask them to write those words and place quotation marks around them to identify the words as a quotation. Help students realize that in the third example, quotation marks should be placed *after* the comma, which sets the quotation apart from the rest of the sentence.

### Independent Practice

Instruct students to write the sentences, placing the quotation marks and commas where they belong to set off the quotations. Remind students that some quotations end with exclamation marks or question marks, and that quotation marks should be placed after.

**Assess and Respond**

**If** students are having difficulty placing quotation marks correctly,

**Then** give students more practice by writing five more sentences like those shown in Independent Practice and having students place the commas and quotation marks where they belong.

### Grouping Options

Pair students having difficulty with a more proficient learner to gain more practice with quotations.

Write statements (for example, *Go to bed.*) on index cards and place them in a pile. Then make another pile of index cards with sentence parts that identify a speaker, such as *Maria says*, or *said Jonah*. Ask the partner with developing skills to choose a statement and rewrite it, placing quotation marks at the beginning and end. Then ask the more proficient partner to choose an index card from the sentence part pile, and have him or her write the sentence part at the beginning or end of the quotation, placing a comma where it belongs.

**OBJECTIVES**

- **Come to discussion prepared, and draw on that preparation to explore ideas.**
- **Ask questions to check understanding.**

## Discuss the Essential Question

Before beginning a group discussion, copy and distribute the "Did I?" checklist, available on **sadlierconnect.com**.

### Leading the Class Discussion

Give students time to think about the questions before the class discussion.

1. Have students review events in the student model.
2. Instruct students to skim paragraphs for descriptions.

## SPEAKING AND LISTENING

### Discuss the Essential Question

**How do writers develop fictional narratives?**

Think about the Essential Question by responding to the questions below. Support your point of view with reasons and experience.

1. How does the writer sequence the story?

   First, the animals gather at the messy playground. They decide to clean it up.

   They work through the night. In the morning, they have a clean playground.

2. What are some words or phrases the author uses to describe events?

   broken swings hung limply; powerful winds; race down the slides;

   sagged with disappointment; fetch sticks; ran back and forth

Use your notes above to discuss the Essential Question in small groups or as a class. Remember to use the rules for being a good speaker and a good listener in the checklist below. When you speak, be sure to explain your ideas fully. As a listener, ask questions and make connections among everyone's comments in order to fully understand the conversation.

***Did I:***

- ☐ Come to the discussion prepared?
- ☐ Follow agreed-upon rules for discussion?
- ☐ Ask questions to check my understanding?
- ☐ Stay on topic?
- ☐ Avoid interrupting others?
- ☐ Listen carefully to others and answer questions?
- ☐ Speak in complete sentences?





### Discussion Skills

Introduce students to sentence starters for building on ideas of others:

- *What you said makes me wonder . . .*
- *What you said reminds me of . . .*

Then give students some sentence starters they can use when asking for clarification:

- *Could you repeat what you said about . . . ?*
- *I'm not sure what you meant by . . .*
- *What evidence do you have for . . . ?*

## CHAPTER 7 REVIEW

This paragraph has mistakes in sentences and agreement. There are incorrect plural nouns and possessive forms, as well as incorrect punctuation of dialogue. Write the paragraph correctly on the lines below.

Lauren has two bunnys, Patches and Hopper. They were in a terrible flood. When the flood came, Lauren put them in boxs and carried them to safety. Lauren whispered You will be okay. Hearing her voice made them feel calm. Patches and Hopper didn't have their favorite grassies, but they did have plenty of water and food. After the flood, Laurens mom suggested that she teach other peoples how to help animals in emergencys.

Lauren has two bunnies, Patches and Hopper. They were in a terrible flood. When the flood came, Lauren put them in boxes and carried them to safety. Lauren whispered, "You will be okay." Hearing her voice made them feel calm. Patches and Hopper didn't have their favorite grasses, but they did have plenty of water and food. After the flood, Lauren's mom suggested that she teach other people how to help animals in emergencies.





### Test-Taking Tips

Give students the following tips to help with taking assessments focused on editing skills.

- Tell students to make a list of the things that they should check for, such as correct spelling of plural nouns, correct form of possessives, and correct placement of commas and quotation marks in sentences that include quotations.
- Encourage students to read slowly. Suggest that they put a pencil under each word as they read to help them focus on one word at a time.

## Introduce the Review

Explain to students that this review will give them an opportunity to apply the language and writing skills that they have studied and practiced in this chapter.

### Language Skills Summary

Explain to students that they are going to use what they learned about all kinds of nouns, including plural nouns, irregular plural nouns, and possessives. Additionally, they will use what they learned about commas and quotation marks in dialogue to make their writing better. Good writers know the rules of grammar and punctuation.

- Have students explain what an abstract noun is. (It is a noun that names something that cannot be seen or held, such as peace or childhood.)
- Ask students to explain how to form plurals for nouns ending in *-x, -ch, -sh,* and how to form plurals for nouns ending in consonant *-y*. (For nouns ending in *-x, -ch, -sh*, add *-es*. For nouns ending in *-y*, change the *-y* to an *-i* and add *-es*.)
- Prompt students to name how forming a possessive of a plural noun ending in *-s* is different from forming a possessive of a singular noun. (For plural nouns ending in *-s*, add only an apostrophe. For singular nouns, add apostrophe *-s*.)
- Ask students to explain where to place quotation marks in a sentence in which someone's words are quoted directly. (Place quotation marks at the beginning and end of the words the speaker said.)

## Writing Process Summary

Remind students that planning helps them organize their ideas before drafting, and revising and editing make a draft better.

**Planning and Drafting**

Have students look at the outline and draft they created earlier (page 165). They should check that the draft covers all the important points in the outline.

**Fictional Narrative Rubric**

| | |
|---|---|
| 4 | The narrative includes: an introduction that sets up the situation, a sequence of events that unfolds naturally, description and dialogue; sequence words; a conclusion that provides closure. There are few or no editing errors. |
| 3 | The narrative has the elements listed under "4" above, though they are executed less successfully. Minor editing errors do not detract greatly from the overall essay. |
| 2 | The piece is missing one or more of the elements required. There are many editing errors, some of which are serious. |
| 1 | The narrative is unfinished or shows a minimal understanding of required elements. Serious editing errors make it difficult to read. |
| 0 | The narrative was not attempted. |

**Self-Assessment: Progress Check**

Have students revisit the Progress Check on page 159 and compare their answers now with the answers they gave before they started Chapter 7.

## CHAPTER 7 REVIEW

**Assignment:** Write a fictional narrative about animal characters.

On the lines below, write your final copy of the fictional narrative draft you created on page 165. Be sure to include dialogue and description to show thoughts, feelings, and actions. Make sure to choose your words carefully and use words to signal the order of events. Include a conclusion that wraps up events in your story. See the Writing Handbook (at **sadlierconnect.com**) for ways to improve your writing as you revise.

Each student should write a fictional narrative that includes animal characters, uses effective technique, includes descriptive details, shows clear event sequences, includes dialogue and descriptions of actions, thoughts, and feelings to show the response of characters to situations, uses temporal words and phrases to signal event order, and provides a sense of closure.





### Digital Connection: Storybooks

Once students have finished writing their stories, they can make storybooks. If computers are available, encourage students to use a computer to write and edit their stories. Then have them choose public domain images they find on the Internet to illustrate their stories. Alternatively, they could use a drawing or painting application to create their own artwork.

Text Types and Purposes

# Write Informative/ Explanatory Texts

CHAPTER 8

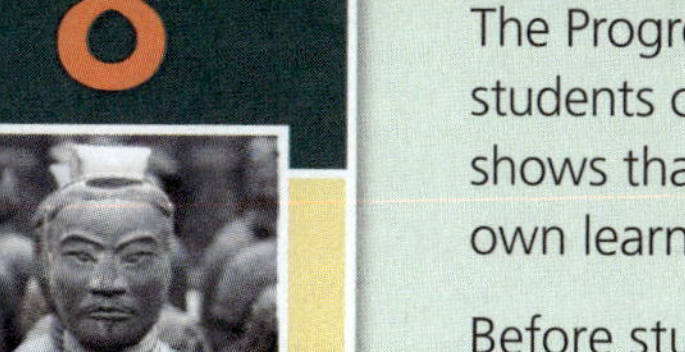

**Focus on Writing** An informational or explanatory text includes facts, details, and evidence.

**Think About Theme** In this chapter, think about what you would write about a history or science topic.

**Let's Get on Our Way!** You can develop a topic using a graphic organizer that organizes a topic and subtopics.

These are the skills you will build in this chapter. Before you begin, check the boxes on the left of any items you can do well now. At the end of the chapter, you will return to this page to use the check boxes on the right to show what you have learned.

**Progress Check** *Can I?*

| Before | Can I? | After |
|---|---|---|
| ☐ | Introduce a topic. | ☐ |
| ☐ | Group related information together. | ☐ |
| ☐ | Use facts, definitions, and details to develop a topic. | ☐ |
| ☐ | Use linking words to connect ideas. | ☐ |
| ☐ | Complete my writing with a concluding statement. | ☐ |
| ☐ | Write using pronouns. | ☐ |
| ☐ | Write using pronouns and antecedents that agree. | ☐ |
| ☐ | Spell high-frequency words correctly. | ☐ |
| ☐ | Use commas in addresses. | ☐ |





**Student Page 173**

## Progress Check

The Progress Check is a self-assessment feature that students can use to gauge their own progress. Research shows that when students take accountability for their own learning, their motivation increases.

Before students begin work on Chapter 8, have them check the boxes next to any item that they feel they can do well. It is fine if they don't check any of the boxes. Tell them that they will have an opportunity to learn about and practice all of these items while studying the chapter. Let them know that near the end of the chapter they will have a chance to reconsider how well they can do each item on this list.

Before students begin the Chapter 8 Review on page 185, have them revisit this page. You can use this information to work with students on any items they don't understand before they tackle the Review.

## HOME ✦ CONNECT...

The Home Connect feature is a way to keep parents or other adult family members apprised of what their children are learning. The key learning objectives are listed, and some ideas for related activities and discussions are included.

Explain to students that they can share the Home Connect page with their parents or other adult family members in their home. Let students know how much time the class will be spending on this chapter so they can plan their time accordingly at home.

Encourage students and their parents to share their experiences using the suggestions on the Home Connect page. You may wish to make a place to post some of this work.

### HOME ✦ CONNECT...

In this chapter, children will learn about **writing to inform or explain a topic** to the reader. Discuss with your child different types of explanatory and informative texts, such as recipes, instruction guides, encyclopedias, informative websites, and textbooks.

Informative writing topics are developed with **facts**, **definitions**, and **details**. Ask your child to tell you about his or her writing topic, and to give details by describing something or defining a term. If your child has difficulty describing a topic, find a related image—an illustration or a photo. Encourage your child to describe the image and then incorporate some of these details into his or her writing.

Think of other topics that interest both you and your child. Together, research and write down facts and details about the topic. Have your child write an **introduction** that explains what the topic is. Then work with him or her to **link ideas** to make the writing flow. Distribute your informative text to friends or other family members.

**On the Go:** Encourage your child's curiosity about topics. Guide him or her to resources that can help answer questions. Model for your child how to use the Internet to search for good sources of information. Talk about different resources you use when you want to find out information or learn how to do something new.

**IN THIS CHAPTER, YOUR CHILD WILL...**

- Learn to write an informative or explanatory text that introduces a topic, groups related information, and ends with a conclusion.
- Use facts, definitions, and details to support the topic.
- Learn to use linking words, such as *also, another, more,* and *but*, to connect ideas.
- Learn specific language skills and use them in writing an explanatory or informative text:
  - Use pronouns, such as *he, we,* or *they*, to take the place of a noun.
  - Check sentences for proper pronoun agreement.
  - Spell high-frequency words correctly.
  - Use a comma between the city and state in an address.

**WAYS TO HELP YOUR CHILD**

Help your child practice using descriptive words by playing a game called "Stretch It." Choose a word such as *frog*. Take turns adding a description to the word, such as *the tiny, wet, slippery, green frog.* Discuss how writers use descriptions to explain and inform.

ONLINE
For more Home Connect activities, continue online at **sadlierconnect.com**





**Student Page 174**

## LEARNING PROGRESSIONS

In this chapter, students will learn how to write an informative/explanatory text on a topic that interests them. In order to learn the skills necessary to craft an informative/explanatory text, students will further develop skills learned in second grade. They should be encouraged to retain these skills, as they will continue to build on them in fourth grade.

**Introducing the Topic**

- Proficient second-grade students should complete the year able to write an informative/explanatory text in which they introduce the topic about which they are writing.
- In grades 3 and 4, students will build on this skill by not only stating the topic of the text in the introduction, but also stating what they will examine about the topic.

**Developing the Topic**

- By the end of grade 2, students should be able to use facts and definitions to develop points in their text.
- Students in grade 3 will be asked to develop their topics with facts and definitions, as well as details, and to group related information together.
- This will prepare them for grade 4, when they will be asked to develop the topic not only with facts, definitions, and concrete details, but also with quotations and other related information and examples, grouping related information together, and adding illustrations and multimedia to aid reader comprehension of the topic.

**Using Linking Words and Phrases**

- In grade 3, students will learn to add linking words and phrases (e.g., *also, another, and, more, but*) to connect ideas in their texts.
- When students move on to grade 4, they will be expected to include more complex linking words (e.g., *for example, because*) in their texts.

**Providing a Concluding Statement**

- In grades 2 and 3, students learn the importance of providing a concluding statement or section.
- In grade 4, students will build on this skill by including a concluding statement or section that relates to the information or explanation presented in the text.

## Writing Handbook

If students need extra practice with writing an informative/explanatory text, refer them to the *Writing Handbook* at **sadlierconnect.com**. The Writing Handbook gives students detailed instruction on planning, drafting, revising, and editing their writing. They will also find tips on producing, publishing, and presenting their writing.

**Essential Question:**
**How do writers develop a topic to inform or explain?**

In this chapter, students will explore how a topic is developed with facts, definitions, and details in order to examine that topic and clearly convey ideas and information about it.

## Theme: Echoes of the Past

Students will continue their investigation of long-ago events as they read and analyze an informative/explanatory text writing model.

## Curriculum Connection: Social Studies

Students will use what they have already learned about human history as they work on their own informative/explanatory text.

## Connect Reading to Writing

Remind students that they read a historical text entitled *King Tut: From Forgotten Pharaoh to Ancient Superstar* in Chapter 2 (Student Book pages 44–49). Review how the author introduces the topic and develops it with facts, definitions, and details.

**OBJECTIVE**

**Write an informative/explanatory text with a clear topic, evidence, linking phrases, and a concluding statement.**

## Introduce: Organizational Structure

Draw students' attention to the informative/explanatory text outline in the left margin, and point out the key elements. Ask students to look for these key elements as you read and analyze the Student Model together.

## Analyze a Student Model

**TITLE:** Tell students that the title of an informative/explanatory text should clearly identify the topic of the essay. You might read the title aloud and then point out the words *King Tut* in the title. Explain that they signal that the text examines something about him. Then you might point out the word *Mystery* in the title and explain that it signals that Janine's text examines a mystery, or something unknown, about King Tut.

**INTRODUCTION:** Help students find the sentences that state the topic: *I know from the title that the text is about a mystery related to King Tut, so I will look for sentences that suggest something mysterious about him.* Help students identify that the last two sentences state the mystery.



**CREATING AN ORGANIZATIONAL STRUCTURE**

Janine used the outline below. It is divided into three sections: introduction, explanation, and conclusion.

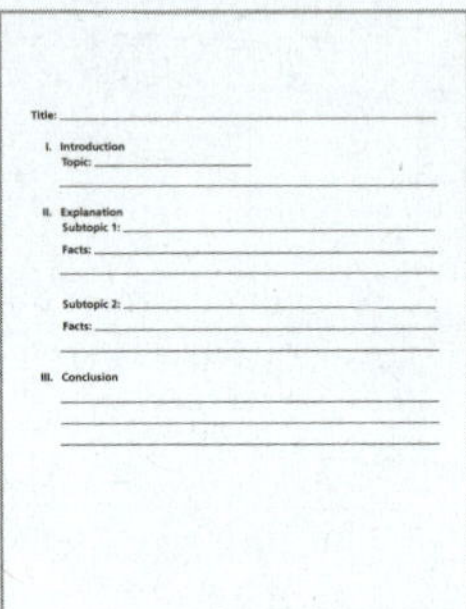
Title: ____________

I. Introduction
Topic: ____________

II. Explanation
Subtopic 1: ____________
Facts: ____________

Subtopic 2: ____________
Facts: ____________

III. Conclusion
____________

# Read a Student Model

Janine has been asked to write an informative/explanatory report about King Tutankhamun, a ruler in Egypt over 3,000 years ago. Janine has used an introduction to state her topic and facts to explain what she learned about King Tutankhamun. As you read her report, think about the topic for your report and how you can use facts, definitions, and details to explain it.

**TITLE**

Identifies the main topic for the reader

**INTRODUCTION**

The introduction states the topic.

***Underline the pair of sentences that tell what this report is about.***

### The Mystery of King Tut

Many people think that all of the kings of ancient Egypt were buried in the pyramids. A huge number of these rulers were actually buried in an area called the Valley of the Kings. The famous King Tutankhamun, or King Tut, was buried there. His tomb and his mummy were discovered in 1922. We have learned many things about King Tut since then. Yet, there are many things we don't know. Everyone loves a good mystery. This may be why people continue to be so interested in King Tut.





## Genre: Informative/Explanatory Texts

Draw students' attention to the base words *inform* and *explain* in the text type "informative/explanatory texts." Then ask students to tell what they think is the purpose of this text type. Point out informative/explanatory texts students may have read, such as an encyclopedia entry or a news article. Be sure students understand that writers write this type of text to examine a topic and to inform or explain something about it to the reader.

Explain that in order to effectively communicate ideas about a topic, a writer must group related information together and develop the topic with facts, definitions, and details. Discuss how it might be tempting to add your own opinion when writing this type of text and why it is important to refrain from doing so—as an opinion would be out of place or feel jarring.

MORE ONLINE sadlierconnect.com

### King Tut's MRI Results

King Tut became a ruler in Egypt when he was young. He ruled for only nine years. In 2013, an MRI was used to look at his mummy. An MRI is a special scanner that takes pictures and sends them to a computer. From the pictures, scientists learned that Tut was around 19 years old when he died.

Many people wonder why King Tut died so young. One rumor said that he was hit from behind. The MRI scans of his head, however, did not show he had been hit. Another idea was that he was hurt in battle. One scan did find a broken bone above his knee. Scientists do not know when this happened, but it could have happened when the mummy was first moved.

### Was King Tut Sick?

Scientists thought King Tut's foot looked odd. In 2003, they took DNA from his mummy. The DNA showed that some of the bone had died. It may have made King Tut limp and use a cane. Still, the scientists do not think this killed King Tut. Scientists also took DNA from an ancient insect in the pyramid. The insect carried a disease called malaria. This disease can be deadly. However, they do not know if this caused his death.

**DEVELOP THE TOPIC**
Facts, definitions, and details help the reader understand the topic.
***In this section, underline a fact and circle a word and its definition.***

**ORGANIZATION**
Related information is grouped together.
***Put boxes around two sentences that tell what scientists learned about King Tut's body.***

**LINKING WORDS**
Linking words (such as *and*, *also*, and *but*) and phrases help connect the ideas.
***Circle the linking words in the section "Was King Tut Sick?"***





## Analyze a Student Model

**DEVELOP THE TOPIC:** Remind students that a fact is something that can be proven, like the date something happened, unlike an opinion, which is someone's idea about something. Ask students to identify a fact about an MRI in the text. ("In 2013, an MRI was used to look at his mummy.") Ask students to identify the type of information Janine provides in the next sentence—a fact, definition, or detail. (definition) Ask students what does she define? (an MRI)

**ORGANIZATION:** Model identifying the information that is grouped together: *I know from the first paragraph that scientists used an MRI to study King Tut's mummy. I'll look for information in this paragraph that tells what they learned from the scans of his body.* ("did not show he had been hit" and had "a broken bone above his knee") Read aloud the first paragraph, adding the first circled sentence from the second paragraph to the end of the first paragraph. Then read aloud the second paragraph, leaving out the first circled sentence. Help students see that the paragraphs do not make sense when related information is not grouped together.

**LINKING WORDS:** Ask students to identify the linking word Janine uses to connect the idea that dead bone in King Tut's foot may have made him limp and use a cane to the idea that scientists do not think this killed King Tut. (*Still*) Point out that this information relates to one test scientists conducted with DNA. Have students identify the linking word Janine uses to show that scientists conducted a second test related to DNA. (*also*) After giving students time to find the third linking word (*However*), ask a volunteer to explain the ideas Janine connects with that linking word. ("malaria can be deadly" and "scientists do not know if this caused his death")

### Support English Language Learners

Help English language learners build and connect to background knowledge before they read this text so that they can focus their energy on comprehending the ideas the author presents rather than on trying to make sense of unfamiliar references.

Be sure English language learners understand that the King Tut discussed in this text is the same King Tut that they read about in Chapter 2. Explain that MRI and DNA are both initialisms. (*magnetic resonance imaging* and *deoxyribonucleic acid*)

Show students pictures and videos related to King Tut, MRIs, and DNA to help them build background knowledge.

## Analyze a Student Model

**CONCLUSION:** Review Janine's conclusion with students. Students should recognize that the questions serve to summarize the ideas in the text; they are not new questions. Students should also recognize that Janine wraps up these ideas with the last sentence, but adds an interesting thought before wrapping up the topic.

## Evaluate a Writer's Work

Have partners discuss the informative/explanatory text. Remind students that the purpose of an informative/explanatory text is to inform or explain something to the reader. Have students recall what Janine stated in her introductory paragraph that she would examine in the text: "We have learned many things about King Tut since then. Yet, there are many things we don't know." Ask students if Janine effectively follows up on this purpose in her text. Have partners share their thinking with the class.

## Model: Organizational Structure

Ask students to think about how the writer might have completed her outline for the informative/explanatory text. On a board or projector, post the outline on page 179. Then have students help you fill in the outline based on the model text. Review the notes in the margins alongside the model text. Fill in the introduction, explanation, and conclusion. Point out that well-written informative/explanatory texts have strong organization, which requires planning and prewriting.

Students will next use the blank outline found in their books to plan their own informative/explanatory text, and then they will draft the text based on their outline.

WRITE INFORMATIVE/EXPLANATORY TEXTS

**CONCLUSION**

The conclusion wraps up the topic by telling what was learned. It also adds an interesting idea related to the topic.

***Underline the concluding statement.***

What caused this young ruler to die? He was not hit in the head. He did not die from a deformed foot. Did he get sick? Was it something else? The scans and tests ruled out some ideas. Yet, we still are not sure what caused King Tut to die so young. As scientists invent new tests and technology, they may find the answers to some of these questions. Until then, King Tut will be remembered as much for what we do know as for what we still wonder.

178 Chapter 8 ■ Text Types and Purposes: Write Informative/Explanatory Texts

### Review: Determining Main Idea and Key Details

Remind students that when they read the historical text "King Tut: From Forgotten Pharaoh to Ancient Superstar," they learned that an author usually points out the main idea in the title and then early in the text. They also analyzed how the author supported the main idea with details.

Ask students to recall the main idea that they identified for this text at the start of the lesson. ("We have learned many things about King Tut since then. Yet, there are many things we don't know.") Then ask them to identify a word or phrase in each subheading that points to the main idea of that section. (*MRI Results; Sick*) Finally, have students identify one detail that supports the main topic in the section "Was King Tut Sick?" (They do not know if malaria caused his death.)

MORE ONLINE sadlierconnect.com

Use an outline like the one below to organize your informative/explanatory essay on a history or science topic that interests you. Then write a first draft of your essay on a separate sheet of paper. Make sure to develop your topic using facts and details and group related information together. Remember to use linking words in your draft to connect pieces of information. Lastly, make sure your draft ends with a conclusion that summarizes your topic. You will use this draft to write your final essay in the Chapter Review section on page 186.

**Title:** ______________________________

I. **Introduction**
   **Topic:** ______________________________
   ______________________________

II. **Explanation**
   **Subtopic 1:** ______________________________
   **Facts:** ______________________________
   ______________________________

   **Subtopic 2:** ______________________________
   **Facts:** ______________________________
   ______________________________

III. **Conclusion**
   ______________________________
   ______________________________





## Differentiate Instruction

Work individually with students who are not yet ready to pick a topic and plan and draft their text on their own. Be sure students understand the meaning of *subtopic*, *fact*, *definition*, and *detail*. Point to an example of each from the Student Model to reinforce understanding. Consider creating a tree diagram (with the topic box at the top, subtopic boxes in the next row, and evidence boxes in the bottom row with arrows leading down) for students to use in place of the outline for organizing ideas to help them "see" how the subtopics relate to the topic, and how the facts, definitions, and details support the subtopics. Help students select a topic from the list of topics the class brainstormed. Then guide them as they complete their tree diagrams to organize their ideas.

## Create: Organizational Structure

### Brainstorming

Tell students that writers write informative/explanatory texts about topics that interest them. Have students name their favorite history and science topics. Make a list of students' topic ideas on the board or projector for them to use as they plan their writing.

### Planning

Students will use the outline on page 179 to plan their texts. Students should first decide on a topic and then fill in what they will examine about the topic.

- Students should decide how to best examine their topics through two subtopics and record facts related to each subtopic.
- Remind students that Janine added an interesting idea about the topic to her conclusion. Ask students what ideas they can add to their conclusions.

### Drafting an Informative/Explanatory Text

Instruct students to refer to their outlines as they draft their informative/explanatory texts on a separate sheet of paper. Remind them to use linking words to connect their ideas.

## Introduce the Writing Process

Remind students that in order to do a good job on an essay, they must plan, draft, revise, and edit it. These are all steps of the writing process. For more on the writing process, see the *Writing Handbook* at **sadlierconnect.com**.

### Assess and Respond

**If** students have difficulty breaking their topic into subtopics,

**Then** have students list facts they know about the topic and help them group the facts into two subtopics, leaving out any facts that do not fit.

**OBJECTIVE**
**Use the correct pronoun in writing.**

## Guided Instruction

Make sure students understand what a noun is and then review how a pronoun takes its place. Explain that *they* in the first example set takes the place of *statues*. Ask students to identify what *he* and *it* take the place of in the next example sets. Have students read each sentence set aloud, emphasizing the nouns and pronouns in bold, to reinforce learning verbally.

## Guided Practice

Help students identify the pronouns in the first two sentences. Then discuss whether each word in the remaining sentences could take the place of a noun, and thus be a pronoun. Allow students to identify the pronoun in these sentences.

## Independent Practice

Challenge students to explain why the pronoun that they selected is correct. Then have them read aloud the sentence, replacing the underlined noun with the pronoun.

### Assess and Respond

**If** students have difficulty identifying pronouns to replace nouns,

**Then** create several two-sentence sets—with the second sentence containing a pronoun replacing a noun (which is underlined) in the first sentence. Have them circle the pronoun in the second sentence that replaces the underlined noun.

## LANGUAGE

### Pronouns

**Guided Instruction** A **pronoun** takes the place of a noun. Some of the most common pronouns are *I, he, she, it, we, they,* and *you.*

***Statues** were found in China.* [noun]
***They** were found in China.* [pronoun]

*The **Emperor** had the statues made.* [noun]
***He** had the statues made.* [pronoun]

*The **book** is from the museum gift shop.* [noun]
***It** is from the museum gift shop.* [pronoun]

**Guided Practice** Write the pronoun in each sentence.

1. We went to the museum to see the Terra Cotta Warriors. ___We___
2. Surprisingly, she knew a lot about them. ___she___
3. Have you heard of the statues? ___you___
4. They are very old statues of warriors. ___They___
5. I liked how each statue looked different. ___I___
6. They are all beautiful. ___They___
7. Jessie and I sketched and photographed the statues. ___I___

**Independent Practice** Replace the underlined words with a pronoun.

1. Mrs. Ling is our teacher. ___She___
2. Mrs. Ling took us to see the exhibit. ___it___
3. Our class saw pictures of the pits where the warriors were found. ___We___
4. The guides told us how they found the warriors. ___They___
5. Mr. Hurd showed us the tools they used. ___He___
6. Jenna and Mae decided to spend more time at the exhibit. ___They___
7. The experience was fascinating! ___It___





### Turn and Talk

During Guided Practice, promote discussion participation by all students by having partners turn to each other and talk over which word in the sentence is the pronoun in sentences 1–7. Have partners take turns sharing the pronoun they selected with the class. Then, after Independent Practice, have different partners turn to each other and discuss the pronouns they chose to replace the underlined words. Have volunteers share the pronouns they chose, explaining their choices.

MORE ONLINE sadlierconnect.com

## Pronoun-Antecedent Agreement

**Guided Instruction** Some pronouns have antecedents. The **antecedent** is the noun the pronoun refers to. The pronoun and antecedent must match. Both must be singular or plural.

*The **scientists** work for **their** museum.*
[antecedent] [pronoun]

*The **scientist** works for **her** museum.*
[antecedent] [pronoun]

**Guided Practice** Correct the sentences.

1. The tourists brought his camera.
   Sample answer: The tourists brought their cameras.
2. Kayla left its camera on the bus.
   Sample answer: Kayla left her camera on the bus.
3. The students took pictures of her visit to the pyramid.
   Sample answer: The students took pictures of their visit to the pyramid.
4. Curt and Diego drew pictures of his favorite sites.
   Sample answer: Curt and Diego took pictures of their favorite sites.

**Independent Practice** Use a pronoun and antecedent in a sentence. Underline the pronoun and its antecedent.

Sample answer: The pyramid had steps leading to its top.





### Support English Language Learners

Reinforce understanding of pronouns for native speakers of Mandarin and other languages that do not rely heavily on pronouns.

First reinforce basic understanding of pronouns. Write the pronouns *I, me, he, him, she, her, they, them, their, we, us, it, its* each on a separate index card. Then write one noun, each on a separate index card, that relates to each pronoun. (Put the students' names on cards for *I, me, we,* and *us.*) Then have students place a pronoun card on top of a noun card to correctly "replace" it. Go on to reinforce understanding of pronoun-antecedent agreement. Have students place a pronoun card after a noun card that it can correctly refer to and use their fingers to "draw" an arrow from the pronoun card back to the noun card.

**OBJECTIVE**
**Use correct pronoun-antecedent agreement in writing.**

### Guided Instruction

Explain that students will build on their knowledge of pronouns in this lesson. Then explain that sometimes a pronoun does not replace a noun; instead it refers back to a noun that comes before it. Have students draw an arrow from the pronoun back to the noun in each example sentence. Discuss how each pronoun matches its noun.

### Guided Practice

Read the first sentence aloud and then model correcting it: *This sentence sounds strange. I know that* his *is a pronoun that refers to a singular, masculine noun, but there is no singular masculine noun before* his *in this sentence. The only noun before the pronoun is* tourists, *so the correct pronoun must be* they*—a plural, gender-neutral pronoun.* Talk students through the second sentence. Then allow them to rewrite the last two sentences on their own.

### Independent Practice

Have students repeat the rules of pronoun-antecedent agreement. Then have them write their sentences.

**Assess and Respond**

**If** students have a difficult time with pronoun-antecedent agreement,

**Then** give students more practice correcting sentences by repeating the process under Guided Practice with additional examples. If needed, provide a list of pronouns to draw from for the first few sentences.

**OBJECTIVE**
**Use correct spelling in writing.**

## Guided Instruction

Explain that when you write a text, you want your reader to focus on the ideas you are presenting in your text. You do not want them to be distracted by spelling errors. Then explain that high-frequency words are words that are used often and that students should memorize how to spell these words. Review the spelling of each word. Point out common misspelling errors for each word (e.g., writing *u* instead of *o* in *another*; leaving out the *i* or writing two *e*'s in the second syllable in *believe*). Have students say and spell each word.

## Guided Practice

Have students cover up the word box at the top of their page. Help students circle the correctly spelled word in the first example. Then have partners work together on the remaining sentences and share their answers with the class.

## Independent Practice

Ask students to write another sentence for each misspelled word, using the correctly spelled version of it.

**Assess and Respond**

**If** students have difficulty finding the misspelled word and spelling it correctly,

**Then** give them additional Independent Practice examples, providing a "correct spelling" word bank to draw from at first.

# LANGUAGE

## Spelling High-Frequency Words

**Guided Instruction** It is important to spell words correctly when you are writing. You should remember how to spell high-frequency words that you use often when you write.

| High-Frequency Words | | |
|---|---|---|
| *another* | *especially* | *question* |
| *believe* | *friendly* | *ready* |
| *caught* | *important* | *thought* |
| *does* | *knew* | *usually* |

**Guided Practice** Circle the correct spelling of the word in parentheses.

1. Chichen Itza is an (importent, important) pyramid in Mexico.
2. Scientists (believe, beleeve) that the Mayans built the pyramid.
3. (Anuther, Another) Mayan pyramid is El Castillo.
4. Pyramids were (espeshelly, especially) important in Mayan society.
5. I never (new, knew) they were so interesting.

**Independent Practice** Find the misspelled word and spell it correctly on the line.

1. Chichen Itza has meny steps leading to the top. many
2. Some peeple like to climb the stairs. people
3. You should place your feet carfully as you climb, so you don't fall. carefully
4. Be reddy for a tough climb, but know that it is well worth it in the end. ready
5. I thougt it was a great day. thought





## Differentiate Instruction

Help struggling students master correct spelling with several activities.

First, have students say the word. Then, have them spell the word, tapping each letter with a pencil tip as they spell it. Finally, have them say the word again. Repeat for each word.

Then show an index card to the student with the word written on it. Hide the word and have the student spell it. Show the word to the student again. Ask the student to explain if he or she spelled it correctly or incorrectly, and identify the misspelling. Repeat for each word.

Finally, give students a handout that lists the spelling words with a misspelling of the word next to it. Have them circle the correct version.

MORE ONLINE sadlierconnect.com

## Commas in Addresses

**Guided Instruction** A comma is used to separate words or ideas. In an address, a comma separates a city from a state.

*Dinosaur National Monument*
*4545 E. Highway 40*
*Dinosaur, CO 81610*

**Guided Practice** Add a comma to the sentences below.

1. Dinosaur National Park is near Boulder, Colorado.
2. On your way to the park, you may want to visit the craters near Twin Falls, Idaho.
3. You can also travel to Salt Lake City, Utah, which is nearby.
4. We traveled all the way from Pittsburgh, Pennsylvania.
5. Next year we plan to go to Portland, Oregon.
6. In San Francisco, California, we can visit my grandparents.
7. They moved to California from Miama, Florida.
8. New York, NY, is the town for me!

**Independent Practice** Using correct punctuation, write your address below.

Answers will vary.





**OBJECTIVE**
**Use commas correctly in addresses.**

### Guided Instruction

Make sure students understand that homes, businesses, and institutions (such as schools and museums) are located in a certain place, and that the place has an address. People use the address to find or send letters to the people in the homes, businesses, or institutions. Then discuss how commas separate words or ideas to clarify information for readers. Point out how if there was no comma in the example address, it would be unclear if *CO* was part of the city name or the abbreviation for the state.

### Guided Practice

Discuss with students why a comma is needed to separate *Boulder* from *Colorado* in the first sentence. Then have partners identify the words that need to be separated in the remaining sentences. Have volunteers share their answers and explain them to the group.

### Independent Practice

Have students explain where they placed the comma and why the information in their address would be confusing if they had omitted the comma.

### Assess and Respond

**If** students have difficulty correctly using commas in addresses,

**Then** give them additional Guided Instruction examples, talking through how to correct the first one, providing corrective feedback for the second one, and allowing them to complete the remaining ones independently.

### Differentiate Instruction

Some students might not be aware that cities or towns are located in states. Display a map to students. Point first to a city or town on the map. Then draw attention to the state the city or town is in. Present the information orally while pointing to the map. For example, *Boulder is located in Colorado.*

Then review the Guided Instruction and Guided Practice examples. For each example, have students identify the city. Then have them identify the state. Reinforce that these are two different ideas—a city and a state—so they need to be separated by a comma to help readers understand the addresses.

## OBJECTIVES

- **Come to discussion prepared, having read the required text, citing evidence when building on others' ideas.**
- **Follow conventions of discourse, including agreed-upon rules for discussion.**

## Discuss the Essential Question

Before beginning a group discussion, copy and distribute the "Did I?" checklist, available on **sadlierconnect.com**.

### Leading the Class Discussion

Give students time to think about the questions before the class discussion.

1. Guide students to identify how the section headings give a clue as to how information is grouped in each section.
2. Have students skim the text for the linking words used to connect ideas.

## SPEAKING AND LISTENING

### Discuss the Essential Question

**How do writers develop a topic to inform or explain?**

Think about the Essential Question by responding to the questions below. Support your point of view with reasons and experience.

1. How does the writer of "The Mystery of King Tut" group related information, or facts, together?
   The author tells us that scientists used an MRI to find out the age and cause of death of King Tut. Then, we learn what scientists know from King Tut's DNA.
2. What linking words does the writer of "The Mystery of King Tut" use to connect ideas?
   The author uses linking words such as "yet," "however," "another," "but," "still," "also," and "as" to connect ideas.

Use your notes above to discuss the Essential Question in small groups or as a class. Follow agreed-upon rules for discussion. Use the organizer below to record what you heard and how you participated.

| Ideas I Agree or Disagree With | | Questions I Asked |
|---|---|---|
| Agree | | |
| Disagree | | |
| **New Ideas I Had During Discussion** | | **Questions I Answered** |
| | | |





### Discussion Skills

Before discussing each question as a class, have partners build on and clarify each other's ideas by sharing their responses to the questions with each other. Have each partner make one statement, building on the other partner's responses to the questions. Then have each student ask their partner for clarification about their responses. Provide sentence starters if necessary. Encourage students to revise their answers based on their discussions with their partners. Then have volunteers share their responses and explain how they revised their responses through building on and clarifying ideas with their partners. As students participate in the discussion, rephrase what they say, adding to it to model building on and clarifying each other's ideas.

# CHAPTER 8 REVIEW

This letter has mistakes in spelling, punctuation, and use of pronouns. Write the paragraph correctly on the lines below.

238 Elm Street
Nashville TN 37240

Dear Dr. Frank,

I would like to ask your a few questuns. I am intrested in how you use planes to map your sites. How did your team members get his information about Peru? Do you beleeve that technology will help you find more artifacts? Thank you for the infermation.

Tomas

238 Elm Street
Nashville, TN 37240
Dear Dr. Frank,
I would like to ask you a few questions. I am interested in how you use planes to map your sites. How did your team members get their information about Peru? Do you believe that technology will help you find more artifacts? Thank you for the information.
Tomas





## Introduce the Review

Explain to students that this review will give them an opportunity to apply the language and writing skills that they have studied and practiced in this chapter.

### Language Skills Summary

Let students know that they are going to use what they learned about pronouns, spelling, and commas to make their writing better. Good writers follow grammar rules, can spell correctly, and understand the mechanics of writing.

- Ask students to tell what a pronoun takes the place of (a noun) and name some common pronouns. (*I, he, she, it, we, they, you*)
- Have students explain the rules of pronouns and antecedents. (The pronoun and antecedent must match. Both must be singular or plural.)
- Prompt students to explain what a high-frequency word is and then to correctly spell one or two high-frequency words. (*another*, *friendly*, *ready*)
- Have students tell what a comma separates in an address. (a city from a state)

## Test-Taking Tips

Give students the following tips to help with taking assessments focused on editing skills.

- Tell students to read the text slowly and mark suspected errors lightly on the text in pencil as they find them. Tell them to then reread the text reconsidering the suspected error they marked. If they decide it is not actually an error, they can erase their marking. If they decide that it is an error, they can mark the error more clearly so that they do not omit correcting it when they rewrite the paragraph.
- Have students read the text backward to help them identify misspelled words.

## Writing Process Summary

Remind students that planning helps them organize their ideas before drafting, and revising and editing make a draft better.

### Planning and Drafting

Have students look at the outline and draft they created earlier (page 179). They should check that the draft includes an introduction, subtopics, and ends with a conclusion.

### Informative/Explanatory Text Rubric

| | |
|---|---|
| 4 | The text clearly introduces the topic and states what the writer will examine in the introduction; groups related information and develops the topic with facts, definitions, and details; concludes by wrapping up what was learned and adds an interesting thought; and uses linking words. There are few or no editing errors. |
| 3 | The text has the elements listed under "4" above, though they are executed less successfully. Minor editing errors do not detract greatly from the overall text. |
| 2 | The text is missing one or more of the required elements. There are many editing errors, some of which are serious. |
| 1 | The text is unfinished or shows a minimal understanding of required elements. Serious editing errors make it difficult to read. |
| 0 | The assignment was not attempted. |

### Self-Assessment: Progress Check

Have students revisit the Progress Check on page 173 and compare their answers now with the answers they gave before they started Chapter 8.

## CHAPTER 8 REVIEW

**Assignment:** Write an informative/explanatory text about a history or science topic that interests you.

On the lines below, write your final copy of the informative/explanatory essay you created on page 179. Be sure to introduce the topic and end with a concluding sentence or paragraph. Make sure to use facts, definitions, and details to explain the topic. Do not forget to use linking words to connect ideas. See the Writing Handbook (at sadlierconnect.com) for ways to improve your writing as you revise.

Students should write an informative/explanatory essay by using facts, details, and definitions. They should group related information together and use linking words to connect ideas. Each student's essay should include an introduction to make the reader familiar with the topic, a middle to develop ideas further, and a conclusion to wrap up the essay.





### Digital Connection: Digital Slide Presentation

Once students have finished writing their essays, they can turn them into digital slide presentations.

Display a sample digital slide presentation that includes a title slide, sections that group related information, and a concluding slide. Point out that the digital slide presentation does not simply display chunks of text on screen; rather, it displays key headings and bullet points, as well as visuals (images and videos), and audio. The presenter clicks through slides that support what he or she says during the presentation.

Have students create their digital slide presentations and present them to the class.

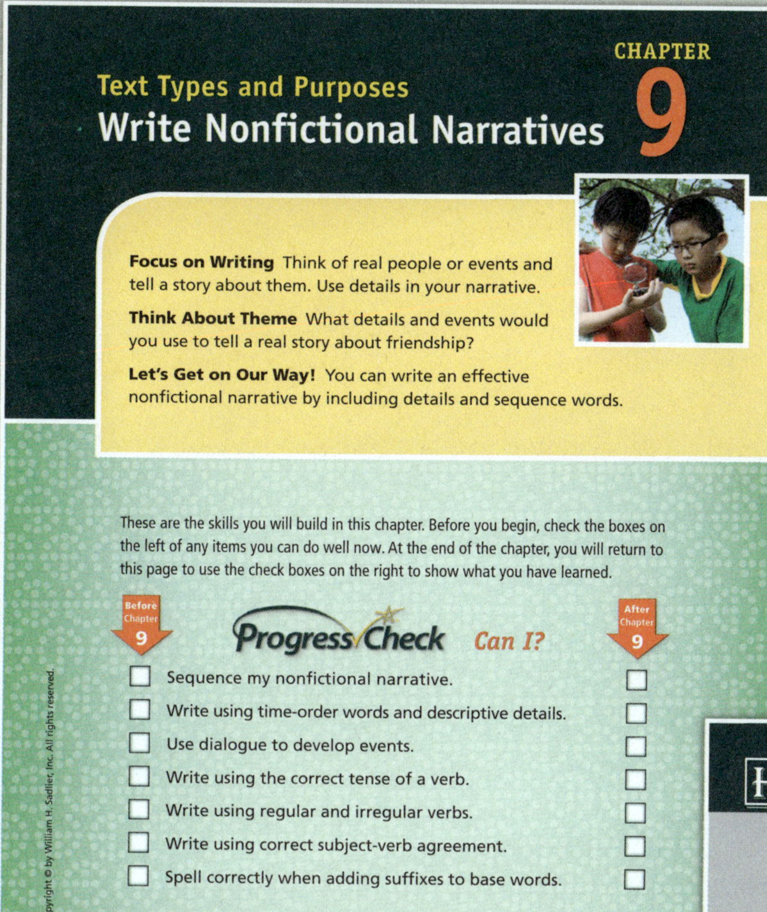

CHAPTER 9

Text Types and Purposes
## Write Nonfictional Narratives

**Focus on Writing** Think of real people or events and tell a story about them. Use details in your narrative.

**Think About Theme** What details and events would you use to tell a real story about friendship?

**Let's Get on Our Way!** You can write an effective nonfictional narrative by including details and sequence words.

These are the skills you will build in this chapter. Before you begin, check the boxes on the left of any items you can do well now. At the end of the chapter, you will return to this page to use the check boxes on the right to show what you have learned.

| Before Chapter 9 | Progress Check — Can I? | After Chapter 9 |
|---|---|---|
| ☐ | Sequence my nonfictional narrative. | ☐ |
| ☐ | Write using time-order words and descriptive details. | ☐ |
| ☐ | Use dialogue to develop events. | ☐ |
| ☐ | Write using the correct tense of a verb. | ☐ |
| ☐ | Write using regular and irregular verbs. | ☐ |
| ☐ | Write using correct subject-verb agreement. | ☐ |
| ☐ | Spell correctly when adding suffixes to base words. | ☐ |



Chapter 9 ■ Text Types and Purposes: Write Nonfictional Narratives

**Student Page 187**

## Progress Check

The Progress Check is a self-assessment feature that students can use to gauge their own progress. Research shows that when students take accountability for their own learning, their motivation increases.

Before students begin work on Chapter 9, have them check the boxes next to any item that they feel they can do well. It is fine if they don't check any of the boxes. Tell them that they will have an opportunity to learn about and practice all of these items while studying the chapter. Let them know that near the end of the chapter they will have a chance to reconsider how well they can do each item on the list.

Before students begin their Chapter 9 Review on page 199, have them revisit this page. You can use this information to work with students on any items they don't understand before they tackle the Review.

## HOME ✦ CONNECT...

The Home Connect feature is a way to keep parents or other adult family members apprised of what their children are learning. The key learning objectives are listed, and some ideas for related activities and discussions are included.

Explain to students that they can share the Home Connect page with their parents or other adult family members in their home. Let students know how much time the class will be spending on this chapter so they can plan their time accordingly at home.

Encourage students and their parents to share their experiences using suggestions on the Home Connect. You may wish to make a place to post some of this work.

### HOME ✦ CONNECT...

In this chapter, children will learn to write about real events and experiences as part of the **nonfictional narrative** form. Explain that many people enjoy recording their experiences in diaries, journals, or blogs. These can be records of special events and experiences. Encourage your child to retell the events of a special experience, such as a trip to the zoo or losing a tooth.

When writing a nonfictional narrative, your child will be asked to **sequence events** in the order they occurred. As your child retells a special event, ask: *What happened first? What happened next? What happened last?* Help your child think of some **descriptive details** about his or her special event. Ask what was said during the event. This practice will add **dialogue** and interest to your child's narrative. Encourage him or her to **provide a good ending** by explaining what made the event special and how he or she felt.

**On the Go:** Show your child examples of child-friendly blogs—perhaps a travel blog or movie blog for family movies. Then, ask your child to write about his or her experiences. Encourage him or her to select one important recent event. If you wish, ask your child to share the blog with family or friends who don't live nearby.

**IN THIS CHAPTER, YOUR CHILD WILL...**

- Learn to write a nonfictional narrative using dialogue, descriptive details, and a clear sequence of events.
- Learn to use time-order words such as *next, then,* and *last* to show the order of events.
- Learn specific language skills and use them in writing a nonfictional narrative:
  - Write verbs to show actions in the narrative.
  - Use the correct verb tense to show when the action happened.
  - Correctly use regular and irregular verbs such as *I blow a bubble* and *I blew a bubble*.
  - Use correct singular and plural subject-verb agreement.
  - Recognize suffixes that change the meaning of a base word.

**WAYS TO HELP YOUR CHILD**

Discuss special events with your child. For example, instead of telling about the weekend, encourage your child just to tell about dinner at Grandma's. Ask questions: *What did it look like? How did you feel?* Descriptive details add to the event.

ONLINE
For more Home Connect activities, continue online at sadlierconnect.com



188 Chapter 9 ■ Text Types and Purposes: Write Nonfictional Narratives

**Student Page 188**

## LEARNING PROGRESSIONS

In this chapter, students will learn how to write a nonfictional narrative about friendship. In order to learn the skills necessary to craft a nonfictional narrative, students will further develop skills learned in second grade. They should be encouraged to retain these skills, as they will continue to build on them in fourth grade.

**Establishing a Situation**

- By the end of grade 2, students should be able to write a narrative in which they recount a well-elaborated event or sequence of events.
- In grade 3, students will learn to use effective narrative techniques, such as by establishing a situation and a narrator.
- When students move to grade 4, they will continue to develop their narrative writing techniques by orienting the reader with a situation and a narrator.

**Dialogue, Details, and Descriptions**

- By the end of grade 2, students will be able to write nonfictional narratives that include details to describe actions, thoughts, and feelings.
- In grade 3, students will build on their abilities by using temporal words and phrases to show the sequence of events.
- During grade 4, students will continue to develop their narrative technique by using transitional words and phrases to clarify sequences of events and concrete words and sensory details to convey experiences.

**Conclusions**

- In grade 2, students learned to provide a concluding statement.
- In grade 3, students will learn to provide a sense of closure to their narrative.
- These skills prepare them for grade 4, when they will learn to provide a conclusion that follows from the narrated experiences and events.

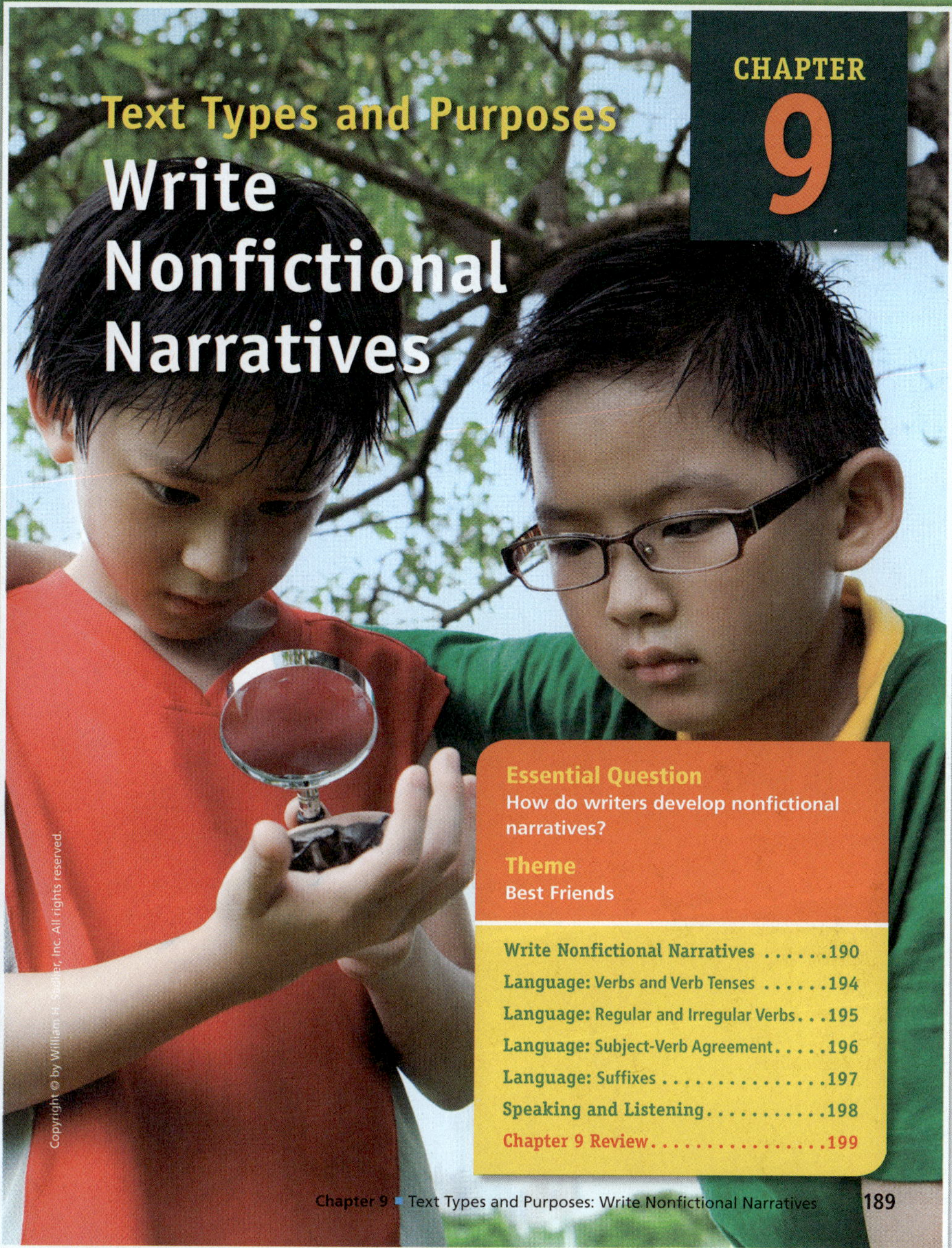

Text Types and Purposes

# Write Nonfictional Narratives

CHAPTER 9

**Essential Question**
How do writers develop nonfictional narratives?

**Theme**
Best Friends







**Essential Question:**
**How do writers develop nonfictional narratives?**

Students will learn how writers craft nonfictional narratives using effective techniques such as dialogue, details, and a clear sequence.

## Theme: Best Friends

Students will write a nonfictional narrative about friendship. The friendship can be with a person or a pet.

## Curriculum Connection: Language Arts

Students will use what they have already learned about reading fictional narratives as they write their own nonfictional narrative.

## Connect Reading to Writing

Remind students that they read several forms of fictional narratives in Chapter 3 including realistic fiction, drama, and poetry. In this chapter, students will build upon what they have learned to write their own nonfictional narrative.

## Writing Handbook

If students need extra practice with writing a nonfictional narrative, refer them to the *Writing Handbook* on **sadlierconnect.com**. The Writing Handbook gives students detailed instruction on planning, drafting, revising, and editing their writing. They will also find tips on producing, publishing, and presenting their writing.

**OBJECTIVE**

**Write a nonfictional narrative that develops a real experience or event using effective techniques, descriptive details, and clear event sequences.**

## Introduce: Organizational Structure

Draw students' attention to the nonfictional narrative organizer in the left margin and point out the key elements. Ask students to look for these key elements as you read and analyze the Student Model together.

## Analyze a Student Model

**EVENT SEQUENCE:** Tell students that a narrator is the person telling the story, and an event is something that happens. *I know that writers tell about events in a narrative.*

*What event is described in the first paragraph?* (The narrator is crying at a skating party because she doesn't know how to skate.) *How does the writer get the reader's attention?* (by describing the balloons and the loud music)

---

WRITE NONFICTIONAL NARRATIVES

**CREATING AN ORGANIZATIONAL STRUCTURE**

Abbey used an outline to organize her nonfictional narrative. It divides the sequence of events into three sections: beginning, middle, and end.

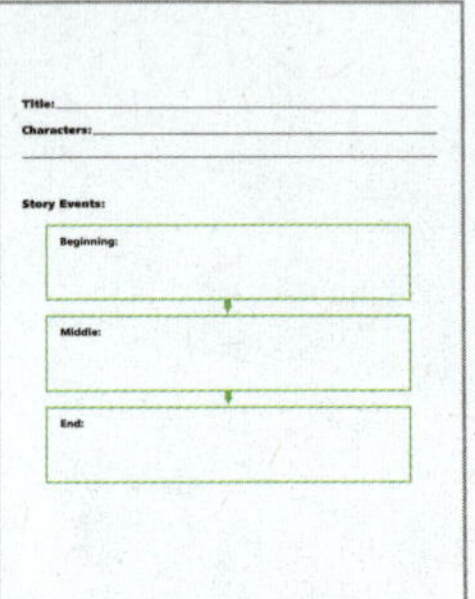
Title:
Characters:
Story Events:
Beginning:
Middle:
End:

**EVENT SEQUENCE**

- The beginning of the narrative introduces the event and the narrator.
- It uses words for effect and gets the reader's attention.

***Underline a sentence that tells what happened at the beginning.***

# Read a Student Model

Abbey is in the third grade. She has been asked to write a nonfictional narrative about a special day with a friend. She has been asked to use a clear event sequence and to describe her thoughts, feelings, and actions. As you read her nonfictional narrative, think about what event you will share and what words you will use to describe the event.

### A Hand to Help

Lots of colored balloons clung to the ceiling. Loudspeakers blared my favorite music. It was a party, so why was I sitting in the middle of the floor crying? It was a skating party, and I had never been on skates before.

My mom had carefully fastened my bubblegum-pink skates. She turned around to help my little brother with his black ones. I tried to stand up, but instead I wobbled and fell on the shiny hardwood floor. My knees buckled and my hands stung as I tried to break my fall. I felt embarrassed.





---

## Genre: Nonfictional Narrative

Explain to students that in a nonfictional narrative, the writer recounts an event or experience that actually happened. By using effective storytelling techniques, such as descriptive details and dialogue, the writer can tell a compelling personal story.

Not all nonfictional narratives are personal stories. History books, newspaper and magazine articles about current events, and biographies are also nonfictional narratives that retell real events not experienced by the writer. These forms of nonfiction narratives require the writer to do research and conduct interviews to get the facts behind the true stories.

MORE ONLINE sadlierconnect.com

As I watched my friends skating effortlessly around and around the rink, I wanted to crawl into a hole. Emma waved from across the room. "Oh no! She's coming over here," I thought.

Emma glided to a graceful stop in front of me. I peeked up at her. She had a big smile on her face.

★ "Would you like to go for a spin?" she asked.

I shook my head no. She tried to bend down closer but lost her balance. Her hands were flying around as she tried to break her fall. Then she ended up on the floor just like me.

Emma laughed. "I think I spend more time falling than I do skating!"

"At least you can stand up. I can't skate at all," I replied.

"You will, too. We'll hold onto the rail until you can go on your own."

Having a friend by my side gave me a lot of confidence. I grabbed the rail and Emma's hand in a tight grip as I slowly pulled myself off the floor. I wobbled but eventually managed to stand on my own two feet. In the beginning, I held on to the rail and pulled myself along.

**DIALOGUE AND DESCRIPTIONS**

- Dialogue shows thoughts and feelings of characters.
- Descriptions give details about how things look, smell, sound, or feel.

***Underline descriptive words in the first paragraph on this page that show how the narrator feels.***

***Put a star next to Emma's first line of dialogue.***

**EVENT SEQUENCE**

The middle of the nonfictional narrative continues the sequence of events in the order they happened.

**TIME-ORDER WORDS AND PHRASES**

Words such as *before, until*, and *eventually* tell when events happen. Use time-order words and phrases to signal the order of events and make the event sequence clear.

***Circle words that show the sequence of events.***





## Analyze a Student Model

**DIALOGUE AND DESCRIPTIONS:** Tell students that the writer uses dialogue to show the thoughts and feelings of the narrator and other people in the narrative. Ask them to point out an example of dialogue in the text. ("Would you like to go for a spin?") Ask how they know the words are dialogue. (The words are set inside quotation marks.)

Point out that the writer includes details of the party to enhance her story. Ask students how these details help them imagine the scene.

**EVENT SEQUENCE:** Point out to students that the events are told in the order they happened. *What happened when Emma tried to bend closer?* (She fell beside Abbey.)

**TIME-ORDER WORDS AND PHRASES:** Tell students that time-order words indicate the order of events in the sequence. Point out the time-order word *as*. Help students identify other time-order words in Abbey's narrative. (*as, eventually, in the beginning*)

### Support English Language Learners

Help English language learners by previewing time-order words. Write this list of common time-order words and phrases on the board: *first second, last, before, after, now, later, next, then, in the beginning, eventually,* and *finally*. Define the words if necessary, and then create a time line showing how they relate to each other. Invite students to tell about something that happened to them recently. Guide them as they retell the event by pointing out the relevant time-order words that will help make the story coherent.

## Analyze a Student Model

**PROVIDE A STRONG ENDING:** Review the end of Abbey's story with the students. Ask if any of them have been in a similar situation, either needing help from or giving help to a friend. *What are Abbey's final feelings about her party that day?* (She learned what a great friend Emma was.) Point out how Abbey's conclusion brings the narrative to a close.

## Evaluate a Writer's Work

Organize a group discussion about Abbey's narrative. Remind students that effective nonfictional narratives include details and dialogue, and use time-order words to show a clear sequence of events. *How well did Abbey include the elements of a good nonfictional narrative?* Students should cite evidence from the Student Model to support their answers. If they don't think Abbey included enough details or dialogue or showed a clear sequence of events, have them explain their thinking.

## Model: Organizational Structure

Ask students to think about how Abbey might have used an organizer to plan for her nonfictional narrative. On a board or projector, post the organizer on page 193. Have students help you fill in the organizer using details from Abbey's narrative. Ask them to include time-order words that tell when events happened.

Students will use the blank organizer in their books to plan their own nonfictional narratives. Once they have completed an organizer, they will draft their own nonfictional narratives based on their notes.

## WRITE NONFICTIONAL NARRATIVES

**PROVIDE A STRONG ENDING**

The ending tells how the events worked out or how the writer felt about the events.

***Underline the words that Abbey used to signal the ending.***

Then, I released my grip on the rail but my hand stayed close to it.

By the end of the party, I was skating around and around with everyone else. It was so much fun to glide and coast. It felt a little like flying. I felt brave for trying something new and scary. I couldn't have done it without my friend. Emma never left my side. She helped me laugh when I would get upset. She cheered me on when I was doing well. It wasn't learning to skate that made the day special. It was learning what a great friend Emma had been to me.

### Review: Distinguishing Literal/Nonliteral Language

Remind students that when they read the realistic fictional narratives in Chapter 3, they learned how to distinguish literal language from nonliteral language. If necessary, remind students that nonliteral language includes figures of speech, such as "bend over backward" or "a green thumb." The meaning of the words taken together is different from the dictionary definitions of the individual words. Tell students that they should consider using nonliteral language in their own nonfictional narratives. Nonliteral language is colorful and can make their writing more interesting.

MORE ONLINE sadlierconnect.com

Use an organizer like Abbey's to plan your own nonfictional narrative about a special day with a friend. Then write a first draft of your story on a separate piece of paper. Don't forget to use dialogue, descriptions, and time-order words in your narrative. You will use this draft to write your final story draft in the Chapter 9 Review section on page 200.

**Title:** ______________________________

**Characters:** ______________________________

______________________________

**Story Events:**

**Beginning:**

**Middle:**

**End:**





## Differentiate Instruction

Struggling students might not yet be ready to write a nonfictional narrative on their own. Form a writing group to support these students.

Lead the group in a shared writing experience in which students brainstorm experiences, decide on a topic, collaborate to complete the organizer, and then draft a nonfictional narrative. Be sure that every member of the group gets a chance to contribute.

## Create: Organizational Structure

### Brainstorming

Remind students that some nonfictional narratives are about the writers' personal experiences. As a class, brainstorm common experiences that students could write about. Make a list of the students' topic ideas on the board or projector for them to use as they plan their writing.

### Planning

Students will use the organizer on page 193 to plan their nonfictional narratives.

- Students should first choose an event or experience to write about.
- Next, they should make a list of the characters that will be in the narrative.
- Have students list the events in chronological order, using time-order words to show the sequence.

### Drafting a Nonfictional Narrative

Instruct students to refer to their organizers as they draft their nonfictional narratives on a separate piece of paper. Be sure students have a beginning, a clear sequence of events, dialogue, descriptive details, and an ending.

## Introduce the Writing Process

Remind students that in order to write their best nonfictional narrative, they must plan, draft, revise, and edit it. These are all steps in the writing process. For more on the writing process, see the *Writing Handbook* on **sadlierconnect.com**.

### Assess and Respond

**If** students have difficulty turning their organizer into a draft,

**Then** draw a flow chart on the board. Ask students to tell you events as you write them in the chart. Then ask students to orally retell the events you wrote by using time-order words.

**OBJECTIVE**

**Use the correct verb tenses in writing.**

## Guided Instruction

Make sure students understand that verb tense helps readers determine when an action happened. Have students study the boldface words in the example, and ask them to identify when the actions happen—in the past, in the present, or in the future. Point out that singular verbs in the present tense end in *-s* or *-es*, but plural verbs in the present tense do not have any suffixes. Verbs in the past tense usually end in *–ed.* Future tense verbs have the helping verb *will* in front of them.

## Guided Practice

Point out how the word at the beginning of each sentence helps identify the tense. Ask students how to change the verb *walk* from the present tense to the past and future tenses.

## Independent Practice

Provide additional examples of sentences with different verb tenses. Have students identify the verb tense in each.

**Assess and Respond**

**If** students are having trouble determining which tense the verb should be in,

**Then** have them look for time-order words such as *yesterday, today, tomorrow, next,* and *before* to help them decide when the action takes place.

# LANGUAGE

## Verbs and Verb Tenses

**Guided Instruction** A **verb tense** tells when an action happens. When an action happens now or regularly, the verb is in the **present tense**.

*Kylie **visits** Beth at her house.*
*Kylie and Sarah **visit** Beth at her house.*

When an action has already happened, the verb is in the ***past tense***.

*Last week, Kylie **visited** Beth at her house.*

When an action is going to happen, the verb is in the ***future tense***.

*Tomorrow, Kylie **will visit** Beth at her house.*

**Guided Practice** Write the correct tense of the word in parentheses.

1. Today, I ___walk___ to Tom's house. (walk)
2. Yesterday, I ___walked___ to Tom's house. (walk)
3. Tomorrow, I ___will walk___ to Tom's house. (walk)
4. Every month, I ___walk___ to Tom's house. (walk)

**Independent Practice** Use the correct tense of the verb in parentheses to complete each sentence.

1. The friends ___work___ on a group project right now. (work)
2. The group ___talked___ about the plans a month ago. (talk)
3. They ___started___ it yesterday. (start)
4. Tomorrow, the boys and girls ___will look___ for poster board and paints. (look)
5. They ___will finish___ the project next week. (finish)





**Support English Language Learners**

Identifying tenses of verbs can be difficult for English language learners, as not all languages conjugate verbs the same way as English. To help students, draw a three-column chart on the board with the headings *Past, Present,* and *Future.* Then fill in a couple of rows with the verb tense forms of a common regular verb, such as *walk* or *wish.* You might also include a row showing the verb tense forms of an irregular verb, such as *run* or *sing.* Call out another verb, and ask a volunteer to come up to the board to write the three tenses in the chart, using the words you wrote in it as models. If time allows, call out other verbs for students to write in the chart. Keep the chart up throughout the chapter.

MORE ONLINE sadlierconnect.com

## Regular and Irregular Verbs

**Guided Instruction** Most verbs form the past tense by adding *-ed* to the end. **Irregular verbs** change their spelling when forming the past tense.

| | | |
|---|---|---|
| *work (regular verb)* | *worked* | *We **worked** on the group project last night.* |
| *come (irregular verb)* | *came* | *We **came** home late.* |

**Guided Practice** Underline the verb that correctly completes the sentence.

1. Two friends (goed, went) to the park.
2. They (brought, bringed) a picnic lunch.
3. After they (eated, ate), they threw away the trash.
4. Then they (took, taked) the water bottles home.

**Independent Practice** Write the correct past tense of the verbs in parentheses on the line.

1. Arjun ____ran____ the race last week. (run)
2. Arjun's friend ____broke____ his leg. (break)
3. Arjun ____pushed____ his friend in a wheelchair. (push)
4. They____knew____ how to finish the race. (know)
5. Their parents ____came____ to watch. (come)
6. The crowd ____saw____ a great race. (see)





### OBJECTIVE

**Use the correct forms of regular and irregular verbs in writing.**

### Guided Instruction

Explain that regular verbs follow a set pattern when changed to the past tense. To change a regular verb from present tense to past, add *–ed* to the word. Give students more examples: *roll, rolled; add, added; allow, allowed; ask, asked.*

Tell students that irregular verbs don't follow a set pattern. Their spelling changes when they shift from present tense to past tense. There is no rule to go by. Students must memorize them. Examples include: *drink, drank; run, ran; forget, forgot; is, was; go, went.*

### Guided Practice

Help students draw on their understanding of how English works. If students can't determine the correct form of a verb, ask them questions like this: *Which is correct? I goed to the park, or I went to the park?*

### Independent Practice

Read aloud each verb in the parentheses and ask students whether it is regular or irregular. Have them form the past tense form of each verb before writing the word in the blank.

### Assess and Respond

**If** students are having difficulty recognizing irregular verbs,

**Then** provide them with a list of common irregular verbs and their tenses.

### Numbered Heads Together

Divide students into teams of four. Give each student a number from one to four. Give each group a list of eight verbs—four regular and four irregular. Have students work together in their teams to identify the verbs as regular or irregular and to form the past tense of each. Then call out a number, and ask all students with that number to stand and identify one of the verbs from the list as regular or irregular and give its past tense. Ask the rest of the class if each student's answer is correct. Work together as a class to reach the correct answer. Repeat until all students have given answers to the class.

**OBJECTIVE**
**Use subject-verb agreement in writing.**

## Guided Instruction

Remind students that the subject is who or what the sentence is about, and the verb tells the action, or what the subject does. Explain that the subject and verb must both agree in number. They must both be singular or plural. Point out that when a subject is singular, the verb usually ends in an *–s*. When a subject is plural, the verb does not end in *–s*.

## Guided Practice

Have students read the sentences. Ask whether the sentence is missing its subject or verb. Remind them to fill in the missing word after checking the subject or verb that is present to see if it requires a singular or plural verb or subject.

## Independent Practice

Provide additional examples of sentences that are missing either the subject or verb. Have students fill in the missing word, making sure it matches the number.

**Assess and Respond**

**If** students are having trouble identifying plural nouns,

**Then** work as a class to generate a list of singular and plural nouns. Write the words on the board. Then have students tell you whether to put the letter *P* for plural or the letter *S* for singular next to each.

# LANGUAGE

## Subject-Verb Agreement

**Guided Instruction** The subject and verb in a sentence must both be singular or both be plural.

- If the subject is a singular noun or pronoun, add *-s* to the verb.

  *The **lizard runs** across the sand.*

- If the subject is a plural noun or pronoun, do not add *-s* to the verb.

  *The **lizards run** across the sand.*

**Guided Practice** Write the word in parentheses that correctly completes each sentence.

1. Many animals ____live____ on or around the cactus. (live, lives)
2. The wren ____makes____ a nest on the branch. (make, makes)
3. The ____owl____ hunts at night. (owl, owls)
4. Some ____insects____ eat cactus. (insect, insects)

**Independent Practice** Correct the mistakes in subject-verb agreement. Write the new sentences.

1. The woodpecker make a hole in the cactus.
   The woodpecker makes a hole in the cactus.
2. Inside the nest, the babies sleeps safely.
   Inside the nest, the babies sleep safely.
3. When the babies leave, other birds uses the nest.
   When the babies leave, other birds use the nest.
4. A woodpecker eat insects.
   A woodpecker eats insects.
5. Gila woodpeckers lives as long as 10 years.
   Gila woodpeckers live as long as 10 years.





## Differentiate Instruction

Some struggling students may have trouble understanding the relationship between a subject's number and the form of the verb it takes. Place students in pairs. Create a set of flash cards that students can use. On four index cards, write a singular or plural subject on the front. On the back, identify the subject as singular or plural. On another four index cards, write a singular form of a verb on the front and the plural form on the back. Mix up the cards. Have students work together to sort the cards to create sentences from the words. The subjects and verbs should agree.

MORE ONLINE sadlierconnect.com

## Suffixes

**Guided Instruction** A **suffix** is a word part that is added to the end of a word to change its meaning. Suffixes can be added to the end of verbs to change them into a different part of speech. Sometimes the spelling of the base word is changed when a suffix is added. Here the *e* is dropped before adding *-ing*.

*I like to **bake** cookies.*
*Mom likes **baking** pies in the winter.*

Suffixes can also be added to nouns and adjectives to change their meaning. When a base word ends in *y* preceded by a consonant, the *y* changes to *i* before the suffix is added.

*What makes you feel **happy**?*
*I feel **happiness** when I play at the park with friends.*

**Guided Practice** Add the suffix to the base word and spell the new word on the line.

1. shop + er ___shopper___
2. cute + est ___cutest___
3. penny + less ___penniless___
4. silly + est ___silliest___

**Independent Practice** Complete each sentence with the correct base word and suffix.

1. He is the ___bravest___ person I know. (brave + est)
2. The child picked up the ___wrapper___ on the floor. (wrap + er)
3. Liam's hair was ___curlier___ than any I've ever seen! (curly + er)
4. Joni would ___happily___ help the young child. (happy + ly)
5. Rene was a ___skater___ in the ice show. (skate + er)





### OBJECTIVE

**Use conventional spelling for adding suffixes to base words.**

### Guided Instruction

Explain that suffixes are letters added to the end of base words to change their meaning. When a suffix is added, the spelling of the base word can often change. Remind students that the best way to learn the spellings of these words is to memorize them. Write several words on the board, and demonstrate how to change their spelling.

### Guided Practice

Help students by reviewing the rules for spelling changes to the words in the activity. When adding *–ing* to a word that ends in *e*, the *e* is dropped. When adding *–er* to a word that ends in a consonant, the final consonant is repeated. When adding *–est* or *-less* to a word that ends in *y*, turn the *y* into an *i*.

### Independent Practice

Have students tell you the rules for adding suffixes to words. Write the rules on the board. Have students consult the board as they write the words in the blanks.

### Assess and Respond

**If** students are having trouble spelling words with suffixes,

**Then** provide them with a list of words with suffixes, and ask students to provide the correctly spelled base words.

### Differentiate Instruction

Struggling students may have trouble forming new words by adding suffixes to base words because the rules for spelling might strike them as arbitrary. Place students in groups of three. Assign each group a suffix—*-y, -er, -est, -less, -ly.* Tell each group to review the rule that applies to the suffix. Then have group members work together to generate a list of five words that use it. Students may consult a dictionary, if necessary. Go around the room and ask students for a word that uses a particular suffix and to spell it. Write their answers on the board.

**OBJECTIVES**

- **Engage effectively in a range of collaborative discussions.**
- **Follow agreed-upon rules of discussion, including asking and answering questions.**

## Discuss the Essential Question

Before beginning a group discussion, copy and distribute the "Did I?" checklist available on **sadlierconnect.com**.

**Leading the Class Discussion**

Give students time to think about the questions before the class discussion.

1. Point students to the body of the Student Model to find time-order words that indicate sequence.
2. Have students skim the narrative for descriptive details.

## SPEAKING AND LISTENING

### Discuss the Essential Question

**How do writers develop nonfictional narratives?**

Think about the Essential Question by responding to the questions below. Support your point of view with details from Abbey's story.

1. What words does the writer use to signal the order of the story?
   then; as; eventually; in the beginning; by the end
2. What are some words or phrases the writer uses to describe events?
   loudspeakers blaring; glided to a graceful stop; her hands were flying around; I grabbed the rail and Emma's hands in a tight grip; I released my grip; glide and coast

Use your notes above to discuss the Essential Question in small groups or as a class. Follow agreed-upon rules for discussion. Use the organizer below to record what you heard and how you participated.

| | Ideas I Agree or Disagree With | Questions I Asked |
|---|---|---|
| Agree | | |
| Disagree | | |

| New Ideas I Had During Discussion | Questions I Answered |
|---|---|
| | |





### Discussion Skills

Remind students of the sentence starters they can use during a discussion that will help them build on each other's reasoning:

- *I am not sure I agree with you. Here's why . . .*
- *I see what you are saying, but I think the evidence shows that . . .*

Then tell students that they are responsible for encouraging everyone in a group to participate. They can use these questions:

- *Would someone like to add to that?*
- *Would you please say more about that?*

## CHAPTER 9 REVIEW

This paragraph has mistakes in the use of regular and irregular verb tenses, subject-verb agreement, as well as suffixes. Write the paragraph correctly on the lines below. Use a dictionary to help you spell the words.

Last week, Kate and I had a lemonade stand. We want to raise money for the hospital that is careing for our sick friend. First, we will ask our parents for permission. Then, we puts together our supplies. Kate mixes the lemonade, and I carefully poured it into the glasses. We selled the tastyest lemonade ever for fifty cents. By the end of the day, we raised twenty dollars. It gave us both great happyness to help our friend.

Last week, Kate and I had a lemonade stand. We wanted to raise money for the hospital that is caring for our sick friend. First, we asked our parents for permission. Then, we put together our supplies. Kate mixed the lemonade, and I carefully poured it into the glasses. We sold the tastiest lemonade ever for fifty cents. At the end of the day, we raised twenty dollars. It gave us both great happiness to help our friend.





## Introduce the Review

Explain to students that this review will give them an opportunity to apply the language and writing skills that they have studied and practiced in this chapter.

### Language Skills Summary

Let students know that they are going to have to use what they have learned about using regular and irregular verb tenses, subject-verb agreement, and suffixes to make their writing better. Good writers follow grammar rules, and they know how to use different kinds of sentences to make their writing more interesting for the reader.

- Have students explain how to form the present, past, and future tense of verbs.
- Ask students to give examples of regular and irregular verbs.
- Ask students how to determine whether verbs and subjects are singular or plural.
- Prompt students to explain how the spelling of a base word changes when they add certain suffixes to it.

## Test-Taking Tips

Provide the following tips to students to help with taking assessments based on editing skills.

- Students should make a list of at least five common editing errors. Then they should read through their answers five separate times, checking for one item on the list each time. Students' lists should include the errors they typically make in their writing, such as capitalization of proper nouns, correctly using easily confused words (*there*, *their*, *they're*), and end punctuation.
- Tell students to place a ruler or piece of paper beneath each line as they check it for errors.

## Writing Process Summary

Remind students that planning helps them organize their ideas before drafting, and that revising and editing make a draft better.

**Planning and Drafting**

Have students look at the graphic organizers and drafts they created (page 193). They should be sure that their drafts include the sequence of events listed in the graphic organizer, dialogue, descriptions, and a strong ending.

**Nonfictional Narrative Rubric**

| | |
|---|---|
| 4 | The narrative includes: characters, a clear sequence of events with time-order words, dialogue and descriptions, and a conclusion. There are few or no editing errors. |
| 3 | The narrative includes the elements listed in "4" above, though they are executed less successfully. Minor editing errors do not detract from the overall piece. |
| 2 | The narrative is missing one or more of the required elements. There are many editing errors, some of them serious. |
| 1 | The narrative is unfinished or shows a minimal understanding of the required elements. Serious editing errors make it difficult to read and understand. |
| 0 | The assignment was not attempted. |

**Self-Assessment: Progress Check**

Have students revisit the Progress Check on page 187 and compare their answers now with those they gave before they started Chapter 9.

## CHAPTER 9 REVIEW

**Assignment:** Write a nonfictional narrative about a special day with a friend.

On the lines below, write your final copy of the nonfictional narrative draft you created on page 193. Be sure to describe your thoughts, feelings, and actions. Make sure to choose your words carefully and use words to signal the order of events. You may also use dialogue to explain events and tell about the characters. Wrap up your narrative with a conclusion. See the Writing Handbook (at **sadlierconnect.com**) for ways to improve your writing as you revise.

Students should write a nonfictional narrative that establishes a situation with characters. They should use detailed descriptions and possibly dialogue to describe events, and the narrative should have a clear beginning, middle, and end. Time-order words should signal event order. The strong ending should provide closure to the events.





### Digital Connection: Online Publishing

Once students have completed their nonfictional narratives, they can publish them online for other classmates, family, and friends to read. Guide students to an appropriate website for publishing their work. Before students post, they should enhance the final versions of their narratives by adding relevant illustrations or photos. Some students might even want to draw their own illustrations, which they can scan into a computer and then paste into their final drafts.

# Text Types and Purposes: Write Opinion Pieces

CHAPTER 10

Text Types and Purposes

## Write Opinion Pieces

CHAPTER 10

**Focus on Writing** In an opinion piece, you state your views about a topic that is meaningful to you. Provide some background context to help explain your views.

**Think About Theme** In Chapter 4, you read about extreme weather. What things would be important to you in a natural disaster?

**Let's Get on Our Way!** To be effective, an opinion piece must be well organized, clearly written, and follow grammatical rules. Opinions should be supported by convincing reasons.

These are the skills you will build in this chapter. Before you begin, check the boxes on the left of any items you can do well now. At the end of the chapter, you will return to this page to use the check boxes on the right to show what you have learned.

Progress Check — Can I?

| Before Chapter 10 | | After Chapter 10 |
|---|---|---|
| ☐ | State my opinion clearly. | ☐ |
| ☐ | Support my opinions with reasons. | ☐ |
| ☐ | Use linking words and phrases to connect my opinion and my reasons. | ☐ |
| ☐ | Include both an introduction and a conclusion. | ☐ |
| ☐ | Write using adjectives and adverbs correctly. | ☐ |
| ☐ | Write using correct spelling. | ☐ |
| ☐ | Write simple sentences. | ☐ |

**Student Page 201**

## Progress Check

The Progress Check is a self-assessment feature that students can use to gauge their own progress. Research shows that when students take accountability for their own learning, their motivation increases.

Before students begin work on Chapter 10, have them check the boxes next to any item that they feel they can do well. It is fine if they don't check any of the boxes. They will have an opportunity to learn about and practice all of these items while studying the chapter. Let them know that near the end of the chapter they will have a chance to reconsider how well they can do each item on this list.

Before students begin the Chapter 10 Review on page 213, have them revisit this page. You can use this information to work with students on any items they don't understand before they tackle the Review.

## HOME ✦ CONNECT...

The Home Connect feature is a way to keep parents or other adult family members apprised of what their children are learning. The key learning objectives are listed, and some ideas for related activities and discussions are included.

Explain to students that they can share the Home Connect page with their parents or other adult family members in their home. Let students know how much time the class will be spending on this chapter so they can plan their time accordingly at home.

Encourage students and their parents to share their experiences using the suggestions on the Home Connect. You may wish to make a place to post some of this work.

### HOME ✦ CONNECT...

In this chapter, children will learn about **writing to express an opinion.** Help your child see all the different types of opinion writing in the world around you, ranging from billboards and signs to movie reviews on websites and editorials in newspapers. Model responding to opinions by giving reasons that you agree or disagree with them.

When writing an opinion piece, it is important to pay attention to the **organization.** A good way for your child to organize his or her piece is to **list a reason to support an opinion,** and then **give details** to explain why that reason is important. Identify reasons and supporting information with your child in a published review or editorial. Decide together if the reasons and supporting details are convincing or not.

**Activity:** Focus on an important community issue. With your child, reach an opinion about it. Then together, write a letter to the editor of a local newspaper or contribute to a blog. In the first paragraph, introduce the topic and state your opinion. In the next paragraphs, give at least three reasons in support of your opinion. In the conclusion, restate your opinion and call for some sort of action. Then sign and submit!

**IN THIS CHAPTER, YOUR CHILD WILL...**

- Learn to write an opinion piece with an introduction, a statement of opinion, reasons supporting it, and a conclusion.
- Learn to use linking words to connect the reasons to the opinion.
- Follow a process when writing an opinion piece, beginning with using an outline to organize ideas.
- Learn specific language skills to use when writing an opinion piece:
  - Use adjectives to describe nouns and adverbs to describe verbs.
  - Spell words using word families.
  - Write a variety of simple sentences.

**WAYS TO HELP YOUR CHILD**

Show respect for your child's opinions. Regularly engage in discussion with your child about topics he or she is passionate about, such as sports, hobbies, or movies. Ask for your child's point of view and follow up with questions requesting reasons: *Why do you say that? Do you know any facts that support your feelings?*

ONLINE — For more Home Connect activities, continue online at sadlierconnect.com





**Student Page 202**

## LEARNING PROGRESSIONS

In this chapter, students will learn how to write an opinion piece on a topic that interests them. In order to learn the skills necessary to craft an opinion piece, students will further develop skills learned in second grade. They should be encouraged to retain these skills, as they will continue to build on them in fourth grade.

| Introducing the Topic | • By the end of grade 2, students should have been able to write opinion pieces in which they introduce the topics or books they are writing about.<br>• In grade 3, students will build on this skill by not only introducing the topics or texts they are writing about, but also creating an organizational structure, such as an outline, to list the reasons behind their opinions.<br>• When students move on to grade 4, their organizational structures will become more complex as they group related ideas to support their purposes. |
|---|---|
| Providing Reasons that Support the Opinion | • Throughout grades 2 and 3, students are asked to master supplying reasons that support their opinions about a certain topic or text.<br>• This skill provides the foundation for what they learn in grade 4. By grade 4, students will need to provide reasons that are supported by facts and details. |
| Using Linking Words and Phrases | • By the end of grade 2, students should have been able to use linking words such as *because*, *and*, and *also* to connect their opinions to their reasons.<br>• In grade 3, students use not only linking words but also linking phrases to connect opinions and reasons, such as *therefore*, *since*, and *for example*.<br>• This prepares students for the more complex linking words and phrases in grade 4, including *for instance*, *in order to*, and *in addition*. |
| Providing a Concluding Statement | • In grades 2 and 3, students learn the importance of providing a concluding statement or section.<br>• This skill prepares them for grade 4, when their concluding statement or section must be related to the opinion presented. |

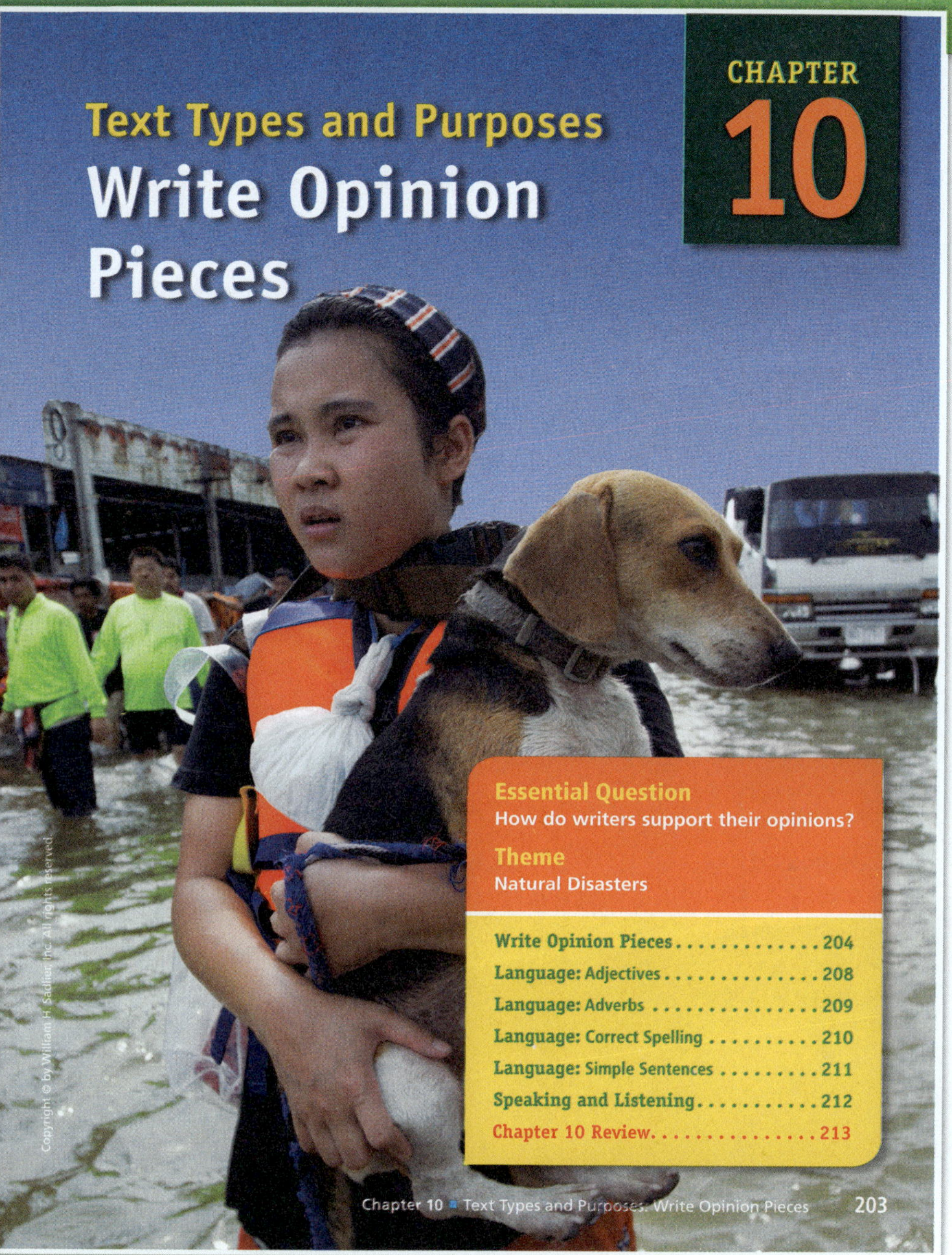

Text Types and Purposes
# Write Opinion Pieces

CHAPTER 10

**Essential Question**
How do writers support their opinions?

**Theme**
Natural Disasters







## Essential Question:
How do writers support their opinions?

Students will learn how opinions are supported with reasons and evidence in order to make arguments more persuasive.

### Theme: Natural Disasters
Students will continue their investigation of natural disasters as they read and analyze an opinion piece writing model.

### Curriculum Connection: Science
Students will use what they have already learned about natural disasters as they work on their own opinion pieces.

### Connect Reading to Writing
Remind students that they read an editorial entitled "Stop the Droughts!" in Chapter 4 (Student Book pages 102–107). Review the author's opinion expressed in that editorial article. Tell students they will be reading and writing an opinion piece in this lesson.

### Writing Handbook
If students need extra practice with writing an opinion piece, refer them to the *Writing Handbook* on **sadlierconnect.com**. The Writing Handbook gives students detailed instruction on planning, drafting, revising, and editing their writing. They will also find tips on producing, publishing, and presenting their writing.

**OBJECTIVE**

**Write an opinion piece with a clear opinion, supporting reasons, linking phrases, and a concluding statement.**

## Introduce: Organizational Structure

Draw students' attention to the opinion piece outline in the left margin, and point out the key elements. Ask students to look for these key elements as you read and analyze the Student Model together.

## Analyze a Student Model

**TITLE:** Tell students that an essay title should tell the topic of the essay and also be interesting enough to grab the reader's attention. You might point out that Ruthie's title is a pun on the saying, "any port in a storm," which roughly means "When things are difficult, do whatever works."

**INTRODUCTION:** Help students find the opinion statement: *I know that the opinion is usually at the end of the introduction and that it might contain words like* I think, I believe that, should, *or* must. Point out that Ruthie, the author, first says something about the topic (natural disasters), then gives some background (her own experience with a hurricane), and finally states her opinion on the topic.

WRITE OPINION PIECES

**CREATING AN ORGANIZATIONAL STRUCTURE**

Ruthie used an outline to organize her essay. It has an opinion, three reasons to support this opinion, and a conclusion.

Title: ______

I. Introduction
a. Background: ______
b. Opinion: ______

II. Supporting Reasons
a. Reason 1: ______
b. Reason 2: ______
c. Reason 3: ______

III. Conclusion

**TITLE**
- Draws the reader into the basic topic

**INTRODUCTION**
- Introduces the topic
- Gives background
- States an opinion

***Underline the writer's opinion.***

# Read a Student Model

Ruthie is a student in Ms. Jenkins's third grade class. Ruthie has been asked to write an opinion piece on what she would do with a pet during a natural disaster. In her piece, she must support her point of view with three reasons. As you read her essay, think about your opinion, reasons, and organization to prepare to write your own opinion piece.

### Any Pet in a Storm!

I know that there are a lot of natural disasters, such as hurricanes, tornadoes, and droughts, all over the world. The only one I can write about with real experience is a hurricane that hit my town last summer. When the hurricane hit, I was very worried about my beagle, Rudy, and what to do with him. My parents said we might have to leave our home without him. I think pet owners should always take their pets with them in a disaster.



204 Chapter 10 ■ Text Types and Purposes: Write Opinion Pieces

## Genre: Opinion Piece

Tell students that a writer writes an opinion piece for a purpose: to give an opinion on a specific topic and to convince readers to agree with this opinion. Sometimes the writer also wants to convince the reader to do something after reading.

To convince readers, the writer constructs a strong argument in support of his or her opinion. The writer gives solid reasons to support the opinion and uses information such as facts, examples, and personal experiences to support each reason. Whether the reader will agree with the writer depends on how good the reasons and support are.

MORE ONLINE sadlierconnect.com

First of all, our pets depend on us for everything—their food, their shelter, their health, and their happiness. These things don't change just because there is an emergency. We must take care of our pets no matter what! How would you feel if you were left alone in a scary emergency?

**LINKING PHRASE**

- Use linking words and phrases to link reasons to the opinion.

**REASON 1**

- Provide reasons that support the opinion.
- Ruthie uses *First of all* to link her reason and opinion.

Also, I know my dog, Rudy, is a part of the family. He comes on trips with us, eats dinner at the same time, and sits on the couch with me as I read. When I am sad, he always cheers me up, and I love him so much. Even thinking of leaving him behind in a hurricane gives me nightmares—imagining him hungry, scared, and alone.

**REASON 2**

***Underline Ruthie's second reason.***

Finally, it can be dangerous for other people when abandoned animals are trapped or roaming around. Imagine a rescue worker trying to search a house for survivors while a scared dog or cat tries to protect the house. The worker or the pet might get hurt. Also, if hungry animals roam the streets, they could get into trouble, like fighting each other and chasing or attacking people.

**REASON 3**

***Underline Ruthie's third reason for never leaving pets behind.***

***Circle the linking word that connects this reason with Ruthie's opinion.***





## Analyze a Student Model

**LINKING PHRASE:** Explain to students that Ruthie uses a linking phrase (*First of all*) to connect Reason 1 to the opinion that she gives in her introduction. Alert students to watch for other linking words and phrases as they read the rest of Ruthie's essay. (*Also, Finally*)

**REASON 1:** Model identifying Ruthie's first reason: *I'm looking for something that explains why pet owners should take their pets with them in a disaster. I know reasons are usually found near the beginning of the paragraph in an opinion piece.* (First of all, our pets depend on us for everything . . . ) Help students see the close connection between Reason 1 and the opinion statement.

**REASON 2:** If necessary, model identifying the second reason with the same wording as for Reason 1. Ask students to put Reason 2 in their own words. (Pets are part of the family.) Point out that the author uses personal experience as support for this reason. (Her dog goes on family trips, eats dinner with the family, etc.)

**REASON 3:** If students are struggling, model identifying the third reason with the same wording as for Reason 1. Have students state Reason 3 in their own words. (Animals left behind can be a danger.) Point out that Ruthie uses possible situations as support for this reason. Ask volunteers to describe these situations. (pets defending their homes and endangering rescuers; pets fighting each other or attacking people)

### Support English Language Learners

Help English language learners by previewing some basic information that will help students understand this essay. First, be sure they understand that the author, Ruthie, is a young girl who has a pet dog named Rudy. Point out the picture of the beagle on page 204.

Explain that Ruthie is giving her opinion on what pet owners should do with their pets if they have to leave their homes due to a natural disaster. Ruthie is basing her opinion on her own experience with her dog, Rudy, during a hurricane last summer.

## Analyze a Student Model

**CONCLUSION:** Review Ruthie's conclusion with students. Ruthie gives pet owners some advice for planning ahead. Students should understand how this advice connects to the restated opinion in the last sentence. (Ruthie wants readers to take their pets with them during an emergency.)

## Evaluate a Writer's Work

Begin a group discussion about Ruthie's opinion piece. Remind students that the purpose of an opinion piece is to convince the reader to share the author's point of view. First, have students recall Ruthie's point of view: If there is a big storm or other emergency, people should not leave their pets behind. Then ask students if Ruthie was able to convince them. Have them explain their thinking.

## Model: Organizational Structure

Ask students to think about how Ruthie might have made an outline for her essay. On a board or projector, post the outline on page 207. Then have students help you fill in the outline based on Ruthie's essay. Review the notes in the margins alongside the essay. Fill in Ruthie's introduction, supporting reasons, and conclusion. Point out that well-written pieces have strong organization, which requires planning and prewriting.

Students will next use the blank outline found in their books to plan their own opinion pieces, and then they will draft the pieces based on their outlines.

WRITE OPINION PIECES

You should plan ahead for your pets in an emergency. Have a supply kit packed. Make sure your pet has its identification and shots, and plan to go to a safe place that allows pets if you have to leave your home. After you do all of this, you will never have to leave your pet behind in an emergency.

**CONCLUSION:**

- Ruthie's concluding statement wraps up her opinion essay and restates her opening opinion in slightly different words.

***Underline Ruthie's concluding statement.***

206 Chapter 10 ■ Text Types and Purposes: Write Opinion Pieces

### Review: Author's Point of View

Remind students that when they read the editorial on droughts ("Stop the Droughts!" on Student Book pages 102–107), they identified the author's point of view. They looked for evidence that the author used to support that point of view, and they thought about whether they agreed with the author.

Ask students to rephrase Ruthie's point of view. (Animals should not be left behind in an emergency.) Ask them to tell what kind of evidence Ruthie used. (examples from life and her own experience)

MORE ONLINE sadlierconnect.com

Use an outline like the one below to organize your opinion essay about something you care about. Then write a first draft of your essay on a separate sheet of paper. Remember to state an opinion and give three supporting reasons. Be sure to use linking words to connect ideas. You will use this draft to write your final essay in the Chapter 10 Review section on page 214.

**Title:** ______________________________

I. **Introduction**

a. Background: ______________________________

______________________________

b. Opinion: ______________________________

______________________________

II. **Supporting Reasons**

a. Reason 1: ______________________________

______________________________

______________________________

b. Reason 2: ______________________________

______________________________

______________________________

c. Reason 3: ______________________________

______________________________

______________________________

III. **Conclusion**

______________________________

______________________________





## Differentiate Instruction

Some students might not yet be ready to write an essay on their own. Form a writing group to support these students.

Lead the group in a shared writing experience in which the group brainstorms ideas, decides on a topic, collaborates to fill in the outline, and then drafts an essay. Be sure that every member of the group gets a chance to contribute. You might subdivide the essay and assign pieces to individuals or small groups to draft.

## Create: Organizational Structure

### Brainstorming

Tell students that writers write opinion pieces on topics they care about. As a class, brainstorm school and community issues that students have opinions about. Make a list of students' topic ideas on the board or projector for them to use as they plan their writing.

### Planning

Students will use the outline on page 207 to plan their opinion pieces. Students should first decide on a topic and then fill in their opinions.

- Students should write three clear reasons that they believe would be convincing to a reader.
- Remind students that Ruthie gave advice in her conclusion that would make it easier for people to agree with her. Ask students what kind of advice or extra information they can give in their conclusions.

### Drafting an Opinion Piece

Instruct students to refer to their outlines as they draft their opinion pieces on a separate piece of paper. Be sure students have an introduction, three reasons, and a conclusion. Remind them to use linking phrases.

## Introduce the Writing Process

Remind students that in order to do a good job on an essay, they must plan, draft, revise, and edit it. These are all steps of the writing process. For more information on the writing process, see the *Writing Handbook* on **sadlierconnect.com**.

### Assess and Respond

**If** students have difficulty turning their outlines into a draft,

**Then** give students some sentence starters that will help them put their ideas into words.

**OBJECTIVE**

**Use comparative and superlative adjectives in writing.**

## Guided Instruction

Make sure students understand that adjectives give information about the persons, places, or things in a sentence. Explain that adjectives are often used to compare two or more nouns. Have students identify the nouns in the example sentences. (*puppy, dog; puppy, litter*)

## Guided Practice

Have students begin by identifying the nouns in the first sentence. (*rain, barn*) Have them look for any words that tell about those nouns. (*old*) Have students continue identifying the adjectives in the rest of the sentences.

## Independent Practice

Remind students that adjectives usually end in *-er* when one thing is being compared to another, and they end in *-est* when one thing is being compared to two or more. If students struggle, ask them to figure out how many things are being compared in each sentence before choosing their answers.

**Assess and Respond**

**If** students have difficulty with comparative and superlative adjectives,

**Then** give students more practice by acting out simple examples with students; for example, "Joe is taller than Zoe" and "Joe is the tallest student in the class."

# LANGUAGE

## Adjectives

**Guided Instruction** An **adjective** describes or tells about a noun. Adjectives often answer the questions "What kind?" or "How many?"

*The **strong** wind blew down many houses.*

Sometimes adjectives are used to compare. To compare two nouns, add *-er* to the end of most adjectives.

To compare three or more nouns, add *-est* to the end of most adjectives.

*The puppy was **smaller** than the dog.*
*The puppy was the **smallest** in the litter.*

**Guided Practice** Underline the adjectives in each sentence.

1. The rain leaked through the old barn.
2. There were wet puddles everywhere.
3. The cold wind blew through the sides of the barn.
4. Several animals cuddled in the hay.
5. The nasty storm finally ended in the morning.

**Independent Practice** Circle the correct adjective in parentheses to complete each sentence.

1. The calf was the (younger, youngest) animal in the herd.
2. It was the (smaller, smallest) brother of the twins.
3. However, the calf was (smarter, smartest) than the bull.
4. It found the (drier, driest) hay of all in the barn.
5. After the storm, the calf was the (sleepier, sleepiest) animal in the barn.





**Support English Language Learners**

Using comparative and superlative adjectives correctly may be difficult for English language learners who may be inclined to use the words *more* and *most* before adjectives instead of adding endings.

On the board, make a chart showing the forms of several adjectives, such as *high, higher, highest*; *low, lower, lowest*; and *funny, funnier, funniest*. Model how to compare items in the classroom by using these adjectives. Then have volunteers use these adjectives to discuss other items, such as books and pictures.

MORE ONLINE sadlierconnect.com

## Adverbs

**Guided Instruction** An **adverb** describes or tells about a verb. Adverbs often tell when, where, and how.

*The wind blew* ***fiercely****.*
***Then,*** *the rain fell* ***everywhere****.*

Sometimes adverbs are used to compare. To compare two actions, add -*er* to the end of most one-syllable adverbs.

To compare three or more actions, add –*est* to the end of most one-syllable adverbs.

**Guided Practice** Underline the adverbs in each sentence.

1. Yesterday my cat was lost.
2. We looked outside for it.
3. After we won the baseball game, I ran happily all the way home.
4. My cat was on the front porch, meowing loudly.

**Independent Practice** Write the correct adverb in parentheses on the line.

1. The second lightning bolt flashed (quicker, quickest) than the first one.
   quicker
2. The thunder clapped (louder, loudest) when the storm was overhead.
   loudest
3. The storm traveled (faster, fastest) than the one last week.
   faster
4. My little brother fell asleep (easier, easiest) than I did.
   easier
5. I was the one who slept the (sounder, soundest) in my family.
   soundest





**OBJECTIVE**
**Use adverbs that compare and tell when and where in writing.**

### Guided Instruction

Tell students that adverbs give information about actions. Adverbs can compare two or more actions; for example, John ran faster than Kam, and Shel ran the fastest of all.

### Guided Practice

Adverbs answer questions about when, where, and how. Have students identify the action in the first sentence (*was lost*) and the word that tells when. (*Yesterday*) Have students continue underlining adverbs.

### Independent Practice

Adverbs that compare one action to another usually end in -*er*; adverbs that compare one action to two or more other actions usually end in –*est*.

**Assess and Respond**

**If** students have difficulty with the concept of comparative adverbs,

**Then** give students more practice using correct adverbs to compare simple actions.

### Differentiate Instruction

Some students may have difficulty identifying and understanding how to use adverbs in a sentence.

Have students practice using adverbs by writing the Guided Practice sentences on the board. Erase the adverb in each sentence, and have students generate other possible adverbs that could be used to tell where, when, or how. (For example, Tuesday my cat was lost. We looked everywhere for it. I walked quickly back home. My cat was on the front porch, meowing sweetly.)

**OBJECTIVE**
**Use correct spelling in writing.**

## Guided Instruction

Make sure that students understand that all of the example words are related. Point out that the letters *famil* are in each word. Review that *un-* is a common prefix, and *-ity* and *-ize* are common suffixes.

## Guided Practice

Help students identify the base word in the first two items. Point out that the spelling of a base word may change, as when you change a *y* to an *i* before adding *-ed.* Then have students complete items 3 and 4. Answer students' questions as needed.

## Independent Practice

Remind students that the form of the base word needs to make sense in the sentence. Point out that the missing word might take the form of a verb, an adjective, or an adverb.

**Assess and Respond**

**If** students have difficulty spelling related words correctly,

**Then** provide them with more examples of word families, and have them identify common spelling patterns.

# LANGUAGE

## Correct Spelling

**Guided Instruction** When you are writing, it is important to spell the words you use correctly. Use what you know about other words to help you spell new words. You can use word families, syllable patterns, ending rules, and word parts such as suffixes and prefixes to help you spell words.

*family* *unfamiliar* *familiarity* *familiarize*

You can use a dictionary to look up the correct spelling of words. You can also use a dictionary to look up the meaning of the word you are spelling, to make sure you are using the correct form of the word.

**Guided Practice** Write the base word that can help you spell the two words.

| | | |
|---|---|---|
| **1.** taken | mistake | take |
| **2.** retried | trying | try |
| **3.** caring | uncaring | care |
| **4.** interview | viewing | view |

**Independent Practice** Write a word to complete each sentence, using a form of the base word in parentheses.

**1.** I was very excited to get a hamster. (excite)

**2.** I held it very carefully so I wouldn't harm it. (care)

**3.** Mom gave me little food dishes to put in its cage. (dish)

**4.** My hamster loves using its wheel to run around and around. (use)

**5.** I think my hamster's fur is beautiful. (beauty)





**Grouping Options**

Give students an opportunity to learn from peers by creating pairs of students with different levels of spelling ability.

Provide pairs with a list of base words, such as *circle*, *light*, and *fear.* Have the more proficient partner choose a word and then name a related word (for example, *circle—circular*). Have the less proficient partner then write down the related word. Then the more proficient partner should check the spelling, using a dictionary if necessary. Tell partners to switch roles and try again with another pair of related words.

MORE ONLINE sadlierconnect.com

## Simple Sentences

**Guided Instruction** A **simple sentence** has one subject and one verb. It expresses one complete thought or idea.

- Simple: *The ground shakes during an earthquake.*
- Not Simple: *The ground shakes, and buildings move.*

**Guided Practice** Write *simple* or *not simple* to describe each sentence.

1. Yesterday there was an earthquake in our town. simple
2. I grabbed my dog, and we dashed under our table. not simple
3. My dog was shaking so I petted his fur and whispered soft words. not simple
4. None of our family was hurt in the earthquake. simple
5. We helped our neighbors and the volunteers cleaned up the park. not simple

**Independent Practice** Write simple sentences.

1. Sample answer: There were several pets missing after the storm.
2. Sample answer: We helped look for lost pets in the neighborhood.
3. Sample answer: We put posters on trees.
4. Sample answer: Many pets were returned to their families.
5. Sample answer: We were happy to help our neighborhood.





### Differentiate Instruction

Help struggling students understand simple sentences by working with them to create a checklist. Guide students to suggest the following:

- *Is there only one subject?*
- *Is there only one verb?*
- *Does the sentence express a complete thought?*

If students answer yes to all three questions, they have a simple sentence. Tell students to write the checklist on a self-stick note and keep it handy while they are writing their opinion pieces.

**OBJECTIVE**

**Use a variety of sentence types, including simple sentences.**

### Guided Instruction

Make sure that students understand that a simple sentence has one noun, or subject, and one verb. Point out that in the example sentence, the word *ground* is the subject, and the word *shakes* is the verb. Explain that the word *earthquake* is also a noun, but it does not have a verb (the word *shakes* does not tell about it), so it is not the subject. Show students that in the second example, both nouns are subjects since they are each paired with verbs. Two subjects and two verbs mean the sentence is not simple.

### Guided Practice

Point out that words like *and*, *so*, and *because* may join two simple sentences to create a compound—not simple—sentence.

### Independent Practice

Have students repeat the rules of a simple sentence. Then have them write five simple sentences about natural disasters or another topic that interests them.

### Assess and Respond

**If** students have difficulty with the concept of simple sentences,

**Then** provide students with more practice by writing several simple sentences on the board. Ask volunteers to come up to the board to underline the subjects and circle the verbs.

**OBJECTIVES**

- **Engage in collaborative discussion with peers, expressing ideas clearly and in complete sentences.**
- **Follow conventions of discourse, including asking and answering questions.**

## Discuss the Essential Question

Before beginning a group discussion, copy and distribute the "Did I?" checklist, available on **sadlierconnect.com**.

### Leading the Class Discussion

Give students time to think about the questions before the class discussion.

1. Point students to the Student Model introduction and conclusion, where Ruthie has stated and restated her opinion.
2. Have students skim paragraphs 2–4 for Ruthie's reasons and linking words and phrases.

## SPEAKING AND LISTENING

### Discuss the Essential Question

**How do writers support their opinions?**

Think about the Essential Question by responding to the questions below. Support your point of view with reasons and experience.

1. What words did the writer use to state her opinion?

   "I think pet owners should always take their pets with them in a disaster."

2. What reasons did the writer state to support her opinion? How did the writer connect her reason to her opinion?

   Pets depend on us; pets are part of our family; abandoned pets can be dangerous. She used linking words such as *first of all, also,* and *finally*.

Use your notes above to discuss the Essential Question in small groups or as a class. Follow agreed-upon rules for discussion. Use the organizer below to record what you heard and how you participated.

| Ideas I Agree or Disagree With | | Questions I Asked |
|---|---|---|
| Agree | | |
| Disagree | | |
| **New Ideas I Had During Discussion** | | **Questions I Answered** |
| | | |





### Discussion Skills

Remind students of the sentence starters for building on ideas of others:

- *What you said makes me wonder . . .*
- *What you said reminds me of . . .*

Then give students some sentence starters they can use when asking for clarification:

- *Could you repeat what you said about . . . ?*
- *I'm not sure what you meant by . . .*
- *What evidence do you have for . . . ?*

# CHAPTER 10 REVIEW

This paragraph has mistakes in the use of adjectives and adverbs and in spelling. Write the paragraph correctly on the lines below. If you need help, look in a dictionary to check your spelling.

Last night a large storm came through. Dad and I spent the night in the barn careing for the animals. Each animal took cover. The chickens climbed to the higher point in the barn. The cows are our larger animals. Surprisingly, the pigs yelled the louder. The horses were very excitied and jittery. We put blankests on their backs. We tryed to keep them calm. Dad turned on the lights and played some soft music. It was a long night, but I am glad that I could help our animals.

Last night a large storm came through. Dad and I spent the night in the barn caring for the animals. Each animal took cover. The chickens climbed to the highest point in the barn. The cows are our largest animals. Surprisingly, the pigs yelled the loudest. The horses were very excited and jittery. We put blankets on their backs. We tried to keep them calm. Dad turned on the lights and played some soft music. It was a long night, but I am glad that I could help our animals.





## Introduce the Review

Explain to students that this review will give them an opportunity to apply the language and writing skills that they have studied and practiced in this chapter.

### Language Skills Summary

Let students know that they are going to use what they learned about adjectives, adverbs, correct spelling, and simple sentences to make their writing better. Good writers follow grammar rules, and they know how to use adjectives and adverbs to make their writing more interesting to the reader.

- Have students explain why some adjectives end in *–er*. (One thing is compared to one other thing.) Then have them explain why some adjectives end in *-est*. (One thing is compared to two or more other things.)
- Ask them to tell what kinds of things an adverb tells about an action. (when, where, and how it took place)
- Prompt students to name the base word in *caring* (*care*), and have them name and spell related words. (*careful*, *carefully*)
- Ask students how to tell if a sentence is simple. (It has one subject and one verb.)

## Test-Taking Tips

Give students the following tips to help with taking assessments focused on editing skills.

- Students should read each sentence or paragraph carefully and slowly, and then read it softly aloud. Students will be able to identify grammar and punctuation errors from text that doesn't sound correct to their trained ears.
- Tell students to read through each sentence or paragraph several times, each time looking for a specific kind of problem. For example, on the first read they might look for capitalization and punctuation errors, on the second read they might look for agreement errors, and on the third read they might look for incomplete sentences.

## Writing Process Summary

Remind students that planning helps them organize their ideas before drafting, and revising and editing make a draft better.

### Planning and Drafting

Have students look at the outlines and the drafts they created earlier (page 207). They should check that the drafts cover all the important points in the outlines, especially the reasons that support their opinions.

### Opinion Piece Rubric

| Score | Description |
|---|---|
| 4 | The piece includes: a clear opinion statement; three reasons supported by facts, etc.; a conclusion with a restated opinion; linking words/ phrases; sentence variety. There are few or no editing errors. |
| 3 | The piece has the elements listed under "4" above, though they are executed less successfully. Minor editing errors do not detract greatly from the overall essay. |
| 2 | The piece is missing one or more of the elements required. There are many editing errors, some of which are serious. |
| 1 | The piece is unfinished or shows a minimal understanding of required elements. Serious editing errors make it difficult to read. |
| 0 | The assignment was not attempted. |

### Self-Assessment: Progress Check

Have students revisit the Progress Check on page 201 and compare their answers now with the answers they gave before they started Chapter 10.

## CHAPTER 10 REVIEW

**Assignment:** Write an opinion essay about something you care about.

On the lines below, write the final copy of the opinion essay draft you created on page 207. It should start with an introduction and end with a conclusion. Be sure to include reasons that support your opinion. Make sure to use linking words to connect your reasons with your opinion. See the Writing Handbook (at **sadlierconnect.com**) for ways to improve your writing as you revise.

Students should write an opinion essay that clearly states an opinion and includes at least three supporting reasons. Students should use linking words to connect their ideas, and they should provide a concluding statement.





### Digital Connection: Multimedia Presentations

Once students have finished writing their opinion pieces, they can use them as the basis for a multimedia slideshow.

Have students condense their opinions, reasons, supporting evidence, and conclusions into brief statements that can be featured on individual slides. If necessary, review how to use bulleted lists to succinctly convey information. Encourage students to find appropriate images that will illustrate or complement their ideas. Ask students to present their slideshows to their classmates or have them post them online.

Research to Build and Present Knowledge

## Write Research Reports

CHAPTER 11

**Focus on Writing** In a research report, you share your findings about a topic with a larger audience. A research report is based on evidence.

**Think About Theme** You will want to organize the facts from multiple texts to inform your audience.

**Let's Get on Our Way!** A research report uses facts, definitions, and details to explain and develop the topic.

These are the skills you will build in this chapter. Before you begin, check the boxes on the left of any items you can do well now. At the end of the chapter, you will return to this page to use the check boxes on the right to show what you have learned.

- ☐ Conduct a research project. ☐
- ☐ Gather and take notes on information from print and digital sources. ☐
- ☐ Group related information together. ☐
- ☐ Provide information that builds knowledge about a topic. ☐
- ☐ Write using compound sentences correctly. ☐
- ☐ Write using complex sentences correctly. ☐
- ☐ Capitalize the important words in a title. ☐





**Student Page 215**

## Progress Check

The Progress Check is a self-assessment feature that students can use to gauge their own progress. Research shows that when students take accountability for their own learning, their motivation increases.

Before students begin work on Chapter 11, have them check the boxes next to any item that they feel they can do well. It is fine if they don't check any of the boxes. Tell them that they will have an opportunity to learn about and practice all of these items while studying the chapter. Let them know that near the end of the chapter they will have a chance to reconsider how well they can do each item on this list.

Before students begin the Chapter 11 Review on page 227, have them revisit this page. You can use this information to work with students on any items they don't understand before they tackle the Review.

## HOME✦CONNECT...

The Home Connect feature is a way to keep parents or other adult family members apprised of what their children are learning. The key learning objectives are listed, and some ideas for related activities and discussions are included.

Explain to students that they can share the Home Connect page with their parents or the adult family members in their home. Let students know how much time the class will be spending on this chapter so they can plan their time accordingly at home.

Encourage students and their parents to share their experiences using the suggestions on the Home Connect page. You may wish to make a place to post some of this work.

## HOME✦CONNECT...

In this chapter, children will learn about writing a **research report** to share knowledge about a topic. Discuss with your child a topic that you know about, such as repairing a car or baking bread. Share how you continue to learn more. For example, you may read books, talk to other people, or do research on the Internet. Point out that there are a great many resources that can give you the information you need.

Your child will begin the process by **researching a topic.** He or she will use **research materials,** such as books and websites. To practice researching on the Internet, discuss a topic and help your child find good sources of Internet information on it. (Sites ending in .edu and .gov are the most reliable.) As you read information on the topic together, **write down facts and details** that are related. Help your child understand that **related information is grouped together** in a research report.

**Conversation Starter:** A research report is an opportunity to build knowledge on a topic by searching for answers. Discuss these questions with your child: *What is an expert? How does someone become an expert? What are you an expert at? On what topic would you like to become an expert? How might you learn more about that topic?* Emphasize that writing is a great way to learn from and share knowledge with others.

### IN THIS CHAPTER, YOUR CHILD WILL...

- Learn to write a research report that builds knowledge about a subject.
- Gather information by taking notes from print and digital sources.
- Group related information in a report.
- Learn specific language skills and use them in writing a research report:
  - Write compound and complex sentences, using conjunctions correctly.
  - Capitalize the important words in a title.

### WAYS TO HELP YOUR CHILD

Encourage your child to write often and for a variety of purposes. For example, your child can write thank-you notes and letters to family and friends, a journal entry on a scrap-book page, or a list of instructions for taking care of a pet. As your child writes, discuss the purpose for that kind of writing and how it is unique.

ONLINE
For more Home Connect activities, continue online at sadlierconnect.com





**Student Page 216**

# CHAPTER 11 Research to Build and Present Knowledge: Write Research Reports

## LEARNING PROGRESSIONS

In this chapter, students will learn how to research and write a report on the desert. In order to learn the skills necessary to craft a research report, a type of informational text, students will further develop skills learned in second grade. They should be encouraged to retain these skills, as they will continue to build on them in fourth grade.

| Conducting Research | |
|---|---|
| | • Proficient second-grade students should have ended the year capable of participating in shared research and writing projects (e.g., read a number of books on a single topic to produce a report; record scientific observations).<br>• As third graders, students will expand on this skill by conducting short research projects that build knowledge about a topic.<br>• This skill will prepare students for grade 4, when they will conduct short research projects that build knowledge through investigation of different aspects of a topic. |

| Gathering Information | |
|---|---|
| | • In grade 2, students should have learned to recall information from experiences or gather information from provided sources to answer a question.<br>• In grade 3, students will be expected to recall information from experiences, gather information from print or digital sources, take brief notes on sources, and sort evidence into provided categories.<br>• As fourth graders, students will further develop this skill by categorizing information and providing a list of sources. |

Research to Build and Present Knowledge

Write Research Reports

CHAPTER 11

Essential Question

How do writers conduct and present research on a topic?

Theme

Searching for Answers





## Writing Handbook

If students need extra practice with writing a research report, refer them to the *Writing Handbook* at **sadlierconnect.com**. The Writing Handbook gives students detailed instruction on planning, drafting, revising, and editing their writing. They will also find tips on producing, publishing, and presenting their writing.

**Essential Question:**
**How do writers conduct and present research on a topic?**

In this chapter, students will learn how to research and gather information about a topic from multiple sources for the purpose of writing a research report.

## Theme: Searching for Answers

Students will continue their exploration of what it means to search for answers as they read and analyze a research report writing model.

## Curriculum Connection: Science

Students will apply the concept of searching for answers as they research and present information about the desert in their own research report.

## Connect Reading to Writing

Remind students that they read a mystery entitled "The Case of the Missing Fruit" in Chapter 5 (Student Book pages 116–121). Discuss how the characters in the story search for answers about missing fruit. Draw a connection to how students, like the characters, will conduct their own search. Explain, however, that they will search for answers about—or research—a nonfiction topic, the desert, and then write about it.

**OBJECTIVE**
**Research a topic using multiple sources and present the topic in writing with appropriate organization.**

## Introduce: Organizational Structure

Draw students' attention to the research report outline in the left margin. Point out the three subtopics in the outline. Ask students to think about these subtopics as you read and analyze the Student Model together.

## Analyze a Student Model

**TITLE:** Have students read the title. *What can we predict the report is about?* (animals that live in the desert)

**INTRODUCTION:** Help students find the sentence that states the topic: *I know from the title that the report is about life in the desert. That's a pretty big topic that could mean many different things. So, I will look for a sentence that tells me what aspect of life in the desert Bharat focuses on.*

Help students identify that the last sentence in the introduction states what the report is about. Then discuss how Bharat leads up to the topic statement. *Did you notice that Bharat starts his report with a question? That helps engage and get the readers thinking. Then he addresses what readers may be thinking and how it may differ from what is actually true.*

WRITE RESEARCH REPORTS

**CREATING AN ORGANIZATIONAL STRUCTURE**
Bharat used an outline to organize his report. It is divided into three sections: introduction, explanation, and conclusion.

I. Introduction
Topic:
II. Explanation
a. Subtopic 1:
b. Subtopic 2:
III. Conclusion

**INTRODUCTION**
- Bharat introduces the topic at the beginning, leading up to a statement about what the report will be about.

***Underline the sentence that tells what Bharat's report will be about.***

# Read a Student Model

Bharat has been asked to write a research report about the desert. He has researched sources, taken notes, and then grouped related information together. As you read Bharat's research report, think about how you might research your own report about the desert and how you might use the facts, definitions, and details you find to build readers' knowledge.

### Life in the Desert

What do you think of when you imagine a desert? Many people think of sand, rocks, or cacti. They might be surprised to know that the desert is home to many different animals, from snakes to birds to rabbits. The desert presents many challenges to animals. They must be able to survive the strong heat and the limited rainfall. However, many animals are uniquely suited to living in these harsh conditions. Let's take a look at some animals that make their home in and around the saguaro cactus.





## Genre: Research Report

Remind students that the theme of the chapter is "searching for answers." Point out the word *research* within the text type *research report*. Then draw a connection between "searching for answers" and "conducting research." *What is a writer doing when he or she researches something?* Be sure students understand that a writer is looking for answers, in the sense that he or she is trying to find out more about a topic.

Explain that to effectively report on the information a writer has researched about the topic, he or she must present it clearly. This means grouping related information together and developing the topic with facts, definitions, and details. *What other kind of writing has these same requirements?* (A research report is a type of informative/explanatory text.)

MORE ONLINE sadlierconnect.com

### Inside the Cactus

The saguaro cactus has long arms that reach toward the sky. They are covered with a tough coating and spikes. The spikes help to keep water in and animals out. Yet, some animals make their way through these barriers and nest inside the soft flesh of the cactus. For example, the woodpecker uses its beak to peck holes in the trunk and branches. It hollows out the soft inside to make a nest. Later, when the woodpecker leaves, elf owls, purple martins, and sparrows may use the abandoned nest for their home.

**ORGANIZATION**

- Bharat has gathered information about desert life from different sources. Some sources are printed materials. Other sources are digital or online.
- He has grouped related information together, using headings to show each grouping.

***Circle two details about different animals that use the inside of the saguaro cactus.***

### Under the Cactus

Under the saguaro cactus stretches the sandy desert floor. Many animals may be found scurrying across the dry landscape in search of food and water. Several animals eat the cactus's flesh. They include such animals as pack rats, jackrabbits, mule deer, and bighorn sheep. In the late summer, the cactus bears fruit. This fruit is a source of energy for several animals. The saguaro cactus has thick channels inside that hold water for the plant. This channel is a source of water for animals when needed.

**DEVELOP THE TOPIC**

- Facts and other details that Bharat has researched help build readers' knowledge about the topic.

***Underline two facts in the section "Under the Cactus."***





## Support English Language Learners

Help English language learners make sense of the many details about desert life presented in the student model by having them highlight key terms as they conduct a first read and then use the highlighted words to create a drawing of the desert. For example, in the first paragraph, students may highlight the words *sand*, *rocks*, *cacti*, *snakes*, *birds*, *rabbits*, *strong heat*, and *limited rainfall*. After they have created their drawings, show them photographs of desert life. Be sure the photographs you show reflect ideas presented in the student model, such as a woodpecker pecking a hole in a cactus. Point out in the photographs any ideas that students did not include in their own drawings. Then have them read the text again, making additional highlights, and revising their drawings.

## Analyze a Student Model

**ORGANIZATION:** Point out the section headings to students. *Think about the introductory statement that tells what the report is about. Based on the introductory statement and this heading, what do you think this section will tell you about?* (It will tell about animals that make their home in the cactus.) Point out the second section heading. *How has Bharat organized his report?* (He has organized his report by grouping related information.) *So where can we expect to find all the details he includes about animals that live in the cactus?* (We can expect to find those details in the first section.) Ask students to find the first animal that Bharat mentions in this section (the woodpecker). *What information does he provide about the woodpecker?* (It uses its beak to peck holes in the trunk and branches.) Guide students as they look for the detail that relates to how other animals live in the cactus. (Elf owls, purple martins, and sparrows may use the abandoned nest for their home.)

**DEVELOP THE TOPIC:** Model identifying how Bharat builds his topic: *I know from the heading that this section is about animals that live under the cactus. As I read this section, I see that Bharat means the animals that live on the desert floor, not ones that literally live underneath the cactus. He builds this topic by talking about how these animals rely on the cactus for food and water. What is the first fact that Bharat includes to build this idea?* (Several animals eat the cactus flesh.) Point to the sentence "In the late summer, the cactus bears fruit." *Is this a fact or an opinion?* (a fact) *How does this help build this section?* (It helps the reader understand another way some desert animals rely on the cactus for food.) Point out how the first section discussed how the cactus provides shelter, and the second section discusses how the cactus provides food.

## Analyze a Student Model

**CONCLUDING STATEMENT:** Review Bharat's conclusion with students. Students should recognize that Bharat summarizes what readers learn from his report, and then he returns to his opening question by urging readers to broaden what they think about when they think about the desert. Finally, he makes his concluding statement.

## Evaluate a Writer's Work

Remind students that the purpose of a research report is to share information collected about a topic from multiple sources. Have students recall how a research report should group information. (A research report should group related information together.) Have students independently write one sentence telling whether they think Bharat organized his report well. Then have students turn to a partner and share and discuss their opinions about Bharat's organization.

## Model: Organizational Structure

Ask students to think about how Bharat might have taken notes for his research and then written summaries and paraphrases to help complete the outline for his research report. On a board or projector, post the graphic organizer on page 221. Briefly discuss how it works. Then post the outline on page 222. Have students help you fill in the outline based on the model text. Fill in the introduction, explanation, and conclusion. Point out that well-written research reports have strong organization, which requires planning and prewriting.

Students will next use the graphic organizer and outline found in their books to research and plan their own research reports, and then they will draft the report based on their outline.

WRITE RESEARCH REPORTS

**CONCLUDING STATEMENT**
- Bharat's ending wraps up the report by summing up what the reader has learned.

***Underline the sentence that is the concluding statement.***

The desert can be a harsh place to live. The animals living there face many challenges. Despite this, many animals make their homes in the desert. They depend on the natural resources such as the saguaro cactus to survive. So, the next time you think of the desert, you may think of rocks, sand, and cacti. However, you also should think about woodpeckers, hawks, jackrabbits, mule deer, and bighorn sheep. The desert is home to a surprising number of animals.

**Sources:**
https://www.national-park.com/welcome-to-saguaro-national-park/
http://www.nps.gov/sagu/planyourvisit/upload/The%20Saguaro%20Cactus.pdf
"Saguaro," Encyclopædia Britannica

220 Chapter 11 ■ Research to Build and Present Knowledge: Write Research Reports

### Review: Comparing and Contrasting Texts

Remind students that when they read the two fictional stories in Chapter 5, they compared and contrasted them in order to better understand that the two main characters appeared in all three stories but that the setting changed for each story.

Draw students' attention to the sources Bharat noted at the end of his research report. Explain to students that when they conduct research to write their report on the desert, they will need to look at more than one source, just as Bharat did, and then compare and contrast those sources because different sources sometimes contain different information about a topic. Explain that if several sources note the same information about a topic, then students can feel confident that the information is correct.

MORE ONLINE sadlierconnect.com

Use a graphic organizer like the one below to take notes for your research report on the desert. You may use print or digital sources to find information. You will use these notes to create your outline on page 222.

| Source 1 | Source 2 |
|---|---|
| Summarize or paraphrase information: | Summarize or paraphrase information: |





## Differentiate Instruction

Work individually with students who are not yet ready to conduct research. First, review what a source is—a print or digital publication from which you get facts, details, and other information to use in your own text. Then, discuss why one would need to look at several sources, or conduct research, before writing about a topic. *Do you know everything there is to know about the desert? Do you know what kinds of insects live in the desert? Can you name a plant, other than the cactus, that lives in the desert?* Finally, review finding sources, taking notes, and citing sources with students, asking questions to check that they fully understand the role and significance of each step of conducting research.

## Conduct Research

### Finding Sources

Explain to students that they can find sources by looking for books in the library and searching for websites online. Model using key words to search for sources online, and discuss how to determine if an online source is credible. Point out that spelling errors, poor site design, and obvious bias can indicate that the source is not credible.

### Taking Notes

Students will use the graphic organizer on page 221 to record notes as they conduct their research. Explain that there are two ways they can take notes:

- Students can quote directly from the source—writing down the exact words used in the text and putting quotation marks around them.
- Students can summarize or paraphrase the ideas in the source. Discuss how someone else's idea needs to be credited. Point out that if students do not properly credit these ideas in their report, then they will be guilty of plagiarism.

### Citing Sources

Tell students that they need to cite their sources both when they take notes and at the end of their research report. *If you don't cite your sources as you take notes, you might forget which source a fact or detail is from.*

Provide the structure and examples for citing both print and online sources:

- PRINT: Last name, First name. Name of Book. City published in; Publisher, Date published.
- ONLINE: Last name, First name. "Article title." Date published. Website title. Date accessed. URL.

Students should include this information before each summary or paraphrase in their note-taking graphic organizer.

## Create: Organizational Structure

### Brainstorming

Tell students that writers write research reports about topics that they want to know more about. As a class, have students name aspects of the desert they want to know more about. Make a list of students' topic ideas on the board for them to use as they plan.

### Planning

Students will use the outline on page 222 to plan their text. After conducting their research, students should write down their topic and what they will examine about the topic.

- Students should divide their topic into two subtopics and record information from their organizer related to each subtopic.
- Have students recall that Bharat summed up the information presented in his report in his conclusion. Ask students how they might sum up their report.

### Drafting a Research Report

Instruct students to refer to their outline as they draft their research report on a separate piece of paper. Be sure students have an introduction, explanation, and conclusion.

## Introduce the Writing Process

Remind students that in order to do a good job on an essay, they must plan, draft, revise, and edit it. These are all steps of the writing process. For more on the writing process, see the *Writing Handbook* at **sadlierconnect.com**.

### Assess and Respond

**If** students have difficulty writing a conclusion in their outline,

**Then** have them sum up the ideas in their outline to a partner to help them think through how to conclude their report.

## WRITE RESEARCH REPORTS

Use an outline like the one below to organize your research report about the desert. Then write a first draft of your report on a separate sheet of paper. Be sure to take good notes and group related information together. You will use this draft to write your final research report in the Chapter 11 Review section on page 228.

**I. Introduction**

Topic:

________________________________________

________________________________________

**II. Explanation**

**a.** Subtopic 1:

________________________________________

________________________________________

________________________________________

________________________________________

**b.** Subtopic 2:

________________________________________

________________________________________

________________________________________

________________________________________

**III. Conclusion**

________________________________________

________________________________________

________________________________________

________________________________________





### Differentiate Instruction

Work individually with students who do not understand how the note-taking graphic organizer relates to the outline. Have them review their notes, color-coding related information. Then help them decide, based on the subtopics that emerge from their color-coding, how best they can convey the information they have researched about their topic through two subtopics. Help them enter those two subtopics on the outline. Then help them pick the best facts and other details from their notes related to their subtopics and enter them on the outline. Guide them as they note a conclusion.

MORE ONLINE sadlierconnect.com

## Compound Sentences

**Guided Instruction** A **compound sentence** combines two simple sentences that have related ideas. A connecting word called a **conjunction** (*and, but, or*) joins the two sentences. Always use a comma before the conjunction in a compound sentence.

Read these related sentences.

*Some desert plants have needles. Not all plants have them.*

To write these two sentences as a compound sentence, use a conjunction.

*Some desert plants have needles, but not all plants have them.*

**Guided Practice** Complete each sentence using a conjunction (*and, but, or*).

1. We will camp in the desert, ___or___ we will go to the beach.
2. I like camping in the desert, ___but___ it can get cold at night.

Make each pair of sentences into a compound sentence.

3. Be sure to bring sunscreen. You might get a sunburn.
   Be sure to bring sunscreen, or you might get a sunburn.
4. You should wear hiking boots. You might want a hat.
   You should wear hiking boots, and you might want a hat.

**Independent Practice** Write two of your own compound sentences. Use a different conjunction in each sentence. Be sure to use a comma before the conjunction.

1. Sample answer: We can have a snack, and then we can go hiking.
2. Sample answer: We can sleep on cots, or we can use air mattresses.





### Turn and Talk

After completing the activities, have partners engage in a compound sentence game. Hand out a set of index cards to each pair. Each set of index cards should include one index card for each conjunction (*and, but, or*), as well as one index card for each of six sentences of your choosing. (Vary the sentences so every pair has a different set. Check each set to make sure three logical sentences can be created from the index cards.) Ask students to create three compound sentences with the cards by connecting two sentence index cards with a conjunction index card. Challenge them to make necessary capitalization and punctuation corrections. Then have pairs share their sentences with the class.

**OBJECTIVE**
**Use compound sentences in writing, employing coordinating conjunctions as necessary.**

### Guided Instruction

Review that a simple sentence has one subject and one verb to express one complete idea. Explain that a **compound sentence** is made up of two simple sentences connected by a conjunction to express two related ideas. Have students underline the simple sentences in the second example, circle the conjunction, and put a box around the comma. *How are the two ideas related?* (They are both about plants.)

### Guided Practice

Model completing the first sentence with a conjunction. Explain why you choose *or*. Have students test the different conjunctions for the second sentence. Then discuss why *but* is the best fit. Have partners write sentences for items 3 and 4 and explain their answers.

### Independent Practice

After writing their own sentences, have partners see if they can rewrite each other's sentences using a different conjunction and explain why they could or could not replace the conjunction.

**Assess and Respond**

**If** students have difficulty writing compound sentences,

**Then** give students more practice completing and writing sentences by repeating the process under Guided Practice with additional examples.

**OBJECTIVE**
**Use complex sentences in writing, employing subordinating conjunctions as necessary.**

## Guided Instruction

Explain what a **complex sentence** is. Use the second example to point out how the complete idea from the first example, *We went on a hike*, no longer expresses a complete idea when the subordinating conjunction *before* is added to it. *What are you left wondering?* (What happened before the hike?) Explain that adding the subordinating conjunction turns the simple sentence into a subordinating clause. Point out that the first part of the sentence (*We filled our water bottles*) is still a complete idea, and it is the independent clause portion of the complex sentence.

## Guided Practice

Help students test the subordinating conjunctions for items 1 and 2. Have pairs write sentences for items 3 and 4. Ask students to explain their responses and identify the independent clause, dependent clauses, and subordinating conjunction in each sentence.

## Independent Practice

Have students explain what a complex sentence is before writing their sentences. Ask them to identify the parts of their sentences.

**Assess and Respond**

**If** students have difficulty with the concept of complex sentences,

**Then** review additional examples with parts that are labeled "independent clause," "dependent clause," and "subordinating conjunction."

# LANGUAGE

## Complex Sentences

**Guided Instruction** A **complex sentence** is made up of two related ideas joined together by a subordinating conjunction. Some common **subordinating conjunctions** are *after, as if, because, before, since, though,* and *when.*

Read these related sentences.

*We filled our water bottles. We went on a hike.*

To write these two sentences as one complex sentence, use a subordinating conjunction.

*We filled our water bottles* ***before*** *we went on a hike.*

**Guided Practice** Complete each of these complex sentences. Use the subordinating conjunction *until* or *because*.

1. We will walk on the path ___until___ we get to the ranger station.
2. ___Because___ we had hiked for so long, I was really tired.

Make each pair of sentences into a complex sentence using a subordinating conjunction.

3. Beth led our hike. She had the map.
   Sample answer: Beth led our hike because she had the map.
4. We were lost. We used our compass.
   Sample answer: Since we were lost, we used our compass.

**Independent Practice** Write two of your own complex sentences using a subordinating conjunction.

1. Sample answer: After we hiked, we all rested.
2. Sample answer: Dad pointed out animals when he saw them.





## Support English Language Learners

Complex sentences might seem overwhelming to English language learners. Point out the subject/verb/object pattern in complex sentences to help students see these sentences as more approachable. (This will be especially useful to native speakers of Vietnamese and Hmong—languages which also follow the subject/verb/object pattern.)

Build sentences with these students, starting with a simple subject/verb/object sentence. Label the sentence parts, and discuss why it is a simple sentence. Use it as a base for writing a compound and a complex sentence. Discuss the definition of each sentence type, and label the sentence parts. Repeat until understanding of complex sentences (particularly in how they differ from compound sentences) is clear.

MORE ONLINE sadlierconnect.com

## Capitalization

**Guided Instruction** A title tells the name of a book. The first word and all the important words are capitalized. Words such as *a*, *an*, *and*, *but*, *for*, *in*, *of*, *or*, *the*, and *to* are not capitalized unless they are the first word.

*A Guide to Deserts*
*Camping in the Desert*

**Guided Practice** Circle the letters that should be capitalized in each title.

1. *ants and other desert insects*
2. *a bird lover's look at deserts*
3. *looking for snakes*
4. *the hidden life of desert animals*

**Independent Practice** Write each book title correctly.

1. *look at the sand and rocks*
   *Look at the Sand and Rocks*
2. *lizard's big adventure*
   *Lizard's Big Adventure*
3. *ollie owl flies at night*
   *Ollie Owl Flies at Night*
4. *what's under the rock?*
   *What's Under the Rock?*
5. *a really hot day and a cold night*
   *A Really Hot Day and a Cold Night*





### Differentiate Instruction

Some students might find it difficult to remember when an article or preposition should be capitalized in a book title.

Give students a list of ten made-up or real book titles with the important words capitalized but all the articles and prepositions in lowercase, regardless of placement. Use this title, or one like it, as the first title:

- the Sun Shines Brightly in the Morning

Correct the capitalization error and discuss why the first *the* needs to be capitalized, but the *in* and the second *the* do not need to be capitalized. Then have students correct the remaining titles, explaining their choices.

**OBJECTIVE**

**Capitalize titles correctly in writing.**

### Guided Instruction

Hold up a book. Read the title. Ask students to name which words in the title are capitalized. *Do you think the author made up his/her own mind about which words to capitalize? Or do you think there are rules for which words to capitalize in a title?* (There are rules.) Explain that the rules are the same whether the title appears on the actual book, such as the one you are holding, or is noted in print, such as in a review of the book. Discuss the rules for capitalization of titles. Then have students explain why *to*, *in*, and *the* are not capitalized in the examples.

### Guided Practice

Model circling the letters that should be capitalized in the first sentence. Have partners circle the letters in the third and fourth sentences and share their choices. Then guide students as they circle the letters in the last sentence independently.

### Independent Practice

After students have written each book title correctly, challenge them to come up with a title for the sequel to each book and to write it down using correct capitalization.

**Assess and Respond**

**If** students have difficulty identifying which words in a title to capitalize,

**Then** discuss additional Guided Instruction examples before giving them additional Guided Practice examples.

**OBJECTIVES**

- Ask questions to check understanding.
- Express ideas clearly.

## Discuss the Essential Question

Before beginning a group discussion, copy and distribute the "Did I?" checklist, available on **sadlierconnect.com**.

### Leading the Class Discussion

Give students time to think about the questions before the class discussion.

1. Direct students to the research report title and introductory paragraph to identify the topic the writer developed.
2. Guide students to identify how the section headings give a clue as to how information is grouped in each section.

## SPEAKING AND LISTENING

### Discuss the Essential Question

**How do writers conduct and present research on a topic?**

Think about the Essential Question by responding to the questions below. Support your point of view with reasons and experience.

1. What topic did the writer develop into a research report?
   Sample answer: The writer talked about animal life in the desert, especially how animals use the saguaro cactus to survive.
2. How did the writer group related information together?
   Sample answer: The writer used two categories: the animals found in the saguaro cactus, and the animals found under the cactus. He used headings to show how the ideas were related.

Use your notes above to discuss the Essential Question in small groups or as a class. Follow agreed-upon rules of discussion. Use the organizer below to record what you heard and how you participated.

| Ideas I Agree or Disagree With | | Questions I Asked |
|---|---|---|
| Agree | | |
| Disagree | | |
| **New Ideas I Had During Discussion** | | **Questions I Answered** |
| | | |





### Discussion Skills

Remind students that asking questions is a vital part of any discussion. Be sure students understand that asking questions is important not only for the person who does not understand something, but also for the person who is attempting to express his or her ideas. Give students these questions to ask when they want a speaker to clarify or explain a point:

- *Can you please repeat what you said about … ?*
- *I'm not sure I understand. Can you restate your idea?*
- *Can you explain why you made that connection?*

## CHAPTER 11 REVIEW

This paragraph has mistakes in compound and complex sentences and in capitalization. Write the paragraph correctly on the lines below.

We read the book the deserts of texas in class. The book had many interesting facts it showed lots of beautiful pictures. This book was helpful, because we are writing desert reports. Today, our teacher showed us pictures of desert flowers. I was surprised at how many there are. Tomorrow, we will read a book called I live in the desert. The book tells about different desert animals. After that, we will share what we learned. We may create a poster about desert animals or we may write a report about them.

We read the book The Deserts of Texas in class. The book had many interesting facts, and it showed lots of beautiful pictures. This book was helpful because we are writing desert reports. Today, our teacher showed us pictures of desert flowers. I was surprised at how many there are. Tomorrow, we will read a book called I Live in the Desert. This book tells about different desert animals. After that, we will share what we learned. We may create a poster about desert animals, or we may write a report about them.





### Test-Taking Tips

Give students the following tips to help with taking assessments focused on editing skills.

- Tell students to make a list of what they are checking for, and then read the passage multiple times, focusing on one type of correction on the list each time.
- Explain to students that if they read slowly they are less likely to skip over subtle errors that need correcting.
- Have students mark suspected errors lightly in pencil and then reread to confirm whether they are errors, and, if so, mark them darkly.

## Introduce the Review

Explain to students that this review will give them an opportunity to apply the language and writing skills that they have studied and practiced in this chapter.

### Language Skills Summary

Let students know that they are going to use what they learned about compound sentences, complex sentences, and capitalization of titles to make their writing better. Good writers follow grammar rules, can spell correctly, and understand the mechanics of writing.

- Ask students to tell what a compound sentence is. (A compound sentence combines two simple sentences with a conjunction.) Have students give examples of conjunctions. (*and*, *but*, *or*) Ask students to tell how many thoughts a compound sentence expresses. (two or more)
- Have students name the part of speech that connects the two ideas in a complex sentence. (a subordinating conjunction) Ask students to give examples of subordinating conjunctions. (*after*, *as if*, *because*, *before*, *since*, *though*, *when*) Prompt students to explain how a complex sentence differs from a compound sentence. (A complex sentence contains a complete thought and a dependent thought. The dependent part of the sentence cannot stand alone as its own sentence.)
- Prompt students to explain the rules for capitalizing the title of a book. (The first word and all the important words are capitalized. Words such as *a*, *an*, *and*, *but*, *for*, *in*, *of*, *or*, *the*, and *to* are not capitalized unless they are the first word.)

## Writing Process Summary

Remind students that planning helps them organize their ideas before drafting, and revising and editing make a draft better.

**Planning and Drafting**

Have students look at the outline and the draft they created earlier (page 222). They should check that the draft includes an introduction, groups related information in the explanation section, and ends with a conclusion.

**Research Report Rubric**

| | |
|---|---|
| 4 | The text clearly identifies the topic of the report in the introduction; groups related information and builds knowledge about the topic with facts, definitions, and details; provides a conclusion that wraps up what is learned from the report; and lists sources at the end of the report. There are few or no editing errors. |
| 3 | The text has the elements listed under "4" above, though they are executed less successfully. Minor editing errors do not detract greatly from the overall essay. |
| 2 | The text is missing one or more of the required elements. There are many editing errors, some of which are serious. |
| 1 | The text is unfinished or shows a minimal understanding of required elements. Serious editing errors make it difficult to read. |
| 0 | The assignment was not attempted. |

**Self-Assessment: Progress Check**

Have students revisit the Progress Check on page 215 and compare their answers now with the answers they gave before they started Chapter 11.

## CHAPTER 11 REVIEW

**Assignment:** Research and write a report about a desert topic.

On the lines below, write your final copy of the research report draft you created on page 222. Be sure to group related evidence together. As you write, use the evidence you have found to build knowledge about the topic. Remember to list your sources at the end of the report. See the Writing Handbook (at **sadlierconnect.com**) for ways to improve your writing as you revise.

Students should write a research report that clearly states the topic, groups related evidence together, and builds knowledge about the topic through a clear presentation of the evidence. Students should use at least two sources and cite the sources used.





### Digital Connection: Social Media

Once students have finished writing their research reports, they can use information from their reports to contribute to a social media account.

Establish a class social media account. Call the account: *The Desert! Did You Know . . .* Or have students vote on another title for the account. (Discuss which words to capitalize in the title.)

Then have students contribute their favorite facts about the desert from their reports to the site. Make sure every student contributes at least one fact. Encourage students to add photographs. Have a discussion about what students learn from other students' posts.

**A**

**abnormal** strange; weird
**absorb** to take in something; suck up
**Acropolis** the fortified section of an ancient city
**adapted** changed to fit a new situation
**admiring** looking at with enjoyment
**amends** payment for something one has done wrong
**archaeologist** someone who studies past human life by analyzing objects the people left behind
**architecture** a style of building
**artificial** made by humans; not natural
**assign** give; appoint
**asteroid** space object made of rock
**astronomer** a person who studies the stars and planets
**atmosphere** the layer of air around Earth

**B**

**bandits** robbers or thieves
**barrier** wall or other structure that blocks off something
**betray** to be disloyal to
**bond** connection; attachment
**bouquet** a bunch, referring to flowers
**bow** the front of a ship
**burden** something that is hard to bear or put up with

**C**

**cactus** a thick-stemmed plant with thorns
**calculation** the use of math or logic to figure something out
**captive** a person held against his will
**category** group, class
**centimeter** a small unit of measurement
**chamber** a room
**chirped** made a high, sharp sound
**classification** the placing of similar objects in groups; organization
**comet** an icy object in space
**condense** shrink; come together
**conserving** saving; using less of
**constellation** a group of stars that seems to make a picture
**contaminated** dirty or unhealthy
**continent** giant landmass
**cordially** in a friendly manner
**core** center
**crater** hole; hollow
**craze** something that is briefly popular
**crew** team; staff
**curious** odd, strange
**custom** the usual way of doing something







**D**

**dangerous** something that can be harmful
**dazzled** to be impressed
**debris** broken pieces; trash
**decorated** made beautiful
**degree** an amount or intensity
**desert** leave and not return to
**destroy** knock down; wreck
**devastating** causing terrible harm
**diameter** the distance across a circle or sphere
**disaster** terrible event
**dreary** gloomy, bleak
**dropped in** stopped in; visited
**dwarf planet** a space object smaller than a planet and bigger than an asteroid

**E**

**ellipse** an oval [illegible]
**embrace** a hug
**endangered** rare; about to vanish
**environment** nature; surrounding area
**envoy** a representative or leader
**evaluate** examine and decide
**evidence** proof; facts
**excess** extra
**expanse** a large surface
**expansion** the process of becoming bigger
**experiment** a test done to find something out
**exploration** discovery
**expression** look on someone's face
**extinct** no longer living or existing

**F**

**faithful** loyal and devoted
**fate** the overall situation that someone is left in
**feuds** a long fight or dispute
**firmness** the quality of showing certainty
**fractured** broken or cracked

**G**

**gravitational pull** the pull of an object's gravity on another object
**gravity** the pull each object has on another object

**H**

**hammock** a sling bed
**healthy** well and strong

**I**

**inhabitant** one that lives in a place
**inspect** to take a close look at
**inspiring** bringing about good feelings
**instructor** teacher
**intact** unbroken; not damaged
**interior** an inner part, inside
**invade** to enter and occupy a place





**What should students know about using glossaries, dictionaries, and other reference materials to learn words?**

## How to Use the Glossary

This glossary is a cumulative list of the boldfaced Words to Know from the reading selections. The definitions reflect the words' meanings as they are used in those selections. The glossary is intended as a quick reference for students. To find parts of speech, pronunciations, word origins, and alternative definitions, students should consult a print or online dictionary.

## Guided Instruction

Make sure students understand that a glossary is an alphabetical list of words with definitions that appears at the end of a book, usually a nonfiction book or textbook. Point out that the purpose of a glossary is to provide the spellings and definitions of key words used in the book. Help students understand the connection between this glossary and the Words to Know by directing them to open their books to page 12. Ask students to identify the first of the Words to Know—*numerous*. Then have them search for the word in the glossary (page 231). Ask a volunteer to read aloud the word's definition. Repeat the process with another Word to Know from the same or a different page.

Then compare the glossary to a dictionary. Explain that dictionaries include pronunciations, parts of speech, word origins, and all the meanings of the word. Show students a dictionary entry for the word *numerous* and have them compare and contrast it to the glossary entry.

Encourage students to create a word log as they read the selections in the Student Book. Have them write each word and its meaning after checking the glossary. Encourage them to then consult a print or online dictionary for more information, such as the word's pronunciation, its various parts of speech, and additional meanings.

# GLOSSARY

## Guided Practice

Extend the comparison between this glossary and dictionaries by having students participate in a word scavenger hunt. Place students in teams of three. Then randomly assign each team three words from the glossary (pages 229–232). Tell teammates to divide up the words and complete the following tasks:

- Locate the word and its specific meaning in the glossary.
- Use a dictionary to find the word's part(s) of speech, origins, and at least one alternative meaning.
- Record one or two interesting additional facts about the word, such as original meaning(s), multiple meanings, spelling peculiarities, and so on.

Assign bonus points to the team that provides the most information about its words accurately. As a class, discuss each team's findings.

## Independent Practice

Have students meet in small homogeneous groups to conduct informal spelling bees. One student in each group should begin by choosing a word from the glossary and saying it aloud. Another teammate then volunteers to spell it. If that student spells the word correctly, he or she then gets to select the next word for another teammate to spell. Each teammate should have an opportunity to choose and spell a word. Misspelled words should be added to students' word logs. Each group should have access to a print or online dictionary to aid with pronunciations.



**investigate** look into something
**isolated** alone
**ivied** covered with a green vine called ivy

**J**

**judging** making a decision

**L**

**lad** an old-fashioned word for boy
**levee** a river wall to stop flooding
**livelihood** the ways one supports oneself

**M**

**massive** very large and heavy
**mature** grown-up; adult
**megalith** a very large stone used in ancient cultures as a monument
**mighty** possessing great strength or size
**mnemonic** clue that helps you remember
**mobility** ability to move around
**monument** something made in memory of a person or event
**motive** something that causes a person to take a certain action

**N**

**nonprofit organization** a business with the goal of helping people, not making money
**notable** special or remarkable
**numerous** many in number

**O**

**observation** noticing things
**orbit** path around the sun
**orientation** knowing where you are and how to go
**orphanage** a place where children who have lost their parents live together
**outskirts** edges, borders, limits

**P**

**pensive** to be thoughtful
**perplexed** puzzled, confused
**plentiful** characterized as having more than enough
**pompous** exceedingly proud
**poring** studying or looking at carefully
**prairie** grassy plains
**precious** having great value
**predict** guess what will happen next
**prehistoric** taking place before the time of recorded history

**Q**

**quarrel** to fight
**quarry** a place to dig up stone

**R**

**rainforest** a tropical forest that receives lots of rain and has very tall trees
**rambling** long and wordy
**rebelling** acting in opposition to







**reflecting telescope** an instrument that uses mirrors to look at faraway objects
**refracting telescope** an instrument that uses lenses to look at faraway objects
**remark** to make a statement or comment
**report** a detailed description or statement
**review** look over again
**rodents** small mammals with sharp teeth
**ruins** parts of a building or other structure that remain after a destructive event

**S**

**safeguard** to protect
**sarcophagus** a stone coffin
**scarlet** of a bright red color
**severe** strong; terrible
**similar** almost the same
**snare** a trap set for birds
**snowmelt** water from melting snow
**so-called** a name or term commonly given to something
**society** a group of people who share values, traditions, and laws
**solar system** the system of the sun and the planets and other orbiting objects
**solemn** serious, formal
**specialist** an expert in a certain field
**splendid** impressive, excellent
**spray** a tree branch, often flowered
**squinting** looking at with partially closed eyes in order to see more clearly
**steed** a horse that is ridden by a person
**straggled** trailed off
**superior** higher in rank or status
**suspense** anxious waiting
**suspicious** distrustful, having doubts
**system** arrangement, organization

**T**

**technology** electric or digital products
**tilted** slightly turned
**tomb** a room used as a grave
**ton** a measure of weight for 2000 pounds
**treason** the act of betraying or showing disloyalty to one's country
**trident** a fishing spear with three prongs
**tropical** of or occurring in the tropics

**U**

**united** acting as one
**universe** everything that exists in space
**urgent** requiring immediate action

**V**

**vapor** mist; haze
**vein** line of mineral through rock
**vengeful** looking to pay back a wrong or injury

**W**

**wildfire** fire that burns wild land
**wildlife** wild animals
**woe** sorrow
**worshipping** participating in a ceremony to show deep respect

# Notes